Urban Lawyers

URBAN LAWYERS

THE NEW SOCIAL STRUCTURE OF THE BAR

John P. Heinz, Robert L. Nelson,
Rebecca L. Sandefur,
and Edward O. Laumann

THE UNIVERSITY OF CHICAGO PRESS

CHICAGO AND LONDON

John P. Heinz is the Owen L. Coon Professor of Law at Northwestern University and Senior Research Fellow at the American Bar Foundation. Robert L. Nelson holds the MacCrate Research Chair in the Legal Profession and is director of the American Bar Foundation and professor of sociology and law at Northwestern University. Rebecca L. Sandefur is assistant professor of sociology at Stanford University. Edward O. Laumann is the George Herbert Mead Distinguished Service Professor of Sociology at the University of Chicago.

The University of Chicago Press, Chicago 60637
The University of Chicago Press, Ltd., London
© 2005 by The University of Chicago
All rights reserved. Published 2005
Printed in the United States of America

14 13 12 11 10 09 08 07 06 05   1 2 3 4 5

ISBN: 0-226-32539-3 (cloth)
ISBN: 0-226-32540-7 (paper)

The University of Chicago Press gratefully acknowledges a subvention from the American Bar Foundation in partial support of the costs of production of this volume.

Library of Congress Cataloging-in-Publication Data

Urban lawyers : the new social structure of the bar / John P. Heinz . . . [et al.].
    p. cm.
  Includes bibliographical references and index.
    ISBN 0-226-32539-3 (cloth : alk. paper)—ISBN 0-226-32540-7 (paper : alk. paper)
    1. Lawyers—Illinois—Chicago—Social conditions. 2. Practice of law—Illinois—Chicago—Sociological aspects. I. Heinz, John P., 1936– II. Title.

KF298.U73 2005
340'.023'73—dc22

                                                              2005000625

Lawyers are now to a greater extent than formerly business men, a part of the great organized system of industrial and financial enterprise. They are less than formerly the students of a particular kind of learning, the practitioners of a particular art. And they do not seem to be quite so much of a distinct professional class.

James Bryce, "America Revisited" (1905)

Suppose, having entangled yourself every now and then over four decades or so in the goings-on in two provincial towns . . . you wished to say something about how those goings-on had changed. You could contrast then and now, before and after, describe what life used to be like, what it has since become. You could write a narrative, a story of how one thing led to another, and those to a third. . . . You could invent indexes and describe trends: more individualism, less religiosity, rising welfare, declining morale. . . . You could describe the transformation of institutions, structures in motion: the family, the market, the civil service, the school. You could even build a model, conceive a process, propose a theory. You could draw graphs.

The problem is that more has changed, and more disjointly, than one at first imagines. . . . What we can construct, if we keep notes and survive, are hindsight accounts of the connectedness of things that seem to have happened: pieced-together patternings, after the fact.

Clifford Geertz, After the Fact (1995)

Contents

Tables and Figures

Tables

Figures

Preface

The obvious analogue of this book, ungenerous colleagues notwithstanding, is not *Halloween: Part 8* but *Twenty Years After*, Dumas' sequel to *The Three Musketeers*. In the mid-1990s, three of the authors of the present work had just published a weighty study of Washington lobbyists and were looking around for another adventure. The three had committed an outrage or two against the Chicago bar twenty years earlier and lived to tell the tales, and so they thought they might risk another. Like the musketeers, however, they had grown old (some more than others) and wise enough to know that they needed the help of a younger, hardier scholar. Fresh ideas are, of course, to be mistrusted, but it does little harm to give one an airing now and again. And there was, after all, a fourth musketeer.

One of the more eccentric authors of this book wanted to title it "The Raveling of the Bar." Saner heads prevailed. (It is a minor mystery of the English language, by the way, that "raveling" and "unraveling" mean exactly the same thing. The survival of both forms seems improbable and, although the principle of parsimony would predict a preference for the shorter word, in common usage *un* appears to be dominant. This can be attributed to a preference for negation—which brings us back to the bar.)

Lawyers, of course, take pride in their ability to negate almost anything, including each other. Even the term *lawyer* embodies contradictions. It is used to refer to an impressive range of social roles, many of which are in conflict. Some of these roles are elevated, others are generally disparaged; some serve capital, others serve labor; some are in the employ of the state, others seek to frustrate the state at every turn; some are rewarded with substantial wealth, others earn a minimal wage; some celebrate rhetorical skills in public fora, others (at least equally skilled) whisper in private, and yet others draft documents that make James Joyce seem succinct. *Lawyer* can be defined relatively precisely, if not helpfully, as one who holds a particular license. But many persons who are licensed do not practice law, and some who are not licensed pretty clearly do. The label, thus, is not very descriptive. But this book seeks to deal with the full range and variety of the persons who held law licenses in one major American city in the last quarter of the twentieth century.

The title of part 1 of this book, "The Professions of the Bar," should perhaps have been reserved for an essay on legal ethics or professionalism, where it would have a bit of bite, a clear double-meaning. For better or worse, we do not have much to offer here concerning the official statements or ideology of the bar. We do, however, have data on the consequences, in practice, of the bar's prevailing norms—consequences such as the characteristics that distinguish those who are admitted to the profession from those who are not, the nature of lawyers' career paths, and the distribution of income and other rewards within the profession. We also have some information on the political values endorsed by lawyers, and on which sorts of lawyers embrace which views, but our research reveals more about what lawyers do than about what they say.

The rate of change in the legal profession does not leave a scholar much latitude for contemplation. By the time one completes the work, the profession has moved on. Nonetheless, we took our time—in truth, we had very little choice about it. That is the way we are built and the way this work is done. If one does not take care in sifting the data, in questioning it, one will end with a mess—and a misleading, inaccurate mess at that. Some numbers reveal their secrets slowly.

The work would never have been completed without the assistance of a legion of friends, scholars, lawyers, students, data analysts, secretaries, editors, publishers, and funders. Many would no doubt prefer anonymity, but it is time for them to be counted.

The American Bar Foundation is truly a remarkable institution. Apart from good weather, it provides everything a scholar could want: intelligent and congenial colleagues, expert assistance, intellectual stimulation, a well-heated room, devastating criticism, and generous funding. We are fortunate to have worked there.

Grants to the foundation from the American Bar Endowment were the principal source of financial support for the project. Generous support was also provided by Northwestern University's Institute for Policy Research, the National Science Foundation (SBR-9411515), Northwestern Law School's Summer Faculty Research Program, Class of 1962 Reunion Gift Fund, the Law School Admission Council, and the Chicago Bar Foundation.

We are profoundly grateful to the hundreds of Chicago lawyers who agreed to participate in this research. The contribution of their valuable time and energies to a long, demanding interview was a real sacrifice. No doubt, many of them intended it to be a service to their profession. We hope that may prove to be the case.

Paul Schnorr was a partner in the design of the 1994–95 survey, in its execution, in the coding of the data, and in the early stages of the analysis. He is a coauthor of chapter 9. He departed from the project in 1996, moving first to urban challenges and later to greener pastures. We owe him a great debt.

Kathleen Hull was our project manager through most of the data analysis. She kept track of all of the codes and recodes, meticulously, saved us from disaster, and brought her keen intelligence to the interpretation of the findings. She is a coauthor of chapters 6 and 11. When Kathy left to pursue her own career, her duties were assumed, most ably, by Monique Payne. She, too, made numerous contributions to the analyses, and she is a coauthor of chapter 8. Ethan Michelson, before undertaking his seminal work on the legal profession in China, was a research assistant on this project, and he devised novel solutions to important analytic problems. He is a coauthor of chapter 2. While a law student at Northwestern University, Ava Harter wrote a senior research paper on lawyers' job satisfaction (or dissatisfaction). Parts of her research contributed to chapter 11, and she is a coauthor of that chapter.

We owe special thanks to Katherine Harris (not the Florida politician), Katie Heinz, and Katie Randhava, who provided expert assistance at several stages of the project. They performed their varying roles with remarkable single-mindedness. Katherine organized the interviews—she scheduled them and rescheduled them, assigned interviewers, cajoled reluctant respondents, and reviewed the completed interviews for quality. Katie Heinz coded and cleaned data, chased down missing pieces, and imposed order on chaotic files. Katie Randhava analyzed the data with architectural precision. In the process, we came to regard them as members of the family.

Other research assistants who made important contributions to the work were Sarah Babbitt, Jessica Bornemann, Jeannette Chung, Charles De Boer, Andrew Garth, Brian Gran, Roman Hoyos, Tamara Kay, Harris Kim, Mellissa Kotlen, Carlos Manjarrez, Benton McCune, Heather McIndoe, Wamucii

Njogu, Shepley Orr, Nealon Scoones, Gregory Scott, Jessica Thurk, Zenita Wickham, and Jeanette Wise. Interviewers, who skillfully administered a long and complicated set of questions, included Jeffrey Ahmadian, Diane Clay, Audrey Davis, Erin Fuller, Christine Garza, Lia Grube, Benjamin Nagin, Alina Oh, Eric Phillips, Melanie Roberson, Michael Sapienza, Brett Stockdill, and Johanna Womack. Some of the research assistants named above also conducted interviews.

In the later stages of the project, an extraordinarily talented group of students assisted in the data analyses—Brian Caouette, Rachel Kotzian, Dan Schulman, Benjamin Swoboda, Asha Thimmapaya, and Ryan White. We are indebted to them for the great care and skill they brought to their work.

In addition to the advice of many colleagues at the American Bar Foundation and our universities, we have especially profited from consultation with Richard Abel, Michael Abramowicz, Fred Aman, Carl Auerbach, Charlotte Crane, Ronit Dinovitzer, William Elwin, Tyrone Fahner, Kenneth Gaines, Marc Galanter, Bryant Garth, Judge Robert Gettleman, Gillian Hadfield, John Hagan, William Heinz, Donald Hilliker, Kenneth Janda, Gary Johnson, Arnold Kanter, Stewart Macaulay, Robert MacCrate, Joanne Martin, Carrie Menkel-Meadow, Thomas Morsch, Dawn Clark Netsch, Sara Parikh, Marshall Patner, Daniel Polsby, Milton Regan, David Ruder, Susan Shapiro, Carole Silver, Wesley Skogan, Rayman Solomon, Ann Southworth, Bruce Spencer, Joyce Sterling, Robert Stout, David Van Zandt, Stephen Warner, Wayne Whalen, Stanton Wheeler, and David Wilkins. We also benefited from critiques by two anonymous but conscientious and keenly perceptive scholars who read the manuscript for the University of Chicago Press.

In the early summer of 2004, Benno Weisberg gave the penultimate draft an especially close reading, resulting in a nineteen-page (single-spaced) memo with scores of comments and corrections. Money could not buy that kind of effort. Marcia Lehr, of the Northwestern University Law Library, was remarkably resourceful in chasing down elusive sources and materials. Her assistance went well beyond the call of duty. In the early stages of the project, all of the word processing was done by Laurie Wessel with great efficiency and unfailing accuracy. In more recent years those duties fell upon Anne Godden-Segard, who bore the burden of producing this manuscript. In particular, it was her lot to cope with one of the authors who repeatedly insisted upon changing the text, changing it again, and then putting it back to the way it was in the first place. That she did so cheerfully is a great testament to the British sense of humor (or humour).

We are also grateful for the beneficent attentions of the University of Chicago Press. John Tryneski, the Editorial Director for Social Sciences and

Paperback Publishing, provided sage editorial advice and a steady guiding hand, and he led us through an editorial process in which we made substantial revisions of multiple drafts. Deborah Oliver's copyediting was both expert and meticulous, in the best tradition of that demanding craft. The book's figures were prepared by Catherine Zaccarine, who illuminated the darkness. Many of these presentations are complex, necessarily, but her skillful work has made a difficult text more comprehensible.

It is daunting to tote up this effort, expended by so many skilled and generous colleagues. We are all too conscious of the substantial likelihood that the final product fails to take full advantage of the riches available to us. Organizing the resources—the data and the expert knowledge—was, itself, a formidable task. Inevitably, we made choices. We pursued some paths and rejected others. Different scholars would, we know, have made different choices. But here it is, at long last.

Our family and friends had to put up with us while we were doing this work. (Well, maybe they didn't *have* to, but they did.) It is conventional to thank them for their sufferance. But it is not at all clear that we were more difficult during this project than we usually are. Indeed, the hours devoted to the work kept us out of their way. Perhaps they should thank the American Bar Foundation for keeping us occupied.

Some of the chapters in this book include material adapted from previously published articles. Chapter 2 is a revision of John Heinz, Robert Nelson, Edward Laumann, and Ethan Michelson, "The Changing Character of Lawyers' Work: Chicago in 1975 and 1995," *Law and Society Review* 32 (1998): 751–76. Chapter 4 draws on Rebecca Sandefur, "Work and Honor in the Law: Prestige and the Division of Lawyers' Labor," *American Sociological Review* 66 (2001): 382–403. Chapter 9 is adapted from John Heinz and Paul Schnorr, with Edward Laumann and Robert Nelson, "Lawyers' Roles in Voluntary Associations: Declining Social Capital?" *Law and Social Inquiry* 26 (2001): 597–629. Chapter 10 is a revision of John Heinz and Edward Laumann, with Robert Nelson and Paul Schnorr, "The Constituencies of Elite Urban Lawyers," *Law and Society Review* 31 (1997): 441–72. Chapter 11 is based upon John Heinz, Kathleen Hull, and Ava Harter, "Lawyers and Their Discontents: Findings from a Survey of the Chicago Bar," *Indiana Law Journal* 74 (1999): 735–58. Parts of chapter 12 appeared in John Heinz, Robert Nelson, and Edward Laumann, "The Scale of Justice: Observations on the Transformation of Urban Law Practice," *Annual Review of Sociology* 27 (2001): 337–62.

Other publications that use data from the 1994–95 Chicago survey are Kathleen Hull and Robert Nelson, "Gender Inequality and Law: Problems of

Structure and Agency in Recent Studies of Gender in Anglo-American Legal Professions," *Law and Social Inquiry* 23 (1998): 681–705; Rebecca Sandefur and Edward Laumann, "A Paradigm for Social Capital," *Rationality and Society* 10 (1998): 481–501; Rebecca Sandefur, Edward Laumann, and John Heinz, "The Changing Value of Social Capital in an Expanding Social System: Lawyers in the Chicago Bar, 1975 and 1995," in *Corporate Social Capital and Liability*, edited by Roger Leenders and Shaul Gabbay, 217–33 (Norwell, Mass.: Kluwer Academic, 1999); Kathleen Hull, "Cross-Examining the Myth of Lawyers' Misery," *Vanderbilt Law Review* 52 (1999): 971–83; Kathleen Hull, "The Paradox of the Contented Female Lawyer," *Law and Society Review* 33 (1999): 687–700; Kathleen Hull and Robert Nelson, "Assimilation, Choice or Constraint? Testing Theories of Gender Differences in the Careers of Lawyers," *Social Forces* 79, no. 1 (2000): 229–64; Ethan Michelson, Edward Laumann, and John Heinz, "The Changing Character of the Lawyer-Client Relationship: Evidence from Two Chicago Surveys," in *The Management of Durable Relations*, edited by Werner Raub and Jeroen Wessie (Amsterdam: Thela/Thesis Publications, 2000); Harris Kim and Edward Laumann, "Social Capital, Embedded Status, and the Endorsement Effect: Income Stratification among Chicago Lawyers, 1995," in *Research in the Sociology of Organizations* 20:243–66; and Harris Kim, "The Changing Patterns of Career Mobility in the Legal Profession: A Log-Linear Analysis of Chicago Lawyers, 1975 and 1995," in *Legal Professions: Work, Structure and Organization*, 3:3–24, The Sociology of Crime, Law, and Deviance series, edited by Jerry Van Hoy (Greenwich, CT: JAI Press, 2001).

PART I
The Professions of the Bar

Chapter 1
Chicago Lawyers Revisited

There was a time, long ago, when the bar was a largely undifferentiated mass of independent practitioners. Lawyers, whether they were in villages or in cities, worked in small "law offices," occasionally with a partner or two but more commonly alone. By one count, in 1872 only one American law firm had as many as six lawyers and only three had five (Hobson, in Gawalt 1984, 7). In the last decades of the nineteenth century, however, concentration of business enterprise in corporations led to a corresponding concentration of their lawyers in firms relatively specialized to the practice of "corporate law." By 1933, Karl Llewellyn could observe that the "best brains" of the urban bar had "moved masswise out of court work, out of a general practice akin to that of the family doctor, into highly paid specialization in the service of large corporations" (Llewellyn 1933, 177). A quarter of a century later, 20 New York firms had 50 or more lawyers (Smigel 1969, 358). At that time, however, the majority of American lawyers still practiced alone. In 1948, about 61 percent were in solo practice (Sikes 1972, 10–12). As late as 1967, of 143,000 law firms in the United States, 122,000 consisted of a sole practitioner (Census 1970, cited in Abel 1989, 304).

Sole practitioners, commonly referred to as "solos," and corporation lawyers practicing in large firms are the polar opposites of the legal profession. They represent the extremes of the hierarchies that separate lawyers and sort them into distinct social and professional roles. But there is a considerable range of variety between these extremes—lawyers employed by government, local, state, and federal; lawyers who work in banks, software companies, or real estate firms; lawyers employed by labor unions; lawyers practicing in small firms that specialize in personal injury or divorce or criminal law; lawyers practicing in quite different small to medium-sized firms that specialize in intellectual property, bankruptcy, or admiralty; public defenders, who represent poor people accused of crimes; neighborhood legal services lawyers, who represent poor people with any of a wide variety of legal problems; "cause lawyers" who represent the National Abortion Rights Action League or the National Right to Life Committee; and, importantly, lawyers engaged in work other than the practice of law.

Despite the diversity of these roles, however, during most of the twentieth century some factors tended to pull American lawyers together, to give them a common professional identity. One of these factors was their shared social status and social origins. In spite of lawyer jokes (Galanter 1998) and antipathy toward "shysters" and "ambulance chasers," lawyers as a whole enjoyed the prestige of membership in one of the traditional "learned professions." Their years of education, usually at institutions of some substantial repute, conferred authority and standing. They were required to pass a licensing examination, the "bar exam," more rigorous at some times and places than at others ·(Abel 1989), but generally designed to weed out incompetents. Lawyers were also, by and large, drawn from a relatively narrow stratum at or near the top of the American social order. Their parents had usually held professional or managerial positions (Heinz and Laumann 1982, table 6.3, 190), and the lawyers themselves were relatively wealthy, overall, although there was always considerable inequality in lawyers' earnings. Thus, the privileged social and economic standing of American lawyers tended to set them apart and to give them a shared identity as members of a professional elite.

This socioeconomic exclusivity was reinforced by racial, ethnic, religious, and gender exclusivity as well. For much of the twentieth century, American lawyers were disproportionately likely to be white, male, Protestant, and of northern European ancestry (*Yale Law Journal* 1964; Auerbach 1976). They grew up in similar neighborhoods, attended similar schools, and worshiped at similar churches. Not surprisingly, these backgrounds led them into relatively homogeneous social networks. Their friends and professional colleagues tended to be much like them (Heinz and Laumann 1982, chap. 7). Job openings in the legal profession were routinely filled through the "old-boy network." When lawyers did not fit the standard profile—as, for example, by being female or Jewish—they tended to pursue distinct career paths, gravitating toward settings and specialties where they were disproportionately concentrated with others who shared their characteristics (Carlin

1962; Ladinsky 1963a, 1963b). By the middle of the twentieth century, Jews had succeeded in entering the bar in substantial numbers, but they often did not have access to the most prestigious firms and the most highly valued specialties. Women did not enter the profession in great numbers until the last quarter of the century, and the degree of their integration into the institutions of the bar is one of the subjects dealt with in this book.

The shared family backgrounds, education, and life experiences of American lawyers tended to give them a common outlook on social and political issues. In spite of their representation of varying clientele, often with opposing interests, lawyers displayed a surprising degree of unanimity on issues of the day. A 1975 study of Chicago lawyers, for example, found that 87 percent of a random sample agreed with the proposition that "all Americans should have equal access to quality medical care regardless of ability to pay" and 78 percent endorsed the view that "one of the most important roles of government is to help those who cannot help themselves, such as the poor, the disadvantaged, and the unemployed" (Heinz and Laumann 1982, table 5.1, 139). Lawyers tended to be more liberal than persons in other occupations of comparable socioeconomic status (Laumann, Marsden, and Galaskiewicz 1997), and their characteristic regard for "due process" and civil liberties separated them from the general population.

In addition to the social factors that drew lawyers together, a set of distinct professional interests gave lawyers common cause, and an increasing range of organizational activities gave them opportunities to meet and pursue their objectives. The American Bar Association was founded in 1878, and in the twentieth century it grew into a large and powerful organization (Rutherford 1937; Melone 1977). State and local bar associations, which sponsored numerous (virtually constant) discussions of professional concerns, also burgeoned (Halliday 1987; Powell 1988). One of the common interests of lawyers (or, at least, of many lawyers) was preventing other occupations from trespassing on the market for lawyers' work—that is, preventing the "unauthorized practice of law." For many years, lawyers attempted to prohibit real estate agents and title insurance companies from preparing the documents needed for a sale of property. More recently, law firms have been concerned about "legal work" done by accounting firms (see chap. 12). Thus, the maintenance of boundaries between law and other, potentially competing occupations was an interest that many lawyers shared (Abbott 1988). Many also had an interest in building networks for the referral of cases from general practitioners to specialists or from one sort of specialist to another. A broad range of contacts thus served the needs of both the generalists and the specialists, and these ties provided communication among lawyers and tended to reinforce the integration of the bar.

There is reason to believe, however, that many of the factors that once produced cohesion among lawyers now have less force. This book examines evidence suggesting that the bar is not as unified—in its social characteristics, its political values, or its professional interests—as was once the case. Indeed, the evidence may suggest that the legal profession is now dividing into several distinct occupations. But the demise of the bar has been forecast so many times, prematurely, as to give us pause. The relativity of judgments about the nature and degree of change in the character of the bar—for example, about whether the bar has become less professional or more bureaucratic—becomes strikingly apparent as soon as one examines nineteenth- and early twentieth-century commentary, such as the quotation from Lord Bryce that is an epigraph to this book (see also Gordon 1988; Solomon 1992).

We assess, here, the nature and degree of change in the Chicago bar over a twenty-year period. Most of the evidence is drawn from two surveys, the first conducted in 1975 and the second in 1994–95. In each, personal interviews were conducted with a random sample consisting of nearly eight hundred lawyers drawn from all types of practice. The two samples are independent cross sections. That is, the same lawyers were not reinterviewed; therefore, this is not a "panel" study. Both samples include solo practitioners, lawyers in firms, corporate house counsel, government lawyers, public defenders, judges, law professors, and lawyers who were retired, unemployed, or engaged in occupations other than law.

Although the book principally relies on the comparison of data from the two Chicago surveys, we also draw on other scholarly literature on lawyers and on press reports in order to present a broader picture. Because the 1975–95 period is not a long historical frame, we would not expect all of the changes that are interesting and important to have run their course within that time. Indeed, the trends of major significance certainly had identifiable antecedents before 1975 and continuing developments after 1995, and we will want to attend to those where they help to complete the story.

The findings from the 1975 survey were reported and interpreted in a previous book (Heinz and Laumann 1982), which argued that much of the differentiation within the Chicago bar could be understood as a distinction between lawyers who represented large organizations and those who represented individuals or the small businesses owned by individuals: "The two kinds of law practice are the two hemispheres of the profession. Most lawyers reside exclusively in one hemisphere or the other and seldom, if ever, cross the equator" (319). The more cautious passages of that work acknowledged that "the client type distinction is too crude and too simple to account for the full complexity of the social structure of the profession" and that there were, "in some respects, larger differences within the hemispheres than between them" (321), but the "two-hemispheres" metaphor captured the attention of the book's audience and the image has become a frequent point of reference in the scholarly literature.

The 1995 survey, then, provides data with which we can evaluate the validity (or the continuing validity) of the "two-hemispheres" hypothesis. As we have noted, there are reasons to think that the legal profession was less cohesive in the 1990s than in the 1970s. While urban lawyers may well have become subdivided into smaller clusters, however, the division between the two classes of clients—between large organizations, on one hand, and individuals and small businesses, on the other—endures. Note that this distinction, unlike wealth, is conceived of as a dichotomy. Organizational size is a matter of degree, of course, but the distinction between organizations and individuals is a matter of substance as well as form. One might argue that small corporations, even publicly held ones, are more akin to partnerships than they are to large corporations, but the difference in form has legal content, and it alters the nature of the lawyers' work and the relationship between lawyer and client. Where the owners of corporations (the shareholders) are distinct from the management of the company, lawyers' relationships with management are more difficult and ethically complex than are lawyers' relationships with owner-operators. Corporations issue securities, and they are subject to a multiplicity of reporting requirements at the federal, state, and local levels. Moreover, corporations pay corporate tax, and the rules and procedures differ from those that apply to the taxation of individuals. Other large organizations (governmental institutions, labor unions, trade associations, professional organizations) are also subject to special rules and reporting requirements, and lawyers' relationships with these clients are often more akin to their relationships with corporations than to those with individual clients.

Lawyers employed by large law firms do, of course, handle legal work for individuals as well as for corporations—often for the individuals who are officers of their corporate clients. Some large firms have probate departments, many handle individual income tax problems for favored clients, and a few will even work on clients' divorces. To the extent that this occurs, the corporate and the personal client sectors of the bar are drawn closer. But there is a division of labor within these firms, and the lawyers who do the corporate work may not be the same ones who handle personal matters. If lawyers' work has become increasingly specialized—if lawyers who do securities work are now less likely to do probate or commercial law as well—this will tend to separate the sectors of the bar. Fewer lawyers will cross the boundaries.

Lawyers can, of course, be sorted in other ways. For example, one might distinguish trial lawyers or "litigators" from office lawyers, or "employed" lawyers (i.e., corporate house counsel and government lawyers) from independent practitioners who work in law firms or in solo practice. In her study of solo and small-firm lawyers in metropolitan New York, Carroll Seron (1996) divided the sample into "entrepreneurs," "experimenters," and "traditionalists," based primarily on the nature of their business practices. John Hagan and Fiona Kay's (1995) study of lawyers in Toronto and in the province of Ontario used a typology that categorized practitioners by the degree to which they possessed "autonomy" and social power (35–40). All of these distinctions may well be useful, depending on one's analytic purpose.

In part (but by no means entirely) because of an increase in demand for lawyers' services (Sander and Williams 1989), the bar grew very substantially during the last decades of the twentieth century. The number of lawyers in the United States increased from about 355,200 in 1970, one for every 572 persons in the population (Sikes, Carson, and Gorai 1972, 6, table 2), to about 1,066,000 in 2001, one per 264 persons (Carson 2004). In Cook County, the number of resident lawyers increased from 19,072 in 1976 (Attorney Registration and Disciplinary Commission 1977, 1) to 35,704 in 1994 (Attorney Registration and Disciplinary Commission 1995, 5), an increase of 87 percent, while the county's population decreased modestly.[1] Overall, expenditures on legal services in the United States increased by 309 percent between 1972 and 1992.[2] This rate of increase was twice that of the gross national product during the same period and even exceeded the percentage increase in spending for health services (Litan and Salop 1992, 2 and fig. 1).

The increase in the scale of the profession—both in the size of the organizational units and in overall size—also tends to weaken the coherence of the bar. That is, as the numbers grow, the probability of chance transactions between any given pair or any given sets of lawyers decreases. Since individual lawyers' circles of acquaintance are unlikely to expand to the same extent as the growth of the bar, there will be an increasing number of their fellow lawyers with whom they have no ties. Thus, communication is likely to be restricted to more narrow slices of the whole. The bar, therefore, has become more diverse and less well integrated.

The rapid growth of large law firms unsettled established ways of doing business, and to some extent presented new options for firm management. Some firms aggressively expanded, opening or acquiring multiple offices in the United States and abroad, and "rationalizing" or bureaucratizing their management structure with professional managers and an elaboration of formal procedures. Other firms grew slowly if at all, remained local or regionally based, and retained a more informal, more personal management style. These organizational strategies were often shaped by the particular market or clientele that the firm sought to reach and by the firm's specialties (see chapter 5). For example, a firm specializing in litigation will usually have a higher ratio of junior lawyers and paralegals to senior lawyers than a firm specializing in tax work (Kordana 1995). Preparation for complex litigation often involves sifting and sorting through mounds of documents, a task that may be efficiently performed by relatively less experienced labor, while the client who seeks tax advice is buying individualized expertise and judgment. Moreover, as organizations grow, they are likely to adopt a clear division of labor. Instead of being built around dominant seniors, they create departments defined by substantive expertise or skill types—for example, tax, litigation, real estate, or mergers and acquisitions.

Specialization of work changes the lines of communication within the profession. Some lines are severed, some are reconstituted. When each lawyer deals with a broad range of types of law, then the set of lawyers brought together to handle a problem is likely to be determined by availability and by client affinities, and thus the set will change from case to case. But if work is organized by departments that are defined by legal subject or skill type, lawyers will spend most of their time talking with fellow specialists. When "corporate work" evolves into securities, antitrust, corporate tax, and intellectual property, this separates fields of law (and sets of practitioners) that were formerly brought together.

In 1975, the legal profession was relatively stable. Although it was then on the brink of rapid change (the entry of women, explosive growth), most of that change was yet to come. The social hierarchies within the profession that had evolved since the middle of the nineteenth century were still in place (but not firmly, as we shall see), and a survey of a cross section of the bar in 1975 produced a reasonably clear picture of the structure. By 1995, however, the profession had been transformed and was still unsettled. The 1995 Chicago survey drew data from a system in a state of flux. Nonetheless, one can discern order in the patterns of change; the processes do not appear to be random. But it may be a mistake to assume that the structure of the bar will eventually settle into stability once again.

Prior Research

Throughout this book we refer to a substantial, varied body of literature on the social organization of lawyers. The range of the particular debates about lawyers reflects the growth of social scientific interest in the legal profession. The scope of that literature and variety of the issues addressed make a simple summary impractical, but it is useful to locate the 1975 and 1995 surveys in the prior work. Research on lawyers tracks major shifts in the social structure of the bar as well as changing emphases in theories of the professions. In the last quarter of the twentieth century, scholars sought to explain the causes and consequences of the structural changes that were set in motion in the 1970s—the continued expansion of large law firms, the entry of large numbers of women and minorities into the profession, heightened anxiety over the "professionalism" of lawyers and reports of widespread lawyer dissatisfaction, globalization and the export of American-style lawyering, and the creation of new forms of cause lawyering.

From the late 1950s to the early 1970s, the sociology of the professions revolved around an ongoing debate between a "professional dominance" perspective, argued by Eliot Freidson (1970) and Everett Hughes (1958), and a "functionalist" conception of the professions, especially as articulated by Talcott Parsons (1968; see also Ben-David 1963–64; Goode 1957). Functionalists sought to explain the status and social organization of professionals as deriving from the importance of their role in society and the unique forms of knowledge they controlled, while the dominance theorists asserted that professional status was based on the political and economic power of professional groups in the state, the academy, and the market.

Studies of the legal profession reflected this debate. Jerome Carlin's classic study of Chicago solo practitioners, *Lawyers on Their Own* (1962), depicted the harsh realities of solo practice, including the overrepresentation among solos of Jews, recent immigrants, and graduates of lower-status law schools, the difficulties of obtaining business, the problems posed by ethical rules, and the frustrations many solos experienced in trying to establish a professional practice. Carlin's survey of New York City practitioners, *Lawyers' Ethics* (1966), documented on a broader scale the variations in the nature of work, rewards from practice, and ethical issues across practice settings. It debunked the notion that ethical rules and enforcement within the bar were founded on a professional consensus, and argued instead that the rules and enforcement mechanisms were controlled by elite lawyers and were focused on lower status, marginal practitioners, who were driven to questionable practices by financial pressures. Jack Ladinsky's series of articles based on the Detroit area study also documented ethnic and class stratification within the bar (1963a, 1963b, 1964).

While Carlin's and Ladinsky's works were casting doubt on the functionalist model of a unitary profession governed by universal principles, other research argued that lawyers played important roles in mediating conflict and curbing the unreasonable or unjust proclivities of clients. Perhaps most striking was Erwin Smigel's landmark study of elite New York lawyers, *The Wall Street Lawyer* (1964). Smigel documented the anti-Semitism and social elitism of New York City firms, but he adopted Parsons' view of their professional autonomy: the diversity of the client base of Wall Street firms, combined with their expertise, gave them substantial independence from and influence over their corporate clients. Charles Horsky (1952) presented a similar view of Washington lawyers.

Research in the 1970s continued to develop new approaches to studying the social roles of lawyers. Dietrich Rueschemeyer's comparison of German and American lawyers (1973) revealed the distinctiveness of the American legal profession: a much greater proportion of the U.S. lawyers worked in private practice rather than as judges or inside business organizations. The American legal profession was thus more autonomous from business and government and more subject to trends in the private marketplace for legal services. Douglas Rosenthal conducted path-breaking work by examining the relationships between personal injury lawyers and their clients (1974), finding that those lawyers typically controlled their clients, but that more forceful and involved clients sought and obtained larger awards than did passive clients. Jerold Auerbach's critical history of the American legal profession, *Unequal Justice* (1976), provided a sustained look at historical changes in the bar, and asserted that in numerous eras the profession (especially the organized bar) had failed to act in pursuit of a more just system of laws. Auerbach's account brought to light deeply rooted conflicts within the profession about the proper organization of legal education (should it be split between personal client and corporate client fields?), limits on entry to the profession, the political orientation of the bar during 1950s McCarthyism, and support for legal services to the poor.

The 1975 survey of Chicago lawyers sought to determine which groups of lawyers were most influential, whether elite practitioners served as brokers of power within the profession, and whether the Chicago Bar Association and the Democratic Party organization of the first Mayor Daley (Richard J., 1955–76) played important political roles in the profession. Of particular interest was how the political ferment of the late 1960s and early 1970s, which had roiled local politics and led to the formation of a "counter bar association," the Chicago Council of Lawyers (Powell 1979), had affected alignments within the bar. Heinz and Laumann found that elite lawyers inhabited distinct segments of the bar and seldom acted in concert. More fundamentally, they found that even in the mid-1970s, in the post–civil rights era, the bar was highly stratified by client type, field of practice, and the ethnoreligious characteristics of the lawyers. The "two-hemispheres" finding, noted above, contradicted the view of a unitary profession and raised serious questions about the autonomy of lawyers. The book argued that the more prestigious, well-rewarded lawyers—the corporate lawyers—were the least autonomous from their clients.

In the 1980s, a new generation of scholarship proceeded on several fronts:

The growth of the profession. Scholars debated the causes of the rapid growth in the number of lawyers. Richard Sander and Douglass Williams (1989) offered perhaps the most comprehensive economic account, looking at both demand and supply side factors. They documented a rapid rise in real wages for lawyers during the 1970s and 1980s, a reflection of increased demand, but also showed that earnings varied significantly across sectors of the profession. Because potential recruits to the profession may have wrongly assumed that they would obtain the high salaries available only to a small segment of the bar, law schools began to produce "too many" lawyers.

Changes in the organization of law firms. The dramatic growth and managerial restructuring of corporate law firms spurred new studies of large firms and corporate law departments. In *Partners with Power* (1988), Robert Nelson described a shift in the market for corporate legal services away from general service relationships between law firms and corporations toward specialized, transactional work. Nelson also argued, contrary to Smigel's observation about Wall Street firms, that corporate lawyers seldom took issue with their clients and that the autonomy of their firms was circumscribed by the partners who had the strongest connections to corporate clients. Marc Galanter and Thomas Palay argued that the expansion of law firms, and changes from "the golden age" (associated with stable partnerships, lifetime tenure for partners, and restrained competition for new business), were the product of a *Tournament of Lawyers* (1991). The tournament created a built-in growth imperative in each firm, whereby every additional partner required the hiring of new associates. Galanter and Palay's description of the changes in law firms was perceptive and well documented, but several scholars challenged their theoretical explanation for the changes (see, e.g., Kordana 1995; Nelson 1992).

Moreover, some of the literature suggested that there were strong organizational continuities in the management of law partnerships. Emmanuel Lazega's in-depth study of a corporate law firm in the northeastern United States in 1988–91 demonstrated the capacity of collegial firms to achieve effective coordination through informal mechanisms (2001). Certain partners, given their positions in networks of lawyers, could enforce lateral control on their peers. In this way, potentially antagonistic partners worked together to maintain common resources, even as they pursued their own interests. Lazega asserts that collegial governance will remain important in many knowledge-intensive industries, not just law. In discussing the generalizability of his findings, however, he notes that it remains unclear how collegial governance will change in more bureaucratized firms.

The increasing power of lawyers employed in corporations ("inside counsel") stimulated new attention to them. While Jeffrey Slovak (1979, 1980) and Eve Spangler (1986) observed that inside counsel did not possess the same status or independence as outside counsel, by the mid-1980s this proposition was in doubt. Robert Rosen argued that corporate counsel could and did exert considerable influence in corporate decision making (1989, 1999). Nelson and Laura Beth Nielsen, in their study of lawyers in Fortune 1,000 companies in the early 1990s, found that inside lawyers retained their identity as lawyers, but largely adopted the worldview of the businesses in which they worked (2000). If lawyers chose the role of "cop" in the corporation, they risked being excluded from the business decision-making.

Women and minorities. The rapid entry of women into the legal profession beginning in the mid-1970s led to an outpouring of research on their fate. Cynthia Fuchs Epstein (1981) documented the historical barriers to women. Hagan and Kay's surveys of the Ontario bar found that women were less likely to make partner and more likely to plan to drop out of the profession, and that those women who did make partner had better credentials and brought in more clients than many male partners (1995; Kay 1997; Kay and Hagan 1998, 1999). Similar patterns were observed in the United States, as women made up a much smaller percentage of partners than of associates in law firms (see, e.g., Schaafsma 1998; Dixon and Seron 1995; Chambliss 1997). Carrie Menkel-Meadow, in a provocative set of essays, applied feminist theory to data on the legal profession. Using cross-national data, she suggested that women tended to be relegated to low-status legal work, even though the nature of the low-status work varied by society (1989). Menkel-Meadow also theorized about the potential impact of the increase in women lawyers on the way law was practiced (1986). Jennifer Pierce's study of litigators and paralegals found that women did indeed tend to practice differently than men, but that some men adopted an accommodative style, while some women adopted a combative style (1995).

Less research was done on the experience of minorities in the profession. David Wilkins and G. Mitu Gulati sought to explain why there were so few African American lawyers in corporate law firms (1998). They argued that minorities in large firms were caught in the bind between taking too many work assignments and being too cautious, restricting their efforts to work that was too specialized. Neither approach provided a platform for career advancement. They attributed the high attrition rate of minority associates to a partnership structure that based hiring largely on paper credentials and then let associates sink or swim. The tensions confronted by minority associates left them sinking (or at least leaving) more often than swimming (see also Reeves 2001).

Professional associations. Both the trend of events (e.g., Supreme Court rulings striking down bar associations' minimum fee schedules and prohibitions of lawyer advertising) and the scholarship on the profession suggested that the power of the organized bar was in decline. Michael Powell noted that newer, insurgent, dissenting associations challenged the authority of the older organizations (1979), as bar associations yielded control over lawyer discipline to the courts (1986), and as established bar leaders were pressured to provide opportunities for participation and leadership to previously unrepresented elements within the profession (1985, 1988). Theodore Schneyer analyzed the erosion of the power of state bar associations to require membership and the payment of dues (1983) and conflicts within the bar over issues of legal ethics (1989). Not all scholars agreed that the organized bar's power was declining, however. Terence Halliday argued in *Beyond Monopoly* (1987) that the organized bar could, despite these changes, exercise considerable influence over the direction of law by marshaling technical expertise and moral authority.

Contextual variations in practice. A series of studies of lawyers practicing in different contexts underscored the variability of professional practices, even among lawyers working in the same field of law. Donald Landon's research on small-town and rural lawyers in Missouri (1990) and Seron's interviews with suburban practitioners in metropolitan New York (1996) demonstrated that in the personal client sphere the boundary between business and law practice blurred: small-town lawyers often combined the practice of law with ownership of other business enterprises; small-firm suburban practitioners often approached their work in very businesslike terms. Austin Sarat and William Felstiner gained extraordinary access to interactions between divorce lawyers and their clients in California and Massachusetts (1995). They documented the strategies used by the lawyers to control their cases and clients, often by portraying the legal system as arbitrary and potentially irrational. Lynn Mather, Craig McEwen, and Richard Maiman (2001) identified several distinctive types of divorce practices among Maine and New Hampshire divorce lawyers, from generalists to high-volume and low-cost specialists to low-volume and high-cost practices. They found some significant cleavages among the lawyers. Newcomers to divorce practice, often women representing female clients, sometimes did not adhere to the norms of established practitioners (old boys) about negotiated settlements or court procedures. Instead, they adopted a more adversarial style when they thought that informal understandings did not offer their clients adequate support. Nonetheless, Mather and her colleagues concluded that divorce lawyers acted as a kind of professional community that kept lawyers and clients within certain boundaries of acceptable behavior.

Globalization and lawyers. The economics and politics of globalization had sweeping effects on the legal profession in the United States and abroad, and scholars responded with interest. A wave of important comparative scholarship on legal professions began with the publication of three volumes edited by Richard Abel and Phillip Lewis, which brought together essays on lawyers in both the civil and common law worlds and presented alternative interpretive frameworks (1988–89). Large corporate law firms, led by firms in New York and London, began to expand their global reach by opening branch offices in major commercial centers (Silver 2000). In Europe, large tax and consulting firms took the lead in meeting the growing demand for corporate legal services (see Abel 1994; Trubek et al. 1994).

The dynamics of the new competition among American law firms and their European competitors were captured in Yves Dezalay and Bryant Garth's analysis of international commercial arbitration (1996). Dezalay and Garth depicted a struggle between arbitration centered on the "grand old men" of the Paris International Chamber of Commerce and the new style of arbitration favored by American litigators. The book broke new ground both topically and theoretically. It shifted the focus from comparative to transnational lawyering, and it introduced Bourdieu's theory of the field to studies of the legal profession, an innovation that cast new light on the shifting strategies of different groups of lawyers and the relationships between those strategies and the social hierarchies in which lawyers were embedded.

Cause lawyering. Research on the legal profession has long been concerned with public interest lawyering (see Carlin 1962; Handler, Hollingsworth, and Erlanger 1978; Menkel-Meadow and Meadow 1983; Katz 1982) and especially with the conditions under which lawyers can be recruited to represent less advantaged groups in society. The 1990s produced a new body of research examining the activities of lawyers on behalf of particular social movements or public interest groups—work referred to as *cause lawyering.* In two volumes edited by Austin Sarat and Stuart Scheingold (1998, 2001), scholars wrote about the mobilization and consequences of cause lawyering, in the United States and abroad, documenting the range in styles and effects, but suggesting that it had become institutionalized. The research also indicated that cause lawyering was not limited to liberal causes, and that indeed an extensive and active network of conservative lawyers was influential on several types of issues (Heinz, Paik, and Southworth 2003).

Professionalism and lawyer dissatisfaction. In the late 1980s, the organized bar expressed its concern that the rise of lawyer advertising and the growth of corporate law firms were eroding the professionalism of lawyers—especially the public service orientation of the bar. The ABA established a commission to investigate the issue (American Bar Association Commission on Professionalism 1986). This initiative then prompted scholars to examine whether the anxiety over professionalism was a recycling of old rhetoric or a response to something new (see essays in Nelson, Trubek, and Solomon 1992). While some argued that the professionalism campaign was specious or misguided, Freidson, among others, argued that the modern professions were at a pivotal moment in which they might lose their autonomy to bureaucratic encroachments by the state (in medicine, for example, through Medicare) or the market (e.g., through HMOs) (1992). The ABA commission signaled the beginning of a period of controversy within the legal profession about conflicts between traditional professional values and trends toward new forms of practice, such as partnerships combining several professions, or law firms that invest in companies they help to organize and take public.

One strand of the complaints about the changes within the profession was the assertion that large numbers of lawyers were unhappy—that they had become victims of the pressure to work long hours and the erosion of civility in the workplace (see, e.g., Schiltz 1999). The assertion was repeated so frequently and insistently that it took on the character of accepted fact, even though the basis for the claim was dubious (see Hull 1999a).

Theoretical developments. These diverse streams of scholarship cannot be readily ordered according to any one, overarching theory of the professions. Yet much of the scholarship was informed by four primary theoretical frameworks: Larson's market closure theory; Abbott's theory of professional jurisdiction; "new class" theory; and Freidson's theory of professional power.

In 1977, sociological theory concerning the professions was redirected by the publication of Magali Sarfatti Larson's *The Rise of Professionalism*, which presented a sweeping historical model of the growing power of professions in modern society, with emphasis on the American case. The core concept in Larson's analysis is what she refers to as the collective mobility project of the professions. This "project" requires the creation of demand for the profession's service and then control of the supply for that service through standards for professional education, certification and licensure, and regulation of the conditions of professional practice.

Although medicine was more successful than law in "reconciling its internal cleavages because it [medicine] was capable of spreading substantial economic benefits across its fragmented and stratified market," Larson argued that medicine and law shared essential characteristics:

> In both cases, the average independent professional "entrepreneur" is relegated to a marginal position: power and influence flow, in these professions as in society at large, from the state, the corporation, and the national university. These two powerful professions are among the most attractive to the stubborn believers in the receding bourgeois ideology of independence. One of their accessory contributions to the dominant ideology may well be that of maintaining, without too much *actual* encouragement, the flickering flame of the entrepreneurial dream. (1977, 177)

In Larson's view, the social structure of the bar had long been at odds with its professed ideals, and that uneasy tension could be expected to continue so long as lawyers maintained the political power to control the legal marketplace.

Andrew Abbott's *The System of the Professions* (1988) was another influential theoretical contribution. Abbott shifted the frame of reference in the sociohistorical analysis of the professions from an emphasis on mobility projects to the competition among occupations for control of particular types of work. Thus, in Abbott's view, professions stake a claim for "jurisdiction" based on abstract knowledge. The success or failure of a profession (i.e., whether it has wide jurisdiction or only a specialized niche) depends on its knowledge base—its ability to diagnose problems, make inferences from specific cases to general theories, and develop effective treatment. Material resources, political power, and cultural appeals play some part in the competition among professional groups, in Abbott's view, but typically are less important than the effectiveness of a profession's knowledge claims. Abbott compared lawyers in England and America, noting the response of the two to the dramatic expansion in potential demand for legal work in the late nineteenth and early twentieth centuries that was generated by the rise of large commercial enterprises and the administrative state. He argued that the inability of English solicitors to respond quickly to demand (because of their reluctance to certify large numbers of new solicitors) left the field open to competitors, chiefly accountants. The American profession, in contrast, responded by training much larger numbers of lawyers and by building large law firms, which both quantitatively and qualitatively altered the capacity for producing legal work. Abbott demonstrates that conflict among professions is not temporary, recent, or an aberration, but fundamental and continuing. Given competing jurisdictions, as well as struggles for ascendance among different subfields within a profession, it is difficult to predict changes in the social structure of the bar. If lawyers cannot more effectively diagnose and solve clients' problems, they may well lose significant portions of their jurisdiction.

In the 1980s, class-oriented theories of the professions had two distinct foci. "New class" theories—of the sort developed by Ivan Szelényi and Bill Martin (1989)—had an external orientation. These theories contended that previous typologies of class relationships failed to take adequate account of the growing number of professionals and knowledge-workers. Although some traditional professional groups could be expected to align themselves with capitalists, professionals who were involved in the provision of social services—teachers, social workers, psychologists, public health professionals, legal services lawyers—could be expected to favor welfare state policies. Thus, new class theories are primarily concerned with how professional groups align themselves in the political structure. The second strand of class-based theory, by contrast, focused on the internal organization of professions and on working conditions. Derber (1982) and his colleagues argued that, as more professionals have come to be employed in organizations not controlled by professionals, there has been a progressive deskilling or deprofessionalizing of their work. In this view, professionals face the degradation of their occupational status—they increasingly lack control over the objectives they pursue, as well as over the work processes in which they are engaged. As conditions for the free exercise of their skills erode, professionals become dependent on capitalist and state bureaucracies for their livelihood and are increasingly treated as a source of profit for the enterprise or as a cost to be reduced. Spangler's study of lawyers employed by nonlawyer organizations (1986) and Jerry Van Hoy's work on franchise law firms (1997) draw on this perspective.

In later writings, Freidson addressed the argument that the professions had lost power. Ironically, he began to celebrate the ideology of professionalism that he once so enthusiastically debunked. In *Professional Powers* (1986),

Freidson asserted that the professions—in their contemporary, institutional-ized forms—were still enormously powerful in many sectors of social life. He was highly critical of the proposition that the professions had been deskilled or deprofessionalized, and he suggested that aggregate measures of the per-centage of employed professionals or of the degree of specialization by pro-fessionals were not telling indicators of a loss of professional power. Indeed, Freidson argued that if the gatekeeping functions of large private and public organizations are examined, we can see that professionals make the crucial decisions. He took a celebratory turn in *Professionalism Reborn* (1994), a collection of essays. One essay, clearly responding to the dramatic changes in the practice of medicine, argued that the professional model for orga-nizing work and delivering services could and should be defended against market and bureaucratic systems of service delivery. Freidson asserted that the professional model best preserved the autonomous exercise of expert judgment, and in turn advanced the purposes of professional institutions. At least implicit in this normative stance is a conviction that the professions will be able to maintain their distinctive modes of organization in the face of market pressures and the shifting regulatory policies of the state.

The Data

The two surveys of the Chicago bar referred to above—the first in 1975 and a second in 1994–95—were both sponsored by the American Bar Foundation. Random samples were drawn of lawyers in all types of practice, as well as licensed lawyers who were retired, unemployed, or working in other jobs.[3] The geographic boundary was defined as the City of Chicago (not including the suburbs), but the lawyers could, of course, reside elsewhere or have an additional office elsewhere. Face-to-face interviews were conducted with all respondents, 777 in 1975 and 787 in late 1994 and early 1995, almost always in the respondents' offices. Interviews averaged more than an hour in length, in both surveys, and the response rate in both was 82 percent.[4] In 1995, 75 of the respondents (9.6 percent) said that they devoted fewer than ten hours per week to the practice of law. Respondents who were working in nonlegal jobs, who were judges or judicial clerks, or who were retired or unemployed are treated here as not practicing law.[5] In the 1995 sample, the number of practicing lawyers is 674; in the 1975 sample, the number was 699. Thus, the percentage of nonpracticing lawyers in the two samples increases from 10 percent in 1975 to 14 percent in 1995.

We have been able to obtain a limited amount of information about the characteristics of the nonrespondents in both surveys. In 1975, lawyers who

were in solo practice and those who were not members of the Chicago Bar
Association were less likely to be interviewed (Heinz and Laumann 1982,
9–10). In 1995, solo practitioners were again somewhat underrepresented,
as were lawyers in small firms. The 1995 nonrespondents were also significantly older than the random sample, more likely to have graduated from
one of the less prestigious law schools, and less likely to belong to a bar
association. In general, in both 1975 and 1995, it appears that the lawyers
who refused to be interviewed or who could not be contacted tended to be
somewhat more marginal to the profession—they were in less prestigious
positions and less connected to the organized bar—but the underenumera-
tions are relatively small, so that for most purposes we can treat the samples
as representative of Chicago lawyers. But we should remember that the surveys were somewhat more likely to include lawyers who were central to the
profession.

We have also done some analysis of the comparability of the 1975 and
1995 samples. Specifically, we compared characteristics of the respondents
in the 1975 sample with the 1995 respondents who were in practice in 1975.
Thus, we are able to determine whether the 1975 sample and the pre-1975
cohort in the 1995 sample appear to have been drawn from the same population. We found no significant difference between the two groups in place
of birth, size of place of residence during their high school years, or religious
preference. For example, we found that the religious affiliations of the two
groups were: Catholic, 30 percent vs. 25 percent; Jewish 33 percent vs. 34
percent; Protestant, 25 percent vs. 25 percent (note that the 1995 percentages given here refer only to the portion of that sample admitted to practice
before 1975, and that these percentages will therefore not match those in
fig. 1.1). As to differences in the type of law school attended, however, in
the 1995 survey we found substantially fewer graduates of four "local" law
schools located in Chicago (46 percent vs. 34 percent). Since graduates of
these schools do not enjoy, on the average, the same degree of opportunity
within the profession as do respondents from the other school categories
(see Heinz and Laumann 1982, 70, table 3.2.), it is plausible that a greater
proportion of the local school graduates in the pre-1975 cohort may have left
the practice of law by 1995 because of frustration or lack of success. That
is, the rate of attrition from the profession may plausibly be thought to be
higher for local school graduates.

Comparing the 1975 and 1995 samples (fig. 1.1), we see that the percentage of women increased very substantially, from only 3.9 percent in
1975 to 29 percent in 1995. This is clearly one of the biggest differences
in the characteristics of the profession. Historically, the American bar—like

Figure 1.1. Characteristics of Chicago Lawyers, 1975 and 1995 (percentages)

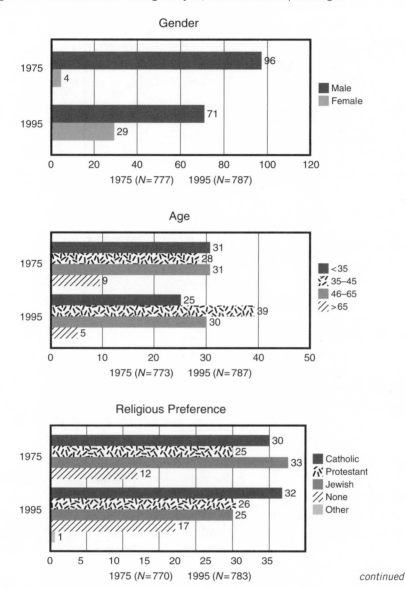

medicine and other elite professions—included few women (Abel 1989, 90–92, 285). Although women had started to enter law schools in substantial numbers in the early 1970s, not many had yet entered practice by 1975. The picture was much different by 1995. The official count of Illinois lawyers does not include an enumeration by gender at the city or county level, but

Figure 1.1 *continued*

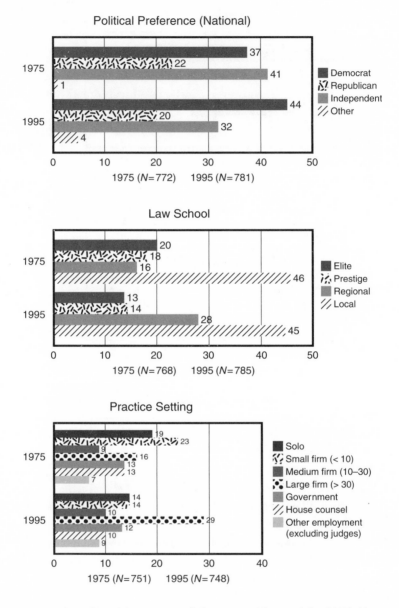

Political Preference (National)

1975 (*N*=772)   1995 (*N*=781)

Democrat
Republican
Independent
Other

Law School

1975 (*N*=768)   1995 (*N*=785)

Elite
Prestige
Regional
Local

Practice Setting

1975 (*N*=751)   1995 (*N*=748)

Solo
Small firm (< 10)
Medium firm (10–30)
Large firm (> 30)
Government
House counsel
Other employment
(excluding judges)

women amounted to 26 percent of the statewide total in 1995 (Attorney Registration and Disciplinary Commission 1996, 4). Nationally, in 1970 only 2.8 percent of the nation's lawyers were women, and this percentage had remained steady since the mid-1950s (Sikes, Carson, and Gorai 1972, 5, table 1). By 1991, the percentage of women had increased to 20 percent (Curran and Carson 1994, 4, table 2), but it was still far from the percentage among law school graduates, which was over 40 percent (American Bar Association 1992, 66).

In 1975, only 22 respondents were members of minority groups, 21 African Americans (2.7 percent of the sample) and one Asian American (0.1 percent) (Heinz and Laumann 1982, 10). There were no Hispanics in the 1975 sample. By 1995, however, additional African Americans and other minorities had gained entry to the bar. The 1995 random sample includes 39 blacks (5 percent), 8 Asians (1 percent), 10 Hispanics (1.3 percent), and 3 other minority lawyers (0.4 percent). Thus, our estimate is that between 1975 and 1995 the Chicago bar changed from 97 percent white to 92 percent white. The age distribution is also of interest (see fig. 1.1). Note that the percentage of respondents over age 65 declined substantially—from 9.1 percent in 1975 to 5 percent in 1995—but recall that this takes place in the context of an approximate doubling of the size of the overall bar. Thus, the number of Chicago lawyers over 65 was somewhat greater in 1995 than it had been in 1975. Note also that, in spite of the rapid growth in the size of the bar, the age category showing an increased percentage is not the youngest group (those under age 35) but those in the 35–45 category. If we look at the year in which the 1995 respondents were graduated from law school, we find that the graduating classes of the mid-1970s each contributed about 20 respondents to the sample. The number reaches 25 in the 1979 graduating class, 30 in 1981, 40 in 1982, and then did not fall below 30 through the end of the series (1993) except in one year, 1983. Thus, the output of the law schools (at least as reflected in the lawyers who enter the Chicago market) appears to peak in the early 1980s and then remain fairly constant. The difference in the age distribution, therefore, may be explained by an increasing tendency to go to law school only after a bit of work experience (see chap. 12).

The biggest difference in the distribution of religious preference in the two samples is the decline in the proportion of Jewish lawyers from nearly a third in 1975 to about a quarter in 1995. Again, however, remember that the size of the bar doubled—thus, there were more Jewish lawyers in Chicago in 1995 than in 1975. The decreasing percentage reflects the rapid growth of the bar over the two decades. The best-informed estimates are that the percentage of Jews in the population of the Chicago metropolitan area in the last quarter of the twentieth century was in the range of 3 percent to 4 percent (Freidman and Phillips 1994; see also Beverly 1954). Since the majority of all Chicago lawyers are recruited from the metropolitan area,[6] when the bar is growing rapidly it would be very unlikely for the prior percentage of overrepresentation of Jews to be maintained. The percentage reported here includes lawyers who identified themselves as Jewish in response to either of two questions: The first asked, "What is your religious preference? That is, are you either Protestant, Roman Catholic, Jewish or something else?"; and the second asked, "What nationality background do you think of yourself as having—that is, besides being American?" In response to the latter question, substantial numbers said "Russian Jewish," "German Jewish," and so on. Lawyers identifying themselves as Jewish in response to either question are included in the percentages reported here.

With respect to political preference, we see a decline in the percentage of lawyers identifying themselves as "independents," from 41 percent in 1975 to 32 percent in 1995, while the percentage calling themselves "Democrats" increases from 37 percent in 1975 to 44 percent in 1995. This change is probably attributable to the fact that the first Mayor Daley was still living at the time of the earlier survey, and many liberals were alienated from the "Daley Organization" and thus identified themselves as independents (Heinz and Laumann 1982, 11–14). For that reason, the 1975 survey distinguished between "national political preference" and "Chicago political preference," and an "independent Democrat" category was provided as an option for responses to the latter question (this was the most numerous category, attracting 40 percent of the respondents; Heinz and Laumann 1982, 13). The distinction between national and local preferences was not used in the 1995 survey. The Republican percentage in 1975 (22 percent) seemed relatively modest, but the Watergate scandal was thought to have depressed Republican identification temporarily. Note, however, that the Republican percentage was even lower (20 percent) in 1995, despite the fact that the latter survey was done at one of the several low points in the popularity of the Clinton administration, not long after the failure of its health-care initiative.

The law school data are grouped in four categories. The elite category includes just six schools: Chicago, Columbia, Harvard, Michigan, Stanford, and Yale (in alphabetical order). In a study of law school reputation in the early 1970s, these schools were ranked in the top five much more often than were others (Blau and Margulies 1974–75), and they remain at or near the top of most such reputational ratings (e.g., *U.S. News and World Report*).[7] The schools in the prestige category are Berkeley, Cornell, Duke, Georgetown, New York University, Northwestern, and four other schools with three or fewer respondents each. In the regional category, alumni of the University of Illinois predominate; this group also includes Indiana, Iowa, Ohio State, Notre Dame, Wisconsin, and several schools with small numbers of graduates in the sample. The local category consists of just four schools, all located in Chicago: Chicago-Kent College of Law, DePaul, John Marshall, and Loyola. These four law schools had trained nearly half of all Chicago lawyers in the 1975 sample, and this remained virtually unchanged in 1995. But note that the percentage of graduates of regional schools increased (from 16 percent to 28 percent) at the expense of graduates of the more highly ranked schools.[8] This reflects the fact that, as the size of the bar increased over the two decades, the enrollments of elite law schools remained constant or grew only modestly.[9]

The most obvious change in the distribution of Chicago lawyers across the various practice settings is the near-doubling in the percentage found in firms with more than thirty lawyers (from 16 percent to 29 percent). The growth of large law firms was clearly one of the most important developments in the legal profession in the last quarter of the twentieth century, and we explore both its causes and its consequences.[10] By contrast, the percentage of solo practitioners decreased from 19 percent to 14 percent, continuing a trend that has been observed for as long as systematic data on the legal profession have been available, and the percentage in firms with fewer than ten lawyers also declined sharply. In 1960, 64 percent of all lawyers, nationally, were solo practitioners, but by 1991 only 45 percent of lawyers were solos (Curran and Carson 1994, 7). In large cities, the proportion was smaller. Note that the share of the profession in house counsel positions declined somewhat (this is contrary to some observations in the scholarly literature; e.g., R. Rosen 1989, 488), while medium-sized firms (10 to 30 lawyers), government legal offices, and respondents who were not practicing remained essentially constant. The number of respondents holding jobs outside the legal profession (e.g., as accountants, bankers, insurance agents, stock brokers, or executives in business firms) was 47 in 1975 (6 percent of the sample) and 57 in 1995 (7 percent of the sample)—these are included in the "not practicing" category in figure 1.1.[11] No retired or unemployed lawyers were included in 1975, but there were 18 in the 1995 random sample. In addition, the 1975 sample included 21 judges and judicial clerks and the 1995 sample included 22. The judges and the retired or unemployed lawyers are not counted in figure 1.1.

Coding and cleaning of the data from the 1994–95 interviews began in the fall of 1995, and the cleaning continued throughout the life of the project. Analyses were done over a period of years. Because cleaning continued as the computations proceeded, the categories used and the distribution of cases across those categories vary marginally from chapter to chapter. We are confident that these differences in coding do not materially affect the conclusions. The most difficult coding decisions concerned lawyers who were less than fully engaged in the practice of law, especially those who practiced law part-time and supplemented their legal work with various sorts of business activity, or who were, in effect, underemployed. The classification of some of those cases is, necessarily, problematic. Fortunately, such lawyers are relatively few.

The Issues

Three interrelated theoretical concerns motivated our research. For convenience, we will refer to these as "professional autonomy," "professional integration," and "social stratification," but the brief labels fail to capture the complexity and subtlety of the issues.

The autonomy theme is, in turn, subdivided into issues concerning the extent of lawyers' control over the content and conditions of their work and issues concerning the degree to which lawyers, individually or collectively, possess influence in the polity or the broader society that is independent of the power of their clients (i.e., the issue is the power of lawyers *qua* lawyers rather than as agents). Everett Hughes asserted that solo practitioners were "the choreboys of their clients" (1958). Is this accurate—either as a characterization of solos or of other lawyers? To what extent are lawyers free, in fact, to refuse cases or clients that come to them? To what extent can they select the strategies that they will pursue and the methods used to implement those strategies? If they are constrained, do the constraints come from clients or from superiors in their own organizations? Do restrictions on autonomy contribute significantly to occupational dissatisfaction among lawyers, or do lawyers place greater weight on other values—perhaps money or status or political power? Do bar associations advance the collective interests of lawyers effectively? How many lawyers, and what types of lawyers, participate actively in the work of bar associations? Do lawyers, in fact, share interests that could be advanced by such collective activity? This last question leads directly to the next theme, professional integration.

To what extent does the legal profession behave as a single entity, with unitary goals and with a sense of professional coherence? Is the work of the profession separated into distinct clusters? If so, how much contact is there among these clusters? Where does that occur? Are the segments divided by the content of the legal doctrines used, by the types of clients served, by the institutions in which the lawyers work, by the lawyers' social or educational backgrounds, or by other characteristics? Do these various groupings of lawyers overlap and, if so, where does that overlap occur? What are the sources of social integration in the bar? Do the elites of the profession—

perhaps the leading practitioners in each field or the political leaders of the bar serve to pull it together? What is the degree and locus of contact among these elites? What are the sources of dissensus? Do social distinctions among lawyers or differences in professional status tend to drive them apart? We are, then, led to the next theme: social stratification.

To what extent do lawyers with systematically different social characteristics—including race, ethnicity, gender, socioeconomic origins—fill distinct roles in the practice of law? Especially, to what extent do they serve clients drawn from distinct social strata? Note that this issue cuts across both of the other themes. Social stratification affects professional independence if lawyers' work options are constrained by their social characteristics or social origins. How many lawyers, for example, have little option but to practice in their own residential neighborhoods, with a practice restricted to neighborhood clients and neighborhood problems? Which sorts of lawyers are most likely to face such constraints? If the allocation of work among lawyers is determined by social criteria (i.e., by the preferences and prejudices of the broader society) rather than by intraprofessional norms or values, then we might say that the independence of the profession as a collectivity is also constrained. Do societal prejudices conflict with professional values, or do they penetrate the professional value system? Social stratification may also affect professional integration if lawyers with distinct social characteristics— especially, minorities and women—are assigned to distinct work roles. Are the social strata of the broader society important determinants of the kinds of work that lawyers do and the places in which they do it, thus interfering with the integration of the profession? How does social stratification, insofar as it is present within the bar, affect the distribution of justice? Do poorer clients get less well-educated, less competent lawyers?

Our answers to these questions must, of necessity, be partial and unsatisfactory. The available data are limited. Although we draw on a variety of sources, we have original data for only one city at two points in time. Moreover, although our interviews were relatively long (averaging 70 minutes for the 787 respondents in the 1995 random sample) and were, no doubt, a substantial imposition upon the patience and generosity of the respondents, the interviews could not deal with all of the issues in sufficient detail to provide definitive answers. Indeed, interviews are surely not the most satisfactory or reliable way to address some of the issues.

How typical is Chicago, and how typical were 1975 and 1995? Might particular events have distorted findings from those times or that place? The short answer is that we cannot be sure. In principle, it is impossible to identify all of the ways in which other times and places might differ. But we do know some things about the context. We know that Chicago is bigger than Omaha but smaller than New York. We know that Chicago has a racially and ethnically diverse population. We know that its economic base is more varied than that of Silicon Valley or Detroit. According to the Census of Service Industries, the growth rate of the legal profession in Chicago was near the middle of the rates in major U.S. cities. Expenditures on legal services in Chicago grew by 327 percent from 1977 to 1997 in constant dollars (U.S. Bureau of the Census 1977, 1997). Over the same period, such expenditures grew by 405 percent in New York, 459 percent in Los Angeles, and 528 percent in Phoenix, but by only 160 percent in Cleveland and 30 percent in Detroit (ibid.). Although the populations of Sun Belt cities generally grew more rapidly than those in the Rust Belt, the rate of growth of legal services in Chicago was the same as that in Miami (327 percent) and similar to that in Pittsburgh (346 percent) (ibid.). Apart from these varying growth rates, however, we know of no reasons to believe that the Chicago bar during the last quarter of the twentieth century differed in significant respects from the bars of other major American cities with diverse populations and economies.

Chapter 2
The Changing Character of Lawyers' Work
With Ethan Michelson

Chicago Lawyers, the book that reported the findings of the 1975 study, argued that the bar was essentially divided into two distinct sectors:

> [M]uch of the differentiation within the legal profession is secondary to one fundamental distinction—the distinction between lawyers who represent large organizations (corporations, labor unions, or government) and those who represent individuals. (Heinz and Laumann 1982, 319)

> The two sectors of the legal profession thus include different lawyers, with different social origins, who were trained at different law schools, serve different sorts of clients, practice in different office environments, are differentially likely to engage in litigation, litigate (when and if they litigate) in different forums, have somewhat different values, associate with different circles of acquaintance, and rest their claims to professionalism on different sorts of social power. . . . Only in the most formal of senses, then, do the two types of lawyers constitute one profession. (Heinz and Laumann 1982, 384)

(Because we refer to this book throughout, we hereafter cite it by title.) But, as noted in chapter 1, there were important changes in the legal profession after 1975. Women entered the bar in large numbers, the overall size of the profession doubled while the organizations within which law is practiced grew at an even greater rate, the management practices of those organizations became more formal and intrusive (Abel 1989, 199–202), and there were substantial changes in the demand for particular types of legal services. Some of these changes have affected the organization of lawyers' work and thus have altered the separation between the sectors of the bar.

Note, however, that separation of work by client type was not the sole basis of the "two-hemispheres" thesis. Rather, that thesis rested in substantial part on the social separation between the two sets of practitioners—in their socioeconomic and ethnoreligious backgrounds, in their educational credentials, in the settings within which they practiced, in their political values, and in their circles of acquaintance and professional association. Those topics are dealt with in subsequent chapters (see especially chaps. 3, 6, 8, and 10).

The 1975 "Two-Hemispheres" Finding: Methodological Issues

Both Chicago surveys presented the respondents with a list of fields of practice and asked them to indicate the percentage of their work time devoted to each of the fields during the past year.[1] The list of fields used in the 1975 interview instruments was, however, ill suited to an assessment of the separation of practice into two client-based hemispheres. The principal defect was that three putative fields—tax, litigation, and real estate—were not differentiated by client type. Respondents indicated only that they devoted time to "tax," not corporate tax, or personal income tax, and so on. When Heinz and Laumann designed the 1975 interview, they did not anticipate the crucial part that client type would play in their analyses. Development of the two-hemispheres thesis was still some years away. As the 1975 data were analyzed, however, it became apparent that the client-type variable was of considerable importance and that the field categories were, especially in these three instances, too crude to capture some of the interesting differentiation.

Consequently, Heinz and Laumann made an effort to separate respondents doing tax, litigation, or real estate work into two classes within each of these three broad categories—to separate lawyers serving primarily corporate clients from those serving individuals or small businesses. Respondents who reported that they received 80 percent or more of their professional income from corporate clients were assigned to the corporate tax, corporate litigation, and corporate real estate fields, and the remaining respondents were placed in general or personal tax, litigation, and real estate (Heinz and Laumann 1982, 32, n. 6). For most purposes, such as analysis of the social characteristics of practitioners in the various fields, this assignment procedure is relatively unproblematic. In analyses of the structure of specialization, however, the procedure does create a problem. The assignment of respondents to either the corporate or the personal side of each of the three areas of practice was mutually exclusive. Thus, there could be no overlap between the two sides. Indeed, the corporate client sides of each of the three categories could not overlap with the personal client sides of any of the three, since the same 80 percent of income criterion was used for each.

Because of the inadequacy of the original list of fields used in the interview, Heinz and Laumann lacked data needed to evaluate the extent of this problem. They knew that a respondent devoted x percent of her time to tax work and derived y percent of her income from corporate clients (and some other percentage from individuals, governments, and other types of organizations), but they did not know whether the respondent did both corporate tax and personal income or estate tax work. Thus, they could not assess the amount of overlap in the practice of these fields.

In the 1995 interviews, this defect was corrected. Tax was disaggregated into four categories: estate and gift tax, federal income tax (personal), federal income tax (corporate), and state and local tax (including property taxes, hotel user fees, sales tax, etc.). Real estate was also divided into four categories: real estate finance and development, landlord/tenant, residential transfers, and zoning and eminent domain. Civil litigation was separated into personal client litigation and corporate client litigation. When the data from the 1995 interviews were in hand, we could see appreciable overlap in the practice of these subfields.

Because the numbers of respondents in some of the new categories are small, a few of those categories have been combined in the following analyses. Corporate income tax and state and local tax are combined in a business tax category, and these are separated from personal income tax and estate and gift tax (personal tax). Real estate finance and development, landlord/tenant, and zoning and eminent domain (business real estate) are distinguished from residential real estate transfers (personal real estate).[2] Thus, we have derived categories that separate the work primarily addressed to the problems of businesses from that primarily addressed to the concerns of individuals.

Using these definitions, we find that in 1995, of the 268 respondents who devoted as much as 5 percent of their time to either corporate or personal litigation, 26 percent (70) did both. Of 152 respondents doing either business or personal real estate work, 24 percent (37) were in both, and overlap among tax practitioners amounted to 22 percent (20) of 89 respondents. The 5 percent time criterion, of course, tells us whether there is overlap at a rather minimal level. If we use a 25 percent time criterion instead, the overlap declines to 13 percent in litigation (22 of 174 respondents), 15 percent in real estate (11 of 74 respondents), and 12 percent in tax (6 of 50 respondents). In sum, about three-quarters of the practitioners in each of these three doctrinal areas do not cross the client-type line for even 5 percent of their time, and only about a seventh devote substantial amounts of time to both types of work.

Since the 1995 data show some overlap in these fields, however, we have now reanalyzed the 1975 data to assess the extent to which the mutually exclusive assignment procedure affected the analyses of the structure of co-practice. But we are necessarily in the position of trading one methodological artifact for another. Given the inadequacy of the original, undifferentiated field categories, we may either choose to split the fields by client type, thereby creating the appearance of greater client separation in the structure of practice, or choose to use the original categories—tax, litigation, real estate—thereby combining work that usually separates by client type and creating a picture of greater overlap than, in fact, exists. *Chicago Lawyers* used the first strategy. We have now pursued the latter.

Figure 2.1 shows the hierarchical clustering of the fields that was presented in the earlier book. Figure 2.2 also uses the 1975 data, but with tax, litigation, and real estate recombined into their original, undifferentiated form. The proximities in both figures are estimated by using the average conditional probabilities of co-practice of the pairs of fields (Heinz and Laumann 1982, 50, 56–58). For example, if the probability of practicing in the banking field is 10 percent given the condition that the respondent does general corporate work, and if the probability that a respondent will do general corporate work given that he does banking is 40 percent, then the average conditional probability of co-practice of those two fields would be 25 percent. As anticipated, the structure in figure 2.2 is less clearly separated by client type because work for the two classes of clients is combined in the three fields. Nevertheless, the cluster at the bottom of the figure, with criminal defense, divorce, personal injury plaintiffs work, and general family practice, includes much of the work that is done primarily for individuals. The two sides of labor law join with this cluster near zero. A small political or government cluster includes municipal law and criminal prosecution, and a more diffuse cluster includes litigation, personal injury defense, civil rights, and public utilities/administrative law.[3] Proceeding up the list, we see a large cluster that includes most of the business law areas; this is subdivided into a financial cluster including commercial, banking, and securities work, and a more general cluster including tax, general corporate, probate, and real estate. A competitive practices or regulation of competition cluster,

Figure 2.1. Hierarchical Clustering of Fields by Co-practice, 1975

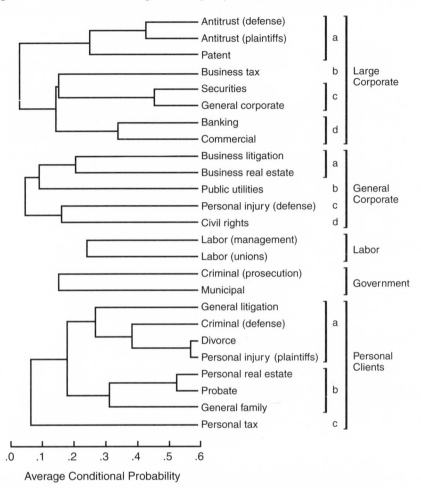

Average Conditional Probability

including patents and trademarks and the two sides of antitrust, joins the other business fields just before zero. Thus, even when the two sides of tax, litigation, and real estate are combined, as in figure 2.2, the separation between the hemispheres is clear.

The analysis presented here, like that used in *Chicago Lawyers*, includes all practitioners who devote 5 percent or more of their time to a field; if there is as much as 5 percent co-practice between two fields, they are treated as overlapping. By this measure, then, overlap is dichotomous: either two fields overlap for a given respondent or they do not. No weight is given to the extent of the co-practice—that is, to the amount of time in each field.

Figure 2.2. Hierarchical Clustering of Fields by Co-practice in 1975, with Litigation, Real Estate, and Tax Recombined

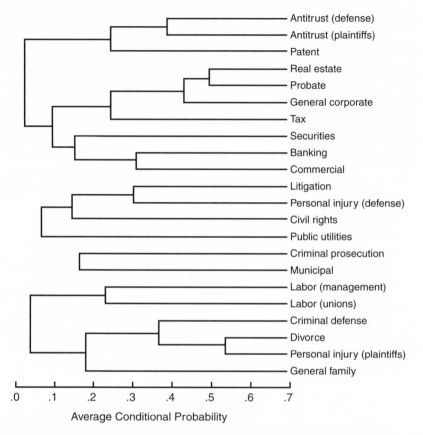

If a respondent devotes 50 percent of her time to securities, 45 percent to tax, and 5 percent to general corporate, in these analyses securities overlaps with general corporate to the same extent that it does with tax. It is possible, then, that the analysis might understate the degree of overlap between pairs of fields in the sense that it does not attend to the concentration of time in cognate fields. To evaluate this possibility, we did additional analyses using an interval measure of the extent of overlap, employing the data on time in each field.[4] For the 1975 data, the resulting hierarchical clustering is much like that presented in figure 2.2. The only difference of any interest is that civil litigation and personal injury defense cluster with the personal litigation fields (criminal defense, divorce, and personal injury plaintiffs work) instead of with civil rights and public utilities. Thus, when time is taken into account, all the main litigation fields cluster together—litigation as a function or skill appears to predominate over the substance of the work. But recall that in these data the civil litigation field is undifferentiated by client type.

1995 Patterns of Co-practice

In figure 2.3, as in figures 2.1 and 2.2, overlap among the fields is measured at the 5 percent level (i.e., 5 percent of the practitioner's time), and co-practice is treated as dichotomous. In these 1995 data, however, the organization of work is subdivided into smaller, more highly specialized clusters that are less clearly separated by the distinction between corporate and personal client types. Note that the fields and clusters do not join as closely in the 1995 structure as they did in 1975. For example, in 1975 (fig. 2.2), divorce joins with personal injury plaintiffs work at .57, and these two fields then join with criminal defense at .39. In 1995, we see this same cluster of fields, but now divorce joins personal injury plaintiffs work only at .31 and criminal defense does not join these two until .22. In the 1995 analysis, criminal prosecution is an isolate; it does not join with any other field. Patents, immigration, and insurance are also near isolates; they do not join other fields until .05 or less. This does not require much co-practice—the connection at .05 between immigration law and the patents and trademarks field is produced by just one respondent, who reported time at the 5–24 percent level in each of the two fields. This respondent practiced in a large firm and did primarily civil litigation for corporate clients, but he was politically active and reported that he also did some pro bono work for groups that he characterized as concerned with "human rights."

In 1995, then, it appears that, in organizing the co-practice of the fields, specialization by client type played a lesser role and substantive or skill-type specialization played a greater role than in the 1975 analyses. Note, for example, that environmental work for defendants joins first with that done for plaintiffs, general civil litigation joins first with business litigation, and personal real estate joins with business real estate. The two sides of labor, however, are not joined here, as they were in 1975,[5] and personal tax joins with probate before joining with business tax substantially closer to zero. The small personal plight cluster—criminal defense, divorce, and personal injury plaintiffs work—joins at .05 with a broader and more diffuse aggregation of fields, including business and general civil litigation, labor union work, the two sides of real estate, and general family practice. The broader aggregation is, in turn, subdivided into two clusters that join only at .10. The other large cluster—from antitrust defense through commercial law—includes most of the business fields. Note, however, that probate and personal tax are found in the midst of corporate fields here.

Figure 2.3. Hierarchical Clustering of Fields by Co-practice, 1995

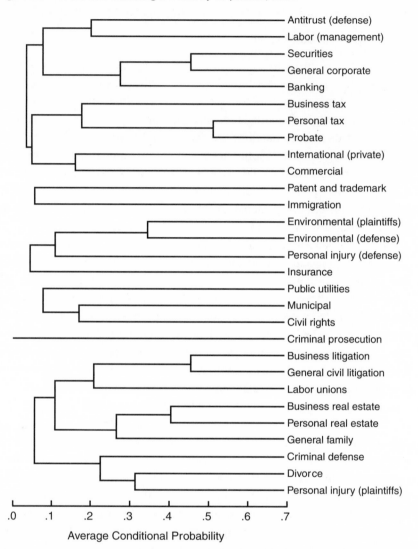

Average Conditional Probability

In an analysis of the 1995 data using our interval measure of time in each field, we again find that the hierarchical clustering closely resembles figure 2.3. The principal difference between the two measures is that, while the business and personal sides of tax and of litigation cluster together in figure 2.3, they separate when time in the field is taken into account. Thus, when we attend to the concentration of lawyers' time, the separation of tax work and litigation by client type becomes more pronounced.[6]

The separation of the hemispheres is still seen in the 1995 data, then, but there is an important difference between 1975 and 1995—in 1995 there is less overlap among the fields.[7] Since the fields became increasingly isolated from one another, we turn next to an analysis of specialization.

Specialization by Field

In 1975, of 687 practicing lawyers responding, 23 percent worked in only one field. In 1995, in spite of the fact that respondents were presented with a longer, more detailed list of fields (forty-two field categories were used in 1995 versus thirty in 1975), 33 percent of 675 practicing lawyers indicated that they worked in only one field. Specialization thus appears to have increased substantially over the twenty years. We computed a specialization index that permits comparison of the degree of specialization by field in 1995 and 1975, controlling for the number of field categories used in the two studies.[8] Figure 2.4 presents twenty-seven fields with data for both years, listed in the order of their degree of specialization in 1975. The specialization index ranges from 0 to 1, where 1 indicates complete specialization (i.e., practice in only one field). Overall (for all fields), specialization increases from .488 in 1975 to .571 in 1995. Note that the index declines in only three of the twenty-seven fields: labor union work, public utilities/administrative law, and environmental work for plaintiffs. In probate, the degree of specialization is constant, and it increases only very marginally in civil rights and business real estate. These fields, of course, then move down in the specialization rank order. The fields that increase most markedly are personal injury plaintiffs work, which moves from eighteenth in rank order to seventh; environmental work for defendants, which moves from twenty-sixth to thirteenth; and commercial, which moves from last place to seventeenth. In sum, specialization increased both substantially and quite generally over the twenty-year period. Note, too, that the corporate fields are not necessarily the most specialized—for example, banking and antitrust defense have a relatively low degree of specialization at both times, and general corporate is in thirteenth place in 1975 and twenty-first in 1995. But family practice and divorce, both of which are personal client fields, are also consistently near the bottom of the list.

While the specialization index used here corrects for the number of field categories in a statistical sense—that is, to permit comparison of 1975 and 1995 index values—the index cannot eliminate the possible effects of response bias resulting from the use of different stimuli in 1975 and 1995. As noted above, the 1995 survey presented respondents with a more highly

Figure 2.4. Mean Specialization Index by Field, 1975 and 1995

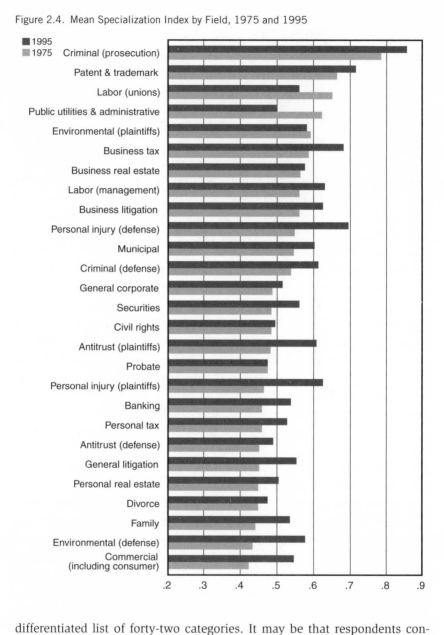

differentiated list of forty-two categories. It may be that respondents confronted with a more detailed set of choices will tend to disaggregate their
work time.[9] Since we find a substantially higher degree of specialization in
1995, however, such a bias (if any) would be conservative. That is, it would
tend to understate or diminish the degree of specialization.

Client Differentiation by Field

Because we have data on the types of clients represented by lawyers practicing in the various fields, we are able to assess more directly the association between particular field categories and the client-type categories. As a first step, let us examine the clientele of respondents who report that they devote 25 percent or more of their time to each of the fields in the 1995 data. Using that criterion, the percentage of clients that are businesses (other client categories are persons—individuals or families—unions, government, and nonprofit organizations) ranges from a mean of 5 percent in criminal prosecution and 8 percent in criminal defense to a high of 91 percent in environmental defense.[10]

Given the 25 percent time criterion, the respondent could be practicing in as many as three other fields. Because the same respondent will be counted in multiple fields, thus reducing variance across the fields, the degree of client differentiation among the fields is quite striking. Figure 2.5 presents the mean percentages of business clients by field. Note that, as one would expect, fields dealing with the personal problems of individuals tend to be the quintessential personal client fields. This is especially the case when the lawyers often represent the poor or those of moderate means, as in criminal defense and personal injury plaintiffs' work. When the clients are more likely to have some money—as, for example, in probate or residential real estate—there is a greater likelihood that the practitioner may represent businesses as well. At the other extreme of the distribution, we see fields that are likely to represent the largest corporations—environmental defense, banking, and patents and trademarks.

But note that some fields of practice serve a more varied clientele. Thus, on the average, 45 percent of the clients served by lawyers who do municipal law work are businesses, while those lawyers also do a considerable amount of work for local governments. Note that 58 percent of the clients of respondents who do personal tax work are businesses and that 72 percent of the clients of those who do corporate tax are businesses. The lawyer who prepares the corporate tax returns for the Smedley Corporation may do the personal returns of Mr. and Mrs. Smedley as well.[11] As indicated in figure 2.5, instead of two hemispheres, we see three broad clusters of fields. Six fields are practiced by lawyers who serve relatively few businesses, while respondents in a larger group of fields (half of the 26) report that two-thirds or more of their clients are businesses, and the remainder of the fields serve a more varied mix. A middle group of fields appears to bridge the extremes.

Figure 2.5. Percentage of Business Clients by Field, 1995

High Group

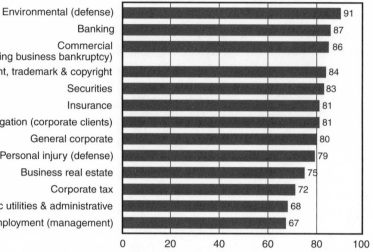

Field	%
Environmental (defense)	91
Banking	87
Commercial (including business bankruptcy)	86
Patent, trademark & copyright	84
Securities	83
Insurance	81
Civil litigation (corporate clients)	81
General corporate	80
Personal injury (defense)	79
Business real estate	75
Corporate tax	72
Public utilities & administrative	68
Employment (management)	67

Middle Group

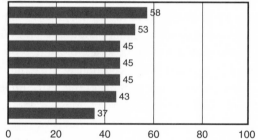

Field	%
Personal tax	58
Environmental (plaintiffs)	53
Municipal	45
Residential real estate	45
Civil litigation (personal clients)	45
Probate	43
Civil rights	37

Low Group

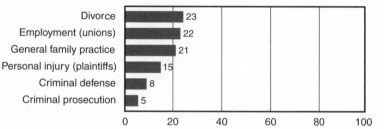

Field	%
Divorce	23
Employment (unions)	22
General family practice	21
Personal injury (plaintiffs)	15
Criminal defense	8
Criminal prosecution	5

Note: Fields with 10 or more lawyers at 25 percent or more time.

In a similar analysis of the 1975 data, we find a greater tendency for the fields to divide into only two clusters, separated by client type.[12]

Allocation of Time in 1975 and 1995

In table 2.1, we compare estimates of the percentages of lawyers' time or effort devoted to the several fields of law in 1975 and 1995.[13] Using a procedure developed by Charles Cappell (Heinz and Laumann 1982, 42 n.8), we derived these estimates from the respondents' reports of the time that they devoted to each field. Since the numbers in the table are percentages of total lawyers' time, the historical comparison is somewhat tricky. There were about half as many lawyers in Chicago in 1975 as there were in 1995. Therefore, if we consider the first field on the list—antitrust defense—our estimate is that the field received 2 percent of lawyers' effort in 1975 and 1 percent in 1995,[14] but since there were twice as many lawyers in Chicago in 1995, the total amount of effort (or time) expended on antitrust defense is about the same in each year. The amount of lawyers' time devoted to business litigation, then, is three to four times larger in percentage terms but amounts to about a sevenfold increase in total effort. Similarly, the total amount of time devoted to criminal defense has not decreased (it has, instead, increased somewhat), even though the proportion decreases from 5 percent to 3 percent. It appears, in fact, that while prosecutors were being outgunned by the defense lawyers in 1975, the two sides of criminal work reached parity by 1995 (in terms of time, at least).

As the number of lawyers doubled, the total amount of effort devoted to almost all of the fields increased—to varying degrees. The only fields in which the amount actually decreased, in absolute terms, were probate and public utilities (which were also among the fields that moved down markedly in the specialization rank order). The biggest increases are seen in the litigation fields. Business litigation has by far the largest increase, but the increase in general litigation is also substantial. In percentage terms, we see decreases in general corporate work (from 11 percent to 6 percent) and in divorce (from 6 percent to 3 percent). Corporate work apparently became more specialized, so that it was less often assigned to the general, undifferentiated category and more often to particular specialties—such as environmental work. The decrease in the percentage of divorce practice probably reflects the fact that the rate of increase in business activity was far greater than that of the Chicago-area population. Note again, however, that these decreasing percentages occurred on a base that was twice as large.

Table 2.1. Estimated Distribution of Legal Effort, 1975 and 1995

Field	1975		1995	
	No. of Practitioners in Field	Estimated % of Total Legal Effort	No. of Practitioners in Field	Estimated % of Total Legal Effort
Corporate client sector	543	53	562	64
Large corporate				
Antitrust (defense)	47	2	20	1
Business litigation	91	4	215	14
Business real estate	74	4	105	6
Business tax	51	3	57	4
Labor (management)	39	2	71	5
Securities	53	2	56	3
Cluster total	256	18	404	32
Regulatory				
Labor (unions)	18	1	31	2
Patents	45	4	44	3
Public utilities and administrative	52	3	20	1
Environmental (plaintiffs)	5	—[a]	17	1
Environmental (defendants)	18	—[a]	39	2
Cluster total	123	9	137	9
General corporate				
Antitrust (plaintiffs)	24	1	9	—[a]
Banking	60	3	49	2
Commercial (including consumer)	102	3	63	3
General corporate	262	11	142	6
Personal injury (defendants)	73	4	80	7
Cluster total	396	22	282	18
Political				
Criminal (prosecution)	20	2	25	3
Municipal	30	1	25	2
Cluster total	46	3	48	5
Personal/small-business client sector	424	40	330	29
Personal business				
General litigation	90	3	123	5
Personal real estate	152	6	84	3
Personal tax	57	2	52	2
Probate	195	8	79	3
Cluster total	296	19	230	13
Personal plight				
Civil rights	41	2	45	2
Criminal (defense)	91	5	41	3
Divorce	153	6	52	3
Family	84	3	62	3
Personal injury (plaintiffs)	120	6	87	6
Cluster total	296	21	208	16
Other fields and unassigned time	162	7	170	7
Total	699	100	675	100

Note: The number of practitioners is defined as all respondents who devoted at least 5 percent of their work to the field. For estimation procedure, see Heinz and Laumann 1982.
[a] Less than one half of 1 percent.

Overall, the corporate client fields grew more rapidly than the personal client fields, and the hemispheres became more unequal in size. In the 1975 data, the estimate is that 53 percent of lawyers' time was allocated to the corporate fields (including work for nonbusiness organizations, such as unions and governmental entities), while 40 percent was devoted to the personal client fields and another 7 percent was not clearly assignable or was spread across a variety of small fields. By 1995, the disparity between the two sectors had increased considerably. As shown in table 2.1, the corporate sector consumed more than twice the amount of Chicago lawyers' time devoted to personal and small-business client work in 1995 (64 percent versus 29 percent). Our estimates of the percentages of time devoted to corporate and individual clients in 1995 correspond remarkably closely to the U.S. Census report of the amount of income that lawyers in the Chicago Metropolitan Statistical Area derived from such clients in 1992. The census reported that 27.9 percent of Chicago lawyers' 1992 receipts came from individuals, 60.1 percent from businesses, and 4.5 percent from government (the remainder came from three small categories; U.S. Bureau of the Census 1996a, 4–446, table 49). The extraordinarily close correspondence of the two estimates, drawn from entirely different data sources, is impressive, but it should be viewed with some caution. If time is equivalent to income, does this suggest that hourly wages are the same in the two sectors? This seems implausible (see chap. 7). Several other factors vary here—for example, the metropolitan area may include a higher proportion of individual client work than does the city.

The large-corporate cluster of fields increased most—from 18 percent of the total in 1975 to 32 percent in 1995—while the personal business and personal plight clusters both declined. One might speculate that some or all of the shift from personal client work toward corporate work between 1975 and 1995 is attributable to a movement of middle-class population from the city to the suburbs. Given "white flight," so the thesis goes, lawyers are likely to have followed the clientele. This would explain, for example, the decline in trusts and estates practice in the city. But the U.S. Census data indicate that the percentage of lawyers' income received from individual clients (persons) declined nationally, while the percentage received from businesses increased substantially. Receipts from individuals decreased from 52.2 percent of total U.S. lawyer receipts in 1972 to 39.6 percent in 1992, while receipts from businesses increased from 42.0 percent to 50.9 percent (and receipts from government increased from 2.9 percent to 3.8 percent) (U.S. Bureau of the Census 1976 and 1996a). The distribution of Chicago lawyers' receipts is similar to that in several other major cities, though not in all. In Sacramento, receipts from individuals decreased modestly from 50.4 percent of the total in 1982 to 46.3 percent in 1992, while receipts from businesses increased from 38.8 percent to 45.2 percent. In Los Angeles, receipts from individuals fell markedly from 46.2 percent in 1982 to 31.0 percent in 1992, while receipts from businesses from rose 49.5 percent to 56.6 percent. In Philadelphia, however, the percentage of receipts from the two categories of clients was virtually unchanged from 1982 to 1992 (varying only from 45 percent to 47 percent for each), and in Phoenix the changes were also modest (individuals fell from 43.3 percent to 38.3 percent, while businesses rose only from 51.7 percent to 53.7 percent) (U.S. Bureau of the Census 1986 and 1996a). The largest city in this set, Los Angeles, displays the pattern most similar to that of Chicago.

Moreover, available data do not appear to indicate a great shift of lawyer population from the city to the suburbs. Official counts of Illinois lawyers first became available from the Attorney Registration and Disciplinary Commission (ARDC) in 1976. According to those reports, the number of lawyers in Cook County increased from 19,072 in 1976 to 36,158 in 1995, while the lawyer population in the five surrounding collar counties of the metropolitan area increased from 2,156 to 7,008 (Attorney Registration and Disciplinary Commission 1977 and 1996). The collar counties had a larger percentage increase, on a much smaller base, but they grew by fewer than 5,000 lawyers while Cook County increased by more than 17,000.[15]

Conclusion

The separation of American lawyers into functional categories has a long history. Early in the twentieth century, a report sponsored by the Carnegie Foundation recommended the creation of an "inner bar" that would handle complex business transactions and would be separate from the "general body of practitioners" handling smaller cases and personal problems (Reed 1921, 237–39). The two sorts of lawyers were to be trained in different schools, with different curricula. The report was not favorably received by the bar (Auerbach 1976, 111–12), but a similar division of practice evolved, de facto. The kinds of work that lawyers do, the style of their work, and the places in which they do it differ greatly. Lawyers who handle the divorces and automobile accidents of a neighborhood clientele may also draft wills or close the sales of homes, but they are unlikely to work on mergers of large companies or to deal with the tax problems of major real estate developers.

The specialization of practice tends to create boundaries for professional relationships among lawyers, but it is possible that the degree of cohesion of colleague networks or work groups may be increasing in some parts of the profession and decreasing in others. If most of the practitioners in a field of law do that work only occasionally, so that there is a constantly changing cast of characters, then stable relationships are unlikely to form. By contrast, when larger numbers of lawyers devote the major share of their efforts to the field, then they are more likely to come into frequent contact with other repeat players, and it becomes efficient for them to invest the time and effort necessary to establish continuing working relationships with those other lawyers. In the personal client sector, specialization by field may be leading to the development of stronger, more stable sets of relationships. Lynn Mather et al. observed the development of regular lines of communication and of a sense of community among divorce lawyers in Maine and New Hampshire (Mather, McEwen, and Maiman 2001). Among personal injury plaintiffs lawyers in Chicago, Sara Parikh (2001) found clear, well-established referral and advice networks, in which the players knew their places in the pecking order. In our data, we observe especially large increases in the specialization index (fig. 2.4) in personal injury plaintiffs work (from .460 to .622, moving from eighteenth to seventh place in the rank order), in personal injury defense (from .546 to .694, moving from tenth to third), and in criminal defense (from .536 to .612, moving from twelfth to eighth). In the personal client sector of practice, therefore, specialization increased markedly, and we would thus expect increased incentives for communication among specialists. But communication across the fields may, at the same time, have decreased—specialists in divorce, criminal defense, and personal injury will have little occasion for professional interchange across fields, except perhaps for client referral.

In the corporate client sector, with the exception of labor union work, public utilities/administrative law, and environmental work for plaintiffs, we also observe increases in specialization by field, but it is not entirely clear how these changes might have affected the stability and coherence of work groups in corporate practice. If the organization of corporate law firms moved from structures that were predominantly hierarchical, built around small numbers of dominant senior partners, toward formal bureaucracies, with departments based on doctrinal specialties and/or skill types (see chap. 5), then this would suggest a change from practice groups organized by the particular needs of the clients served by each of the dominant partners, in the older model, to groups built around particular transactions or pieces of business. In the latter, newer model, the teams that work on the cases would be assembled from the relevant departments in varying combinations. If this is correct, then the work groups would become less stable, changing from transaction to transaction.[16] If departmentalization of large law firms leads to the separation of specialists from lawyers in other fields, then ties among these sets of practitioners will be less common. Note that both of these developments—unstable work groups and departmentalization—suggest weaker ties across fields within the corporate sector. The extent to which this occurs will depend on the degree of functional interdependence among the specialties.

It may be that lawyers were always likely to spend the greater share of their time with fellow specialists (to the extent that field specialization existed) but that their contact with practitioners outside their own fields became more varied and shorter-term with the shift from client-based to transaction-based work groups. If that is true, then cross-field ties may have become more extensive but less strong (i.e., there will be more "weak ties"; Granovetter 1973). When work groups are assembled for particular transactions (as opposed to ongoing groups built around ongoing clients), the same lawyers may or may not work together. The assembly of teams will depend on the power within the firm of the partners competing for assistance and the degree of influence of the particular clients (see chaps. 5 and 12).

Although demand for legal services to corporations and other large organizations has grown far more rapidly than demand for services to individuals and small businesses, entry into the market is easier in the latter types of practice. Any lawyer can hang up a shingle and seek clients in auto accident or refrigerator repossession cases, but it is difficult for lawyers to obtain access to the places where corporate legal services are delivered. Lawyers in personal client fields, for the most part, do not have the option of moving into corporate work. Some practitioners in corporate fields, however, can and do represent individuals. Even the largest law firms work in selected areas of personal client practice, often for the individuals who are officers of their corporate clients. Some of these law firms have probate departments, many handle individual income-tax problems for favored clients, and a few will work on clients' divorces. To the extent that this occurs, the corporate and the personal client sectors of the bar are drawn closer. But there is a division of labor within law firms, and the lawyers who do the corporate work may not be the same ones who handle personal matters. If lawyers' work has become increasingly specialized, this will tend to separate the sectors of the bar. Fewer lawyers will cross the boundaries.

Is the legal profession still divided into hemispheres? *Hemi* means half, and it is now hard to argue that the two parts are approximately equal in size, at least in Chicago (and probably in other large cities). By our estimate, the amount of Chicago lawyers' time devoted to corporate fields and to fields serving other large organizations is more than twice that devoted to personal client fields. But the relative size of the sectors is probably not an important part of the thesis—this will vary with the size and character of the jurisdiction in any event—and we have not yet assessed the degree of socioeconomic, ethnoreligious, educational, and political separation. We turn next to those social characteristics.

Chapter 3
Integration and Separation

There are, to be sure, valid reasons to think of lawyers as belonging to one profession. Lawyers, after all, share a body of basic legal knowledge, a peculiar professional language, and a common license. With rare exceptions, they are licensed to practice *law*—not criminal law or corporate law, but law in general. In form, at least, lawyers subscribe to a common code of ethics. They are also drawn together by networks of relationships that facilitate the referral of cases to lawyers with appropriate specialties, and they belong to bar associations that serve their common interests. Their educational background has standard elements, and the law school educational experience is reputed to be unusually powerful or formative. Although some law schools have far greater resources than others, most of their sermons come from the same text—they base their courses on the same compilations of appellate cases, and their first-year curricula emphasize the fundamental areas of Anglo American common law (contracts, torts, crimes, and property), usually supplemented by constitutional law and civil procedure.

But the division of lawyers into classes has a long history. The familiar British distinction between barristers and solicitors has existed for almost four centuries (although that distinction has now been blurred by new English rules of practice; Gibb 2003, Rufford 1998). American lawyers, too, have long been divided. The narrator of Herman Melville's story *Bartleby, the Scrivener: A Story of Wall Street* describes himself as "one of those unambitious lawyers who never addresses a jury, or in any way draws down public applause; but in the cool tranquility of a snug retreat, do a snug business among rich men's bonds and mortgages and title-deeds" (1996, 14). That was first published in 1853.

If lawyers' work is organized by demand from distinct types of clients (see chap. 2), and if the social differences among the clients are pronounced—for example, large corporations versus small businesses versus unemployed laborers versus wealthy suburbanites—then the lawyers serving these different classes of clients are likely to inhabit separate social worlds. Lawyers who represent wealthy institutions will seldom have occasion to interact with lawyers for the dispossessed. Although the social status of lawyers who serve the poor will almost always be more elevated than that of their clients, those lawyers are unlikely to live in penthouses. Social distinctions among the lawyers' clients are commonly reflected, to one degree or another, in the characteristics of their lawyers.

But what are the consequences, if any, of these social distinctions among lawyers? Our answers to this question must of necessity be more speculative. Some things, however, are reasonably clear. The consequences might be of at least two kinds: consequences for the clients, in the quality and quantity of the services they receive; and consequences for the legal profession itself.

Wealthier clients tend to make for wealthier lawyers and may also permit the lawyers' work to be defined in ways that present a greater degree of intellectual challenge. It takes time to deal with novel legal issues—indeed, it takes time to identify them. If clients lack funds, their problems are likely to be defined as routine. The incentive will be to dispose of matters as quickly as possible. Rich clients, however, can afford to pay for (and may even want) carefully crafted, original solutions. Lawyers who serve the wealthy have multiple advantages, therefore. They not only fatten their pocketbooks, they get the satisfaction of doing creative work. If lawyers value money and intellectual satisfaction, those who can get high-end work will take it (see chaps. 7 and 11). Those who cannot will either do what is left or leave the profession. But perhaps lawyers also care about public service or justice or emotional satisfaction. It is not clear that all of them seek to maximize their wealth. In any event, lawyers have several career options other than the extreme high-end or low-end work. Many lawyers work between the north and south poles of the bar, by necessity or by choice, as prosecutors, estate planners, income tax advisors, or inside counsel at local businesses or local unions.

Credentials play an important role in determining career opportunities. Jobs in the organizations and institutions where the remunerative, intellectually challenging work is done are difficult to get without good grades at a prestigious law school or a record of proven success. Entry-level candidates with mediocre grades at mediocre schools need not apply. Educational opportunity being what it is (in the United States, and elsewhere), persons with prestigious law degrees are likely to be socially advantaged, as well. They are more likely to have a privileged socioeconomic background, to have been born into an upper-class or upper-middle-class family, and to have useful social connections. Potential lawyers from modest origins, lacking connections, are less likely to find the path to the best schools, and job candidates with credentials at the extremes of the hierarchy, as we will see, do in fact tend to be sorted into positions at the poles of the profession. Thus, wealthy clients tend to get lawyers who are better trained and more influential. The poor are lucky to get any lawyer at all.

As to the consequences of this social stratification for the profession itself, it seems likely that lawyers who inhabit separate social worlds and who seldom deal with one another in their professional work would find it difficult to pursue a common agenda on issues of public policy, even on issues of special concern to lawyers. Although lawyers occupy positions of importance in U.S. government and in the financial world, they will be unable to exploit their full potential for influence if they cannot unite on a course of collective action. Typically, each of the contending interest groups engaged in policy controversies has a phalanx of lawyers who serve as their allies or advocates, and this assures that lawyers who are active on such matters will be divided by their client allegiances (Heinz, Paik, and Southworth 2003).

For example, in the battle over the alleged "litigation explosion," lawyers could be found on both sides of the issue (see, e.g., Haltom and McCann 2004). Some, employed by insurance companies or more generally sympathetic to the corporate establishment or the Republican Party, supported the argument that Americans were rushing to court at the slightest provocation, runaway juries were awarding absurd sums to plaintiffs who found McDonald's coffee too hot, and the threat of tort claims was making park districts remove playground equipment and forcing doctors to abandon obstetrics practice. Other lawyers, who earned nice livings from contingent fees in their work for plaintiffs in personal injury cases, were inclined to defend the right of citizens to seek legal redress in the courts and the established role of juries in punishing malefactors through the award of punitive damages. Similar divisions of lawyers enlisted on the question of whether class action suits—against manufacturers of asbestos products, the Dalkon Shield IUD, silicon breast implants, or Firestone tires—should be restricted (Glater 2003b).

Another example is the continuing struggle between the legal and accounting professions for control of work done by both (e.g., tax advice) and for ownership of the organizations in which that work is done (see chap. 12). Many lawyers compete or potentially compete with accountants and other consultants, and those lawyers have sought to eliminate the competition by using licensing restrictions and statutes prohibiting the "unauthorized practice of law." Other lawyers, however, were eager to cooperate with the accountants—they saw mergers with accounting firms (creating "multidisciplinary" partnerships) as a way to reach new clients and expand the scope of their practice. Lawyers working as inside counsel in corporations that purchase services from outside law firms (as do most corporations) were eager to encourage the law firms' competitors. The general counsel of McDonald's Corporation, commenting on the move of accounting firms into the market for legal advice, noted: "Anything that enhances competition for legal services, from my point of view, is a good thing. . . . We use Ernst & Young for a lot of tax advice we might have gone to lawyers for" (Merrion 2000, 15, 20). On this issue lawyers were, as on so many things, divided by both their own and their clients' interests.

Integrative Mechanisms

Counteracting the interests and allegiances that divide lawyers, however, are factors that tend to draw them together. The opening paragraph of this chapter referred to some of the formal or legal mechanisms that treat the law as one profession—common licensing, ethical rules, and educational requirements. More important, perhaps, are the social affinities that create contact and community of interest among fields of law. Like some of the divisive forces, some of these integrative mechanisms derive from the influence of clients. Lawyers in complementary specialties, for example, may work together if they serve the same client—a tax expert and a real property specialist may collaborate on the acquisition of land for a major real estate development. Fields of law that work on related problems have incentives to create channels of communication, and these incentives are stronger if the problems recur in the lawyers' practice. The need for communication across fields probably occurs less often in a slip-and-fall case or a criminal matter than if the client is a multinational manufacturer who has a continuing need for tax, securities, environmental, and employment law advice. The boundaries among personal client fields may therefore be more distinct.

Doctrinal and skill or task-type similarities also create affinities. For example, trial lawyers may have more in common with one another than they do with office lawyers. But how often do lawyers doing trial work in various fields have occasion to communicate? And how often do they move from one field to another? The question of whether a particular skill is transferable across fields is empirical, and it may be difficult to discover the facts necessary for an answer. Suppose we wanted to know whether special skill in drafting appellate briefs in criminal cases could be easily transferred to brief writing in corporate litigation. One might be able to measure the extent of mobility of lawyers from the former field to the latter (and we have data that will permit us to do that, albeit imperfectly), but this would not tell us whether the inherent nature or character of the skill (i.e., strategic organization of an argument and persuasive written advocacy) is the same in both fields. It is possible that even if the talents required were essentially similar, the social gulf between fundamentally different kinds of clients might hinder mobility across the two fields.

Similarly, fields that share doctrine (elements of law) might or might not be well integrated. For example, several areas of federal regulatory law are governed by the Administrative Procedure Act. Precedents interpreting and implementing the act—concerning procedures in rulemaking and adjudicative proceedings—commonly apply in more than one substantive area of regulation. But is "administrative law" in fact a specialty in practice? Is knowledge of the administrative procedures used in broadcasting cases often applied by those same lawyers to natural gas regulatory proceedings? Or does the lack of overlapping networks between broadcasters and natural-gas producers mean that lawyers will seldom have an opportunity to make that move? If there were a great deal of lawyer mobility between broadcast cases and natural-gas cases, the two areas of regulation would probably not be, functionally, separate fields of practice. That is, if there is a very high degree of overlap in the practitioners active in two substantive areas of the law, it would suggest that the two areas are part of one line of work, one career.

Some fields are more distinct than others. Admiralty, patents, public international law, and criminal prosecution are all quite well defined, but civil litigation and general corporate work are not. This may be a function of several variables: the degree of specialization in that work, the distinctiveness of the types of clients served, the social distinctiveness of the lawyers in the field (their social class of origin, ethnoreligious identification, etc.), and the nature of the paths through which lawyers are recruited to the field (i.e., the channels of entry and the barriers). As we saw in chapter 2, however, the principal factor organizing the structure of specialization and co-practice of the fields is the nature of their clientele. Lawyers doing environmental work may share clients with lawyers doing commercial law, but the clientele of the environmental specialists is less likely to overlap with that of divorce lawyers. Similarly, estate planning will not have much contact with public utilities work. The social types of clients tend to create separate markets for lawyers.

Relatively few lawyers are true generalists. Of the 674 practicing lawyers in the 1995 sample, only 30 (4.5 percent) did not devote as much as 25 percent of their time to any one field. By contrast, a third of the practicing lawyers said that they worked in only one field, and 488 of the 674 (72 percent) indicated that they devoted half or more of their time to one field. This is another measure of the specialization by field discussed in chapter 2.

In addition to exchanging information, fields that work on related issues and thus are functionally interdependent may also exchange cases—the lawyers may want to have reliable referral partners to whom they can send clients (and from whom they may, in turn, receive work). Referral networks thus bring the fields into contact and create another reason for communication across fields (or even within fields; Mather, McEwen, and Maiman 2001; Parikh 2001), but the separate fields have an interest in maintaining the boundaries. Lawyer A is unlikely to send cases to lawyer B if A thinks B is willing and able to do work that A would like to have. The continuing referral partnership depends upon an understanding (implicit or explicit) that the recipient will not seek to do work for the client beyond the scope of the matter referred.

In the 1995 survey, we asked how respondents obtained their clients—whether through direct personal contact, referrals by previous clients, referrals from other lawyers, or other means. In most fields, about half to two-thirds of the practitioners reported that they "sometimes" or "often" got new clients through lawyer referrals. In a few fields, however, the percentage was notably higher. About four-fifths of the practitioners of patent law and personal injury work for plaintiffs said that they obtained clients from other lawyers at least "sometimes." Both of these fields had high scores on the specialization index in 1995 (see chap. 2, table 2.1), and both are kinds of work that nonspecialists are not, ordinarily, eager to do—patent work requires abstruse knowledge that is costly to acquire, and personal injury plaintiffs work requires the ability (and willingness) to do jury trials. By contrast, relatively few respondents in banking, corporate tax, and personal injury defense (only 36 percent to 38 percent) reported that they obtained clients through other lawyers that often. These fields get most of their clients through networks of relationships among the businesses they represent. The contrast between the two sides of personal injury practice is instructive. Plaintiffs' lawyers have a well-developed system for the referral of cases up or down in the lawyer hierarchy—the bigger, more complex, more remunerative cases are referred to the most experienced lawyers and, in return, routine cases are sent down the ladder to journeymen (Parikh 2001). Defense work, however, is concentrated in medium-sized specialty firms, each of which has a continuing relationship with a particular insurance company or set of companies and thus is not dependent upon lawyer referrals.

Although referrals provide contact among the fields, they do not necessarily promote social similarity among them. The referral relationship may in fact be more stable if the separation among the fields is clear, and social distinctions serve to mark those boundaries. At some times and places, for example, lawyers of an identifiable ethnoreligious background have been concentrated in particular specialties. Notably, Irish Catholic lawyers have created litigation specialty firms. One of the most prominent of these firms was Donovan, Leisure in New York (Powell 1988, 70–71), which grew to a large firm before closing its doors in the late 1990s.[1] A more recent example in Chicago was Phelan, Pope, and John, which prospered for a time in the last quarter of the twentieth century before also closing. These firms did both corporate and commercial litigation, while other "Irish firms" have specialized in personal injury work or criminal defense. Why do ethnoreligious concentrations occur in particular fields or particular firms? Do family networks of contacts lead people from distinct social origins into distinct career paths? Or do identifiable groups end up in some practice settings because they were excluded from others? Or do the law schools serve as the recruitment mechanism or the gatekeepers, with certain law schools having an ethnic character (e.g., the Catholic[2] schools) and feeding limited markets? (See fig. 3.3, below.)

Bar Associations

The organized bar might also pull the profession together. At some times, at least, it has certainly made a conscious effort to do so (Halliday 1987). But bar associations often have difficulty taking decisive action because of the variety of lawyers among their members. As early as 1921, a report to the Carnegie Foundation observed that the bar was "so disunited within itself as seriously to impair its capacity to formulate—let alone to realize— professional ideals" (Reed 1921, 215). There are, of course, two classic ways for an organization to address a problem of this sort. One is to limit the membership of the association to those who are (relatively) of like mind, but an association representing only a narrow segment of the bar sacrifices some of the influence that might come from numbers and a broader constituency. The other solution is to place the leadership of the association firmly within the control of a limited, not fully representative segment of the membership—usually, the elite. But this will tend to weaken the legitimacy of the organization's initiatives, and the oligarchy might prove unstable if the rank and file should mount a challenge.

Both strategies of exclusion have been pursued, nonetheless. For many decades, the membership of the Association of the Bar of the City of New York was disproportionately drawn from the profession's elite, that is, WASPs from large law firms with large clients (Powell 1988, 37–41, 69–78), and the 1975 Chicago survey found that lawyers were significantly more likely to be members of the American Bar Association if they were Protestants, graduates of elite law schools, in large law firms, or highly paid (Heinz and Laumann 1982, 235, table 8.1). In the 1995 Chicago data, the elite law school and large firm bias in ABA membership remains (and, indeed, is even stronger)—of the graduates of elite schools, 71 percent were members of the ABA; of local school graduates, only 48 percent were members; three-quarters of the respondents who worked in firms with more than a hundred lawyers were members, but only 37 percent of those in solo practice and 41 percent of those in government jobs. The ethnoreligious difference in ABA membership, however, was not present in 1995.

The leadership of bar associations has also been dominated by certain elites. The 1975 Chicago survey found that leadership positions in the Chicago Bar Association had been held by 25 percent of the graduates of elite law schools but by only 9 percent of the graduates of local schools, and by 28 percent of those in the highest income category but none of those in the two lowest income ranges (Heinz and Laumann 1982, 240, table 8.3). In the 1995 data, religious preference is significantly associated with the probability of bar association leadership. Of lawyers who were either Episcopalian, Presbyterian, or Congregationalist, 42 percent had held a leadership position in some bar association, but only 18 percent and 19 percent of Catholic and Jewish respondents, respectively, had held such positions.[3]

The relationship between bar association activity and the size of the firms within which the lawyers practiced, however, suggests a story that runs counter to these observations about elite leadership. In 1995, solo practitioners were significantly more likely than those in large law firms to have held office or chaired a committee in a bar association. Of solo practitioners, 32 percent had held one or more of these leadership positions; of those in firms with more than thirty lawyers, only 18 percent had.[4] Among lawyers in the larger firms, those in firms with fewer than a hundred lawyers were significantly more likely to report that they regularly attended bar association meetings than were those in firms of one hundred or more.[5]

Patterns of membership in the organized bar have been increasingly influenced by changes in the organization of work. As we noted in chapter 2, specialization increased markedly in the Chicago bar from 1975 to 1995—lawyers were more likely to concentrate their time in a particular field or a smaller group of fields, and consequently there was less overlap among the sets of practitioners active in the various practice areas. General-membership bar associations, therefore, might have become (or have been perceived as) less relevant. But associations adapted to these changes by creating a wide range of committees and sections addressing concerns of specialized groups of practitioners, and the Chicago data indicate that membership was quite stable in both the ABA and the CBA. Just over half of the respondents reported ABA membership and just over 60 percent were in the CBA in both 1975 and 1995. Membership in the Illinois State Bar Association, however, declined from 65 percent of respondents in the first survey to 45 percent in the second. Responses to the surveys indicate a large increase in the number and variety of bar associations—especially, in those organized to promote the interests of particular specialties. In 1975, only eight associations of lawyers in substantive or skill-type practice areas (e.g., the American Patent Law Association, the Association of Life Insurance Counsel, and the Federal Communications Bar Association) had members among the respondents. In the 1995 survey, however, Chicago lawyers reported membership in a total of twenty-three such organizations, including associations of corporate counsel, trial lawyers, intellectual property lawyers, immigration lawyers, appellate lawyers, elder lawyers (i.e., lawyers practicing "elder law"), employment lawyers, health lawyers, and transportation lawyers. This development, then, is consistent with the observed increase in specialization of function in the bar.

There was also a substantial increase in the number of bar associations organized by race, sex, ethnicity, religion, and sexual preference—associations of Jewish, Catholic, female, black, black female, Greek, Italian, Hispanic, Asian, Mexican American, and gay and lesbian lawyers. While six such associations were mentioned by respondents in 1975, membership was reported in fifteen associations based on these categories in 1995. This increase, no doubt, reflects the growing number of lawyers drawn from previously excluded social groups. Thus, both the greater diversity of lawyers and the specialization of work appear to have led to a proliferation of lawyers' organizations.

In spite of the increasing number of associations, the overall percentage of lawyers reporting bar association membership declined somewhat. In 1975, only 10 percent of respondents belonged to no bar association; in 1995, this had nearly doubled, to 18 percent. Membership in three or more professional associations was reported by 44.4 percent of respondents in 1975. Notwithstanding the increasing variety of choices available, this declined to 37.9 percent in the second survey.

Law School Stratification

If all law schools train their students for the same job—the general practice of law—this will tend to unify the profession. But the schools could specialize in training for particular segments of the market and thus, in effect, limit graduates' options. The curricular choices of the law schools might, therefore, contribute to either the unity or the segmentation of the profession. Using the school categories in chapter 1, of the six law schools in Chicago, the University of Chicago is elite, Northwestern University is in the prestige category, and the Chicago-Kent College of Law (now affiliated with the Illinois Institute of Technology), De Paul University, John Marshall (a freestanding law school), and Loyola University are local schools. Together, the six schools supplied 68 percent of the respondents in the 1975 Chicago survey and 58 percent of the 1995 sample.

Ryan White (2002) found that, after the first year of introductory courses, the curricula of these six schools differed substantially. In 1995, 27 percent of all courses offered at the University of Chicago were in legal history, jurisprudence (philosophy), or comparative law (foreign legal systems). No other school devoted more than 10 percent of its curriculum to such courses. By contrast, only 3 percent of the courses at the University of Chicago were devoted to clinical instruction and similar skills-training subjects, but the four local schools allocated 11 to 17 percent of their courses to such training. Local schools apparently also sought to develop specialties or market niches. The offerings of De Paul in health law, Loyola in family and poverty law, and Kent in environmental law were more than double those at any other school. If a school lacks sufficient resources to compete with wealthier schools across the board, one possible strategy is product differentiation: the development of notable depth in a particular field or set of fields that will attract potential students with a strong interest in that specialty. In sum, White found that the schools appeared to design their curricula for distinct segments of the market.[6]

There is strong evidence from both Chicago surveys that graduates of highly ranked schools are more likely to practice in large law firms. Table 3.1 shows the extent of the representation of the four school categories in firms of different sizes and in two other practice settings.

Table 3.1. Distribution of Graduates of Four Law School Categories across Practice Settings, 1975 and 1995 (percentages)

						1975			
School	Solo	Firm 2–9	Firm 10–30	Firm 31–99	Firm 100 +	Internal Counsel	Government	Total[b]	(N)
Elite	12	17	25	39	51	18	4	20	(138)
Prestige	11	12	24	32	21	17	20	17	(118)
Regional	11	12	25	14	21	25	21	17	(115)
Local	65	59	26	15	7	40	56	46	(313)
Total[a]	99	100	100	100	100	100	101	100	
(N)	(141)	(180)	(72)	(59)	(57)	(98)	(77)		(684)

							1995			
School	Solo	Firm 2–9	Firm 10–30	Firm 31–99	Firm 100–299	Firm 300 +	Internal Counsel	Govt.	Total[b]	(N)
Elite	10	7	16	8	18	30	16	2	14	(88)
Prestige	8	7	11	17	22	24	12	9	13	(86)
Regional	25	21	25	38	33	29	36	22	28	(182)
Local	58	66	49	38	26	17	37	67	45	(295)
Total[a]	101	101	101	101	99	100	101	100	100	
(N)	(105)	(107)	(76)	(64)	(76)	(89)	(76)	(58)		(651)

[a] Due to rounding error, some columns do not total exactly 100 percent.
[b] These percentages do not match those in figure 1.1 because the figure shows data from all respondents, but this table includes only practicing lawyers. Judges and legal services lawyers are not included here.

In the 1975 data, we see that 65 percent of the solo practitioners had attended a local school, but only 7 percent of the lawyers in firms of 100 or more had done so. By contrast, 12 percent of the solo practitioners were graduates of elite schools, whereas 51 percent of the lawyers in the largest firms had gone to those schools. In 1995, the differences were somewhat less extreme but still pronounced. The percentage of the bar drawn from elite schools decreased (from 20 percent in 1975 to 14 percent in 1995) because those schools did not grow as much as the bar, but in 1995 the percentage of elite graduates in the largest firms was still more than twice as high as their overall share. Note, however, that the representation of local schools in large firms did increase substantially, perhaps because those firms were growing so rapidly that they found it necessary to recruit more widely— that is, they were unable to get sufficient numbers of lawyers from their usual, more elite sources. In 1995, firms with 100 to 299 lawyers in fact employed more graduates of local schools than of elite or prestige schools, but local schools were still greatly underrepresented in the big firms and greatly overrepresented among solo practitioners and in the smallest firms.

The local school percentage in firms with 2 to 9 lawyers was even greater in 1995 than in 1975. In both years, graduates of elite schools were greatly underrepresented in government jobs and local schools had far more than their share of those jobs. In house counsel positions, regional schools were somewhat overrepresented and local schools modestly underrepresented in both years. Thus, again, the stratification within the bar was clear. Over the two decades between the Chicago surveys, there were changes at the margins, but the recruitment hierarchy remained quite stable.

We have also analyzed the effect of the type of law school attended on lawyers' income and on attainment of the status of partner in a large law firm.[7] Because both partnership and income are correlated with age (older lawyers are more likely both to be partners and to have higher incomes), we controlled for age in these analyses, and we will report here the predicted probabilities where age is held at the mean, which was 44.45 in 1975 and 42.86 in 1995. The analyses dichotomized the law school categories, comparing graduates of schools in the elite and prestige categories with those from regional and local schools.

We found that graduates of these two broad classes of schools had very different rates of partnership in large law firms.[8] In the 1975 data, the overall predicted probability of partnership in a firm of thirty or more lawyers for a respondent at age forty-four was 8 percent. For graduates of elite and prestige schools, however, this probability was 17 percent, while for those from regional and local schools it was only 2 percent. In the 1995 survey, the overall probability was somewhat higher—the predicted probability of partnership in a firm with one hundred or more lawyers[9] was 11 percent for the full random sample at the mean age—but the difference between the two classes of schools remained very strong. For graduates of elite and prestige schools, the partnership probability was 21 percent, but for those who had attended regional or local schools it was only 8 percent. Although the predicted probability that a regional or local school graduate would become a partner in a large firm by the time he or she reached the mean age increased substantially from 1975 to 1995, the gap between lawyers from those schools and the elite or prestige school graduates was still large.

For the income analysis, we computed the probability that graduates of the two groupings of schools would have an income in the top quartile of the income distribution for the total sample, and we found that the relationship between income and the law school categories was significant in both surveys.[10] It was, however, somewhat less strong than that between law school and partnership. By the time a graduate of an elite or prestige school reached the mean age in 1975 (age forty-four), his or her probability

of having an income in the top quartile was 41 percent. For those from regional and local schools, it was 31 percent. In the 1995 sample, the income
difference between the school categories was even more substantial. In 1995,
the predicted probability of an elite or prestige school graduate being in the
top quartile was 34 percent, at the mean age, but for those who went to
regional and local schools it was only 20 percent. Thus, the gap between the
school categories widened from 10 percentage points in 1975 to 14 points in
1995.

It is not clear whether the differences between the two classes of schools
are attributable to the inherent abilities of the people attending them, to the
credentialing or validation effects of the schools themselves, to the quality
of the training that the schools provide, or to the channeling to differing
schools of students with systematically varying social advantages. Indeed,
each of these factors may play a part, and they may combine to produce
the hierarchical effects. If the partnership and income differences reflect inequality in opportunities open to graduates, it appears that the inequality
did not diminish and may in fact have increased.

Ethnoreligious Differences

The 1975 survey found striking (indeed, we think, startling) differentiation
in the social characteristics of lawyers active in the various fields, and that
differentiation was organized in a consistent hierarchy. For example, in 1975
Jewish respondents constituted only 14 percent of the respondents who devoted a quarter or more of their time to securities work but 56 percent of
those who did a comparable amount of divorce work. By contrast, 36 percent
of the securities lawyers were Episcopalians, Presbyterians, or Congregationalists, but only 2 percent of personal injury plaintiffs lawyers and none of
the divorce lawyers were affiliated with those denominations. (These three
Protestant denominations, referred to as type I Protestants, tend to include
disproportionate numbers of persons with high social status, drawn from
older immigrant stock; Pope 1948; Demerath 1965.) Similarly, 53 percent of
the prosecutors in the sample but only 9 percent of the securities lawyers
were Catholics. Figure 3.1 presents data on ethnoreligious characteristics of
practitioners in six selected fields of law in 1975 and 1995. In 1975, the
percentage in type I Protestants tends to be high in fields where the Jewish percentage is low. But not without exception. Among practitioners of
banking law, where type I Protestants were substantially overrepresented
in 1975, Jews were present in about the same proportion as in the overall bar. Note also, in 1975, the strong overrepresentation of Catholics in

Figure 3.1. Ethnoreligious Differentiation among Selected Fields, 1975 and 1995 (percentages)

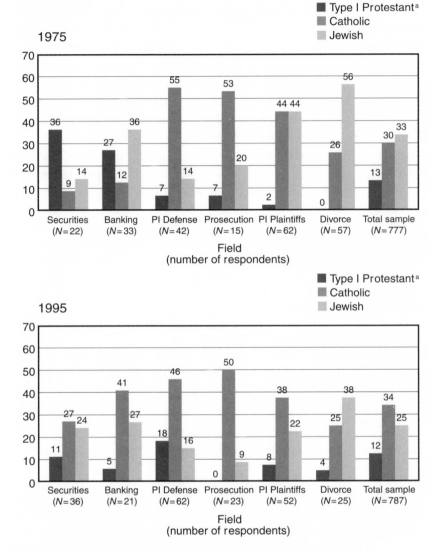

Note: Characteristics of respondents who devoted 25 percent or more of their time to each field.
[a] Episcopalians, Presbyterians, and Congregationalists.

the litigation fields (criminal prosecution and both sides of personal injury work) and their underrepresentation in securities and banking. The pattern in 1995 is generally similar, but much less strong. The overrepresentation of type I Protestants in securities and banking completely disappears in 1995. Catholics were still overrepresented in litigation, especially in prosecution and personal injury defense, and Jews were still overrepresented in divorce work, but less strongly than in 1975. In securities, banking, and personal injury plaintiffs work, in 1995 Jewish lawyers were represented in approximately the same percentage as in the overall bar. Thus, the ethnoreligious differences among these fields diminished, but considerable differentiation remained.

Some of the ethnic distinctiveness of particular fields of practice is attributable to differences in the extent to which each of the Chicago area law schools supplied lawyers to those fields, combined with the ethnoreligious characteristics of the students at those schools. If we examine the distribution of ethnic groups in the graduates of the six Chicago schools, we see some pronounced differences. Of the University of Chicago graduates in the 1975 sample, 46 percent were Jewish and only 3 percent were of Irish descent. Loyola graduates display the opposite pattern—12 percent were Jewish and 35 percent were Irish. The pattern at those schools in 1995 was similar, but less extreme. Figure 3.2 presents the percentages of respondents identifying as either Jewish or Irish among the graduates of all six schools. Note that Jewish respondents were overrepresented among the graduates of both of the more highly ranked law schools in both years, and also overrepresented at two of the local schools in 1975 (De Paul and Kent), but at only one of them (Kent) in 1995. But graduates of Irish descent were underrepresented at both Chicago and Northwestern in 1995, and were overrepresented among graduates of three of the four local schools.[11] Thus, Jews appear to have secured access to the more prestigious educational institutions, while Irish respondents did not.[12]

Race, Gender, and Family Background

We also analyzed the race, sex, and ethnoreligious identification of graduates of the full range of law school categories. The numbers of women and of racial minorities in the 1975 sample are small, but the patterns are sufficiently clear to be of interest.

The twenty-eight white females in the 1975 random sample had a higher percentage of graduates of elite schools than did any other social group (32 percent) and the lowest percentage of local school graduates (39 percent). The minorities (twenty African Americans and one Asian American) had the opposite pattern—the lowest percentage of elite school graduates (14 percent) and the highest percentage of those from local schools (62 percent). The representation of graduates of elite and prestige schools among Jewish males was similar to that among other white males, but the Jewish

Figure 3.2. Jewish and Irish Respondents among the Graduates of the Six Chicago Law Schools, 1975 and 1995 (percentages)

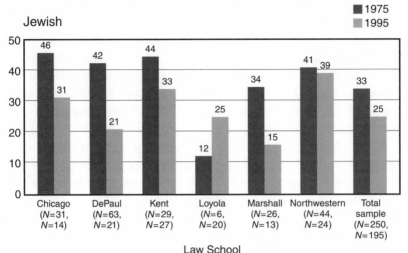

Jewish

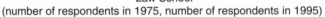

Law School
(number of respondents in 1975, number of respondents in 1995)

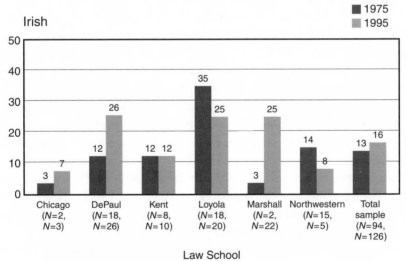

Irish

Law School
(number of respondents in 1975, number of respondents in 1995)

respondents had a higher percentage of local school graduates (50 percent versus 44 percent).

To obtain additional respondents in racial and ethnic minority groups, the 1995 random sample was supplemented by two oversamples, one of African Americans and one of Hispanics. The Hispanic oversample was selected by identifying Spanish surnames and then sampling randomly from that list.[13] Because there was no comprehensive list of African American lawyers in Chicago, however, that oversample was selected through a modified snowball sampling technique—when an African American lawyer was interviewed in the random sample, that respondent was asked to identify other African Americans in several practice contexts.[14] The list of nominees was then sampled within each practice context, resulting in a stratified sample. Like most snowball samples, this one probably has a bias toward the inclusion of persons of higher status: respondents asked to nominate others are likely to identify persons who are visible or notable. In some of the analyses reported here, we have merged the two minority oversamples with the random sample, which results in a total of seventy-three African American and forty-one Hispanic respondents, but we will want to recognize the bias. The larger number of women in the Chicago bar in 1995 also makes it possible to distinguish, in some analyses, between males and females in both the Jewish and "other white" categories.[15]

The biggest change in the 1995 findings is in the distribution of women across the law school categories. While women had the highest percentage of graduates of elite schools and the lowest percentage of local school graduates in 1975, in 1995 this was true only of Jewish women. Other white females had a low percentage of elite school graduates in 1995 (7 percent) and a high percentage of graduates of local schools (53 percent). It may be useful here to speculate about the processes that could have produced this change. First, as larger numbers of women were drawn to the legal profession, self-selection effects may have diminished. That is, when very few women entered the bar, perhaps only those who were exceptionally well qualified chose to apply to law schools; as their numbers grew, however, the women's credentials increasingly resembled those of men. Second, the larger numbers of women recruited to the bar in the 1970s and 1980s may have come from more varied family backgrounds, perhaps less privileged than was formerly the case. Or, at the earlier time, local and regional schools may have been less willing than elite or prestige schools to admit women. Or, if more of the women in the 1995 sample were married before they went to law school, their geographic mobility and thus their choice among schools may have been limited by their husbands' employment. It is also possible that, because of greater discrimination against women in 1975, women then felt that they had greater need of elite school credentials in order to improve their job prospects. Unfortunately, because of the small number of women in the 1975 sample, we are unable to test these various hypotheses with any confidence.

There were not large differences in 1995 between the types of schools attended by Jewish males and other white males—for example, 44 percent and
45 percent, respectively, had graduated from local schools. Of the seventy-
three African American respondents in the combined sample (i.e., including
the oversample), however, relatively few (11 percent) attended elite schools
and a high percentage (41 percent) came from regional schools. Many of the
regional schools are in public universities, whereas most of the schools in
the other categories are private institutions that might be less affordable for
students from families of limited means (see fig. 3.3). Because the African
American oversample is biased toward the inclusion of more noteworthy
lawyers, it is likely that these findings overstate the prestige of the schools
attended by black lawyers in the Chicago bar, even though we find only a
modest percentage of elite school graduates.[16] Hispanic lawyers had a very
high percentage of local school graduates (59 percent), which suggests that
living at home and going to school at night while holding a job was an option
for disadvantaged minorities.

Socioeconomic status of origin has important effects on educational opportunity. In 1995, for example, 78 percent of the lawyers who had attended
elite law schools came from families in which the father was in a professional, technical, or managerial occupation, while for graduates of local
schools that percentage was 20 points lower. Moreover, family background
is clearly related to other social characteristics of the lawyers. Figure 3.3
summarizes the relationships between father's occupation and four social
groupings in the 1975 and 1995 random samples. Lawyers in the minority
groups were more likely, in both years, to have had fathers employed in occupations of lower socioeconomic status. But in 1975, women and minorities
had the highest percentages of lawyer fathers: 19 percent each. Since barriers
to entry into the profession were then especially high for women and minorities, those whose fathers were lawyers may have enjoyed relative advantages
of either access or motivation. In 1995, however, as the barriers became less
formidable, occupational inheritance appears to have become less salient.
Note also that Jewish males had the highest percentage of fathers employed
in professional, technical, or managerial occupations—82 percent (including lawyer fathers) in 1975, and an even higher percentage (87 percent) in
1995. Moreover, Jewish women were considerably more likely to come from
families of high socioeconomic status (as measured by father's occupation)
than were other white females in the Chicago bar. If we separate the ethnoreligious groups in the white female category used in the figure, we find that
91 percent of the Jewish women in the 1995 sample had fathers employed in
such high-status occupations (the 1975 sample had too few women to permit

Figure 3.3. Father's Occupation by Social Groups, 1975 and 1995 (percentages)

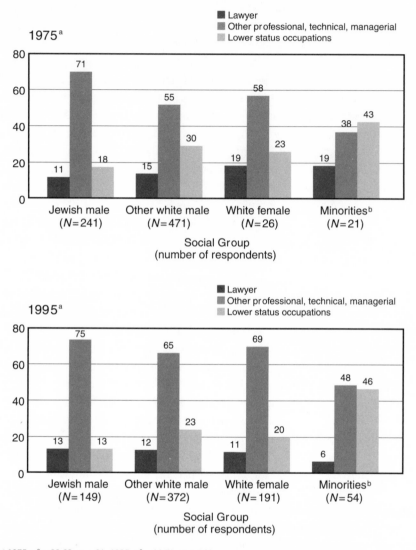

[a] 1975: χ^2 = 20.68, $p <$ .01; 1995: χ^2 = 26.71, $p <$ .001.
[b] 1975: 20 African Americans and one Asian American; 1995: 39 African Americans and 15 Hispanics/Latinos.

this analysis). The most important observation here, however, is certainly that lawyers who are African American (or, in 1995, Hispanic) are far more likely than others to have had fathers who were employed in occupations that were less remunerative and that required less schooling.

Given the correlation between father's occupation and type of law school attended, and the further relationship between law school and practice context, income, and the likelihood of partnership, we should expect there to be a strong relationship between social background and the hierarchy of career opportunities in the legal profession. It exists. We analyzed the probabilities of becoming a partner in a large firm and of having an income in the top quartile in both 1975 and 1995.[17] In 1975 the predicted probability that a white male respondent who was a type I Protestant would be a partner in a firm with thirty or more lawyers by the time he reached the mean age (forty-four) was 14 percent. For other white Christian males (type II Protestants—i.e., other Protestant denominations—and Catholics), however, this probability was only 9 percent. For white females, it was 4 percent; for Jewish males, 3 percent; and for African Americans it was less than 1 percent. So it appears that in 1975 race, religion, and gender were associated with differential rates of partnership in large law firms, but, because of the small numbers of women and minorities in the sample, only the finding with respect to Jewish males is significantly different from that for white male type I Protestants.[18] In the 1995 random sample, although all the probabilities of partnership are larger, the pattern is much the same and the differences become statistically significant. The predicted probability that a white male type I Protestant would be a partner in a firm with a hundred or more lawyers by age forty-three (the mean age in the 1995 survey) was 26 percent. For other Christian males, this decreased by half to 13 percent. For Jewish males, it was 11 percent; for white females, only 6 percent; and for African Americans it was 3 percent.[19] If we include the minority oversamples, we then have enough Hispanic respondents to produce a statistically significant finding for that grouping, and the partnership probability in the group is the same as that for African Americans.

We did a similar analysis of the probability of having an income in the top quartile. In 1975, the probability was 37 percent for white male type I Protestants at the mean age. The percentage was essentially the same for other white males—other Christian and Jewish males both had probabilities of 35 percent. For white females and African Americans, however, the rates were 9 percent and 20 percent, respectively. Because of the small number of African Americans in the 1975 sample, the difference in their income was not statistically significant, but the probability that a woman would have an income in the top quartile was so low that that difference reached conventional levels of statistical significance in spite of the small number of women in the sample ($p < .05$) The pattern in 1995 was similar, but the probabilities of women and African Americans having a top quartile income declined even further as their numbers in the profession grew. The predicted probability that a white male type I Protestant would have an income in that range by age forty-three was 44 percent, and Jewish males again did not differ significantly, although their probability was 11 points lower, 33 percent. The rate of Christian males other than type I Protestants was only a few points less, at 30 percent, but this difference was sufficient to move it across the line drawn by the usual significance standard.[20] The predicted probabilities for women and African Americans, however, were even lower than in 1975—only 7 percent and 5 percent, respectively ($p < .001$, for both). Hispanic respondents in the random sample had a probability of top quartile income that was far below that of white males, 15 percent, but somewhat higher than that of women and African Americans.[21]

Thus, in summary, we find that the type of law school attended appears to have had powerful influence on the lawyers' recruitment by law firms of differing size and on their chances of becoming a partner in a large firm or of earning an income that ranked in the top quartile of the distribution within the profession. Law school credentials were, in turn, associated with personal characteristics of the lawyers. The women in the 1975 sample (a small number, highly self-selected) were disproportionately likely to have gone to elite schools, but the larger number of women in 1995 had quite different educational credentials—a low percentage of elite school graduates and a high percentage from local schools. Thus, as the number of women entering the profession grew, the circumstances of their education and their resulting position within the professional hierarchy deteriorated. Jewish women, however, were the exception: they continued to have elite credentials. Minorities, whether African American or Latino, had low percentages of elite school graduates and high percentages from local and regional schools in both 1975 and 1995. Family circumstances appear to have affected school selection—lawyers whose fathers held high-status positions were more likely to have attended prestigious law schools—and this factor, again, worked to the disadvantage of minorities and to the relative advantage of white men and women.

In our analysis of the probabilities of attaining partnership in a large law firm, however, we saw a further refinement of this stratification system. Males from the old-immigrant-group Protestant denominations (type I) had a significantly higher probability of partnership in a large firm in both 1975 and 1995 than did those who were Jewish, and they had a higher probability in 1995 than any other social groupings—other Christian men, white females, African Americans, or Hispanics. As to income, high-status Protestant males again had the greatest likelihood of success, although their probability of reaching the top quartile of the distribution did not differ significantly from that of other Christian or Jewish males in 1975. In 1995, the income difference was stronger—men who were type I Protestants had a significantly higher probability of a top quartile income than did other Christian males and a much higher probability than did white females, African Americans, or Hispanics. Thus, social stratification, reflecting categories salient in the broader society (race, religion, gender, ethnicity, socioeconomic background), was significantly related to career opportunities in the Chicago bar, and this opportunity structure persisted from 1975 to 1995.

Practice Setting

If the more prestigious legal work or the work done on behalf of influential clients tends to be concentrated in particular practice settings, while the more routine work or work for relatively powerless clients is associated with other settings, then the status (and, perhaps, power) differential between the types of practice will be reinforced by organizational or institutional barriers. In order to be a plausible candidate for a distinct type of legal work (e.g., work on corporate mergers), it is often necessary for a lawyer to be affiliated with a particular kind of institution (e.g., a large law firm), and the employment decisions of such institutions are therefore likely to control access to the same kinds of work. Organizations are gatekeepers for entry into those fields of law. If the managers of the organizations have a preference for colleagues or employees of a specific ethnicity, race, gender, social class, law school pedigree, or political affiliation, those preferences will be reflected in the characteristics of the practitioners in the field.

Table 3.2 uses the 1995 data on time devoted to each of the several fields (see chap. 2, table 2.1) and then allocates the effort to the categories of organizations in which the work is done. This indicates the extent to which differing fields of law are practiced in different contexts. We find that work in the corporate fields tends to be concentrated in larger law firms and in the offices of lawyers employed within the client organization. Of the public utilities work, 41 percent was done in firms with 300 or more lawyers. Of banking law work, 44 percent was located in the legal departments of banks, and more than half of all municipal work was done in firms with 100 to 299 lawyers. Patent work, however, was concentrated in firms of moderate size, and antitrust work for plaintiffs also tended to be located there. By contrast, note the strong tendency of personal client work to cluster at the left side of the table—that is, to be done by solo practitioners or in the smallest firms. Those two contexts account for 80 percent of divorce work and 72 percent of personal real estate practice, for example. With the exception of 15 percent

Table 3.2. Distribution of Work in Each Field across Practice Settings, 1995 (percentages)

	Solo	Firm 2–9	Firm 10–30	Firm 31–99	Firm 100–299	Firm 300 +	Internal Counsel	Govt.
Large corporate								
Antitrust (D)	—	—	15	28	20	15	18	—
Business litigation	—	15	17	13	17	21	—	—
Business real estate	25	—	—	10	13	16	19	—
Business tax	—	19	—	—	—	29	19	14
Labor (management)	—	—	28	11	—	14	14	16
Securities	—	—	—	—	26	26	26	—
Regulatory								
Labor (unions)	17	13	16	11	12	—	11	15
Patents	—	—	27	43	18	—	—	—
Public utilities	—	—	15	—	—	41	11	16
Environmental (D)	10	—	15	13	20	18	19	—
Environmental (P)	20	—	—	—	—	20	—	34
General corporate								
Antitrust (P)	21	—	—	40	—	17	—	—
Banking	—	—	10	—	—	19	44	—
Commercial	—	25	—	—	15	25	14	—
General corporate	12	15	10	—	17	14	28	—
Personal injury (D)	—	11	21	21	11	13	10	—
Political/government								
Criminal (P)	—	—	—	—	—	—	—	90
Municipal	—	—	—	10	52	23	—	
Personal business								
General litigation	32	27	11	12	—	—	—	—
Personal real estate	54	18	—	—	—	—	10	—
Personal tax	19	19	—	20	—	15	13	—
Probate	23	33	—	—	—	—	13	—
Personal plight								
Civil rights	22	—	—	10	18	—	—	20
Criminal (D)	36	12	—	—	—	10	—	35
Divorce	49	31	—	—	—	—	—	—
Family	26	31	—	—	—	—	—	23
Personal injury (P)	30	50	13	—	—	—	—	—

Note: Practice settings in which less than 10 percent of the field's work is done are indicated by a dash.

of personal tax work, 10 percent of criminal defense, and 18 percent of civil rights practice, no substantial amount of work in a personal client field was done in a law firm with 100 or more lawyers.

We should not overstate the case, however. None of these practice settings appears to have a real monopoly on a field of legal work other than criminal prosecution. Even in fields like public utilities and banking, 15 percent and 10 percent respectively of the fields' work was found in firms with only ten to thirty lawyers. The 1975 data are similar, except that more corporate work was done in firms with two to nine lawyers. Over the twenty years between the two surveys, the corporate fields of practice became even more concentrated in large firms.

In 1995, we asked the respondents whether they had ever worked in other fields and, if they had, to indicate those fields. Relatively few lawyers had moved from litigation to office practice or from business fields to those serving individuals, except for the crossover in the subspecialties of tax, litigation, and real estate work (see chap. 2). Of lawyers devoting 25 percent or more of their time to banking law, 43 percent had also done commercial law, a third had done business real estate work, and another third had worked on general corporate matters (less specialized corporate law). Of those doing commercial law, a quarter had experience in general corporate work, nearly a third had done business litigation, and about a quarter had worked in general family practice. Of the securities lawyers, a third had experience in general corporate work, but very few had done anything else. By contrast, the lawyers doing criminal defense, divorce work, or general civil litigation were likely to have worked in a variety of fields. Many of the criminal defense lawyers had also done civil litigation, had previous experience as prosecutors, or had done divorce work, personal injury work for plaintiffs, personal real estate practice, or a general family practice. Those currently handling divorce cases had worked in an even greater range of fields, including labor law and business real estate in addition to those in which the criminal defense lawyers had practiced. Those doing general civil litigation often had experience in other litigation fields, including business litigation, criminal defense, criminal prosecution, divorce, and both sides of personal injury work. Both skill-type specialization and client-type specialization tended to be maintained during the course of the lawyers' careers. The limited amount of movement of personnel across those boundaries, then, means that work experience, which might provide a basis for communication and shared values or a common understanding of lawyers' roles, is not likely to bridge those divides.

Structure and Opportunity

Lawyers in various areas of practice may be drawn together if they share social origins or a common law school experience, serve the same clients, deal with the same legal doctrines, share a particular skill, participate together in a referral network, or pursue common objectives through the organized bar. As we have seen, however, the extent to which this occurs may have diminished. The work of lawyers tends to be specialized, and to have become more specialized (see chap. 2, fig. 2.4). Lawyers specialize in particular types of clients as well as in fields because the organizations in which they work typically serve only a limited range of clients. This restriction of practice usually occurs early in the lawyers' careers, often when they get their first jobs. In later chapters, we analyze in greater detail the prestige of different types of practice (chap. 4), the relationships of lawyers' career paths to their social characteristics (chap. 6), the level of income earned in the various practice areas (chap. 7), the job satisfaction of lawyers in those areas (chap. 11), and the social and political values of lawyers doing different types of work (chap. 8).

But the findings presented thus far have already begun to shed light on the three major themes introduced in chapter 1: professional autonomy, professional integration, and social stratification. The ability of Chicago lawyers to choose the types of clients they will or will not serve is severely restricted by their access to particular practice settings. Corporations that generate securities law problems send that work to large law firms or to their own inside counsel; plaintiffs in personal injury cases, by contrast, are usually not welcome in large law firms, so such work is done almost exclusively by solo practitioners and the smallest firms. For the most part, lawyers do not choose their clients. If they have a choice, it is a choice of practice settings.

The integration of the profession is not greatly advanced by the efforts of bar associations. Instead, the associations appear to be yet another arena in which interest groups within the bar contend for power. In both 1975 and 1995, more than half of the survey respondents belonged to the American Bar Association and three-fifths to the Chicago Bar Association, but the elites of the profession were far more likely to be members than were those in solo practice or government jobs. As specialization of practice increased, a greater number of specialized bar associations came into being, but the percentage of respondents who belonged to no bar association nearly doubled nonetheless.

Although there was less ethnoreligious segregation among the fields of law in 1995 than there had been in 1975, social stratification within the bar remained well defined. When women and minorities entered the profession in substantial numbers, they tended to replace Catholics and Jews on the lower rungs of the ladder. As we report in chapter 6, women often managed to get jobs in law firms, but they seldom advanced to partnership. The few who entered the legal profession before 1975 were highly self-selected and tended to have elite credentials, but the much larger number of women entering after 1975 were disproportionately likely to have attended a local law school, and their probabilities of attaining partnership or a high income were less than a quarter of those of type I Protestant males. The law school hierarchy continued to affect career opportunities, and access to the school strata was determined in important part by social status of origin, as indicated by father's occupation. In multivariate analyses, however, we found that the lower professional attainment of some social groups was not explained by law school effects—net of law school and age effects, women, African Americans, and Hispanics had significantly lower probabilities of top-quartile income, partnership in large firms, or for that matter partnership in firms of any size.[22] Thus, their lower rates of success do not appear to be attributable solely to the prestige of their diplomas, but the latter compounds their disadvantage. African Americans and Hispanics were consistently disadvantaged, in every way—in socioeconomic status of origin, in law school prestige, in attainment of partnership status, and in income. Although Jewish men had succeeded in acquiring superior law school credentials, they were significantly less likely to attain partnership in large law firms than were type I Protestant men. If social similarity contributes to cohesion, while dissimilarity organized into systematic strata is conducive to dissensus, the patterns of differentiation in the Chicago bar are unlikely to contribute to a shared sense of common fate or common purpose.

In sum, although the social strata within the profession shifted in some respects, the bar remained clearly stratified. The greater presence of women and minorities in lower-status practice settings and in lower-status roles within their practice settings may, in fact, have defined the hierarchy even more clearly. Gender and race are more obvious social markers than is religion. The boundaries among the strata may be sharper, therefore, than was the case when the distinctions were drawn among varieties of white males. Even though a majority of the prosecutors were Catholics in 1975 (see fig. 3.1), this may not have been obvious to casual observers. As prosecution became women's work, however (in 1995, 57 percent of the prosecutors in the sample were women), the fact was hard to miss.[23] To some degree, the boundaries among the strata and their social meaning—that is, that lawyers with different characteristics and different degrees of social advantage serve systematically different sorts of clients—are likely to be noticed not only by lawyers and judges but by laymen who have contact with the legal system (clients, jurors, police, etc.). We have no data about the observations or attitudes of laymen, but it is reasonable to speculate that segregation of lawyers' roles by race and gender, especially, would create a perception that there are separate systems of justice. The perception would be correct.

PART II
The Hierarchies of the Bar

Chapter 4
Prestige

American lawyers are subject to a complex, growing public mistrust (Galanter 1998, 809–10; Hengstler 1993). A survey conducted in the early 1990s found that confidence in lawyers' ethical standards was about the same as that enjoyed by auto mechanics and substantially less than that accorded accountants, doctors, and bankers (Hengstler 1993). In 1993, 31 percent of Americans surveyed said that lawyers were "less honest" than most people, up from 17 percent in 1986 (Galanter 1998, 809, n. 21). In 1989, a survey found that 21 percent of Americans thought lawyers' ethics were "poor," while only 3 percent thought they were "excellent" (Galanter 1998, 808).

Perhaps the most consistent criticism of the legal profession concerns equal treatment under the law (Sarat 1977). Americans appear to believe that the legal system works unfairly to the benefit of the rich and powerful. In 1998, only 33 percent agreed with the proposition that "[c]ourts try to treat poor people and rich people alike" (M/A/R/C Research 1999, 65). Further, the public appears to doubt that lawyers work as hard for clients who are poor or politically weak as for clients who are wealthy and influential. A survey conducted in the early 1970s found that only 37 percent of Americans agreed with the statement that lawyers "work as hard for poor clients as for clients who are rich and important" (Curran and Spalding 1974).

Public opinion surveys are a valuable source of information about what people believe, but so are the songs people listen to, the television programs they watch, and the jokes they tell. An analysis by Marc Galanter (1998) of 150 years of lawyer jokes found that lawyers were derided for avarice and duplicity, for taking advantage of vulnerable clients, for swindling their professional peers, and for caring more about winning in court than seeing justice done. Lawyers were scorned for offending the honor that the profession was expected to embody. According to Galanter, the most common offense reflected in jokes of recent vintage is a lawyer's violation of another person's trust, as in this one:

> An ancient, nearly blind old woman retained the local lawyer to draft her last will and testament, for which he charged her two hundred dollars. As she rose to leave, she took the money out of her purse and handed it over, enclosing a third hundred-dollar bill by mistake. Immediately the attorney realized he was faced with a crushing ethical decision: Should he tell his partner? (Galanter 1998, 819)

The popular idea that trustworthiness is central to good lawyerly behavior corresponds closely to a classic sociological understanding of the role of professionals in society. Talcott Parsons emphasized what he called the "fiduciary" nature of relationships between the lay public and professionals such as doctors, lawyers, teachers, and clergy. He suggested that, even though the lawyer and client are engaged in a market transaction, relationships between professionals and clients are fundamentally different from ordinary relationships between buyers and sellers. "The standard of *caveat emptor*," which usually applies between consumers and producers, "cannot legitimately be applied" to professional relationships, Parsons argued (1969, 506; 1962).

Because professionals have knowledge and skills that lay people not only do not have but generally cannot evaluate (Parsons 1962; 1968; 1969; Freidson 1984); but see Larson 1977), professionals are required to act on their clients' behalf. When a doctor suggests a course of treatment, the average patient has two choices: accept the doctor's suggestion, or get a second opinion from another doctor.[1] In other professions, the case is largely analogous, but American lawyers have dual responsibilities. In addition to the obligation to look out for client interests—to be, as the lawyers' ethical code puts it, "zealous advocates"—lawyers are responsible to the "greater good" as "officers of the court." The two duties do not always coexist comfortably. The tensions between lawyers' obligations to clients and to society necessarily place lawyers in a morally ambiguous role, one in which they may be damned if they do and damned if they don't.

Three Theories of Honor

Sociological work on the legal profession recognizes three different sets of values that lawyers may embrace, or three different understandings of what lawyers may honor and respect in professional work.[2] The classical theory of professionalism holds that the lawyer's fiduciary role is like the two sides of a coin: one side is the trust lay people have in lawyers' expertise, and the other is the autonomy lawyers enjoy because of that trust and expertise. In this understanding, then, one of the rewards of being a lawyer is being able to control your own work—being able to tell your client what his problem is and how, with your help, it may be solved. During law school and on-the-job training, lawyers are socialized into this role and come to respect its obligations, while enjoying the privileges it affords. In this classical theory, lawyers value expertise, public service, and freedom from client direction and control.

A second perspective suggests that lawyers' values reflect the preferences of the larger society. In this view, lawyers will value work for clients who enjoy high regard in society (Heinz and Laumann 1982; Laumann and Heinz 1977). *Chicago Lawyers* observed that work for corporations was highly valued in the bar, while work for personal clients had lower prestige—lawyers who serve corporations serve "the core economic values of [American] society. [T]he more a field of law serves these values, the higher its prestige will be within the profession" (Heinz and Laumann 1982, 130). Conversely, the more that lawyers serve people whose general social standing is low (the poor, the unemployed, and those without much formal education), the lower will be that work's prestige.

Since powerful clients are presumably able to exercise greater control over their lawyers, the finding that work for powerful corporate clients was prestigious challenged the classical thesis that professionals value autonomy (Nelson and Trubek 1992, 182). Moreover, the corresponding finding—that work for people of low social standing was derogated—tends to contradict the claim that the profession values public service. Instead of the classical values, the client-centered thesis argues that lawyers primarily value service to wealth and power.

A third sociological perspective suggests that what lawyers value is the opportunity to do work that is truly lawyerly. Like the classical theory, this perspective holds that lawyers have a value system distinct from that of the society in which they work (Abbott 1981). The theory argues that professions are organized around cores or "centers" of abstract knowledge (Abbott

1988, 52–58; Shils 1994). The most respected work in any profession is the work that most closely approaches this core, for that work is most professionally pure, in the sense that nonprofessional considerations have been removed.

Andrew Abbott suggests that professional work can be divided into three types: diagnosis, inference, and treatment. During diagnosis, the client's problem is translated into professional terms. Inference reformulates the problem using the abstract knowledge and conceptual apparatus of the profession, and the professional applies or manipulates that knowledge in order to solve the problem, as defined in professional terms. Treatment provides the client with the solution and involves translating the problem from professional terms back into the specific, real-world context of the client. Thus the work of inference is relatively pure, because it gives little weight to the nonprofessional aspects of the client's problem (Abbott 1988, 40, 47, 48). Consider what goes on in a courtroom: The judge's work deals with issues that lawyers have "purified" by redefining them in legal terms—by constructing arguments that apply relevant statutes, precedents, and legal principles—and infers the answer to what has been formulated as a legal question, a dispute defined in the conceptual categories of the profession (Abbott 1981). Thus, judges are more professionally pure than the lawyers who argue before them.

Lawyers do value autonomy, in this view, but they value a peculiarly professional kind of autonomy. The crucial aspect is not autonomy from client control of lawyers' actions, it is freedom from contamination of the legal issues with nonlegal considerations. It is quintessentially legal autonomy. Lawyers' work for different types of clients therefore exhibits variation in professional purity. Work for corporations is more prestigious than work for people because the corporation itself is "the lawyers' creation . . . the muck of feelings and will is omitted from it *ab initio*" (Abbott 1981, 824). By contrast, if the lawyer's client is an angry former spouse, or a dispossessed child, or a distressed victim of malpractice, the lawyer may need to comfort or console the client, often using emotional rather than legal resources, and the lawyer may use the client's grief and pain to sway a jury (Mather, McEwen, and Maiman 2001; Sarat and Felstiner 1995).

The American public appears to believe that lawyers are *supposed to* value public service and to be ethical in their dealings, but that lawyers fail to behave in accord with such values. Classic sociological theory shares the public's emphasis on the fiduciary role of lawyers, and suggests that lawyers respect and value that role. The client-centered perspective, in contrast, suggests that citizen concern about equal treatment is warranted: in a capitalist society with considerable material inequality, lawyers value service to wealthy and powerful organizations above service to individuals, especially if those people are poor and politically or socially weak (Hadfield 2000). The professional purity perspective also suggests that lawyers will be drawn to work for the rich and powerful, but drawn because they value the legal purity and complexity of such work, rather than because they value wealth or power per se.

Prestige

Asked what they value, lawyers would no doubt respond that they embrace all that is virtuous and just, and that they abhor avarice, sloth, and carbohydrates. But another way to assess what lawyers value is to ask what types of legal work they esteem, and what they derogate or dismiss as unprofessional. By examining the distribution of prestige within the legal profession, we may learn about lawyers' professional values.

The relative honor accorded to a certain role or particular task is commonly called *prestige*.[3] Prestige is an entitlement to deference; as such, it has an inherently hierarchical quality (Shils 1994). To have prestige is to receive a kind of respect or admiration from others that requires the making of "invidious comparisons" (Veblen 1994). Without the judgment of "greater" and "lesser," there can be no deference. The deference is "deserved" by being grounded in the values of the group assigning prestige—it is "granted by an individual or a collectivity for performances they consider above the average" (Goode 1978: 7, emphasis omitted). For the granting of deference, "above average" may mean better than most at a given role or task, or it may mean that the role or task itself more nearly approaches the fulfillment of commonly held ideals: "The qualities enjoined by honor provide the link . . . between self and the idealized norms of the community" (P. Berger, B. Berger, and Kellner 1974, 86). So, for example, in groups that value scholarship, the learned will be prestigious and the erudite will be among the most prestigious. Among lawyers, the three theories of the prestige hierarchy reviewed above imply three different sets of values or "idealized norms" that may be reflected in lawyers' invidious comparisons. We have assessed these comparisons, using lawyers' judgments about the prestige of varying fields of law. As part of the Chicago surveys, lawyers were asked to rate the fields in terms of their "general prestige . . . within the legal profession at large."[4] The rating scale had five points, ranging from "poor" to "outstanding." We measured prestige by the percentage of the ratings indicating that the field was "outstanding" or "above average" (referred to below as the *prestige increment score*)—in other words, the percentage of lawyers who think the field enjoys better than average esteem in the bar.

The proposition that aggregate prestige ratings reveal something about lawyers' values assumes consensus. Given the available data, however, we cannot directly investigate the degree of consensus. The prestige item in the surveys asked lawyers about their perception of the prevailing values of the *profession*, rather than about their own views (cf. Bourdieu 1984): lawyers reported on their colleagues, not necessarily on themselves. Nonetheless, if the lawyers' reports reflect distinct reference groups that make substantially different prestige judgments, we would see systematic disagreement. For instance, lawyers who are left-leaning reformers might think that the views of their allies are more representative of the profession than is the case. Such lawyers might tend to believe that work consistent with reformist values— for example, civil rights and civil liberties law, criminal defense, or general family practice serving poverty-level clients—is higher in prestige than other lawyers report it to be. Or, lawyers who work in the large, private-practice firms, where most of the corporate legal work is done, might think primarily of their coworkers when asked to assess the profession's views. Such lawyers might report that banking, general corporate law, and antitrust defense work enjoy higher prestige.

To investigate this kind of dissensus, we examined the relationship between prestige ratings and the respondents' race, gender, age, political affiliation, and score on a measure of economic liberalism. The variables also included the types of clients the lawyer served and the location of the lawyer's own fields of practice within the prestige order. Table 4.1 presents a summary of these analyses. None of the variables produce systematic differences. Correlations of prestige ratings and rankings across the groups of lawyers range from .89 to .99. We found no instances of inversions or other significant reordering of the fields. Such differences as there were in groups' ratings of specific fields generally exhibited what prestige researchers call *occupational egoism*—the tendency to think that one's own work is more highly regarded than others' ratings reveal it to be (Kahl 1957). The increasing social diversity and economic inequality in the legal profession over the two decades does not appear to have been attended by the emergence of disagreement about the profession's status order. Although some Chicago lawyers may reject the values of the profession at large, most appear to have agreed about what those values were.

Even if the mean prestige scores of fields remained the same, however, this result could be produced by opposing extreme scores that tended to

Table 4.1. Correlations of Prestige Ratings and Rankings across Selected Groups of Lawyers, 1975 and 1995

	1975		1995	
	Ratings	Rankings	Ratings	Rankings
Women and men lawyers	NA	NA	.99	.98
Black and nonblack lawyers	NA	NA	.95	.92
Jewish and non-Jewish lawyers	.96	.94	.98	.97
Republican and Democratic lawyers	.91	.91	.98	.97
Republican and Independent lawyers	.94	.92	.99	.99
Democratic and Independent lawyers	.96	.96	.98	.98
Older and younger lawyers	.91	.89	.97	.96
Economically liberal and conservative lawyers	.97	.95	.99	.99
Top and middle thirds of the status order	.98	.95	.99	.99
Top and bottom thirds of the status order	.92	.91	.99	.99
Middle and bottom thirds of the status order	.93	.93	.99	.99
Lawyers serving 75 percent or more business clients, and all other lawyers	.93	.91	.97	.97
Lawyers a majority of whose personal clients are of low social status, and all other lawyers	.91	.90	.97	.96

offset each other. Accordingly, we did an analysis to determine whether there was increasing polarization within the prestige ratings of individual fields. We computed an index of the extent to which the distribution of responses for each field was bimodal, with nearly as many respondents rating the field low as rated it high. In the 1975 data, five fields had high scores on this index; in 1995, only three did.[5] Thus, we did not find evidence of increasing disagreement. As is common in prestige studies of this type, respondents in each period evidence the most disagreement about fields in the middle of the status order (Reiss 1961).

Table 4.2 presents the prestige scores and ranks of the fields in 1995 and 1975. Although the sets of fields used in the two surveys differed somewhat, they have twenty-seven fields in common, and in those fields we see considerable stability. Lawyers in 1975 and 1995 had similar views about what legal work is respected and what is derogated. The rank order and product-moment correlations for the fields included in both surveys are .86 and .88, respectively. But the prestige order does appear to have undergone a crystallization—the inequality or disparity between the scores of the top and bottom fields increased. The last column of table 4.2 notes the fields that had a significantly higher or lower prestige rating in 1995 than in 1975.[6] Of the top nineteen fields in the 1995 status order, all of the significant changes are increases in prestige. Among the fields ranked lower, however, almost

Table 4.2. Prestige of the Fields of Law, 1995 and 1975

| | 1995 | | 1975 | | Significant |
	Prestige[a]	Rank (of 42)	Prestige[a]	Rank[b] (of 30)	Rating Change[c]
Securities	85	1	75	1	(+)
Trademark and copyright	76	2			
International law—private	75	3			
International law—public	71	4			
Patents	71	5	66	4	
Civil litigation—corporate[d]	67	6			
Income tax, corporate federal[d]	67	7			
Antitrust—defendants	66	8	70	3	
General corporate	66	9	59	6	
Real estate—finance and development[d]	61	10			
Antitrust—plaintiffs	59	11	60	5	
Banking	57	12	56	7	
Estate and gift tax[d]	53	13			
Environmental law—plaintiffs	49	14	28	19	(+)
Environmental law—defendants	46	15	29	18	(+)
Civil rights/civil liberties	44	16	32	15	(+)
Municipal law	38	17	46	10	
Employment law—management	38	18	42	12	
Criminal prosecution	35	19	23	22	(+)
Public utilities, administrative law	34	20	53	8	(−)
Business bankruptcy	33	21			
Income tax, personal federal[d]	32	22			
Civil litigation—personal[d]	28	23			
Probate	28	24	52	9	(−)
Commercial law[e]	27	25	28	20	
Real estate—zoning and eminent domain[f]	27	26	11	25	(+)
Admiralty	26	27	46	11	(−)
State and local tax[d]	26	28			
Employment law—labor	18	29	32	14	(−)
Personal injury—defense	17	30	30	17	(−)
Criminal defense	17	31	24	21	
Personal bankruptcy	14	32			
Personal injury—plaintiff	14	33	19	23	
Consumer law—seller/creditor	12	34	11	24	
Real estate—residential transfers[d]	11	35			
General family practice, paying clients	9	36	10	26	
General family practice, poverty clients	8	37	8	29	
Consumer law—consumer/debtor	7	38	8	30	
Real estate—landlord/tenant	7	39	9	28	
Juvenile law	7	40			
Immigration law	7	41			
Divorce	4	42	9	27	(−)

Table 4.2 *continued*

1975 Prestige of Tax, Civil Litigation, and Real Estate[d]		
	Prestige[a]	Rank
Tax	74	2
Civil litigation	40	13
Real estate	30	16

[a] This score is the percentage of responses rating the field as at least "above average" in prestige.

[b] For the rank of tax, civil litigation, and real estate, see the tax, civil litigation, and real estate portion of the table.

[c] In the fields with entries, the difference in ratings between the two periods is significant at $p < .05$, two-tailed test. A plus sign indicates an increase in prestige; a minus sign indicates a decrease.

[d] In the 1975 survey, the following fields were undifferentiated: civil litigation, real estate, and tax. 1995 comparisons with these fields are not appropriate.

[e] In the 1995 survey, this field was listed as "commercial law, Uniform Commercial Code."

[f] In the 1975 survey, this field was listed as "condemnations."

all the significant changes reflect decreases in the share of lawyers rating them as outstanding or above average. The only exception to this pattern is "zoning and eminent domain." This field was listed as "condemnations" in the 1975 survey, and the change in name may have affected the responses. Thus, in their stock of prestige, the rich got richer and the poor got poorer. This parallels a change in income; see chapter 7.

The preference for "establishment" clients, noted in the first Chicago study, appears to have become more pronounced in some cases. In 1995, criminal prosecution had significantly higher prestige than criminal defense, and employment law on the side of management had significantly higher prestige than that done on the side of labor. On the other hand, lawyers appear to have developed a more uniform distaste for both sides of the personal injury bar. In 1975, personal injury work for defendants was significantly higher in prestige than such work for plaintiffs; in 1995, the difference between the two fields had diminished to insignificance.[7]

In both years, all but one of the fields in the top third of the prestige order were fields serving large and powerful organizations, particularly large business corporations. In 1975, the exception is tax (undifferentiated), which includes corporate tax work, and in 1995 the exception is estate and gift tax, ranked thirteenth in prestige, which is work performed primarily for wealthy individuals and families. The lowest third of the prestige order contains numerous personal client fields, many of which involve contact with clients who not only lack wealth and social power but suffer stigmatization:

divorcing couples, children in trouble with the law, criminals, and people facing financial ruin. The fields most closely associated with public service, poverty law, and individual access to justice are spread throughout the lower two-thirds of the status order. Civil rights/civil liberties is in the second third in both periods, as are personal litigation and criminal prosecution. Criminal defense and personal injury plaintiffs work are in the lowest third of the prestige order.

Determinants of Prestige

As we saw in the review of public opinion about lawyers and the legal system, citizens mostly share the classical view of what lawyers *should* value: lawyers *should* most highly regard the fields of law that require expertise, afford autonomy, and serve the greater good. To measure these characteristics of the fields, professors of law at Northwestern University Law School and research scholars at the American Bar Foundation[8] were asked, in both 1975 and 1995, to rate each field of law on five different dimensions: the intellectual challenge of its legal substance; the rapidity with which the relevant law changes; the degree to which lawyers who do the work are motivated by a desire to serve the public good or, in the alternative, by private profit; the reputation for ethical behavior of the lawyers doing the work; and the degree to which lawyers perform their work free of direction from clients or other lawyers.[9]

Table 4.3 presents the ratings of the fields for both years, standardized to the distribution of ratings in the year. The standard scores range from 0 to 100, with 50 the average score and each ten-point change indicating one standard deviation. So, for example, securities law scored 1.4 standard deviations above the mean of the intellectual challenge ratings in 1995 and 1.3 standard deviations above the mean in 1975. As we saw with prestige, the ratings of intellectual challenge, rapidity of change, public service orientation, reputation for ethical conduct, and freedom of action for each field of law are similar in both surveys.[10]

The last row of table 4.3 reports the correlations of the expert rating scores with prestige. In both surveys, intellectual challenge was strongly and positively associated with prestige, but the correlation was even stronger in 1995 than in 1975. The relationships between prestige and public-service orientation, reputation for ethical conduct, and freedom of action were quite similar in the two periods—the ethical conduct score was positively associated with prestige, but the public service and autonomy scores were both negatively associated with prestige. In 1975, the pace at which law

Table 4.3. Experts' Ratings of Characteristics of the Fields of Law, 1995 and 1975

	Intellectual Challenge		Rapidity of Change		Public Service		Ethical Conduct		Freedom of Action	
	1995	1975	1995	1975	1995	1975	1995	1975	1995	1975
Securities	64	63	57	62	36	44	57	57	38	39
Trademark and copyright	61		63		43		61		43	
International law—private	60		63		45		61		44	
International law—public	62		59		63		67		60	
Patents	65	56	51	44	42	45	66	62	45	47
Civil litigation—corporate[a]	51	52	47	48	41	51	48	45	41	55
Income tax, corporate federal[a]	65	67	70	66	40	43	54	55	39	46
Antitrust—defendants	64	64	52	56	37	40	50	53	38	39
General corporate	48	51	50	48	42	44	61	59	40	41
Real estate—finance and development[a]	53	45	46	37	41	43	55	48	42	50
Antitrust—plaintiffs	64	65	52	57	39	46	49	47	58	65
Banking	52	47	57	42	41	42	54	58	38	35
Estate and gift tax[a]	60	67	59	66	42	43	58	55	50	46
Environmental law—plaintiffs	62	61	68	65	67	72	56	58	63	66
Environmental law—defendants	60	61	69	65	41	47	49	51	33	43
Civil rights/civil liberties	57	61	61	65	69	77	71	64	68	70
Municipal law	49	44	41	38	48	45	56	56	40	41
Employment law—management	46	52	53	53	40	45	42	46	33	38
Criminal prosecution	43	48	47	56	66	56	33	47	66	53
Public utilities, administrative law	60	55	56	53	48	48	56	56	45	39
Business bankruptcy	57		53		42		44		42	
Income tax, personal federal[a]	56	67	67	66	48	43	50	55	47	46
Civil litigation—personal[a]	41	52	44	48	50	51	43	45	64	55
Probate	42	45	37	32	50	44	58	57	54	46
Commercial law[b]	49	52	43	48	47	46	52	55	47	48
Real estate—zoning and eminent domain[c]	42	35	40	36	50	43	42	39	46	49
Admiralty	51	52	30	34	43	42	55	62	53	48
State and local tax	49	67	38	66	45	43	48	55	52	46
Employment law—labor	48	53	51	53	58	51	49	47	44	42
Personal injury—defense	40	33	42	42	43	43	43	38	41	46
Criminal defense	48	51	46	57	65	57	38	33	56	64
Personal bankruptcy	42		51		53		37		58	
Personal injury—plaintiff	41	35	41	43	47	43	27	25	68	64
Consumer law—seller/creditor	42	50	45	60	45	46	43	43	44	41
Real estate—residential transfers[a]	30	45	32	37	50	43	49	48	50	50
General family practice, paying clients	38	38	41	41	55	52	50	54	51	55
General family practice, poverty clients	36	38	40	51	74	76	62	61	69	64

continued

Table 4.3 *continued*

	Intellectual Challenge		Rapidity of Change		Public Service		Ethical Conduct		Freedom of Action	
	1995	1975	1995	1975	1995	1975	1995	1975	1995	1975
Consumer law—consumer/ debtor	41	52	48	59	58	65	44	50	59	62
Real estate—landlord/tenant	32	43	35	47	60	55	40	41	53	52
Juvenile law	42		54		68		54		64	
Immigration law	49		58		63		43		60	
Divorce	34	30	43	45	54	50	25	30	55	54
Correlation with prestige[d]	.83	.64	.52	.10	−.54	−.47	.57	.48	−.47	−.47

Note: Fields are listed in rank order of prestige in 1995.

[a] In the 1975 survey, the following fields were undifferentiated: civil litigation, real estate, and tax. Readers should be cautious in comparing detailed fields from the 1995 survey to their undifferentiated counterparts in the 1975 survey.

[b] In the 1975 survey, this field was listed as "commercial law, Uniform Commercial Code."

[c] In the 1975 survey, this field was listed as "condemnations."

[d] The correlations with prestige were calculated on the differing sets of fields used in each survey (in 1995, N = 42; in 1975, N = 30).

changed was essentially unrelated to prestige because some high-prestige fields (banking, patents, general corporate law) had rapidity of change scores near or below average, while some low-prestige fields (both sides of consumer law, both sides of environmental law, criminal defense) were rated as above average. In 1995, however, there was a positive relationship between prestige and rapidity of change.

Table 4.4 presents the results of a multiple regression analysis of prestige[11] using the five characteristics in table 4.3. The results from the two surveys are generally similar. In 1975, the five characteristics account for 70 percent of the variance in prestige; in 1995, they account for 75 percent. Of the five, the strongest predictor is intellectual challenge. Freedom of action and rapidity of change have no effect on prestige, net of their relationships to the other characteristics. The more a field is oriented toward public service, rather than profit, the lower its prestige, again net of other factors. In 1995, the positive relationship between ethical conduct and prestige achieves statistical significance.

Overall, therefore, the classical theory of prestige receives only partial support in these analyses. Lawyers appear to value intellectual challenge and ethical conduct, or at least they perceive that the profession has regard for fields that the experts rated as possessing those attributes, but they do not assign prestige to work that is more oriented to the public good than to

Table 4.4. Professional Prestige and Professional Purity, 1975 and 1995

	1975	1995
Intercept	−2.245*	−3.910***
standard error	(1.040)	(.926)
Intellectual challenge	.072*	.070**
standard error	(.030)	(.021)
ß	.67	.56
Rapidity of change	−.019	0
standard error	(.029)	(.016)
ß	−.17	0
Public service	−.055 +	−.039*
standard error	(.030)	(.019)
ß	−.51	−.31
Ethical conduct	.028	.033*
standard error	(.023)	(.013)
ß	.25	.26
Freedom of action	−.004	−.001
standard error	(.022)	(.017)
ß	.03	−.01
Adjusted R^2	.70	.75
N	30	42

Note: The table presents metric coefficients and their standard errors (in parentheses) and standardized coefficients from OLS regressions of the logit of the prestige increment score.
*** $p < .001$ ** $p < .01$ * $p < .05$ + $p < .10$ (two-tailed tests)

profit. Moreover, net of other characteristics, fields that afford considerable autonomy do not appear to be especially esteemed by lawyers—and, when other characteristics are *not* taken into account, autonomy is negatively associated with prestige. When we control for the level of remuneration in the fields, which is possible only in the 1995 data, the general pattern of relationships between these characteristics and prestige does not change.[12]

Core Economic Values, or Professional Purity

The client-centered theory of the social organization of the legal profession argues that the business or corporate fields of law serve the "core economic values of society" and are prestigious because they do so. In exploratory analyses in the first Chicago study, the authors found that the social status of the individuals served by a field had significant effects on prestige. Comparing that finding with the observation that more intellectually challenging fields were more prestigious, they argued that higher-status personal clients were likely to present lawyers with more challenging legal work, thereby making work for such personal clients more prestigious than work for lower-status clients.

Because of the way the 1975 data were archived, it is not possible to construct field-level measures of client and work characteristics for all thirty of the fields used in the 1975 survey—sufficient data are available for only twenty-one fields. Therefore, we confine the next set of regression analyses to 1995 data. Analyses not presented here, however, suggest that the findings for 1975 are substantively similar. For each field, measures were calculated based on responses from lawyers who reported that at least 5 percent of their work time was devoted to the given field of law.[13] The lawyer's contribution to the field was weighted by the share that he or she contributed to the total amount of work in the field.[14] Because the fields of practice share personnel and the responses of many lawyers are therefore included in more than one field, these measures of the characteristics of the fields present a conservative picture of the differentiation among the fields.[15] They reflect the responses of all practitioners in a field, not merely the specialists.

In these regressions, measures of client type were constructed from the respondents' reports of the proportion of their clients that were businesses and the proportion of their individual clients who were of lower social status (sales and clerical workers, blue-collar workers, or unemployed). The intellectual demands of the work were assessed using respondents' ratings of the level of legal skill required in their work overall—that is, the measure is the percentage of effort devoted to the field by lawyers who reported that their work required so much specialized skill and knowledge that it could not be done by an educated layman.[16] The professional purity thesis argues that lawyers value *specifically legal* work, not merely intellectually complex work. Thus, if work requires specialized skills and knowledge not accessible to an educated layman, this indicates its proximity to the core of abstract knowledge at the center of the profession.

According to the professional purity theory of prestige, the most prestigious work is the most lawyerly work, work that involves use of and contribution to the abstract knowledge of the profession. The courtroom example given earlier suggests that purity varies in different kinds of legal jobs—in that case, between judges and trial lawyers. Professional purity also varies from field to field. In Abbott's terms, the work of a field is pure to the extent that its practitioners devote effort to inference, instead of to treatment or diagnosis.

We may think of inference as a specific bundle of tasks. Some fields require more tasks in this bundle, others less. The specific tasks performed in different fields of law and the way those tasks are organized are conditioned by the substance of the legal matters themselves (Kordana 1995; Nelson 1988, 177). For example, describing legal work performed for businesses, Kordana notes:

> A large corporate matter (e.g., a securities offering or a merger) or a large litigation matter requires a great deal of what can be termed "paperwork." For a corporate matter these tasks include "due diligence" . . . and drafting and proofreading a variety of agreements. For a litigation matter the paper work includes document discovery . . . and exhaustive legal research on the myriad issues involved in or potentially relevant to the dispute.
>
> A relatively smaller proportion of the work to be done by a large firm in a corporate transaction or litigation matter consists of client interaction and strategic, complex legal work. This includes synthesizing and applying legal research results to the facts at hand, using discovery for strategic advantage over the opponents in a litigation matter, ensuring that agreements or settlements successfully meet client objectives, and keeping clients apprised of developments. (Kordana 1995,1924–25)

To the extent that the "paperwork" is professional at all, it falls in the realm of diagnosis—the work of formulating the client's problem as a legal matter and casting that problem in terms of other matters that have legal precedents. Lawyers' relationships with clients consist, in part, of treatment—of translating the legal understanding of the client's problem back into lay terms so the client can understand the progress of the case—and, in part, of work that is entirely nonprofessional, the "business" work of a salesperson dealing with a customer. Kordana's "strategic, complex legal work" is inference, the work that is most professionally pure.

Professional authority differs from managerial authority in important ways. Managerial authority in large law firms—the power to hire and fire, and responsibility for the other administrative work of the firm—is usually shared by a managing partner and committees of partners (see chap. 5; Nelson 1988). Although such authority may or may not confer professional prestige, the distribution of managerial authority bears no necessary relationship to lawyers' substantive areas of practice. Peculiarly professional authority, however, arises because some people "in the normal course of work involving cooperation with others in a division of labor . . . , because of experience or specialized knowledge, direct those others" (Freidson 1986, 143). Fields of law in which work is organized in this hierarchical division of labor provide an opportunity for some lawyers to specialize in "pure legal work" by delegating relatively impure work to other lawyers.

As a measure of the degree to which work in a field of law requires professionally pure, "strategic, complex legal work," therefore, we calculated the percentage of effort in each field contributed by lawyers who reported that they "frequently" or "very frequently" supervised and reviewed the work of other lawyers. Not all the work of supervising and reviewing involves legal inference, of course: some of it consists of the administrative work of dividing tasks among lawyers or the mentoring of new lawyers. Despite its contamination by such tasks, however, this is the best available measure of the degree to which the division of labor within a field would permit lawyers to delegate the work of diagnosis to other lawyers, and thus to pursue professionally purer work.[17]

All fields of law require some office practice, and some also require lawyers to appear in court. As is the case with office work, the purity of courtroom work varies. Trial courts establish facts. Witnesses are called, and evidence is presented and contested. Lawyers argue about the facts and the import or significance of those facts. Appellate courts, however, usually treat the facts as settled. In appeals, lawyers' arguments focus on matters of law, and are therefore relatively professionally pure.[18] As a measure of the degree to which the lawyers in a field did appellate work (by hypothesis, work that is relatively pure), we used their reports of the number of days per month that they appeared in state and federal appellate courts, and we computed the average for the field. To measure the degree to which the work of a field involved (relatively impure) trial court work, we calculated the average number of days per month that its lawyers appeared in trial courts (state and federal). As with other measures of the fields' characteristics, each lawyer's contribution was weighted by his or her time spent in the field.

Table 4.5 presents the results of regression analyses of prestige on these client-type and professional purity measures.[19] Model 1 indicates that expert knowledge and service to businesses are positively associated with prestige, while service to persons of low social status is negatively associated. These three measures alone account for 55 percent of the variance in prestige. Model 2 adds a measure of the income of the lawyers working in each field—the proportion of effort devoted to the field by lawyers whose income was above the average of all practicing lawyers ($132,904 in 1995 dollars). Adding income to the model reduces by 62 percent ($[0.26 - 0.10)]/0.26$) the relationship between prestige and the proportion of clients who are businesses, and the relationship drops to statistical insignificance. It is possible, of course, that lawyer income is a better indicator of client wealth than is the percentage of business clients. Inclusion of this measure of field income, however, does not change the estimated relationship between prestige and

Table 4.5. Professional Prestige, Type of Client, and Professional Purity, 1995

	Model 1	Model 2	Model 3	Model 4
Intercept	−1.772**	−1.718**	−2.694**	−2.441**
standard error	(.613)	(.577)	(.798)	(.808)
Percent business clients	1.179 +	.446		
standard error	(.686)	(.713)		
ß	.26	.10		
Percent lower status personal clients	−3.374**	-3.358**		
standard error	(1.117)	(1.050)		
ß	−.39	−.39		
Lawyer's intellecual challenge	1.770 +	1.188	2.433**	1.820 +
standard error	(.971)	(.944)	(.869)	(.964)
ß	.27	.18	.37	.27
Income above the average for practicing lawyers		2.690*		1.891
standard error		(1.119)		(1.356)
ß		.33		.24
Days per month in trial courts			−.113*	−.106*
standard error			(.050)	(.050)
ß			−.36	−.33
Days per month in appellate courts			2.670*	2.187 +
standard error			(1.226)	(1.259)
ß			.28	.23
Supervising and reviewing the work of other lawyers			2.266*	1.291
standard error			(1.084)	(1.278)
ß			.27	.15
N	40	40	40	40
Adjusted R^2	.55	.60	.53	.54

Note: The table presents metric coefficients and their standard errors (in parentheses) and standardized coefficients (ß) from OLS regressions of the logit of the prestige increment score. Admiralty law and public international law are excluded.
** $p < .01$ * $p < .05$ + $p < .10$ (two-tailed tests)

service to lower status clients. The relationship between prestige and the measure of professional expertise declines when income is controlled, by a third (0.33 = [0.27 − 0.18]/0.27), and also drops to insignificance. One way to interpret these findings is to infer that expert knowledge and service to businesses are prestigious, at least in part, because they are well compensated.

But pay and prestige are often bestowed upon the same recipients. Thus, service to business may be favored not only with higher income, but with the esteem of one's colleagues as well.

The estimates in model 3 in table 4.1 report the results of regressing prestige on measures of professional purity. As before, expert knowledge is positively associated with prestige. The amount of time spent in appellate courts and the degree to which lawyers in the field supervised and reviewed the work of other lawyers are also positively associated. The coefficient for time spent in trial courts, on the other hand, is negative. These four characteristics of lawyers' work account for 53 percent of the variance. Model 4 adds lawyer income. When expertise, responsibility for directing others' work, and court appearances are controlled, the relationship between income and prestige is not statistically significant, though it is in the expected positive direction. On the other hand, when income is controlled, the coefficient for supervising work declines by 44 percent ($[0.27 - 0.15]/0.27$) and drops to insignificance. The relationship between prestige and expert knowledge also declines when income is controlled—by 27 percent ($[0.37 - 0.27]/0.37$). Smaller declines are seen in the relationships between court appearances and prestige. As with the results on the client-type measures, there are two possible interpretations of these findings. If remuneration is valued in and of itself, then part of the reason that professionally purer fields of law enjoy higher prestige is that these types of legal work pay better than the average. Or, again, it may be that income does not "cause" prestige but that its distribution corresponds to the distribution of prestige.

Participation in Prestigious Work

We introduced our analysis of prestige by suggesting that the distribution of honor among lawyers might reveal lawyers' professional values. We turn now to the distribution of lawyers among honored work. Although members of historically excluded groups have made substantial progress in the bar, observers have suggested that the entry of these new groups has not been followed by full integration into the profession (see chap. 3; Chiu and Leicht 1999; Epstein 1993; Hagan and Kay 1995; Lempert, Chambers, and Adams 2000). The bar does not yet reflect the public it serves with "descriptive representation" (Pitkin 1972)—that is, the profession does not "look like America," either in the sense that groups with distinct interests or experiences are proportionally represented in the bar, or in the sense that members of such groups are able to participate fully in the several kinds of work done by lawyers.

One of the findings of the 1975 Chicago study was that external social hierarchies overlaid and reinforced the internal hierarchies of the bar. Lawyers who had higher social standing outside the bar because of their ethnoreligious heritage and class background—that is, white men of northern and western European ancestry, from professional families, whose religious affiliation was mainline Protestant—tended to serve corporate clients. Lawyers who were members of less privileged groups, such as Jews, those of southern and eastern European ancestry, and those from families of lower socioeconomic status, tended to provide services to individuals and small businesses. Jewish lawyers, in particular, were disproportionately concentrated in work that afforded low prestige in the bar (Heinz and Laumann 1982, 205, table 6.6).

Some of these patterns have changed. But women lawyers in the United States today are less likely than their male colleagues to be partners in law firms, and lawyers who are members of racial minority groups are still underrepresented in positions of power and prestige (Hull and Nelson 2000; Lempert, Chambers, and Adams 2000; Wilkins and Gulati 1996).

Figure 4.1 presents an analysis of access to prestigious work by selected groups. The "prestige of practice scores" presented here are the weighted sum of the prestige scores for the fields in which each lawyer practices, with the weights reflecting the share of the lawyer's effort in each field. In 1975, members of historically excluded groups tended to do work of lower prestige. The average prestige of the work done by Jewish lawyers was five points below the overall average, black lawyers were ten points below, and women were five points below. By 1995, however, Jewish lawyers were no longer disadvantaged, and black lawyers had also moved into higher prestige fields. Though the scores of black lawyers continued to be about four points lower than average, that difference is not statistically significant. The larger number of women in the 1995 sample, however, makes their difference from the overall average significant. That women were younger than men on average is unlikely to account for their underrepresentation in prestigious work, since age is unrelated to prestige.[20] Among Chicago lawyers in 1995, women and blacks were less likely to have attended elite law schools, and this is likely to limit their numbers in the prestigious fields. As we noted in chapter 3 and will see again in our analysis of career patterns in chapter 6, law school prestige is an important determinant of where lawyers are hired and thus of their access to prestigious work.

The most prestigious work is done by lawyers working in the largest law firms and by lawyers serving as in-house counsel (see fig. 4.2). Since lawyers in such settings tend to serve larger corporations, for whom the prestigious work is done, this is no surprise. Among lawyers in private practice, average scores are lowest among solo practitioners, those most likely to serve personal clients. But the prestige of the work done by local government lawyers, public defenders, and legal aid lawyers is even lower. Positions in

Figure 4.1. Prestige of Practice Scores by Selected Groups, 1975 and 1995

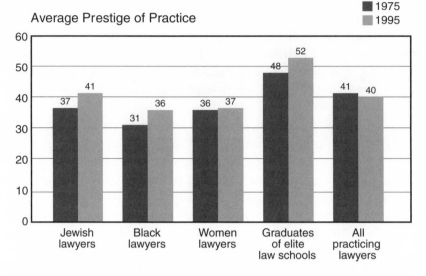

Notes: The following group average scores are significantly different from all other lawyers in the period: For 1975, Jewish lawyers ($p < .001$); black lawyers ($p < .01$); graduates of elite law schools ($p < .001$). For 1995, women lawyers ($p < .05$); graduates of elite law schools ($p < .001$).

local government and in agencies that specialize in service to the poor not only provide lawyers with the fewest opportunities for prestigious work, but are also the most poorly paid in the profession (see chap. 7).

The distribution of prestigious work across practice settings was similar in the two surveys. But the average scores declined in all of the smaller private practice settings—in the two smallest law firm categories, the declines are statistically significant. These declines may reflect the growing complexity of some kinds of corporate legal work, which require larger teams of lawyers (Dunworth and Rogers 1996; Hadfield 2000). Smaller firms may simply not have the staff to handle matters of this magnitude. The declining prestige of practice in smaller firms may also reflect the emergence of a type that was relatively rare in 1975: firms with multiple partners and associates concentrating exclusively or nearly exclusively on low-prestige work, such as personal injury or divorce.[21] But it is also possible that some law firms, especially in the middle range, took on a greater variety of kinds of legal work. Whether for strategic reasons, such as an effort to exploit new markets, or because they were hard pressed, these firms may have become more willing to take work they would previously have sent elsewhere, such as divorce or consumer debt collection.

Figure 4.2. Prestige of Practice Scores by Practice Setting, 1975 and 1995 (averages)

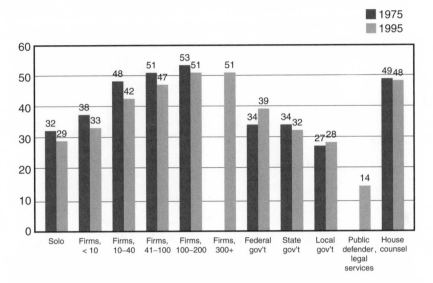

Note: Differences between periods are statistically significant only for firms of fewer than 10 lawyers and firms of 10 to 40 lawyers ($p < .05$, two-tailed). The public defender and legal services category includes lawyers working for legal aid societies.

Conclusion

Lawyers' judgments about the distribution of prestige within the profession do not endorse the fiduciary role that the American public expects. Independence in professional action and commitment to public service are not attributes the profession appears to value highly. Rather, the distribution of prestige reflects respect for service to powerful clients who provide opportunities for both the exercise of arcane skills and a substantial income. The profession is organized by its relationships with clients, the tasks involved in professional work correspond to the varying clientele, and the values of the profession are shaped by those relationships and tasks. Thus, for one reason or another, the legal profession is oriented toward service to wealth and power.

Chapter 5
Organizations

Career trajectories, income, relationships with clients, professional status, and access to resources, including the assistance of colleagues, all largely depend on the nature of the organizations in which urban lawyers work (Leicht and Fennell 1997, 2001; see also Baron and Bielby 1980). The organizational structures and procedures that determine these outcomes, however, and the specific consequences for both the organizations and the individual lawyers, are less clear. Do large practice organizations bureaucratize professional work, erode democratic governance of the firms (Tolbert and Stern 1991), and constrain professional autonomy (Spangler 1986; Derber, Schwarz, and Magrass 1990; Wallace 1995)? Or do large law firms and law departments use a collegial form of governance, perhaps because lawyers or clients especially value it (R. Greenwood, Hinings, and Brown 1990; Waters 1989), or because powerful individual partners and practice groups resist change in the governance structure (Nelson 1988)? How do the tensions between bureaucratization and collegial management—and the mechanisms adopted to deal with such tensions—affect the professional ideologies of lawyers, the organization of their work and the satisfaction they draw from it, and the nature of their commitment to their employing organizations and to the profession? What is the relationship between organizational change and patterns of inequality within and across organizations? Have the imperatives of growth and organizational rationalization ushered in a new era of meritocratic recruitment and advancement (Chiu and Leicht 1999; Kornhauser and Revesz 1995)? Or do we see ongoing disparities between categories of lawyers, especially lawyers differing in race or gender (Hagan and Kay 1995; Kay 1997; Kay and Hagan 1998; Dixon and Seron 1995)?

The Economic Dominance of Large Law Firms

Our data reveal a striking rise in the dominance of large law firms in the practice of business law. Figure 5.1 shows the share of practicing lawyers and of total income commanded by various practice settings, in both 1975 and 1995. The clear winner in the market for legal services was the largest law firms. Note that income share declined in every practice setting except firms with one hundred or more lawyers. The big firms' percentage of total income quadrupled, while the percentage of all practicing lawyers employed by those firms tripled. For solos, house counsel, and the smallest firms, the share of practicing lawyers declined, and firms of thirty-one to ninety-nine lawyers increased their portion of the bar by a bit less than one percentage point. The income share of firms with two to thirty lawyers, however, continued to exceed their percentage of the bar.

Assessment of change in clientele is less straightforward because the measures used in the two surveys differ. In the 1975 interview, respondents were asked to indicate the percentage of their *income* that came from each of several types of clients, including major corporations,[1] medium-sized businesses, and small businesses.[2] In 1995, however, the interview inquired about the proportion of the lawyer's *time* devoted to the various types of clients.[3] Thus, the gauge differs. In spite of this, comparison of findings from the surveys quite clearly indicates that change in clientele occurred. For example, in 1975 a full third of the respondents practicing in firms with one hundred or more lawyers earned three-quarters or more of their income from small businesses, but in 1995 only 1 percent of lawyers in firms of that size devoted as much as 75 percent of their time to such clients. Among solo practitioners, we observe the opposite trend. In 1975, almost half of the solos said that none of their fees came from small businesses, but in 1995 only 29 percent devoted no time to such clients. Fewer than two-fifths of the solo practitioners (38 percent) derived as much as half of their income from small businesses in 1975, but the majority (55 percent) devoted half or more of their time to such clients in 1995 and 43 percent of them devoted three-quarters or more of their time. The percentage of small business clientele (at least as measured by these inconsistent indexes) increased only in firms with fewer than ten lawyers; it decreased in all of the larger-firm-size categories. Large firms did a substantial amount of work for small business in 1975, and

Figure 5.1 Distrubution of Income and of Lawyers, by Six Practice Settings, 1975 and 1995

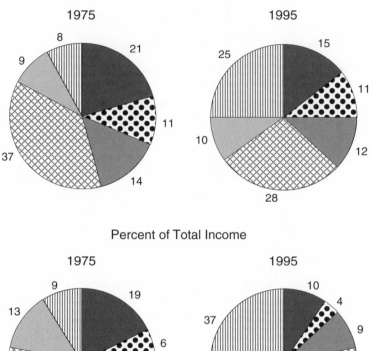

Percent of Practicing Lawyers

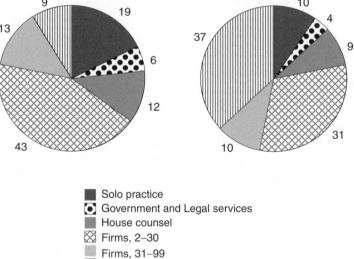

Solo practice
Government and Legal services
House counsel
Firms, 2–30
Firms, 31–99
Firms, 100+

solo practitioners and small firms served a varied mix of types of clients. By 1995, however, the smallest firms were devoting a larger share of their work to small clients, and the largest firms were doing very little work for such clients. Firms at both extremes of size thus came to serve a better-defined slice of the market.

Figure 5.2 shows the distribution across four practice settings of lawyers' effort in selected fields of corporate law. The largest firms increased their share dramatically in all five fields, especially in patent law (or, more broadly, intellectual property) and in business tax work. In 1995, even though firms with one hundred or more lawyers employed only a quarter of the Chicago bar, they did more than half of the securities practice. Firms of two to thirty lawyers gained in share of corporate litigation but lost share in banking, patents, securities, and business tax. Firms of thirty-one to ninety-nine lawyers gained significantly in patent law, probably because patent law firms formerly in the two-to-thirty lawyer category grew into the thirty-one-to-ninety-nine category, but they lost in the other fields. House counsel had a modest gain in banking and a considerable gain in securities work, but it lost share in business tax, corporate litigation, and patents.

Figure 5.3 shows changes in the allocation of effort in selected personal client fields. Solo practitioners and small-firm lawyers continued to dominate lower status, lower paying work. Solos, although only 15 percent of the practicing bar in 1995, did more than three-quarters of all general family practice, more than two-fifths of all divorce work, more than a third of criminal defense, and close to a third of personal injury plaintiffs' work and personal client civil litigation. Firms of two to thirty lawyers were especially dominant in personal injury plaintiffs practice. Larger firms did less than 10 percent of the work in all of these fields except civil litigation for individual clients, but firms of one hundred or more lawyers, which had avoided divorce work in 1975, did a small amount of it in 1995, and they also more than doubled their share of criminal defense work. These increases indicate that divorce cases with substantial property settlements at stake and white-collar criminal defense became more acceptable in corporate law firms. As might be expected, government lawyers, public defenders, and legal services lawyers did a considerable amount of criminal defense and significant amounts of divorce and family law. These data document a simple but important point about the segmentation of the fields of practice: the rise of large law firms and the increase in their share of lawyer income came not from invading the personal client sector of the profession but from increasing their dominance of corporate practice.

Organization-Linked Advantage

A corollary of the growing dominance of large law firms in business law fields is the stronger correlation between income and the types of organizations in which the lawyers worked. In 1975 only 21 percent of the lawyers

Figure 5.2. Effort in Selected Business Law Fields, by Four Practice Settings, 1975 and 1995 (percentages)

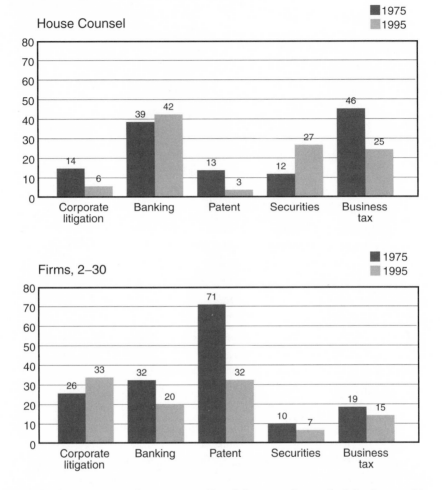

who had incomes in the top quartile of the sample worked in firms with more than thirty lawyers (see chap. 7 for detailed analysis of income). In 1995, however, 37 percent of the top quartile earners worked in firms of one hundred or more.[4] Moreover, multivariate models indicate that organizational type explains a greater share of the income variance at the later time. When we control for age, experience, status of law school attended, law school grades, ethnicity or race, gender, father's occupation, and field of practice, we find significant effects in both 1975 and 1995 for solo practice, government practice, and being a partner. In 1995, we also find significant effects for large-firm practice, mega-firm practice (firms of three hundred or more lawyers), and holding a supervisory rank in nonfirm practice settings.

Figure 5.2 *continued*

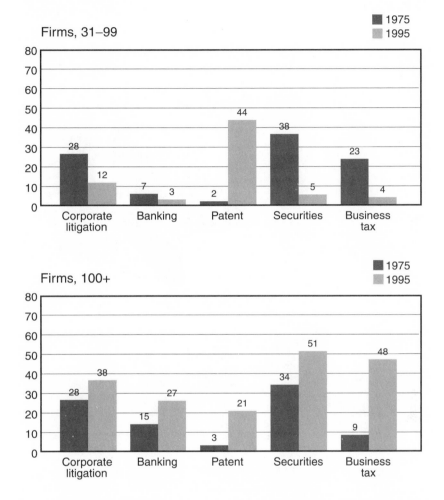

In the 1975 data, models that include the specific fields of law in which the respondents worked explain 5 percent more of the variance in income than do models using practice setting but not field. In 1995, however, the variance explained is unchanged when fields of law are added. So, practice setting does all the work in 1995—field of law adds nothing.

In addition to determining economic rewards, organizations control access to prestigious fields of practice (see chap. 4) and to some of the tools needed for high-quality professional performance. According to information gathered by the *Illinois Legal Times* in 1997, the six Chicago firms that had three hundred or more lawyers within the state employed from 435 to 613 nonlawyers each—the average for these big firms was about 1.5 support

Figure 5.3. Effort in Selected Personal Client Fields, by Five Practice Settings, 1975 and 1995 (percentages)

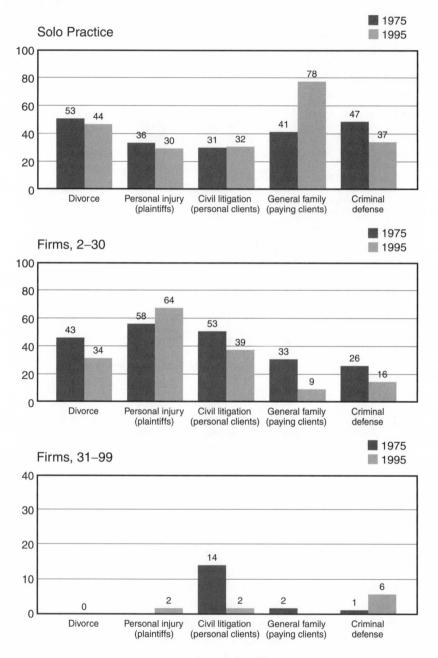

Figure 5.3 *continued*

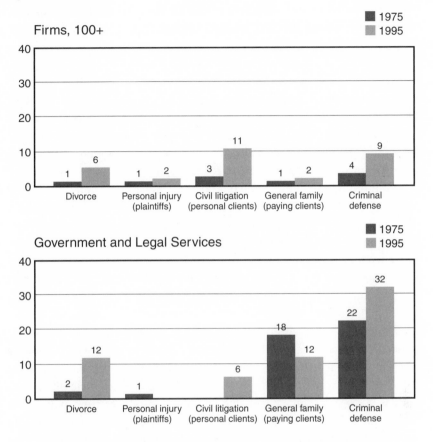

staff persons per lawyer (*Illinois Legal Times* 1997, 20). In 1995, the mean number of nonlawyer personnel regularly used by respondents varied from 1.8 for solo practitioners to 4.9 for lawyers in firms of three hundred or more. One of the advantages of working at a large law firm is that those firms have superior resources. Only about half of the solo practitioners and small-firm lawyers surveyed in 1995 had access to Lexis or Westlaw (computerized legal research tools that are universally available in larger firms).

The organizations that employ lawyers also supply most of the professional colleagues who help produce and perfect the lawyers' work. In 1975, when respondents were asked to identify persons with whom they discussed the law, 78 percent of the colleagues they identified worked in the same type of practice setting as the respondent and a full third worked in the same field. By 1995, inbreeding within practice setting had become even stronger—88 percent of colleagues worked in the same setting—but only 26 percent shared the same legal specialty. Thus, the organizational context appears to have influenced the formation of collegial ties more strongly, while doctrinal expertise was less often the basis of the relationship.

A Typology of Law Firms

With the advantage of hindsight, most of the Chicago law firms that were considered large in 1975 now seem quite modest in size, averaging about forty lawyers. At that size, they were able to encourage one-on-one collegial ties among the principals. The maximum number of one-on-one ties in an organization can be readily calculated.[5] For a firm with forty lawyers, half of whom are partners, there are 190 possible direct ties among the twenty partners—not all of those ties would be close, of course, but a substantial share of them could be established and maintained over time. As the firm grows, the number of ties increases exponentially. To pursue our example, with a fivefold growth in the partners from twenty to one hundred, the number of pairs increases from 190 to 4,950. It is small wonder, then, that new organizational forms emerged to cope with this challenge to traditional collegial relationships.

In the 1995 interviews, respondents in firms with five or more lawyers and those in government and inside-counsel positions were asked about the management of their organizations. The 360 respondents practicing in firms of five or more were drawn from 179 firms. For purposes of classifying the firms into organizational types, we combined responses from individuals within the same firm in order to create firm-level data.[6] Larger firms are more likely to appear in this data set because the odds that any one of their lawyers would be in the random sample are greater than the odds for smaller firms. The resulting set of law firms is therefore properly thought of as a weighted random sample of the firms in which Chicago lawyers worked. Because the initial sampling frame was individual lawyers, not firms, we do not have an ideal set of organizational informants. For example, a young, inexperienced lawyer might provide information that is different from, and perhaps less well-informed than, that provided by a veteran of the same firm. This is an inherent limitation of the research design, but the data are interesting nonetheless. Systematic data on the details of law firm structure and management in a large set of firms are extremely rare.

After considering several strategies for classifying the organizational structures, we settled on four relatively objective measures: whether the firm was organized in departments (e.g., litigation, tax, mergers and acquisitions); whether the firm employed part-time lawyers or permanent associates; whether the firm had a nonpracticing administrator and/or a managing committee (a firm could have neither, one of the two, or both); and whether the firm sought work through competitive bidding (another three-category variable: seldom/never, sometimes, often).

We used these variables in a latent class analysis, a statistical procedure that sorts cases into categories based on similarity in specified characteristics (Clogg 1995; McCutcheon 1987).[7] The model with the best fit identified three classes of firms, which we have labeled "traditional," "hybrid," and "corporate." The characteristics of the three types, as well as data on the size of the firms in each category, are presented in table 5.1. Traditional law firms are seldom organized in departments, use new work statuses less often than do large firms, do not have managing committees or nonpracticing administrators, and seldom bid on work. At the opposite end of the spectrum, corporate firms typically have all of the new management structures and are somewhat more likely (though still unlikely) to engage in competitive bidding. Hybrid firms are intermediate—they often have departments, though less often than do corporate firms; they usually have either a nonpracticing administrator or a managing committee, but not both; and most of them seldom seek work through competitive bidding. Only the "new work statuses" variable does not correspond neatly to this "low," "intermediate," "high" ordering. The new statuses considered here include both permanent associates and part-time lawyers. Again, corporate firms are clearly distinctive (89 percent have these new statuses). But a higher percentage of traditional firms (35 percent) than of hybrid firms (only 3 percent) have such lawyers. The particular statuses, however, may differ across the firm size categories. Firms with only a few lawyers often have a wide variety of work arrangements, of varying degrees of formality. Two small firms may share office space and secretaries, and they are sometimes loosely affiliated. It is common for such firms to seek outside help at times of peak workload or when they get a case that is different from those they usually handle. Arrangements are often ad hoc; on some pieces of work, two lawyers will be "partners," and share fees, and on others they will not. In such circumstances, it is difficult to define "part-time" or nontraditional status. This is very different from big firms that make special arrangements for parents who want to devote a substantial portion of their time to child care (disparaged as "the mommy track") or that have a senior status for semiretired partners (see chap. 12).

Corporate firms are the most numerous: 46 percent of the 179 law firms in the sample are in that category, only 22 percent are hybrid, and 32 percent are of the traditional type. Table 5.1 shows a strong correlation between organization type and organization size. Of traditional firms, 63 percent had

Table 5.1. Characteristics of the Three Classes of Law Firms, 1995 (percentages)

	Traditional (N = 57)	Hybrid (N = 40)	Corporate (N = 82)
Departments, % Yes	26	50	84
New work statuses,[a] % Yes	35	3	89
Management Structure[b]			
Both	0	10	61
One	0	90	39
Neither	100	0	0
Competitive bidding			
Seldom/never	88	90	74
Sometimes	12	0	23
Often	0	10	2
Size of firm			
5–9	63	15	9
10–30	37	55	20
31–99	0	28	30
100–299	0	3	22
300+	0	0	20
Total	100	101	101

Note: All percentages given are the percent of firms, not of individual respondents.
[a] Percent of firms having part-time lawyers, permanent associates, or both of those statuses.
[b] Percent of firms having both a managing committee and nonpracticing administrator, only one of those, or neither.

fewer than ten lawyers and none had more than thirty. Most hybrid firms were also small—70 percent had thirty or fewer lawyers, and only one firm had one hundred or more. The corporate management model predominated among the largest firms. Of firms with at least one hundred lawyers, 97 percent had a corporate structure; none had a traditional structure. Thus, we see substantial variation in organizational form only in firms of ten to ninety-nine lawyers. The partner to associate ratios in the three types of firms also differ: the percentage of partners varies from 61 percent in traditional firms to 48 percent in corporate firms, with hybrid firms between the two (53 percent). Because of the greater size of corporate law firms, many more respondents worked in such firms than in traditional or hybrid firms. Of the 360 who were in firms with 5 or more lawyers, 65 percent worked in firms with corporate management practices.

These numbers are revealing. More than a third of all practicing lawyers (35 percent) worked in firms that conformed to a corporate model. Another 9 percent practiced in hybrid law firms that had some of the corporate characteristics, and 10 percent were in firms of five or more lawyers that conformed to the traditional management model. Richard Abel (1989) once commented that large law firms occupy a position of prominence in the American legal profession that is greatly out of proportion to their numbers. Now, in cities like Chicago, the share of the bar employed in corporate firms reflects a new, tangible form of power within the legal profession. The growing income share that such organizations command and their dominance of prestigious fields of practice have contributed to the success of the diffusion of the corporate model, which has emerged as the exemplar in urban law practice. Moreover, these are not just small law firms that have become big. They have distinctive work structures, distinctive administrative and managerial structures, and a distinctive orientation to the market for legal services.

Democracy and Participation

One of the hallmarks of law firms as an organizational form is that they remain self-governing partnerships, and their collegial character is celebrated in the professions literature (Freidson 1994, 169–83; Gordon and Simon 1992). But scholars and practitioners alike have recognized that the governance of the firms is seldom an ideal form of democracy, a government of equals. Indeed, the firms have been characterized as limited democracies in which the partners who have the closest relationships to important clients possess a disproportionate share of power (Nelson 1988). But the governance of law firms, and the nature and extent of participation in it, has received little systematic study. Emmanuel Lazega (2001) studied a firm in the northeastern United States, and Robert Nelson (1988) studied four firms, all in Chicago. Drawing on published summaries of firm characteristics, Pamela Tolbert and Robert Stern (1991) suggest that firms display relatively high levels of democratic participation. Published descriptions of firms, however, may overstate the level of democratic process. Beyond these sources, we have some valuable but unsystematic descriptions of prominent law firms and of political turmoil within firms (e.g., Caplan 1993). Sources are also scarce concerning the governance structures of law departments in business organizations and in government. Eve Spangler's (1986) study of government and inside-counsel offices suggests that they were bureaucratically governed hierarchies, very different from private partnerships.

The 1995 Chicago survey collected basic data about the management of law firms, government law offices, and the law departments of both profit-making and not-for-profit institutions. Lawyers working in organizations that employed five or more lawyers were asked whether the organization had a managing committee, how that committee was selected, and whether the respondent had experience on the committee or in some other management position. In reporting these findings, we present individual level data, without aggregation to the level of the organization.

As already noted, no traditional law firm had a managing committee, but most hybrid firms and all corporate firms did have such committees. By far the most common method used to select the members of the committees was one-vote-per-partner elections, the most democratic selection process. Nearly half of the lawyers in corporate firms and 36 percent of those in hybrid firms reported such a system. Another fifth to a quarter of the respondents in those categories said that partners' votes were weighted by their share of the partnership. Only a minority of respondents, 5 percent of those in hybrid firms and 12 percent of those in corporate firms, reported that the committee selected its own successors, the least democratic alternative. In government and inside-counsel offices, managing committees were less common: 41 percent of lawyers in government, 60 percent of inside counsel, and 56 percent of public defenders and legal services lawyers said that their organizations had them. Where those contexts had such committees, the selection of members was a managerial prerogative: 80 percent of government lawyers, 61 percent of inside counsel, and 67 percent of public defenders and legal services lawyers reported that management appointed the committee.

Not surprisingly, lawyers who worked in smaller firms were more likely to participate in firm management than were those in larger organizations. Of lawyers in traditional firms, 77 percent said they participated in management decisions. By contrast, only 30 percent of lawyers in hybrid firms and 17 percent in corporate firms reported that they either sat on the managing committee or otherwise participated in firm management.

There are fundamental differences in governance among types of law firms and among other organizations that employ lawyers. In private practice, the managing committee is selected by the partnership; in government and corporations, it is a top-down decision. In smaller, traditional law firms, most lawyers play some managerial role, but such roles were rarely experienced by lawyers in corporate and hybrid firm contexts.

How do these basic differences in the selection of managers and the distribution of managerial experience affect allocative decisions? Figure 5.4 presents some differences across organization types. Most respondents reported that a small group of lawyers made the decisions about compensation. Of lawyers in the three categories of firms, more than half to more than two-thirds agreed with this characterization of the process. Inside counsel were more likely to report hierarchical control, reflecting a fact of corporate life,

Figure 5.4. Features of Governance by Organization Type, 1995 (percentages)

Small Group Divides Profits/Decides Compensation

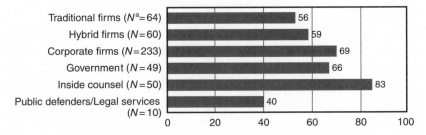

Most Lawyers Decide on Hiring

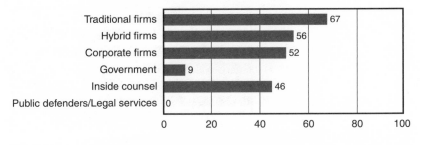

Work Groups Are Autonomous

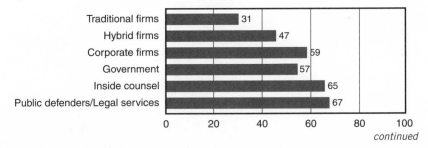

continued

while public defenders and legal services lawyers were the least likely to report that compensation decisions were the province of a few. In the latter practice settings, lawyers were represented by unions. Since there was a union contract, resulting from collective bargaining, compensation decisions were less subject to control by a small group.

We also asked respondents whether "[m]ost lawyers in [the organization] participate to some degree in decisions regarding the hiring of new lawyers." More than two-thirds of lawyers in traditional law firms agreed or strongly agreed with the statement, as did about half of the lawyers in hybrid and corporate firms and in inside-counsel offices. Government lawyers and

Figure 5.4 *continued*

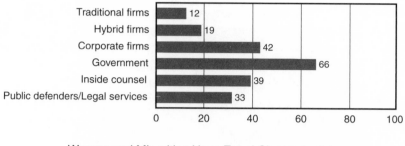

Work Group Affects Access to Power

Traditional firms 12
Hybrid firms 19
Corporate firms 42
Government 66
Inside counsel 39
Public defenders/Legal services 33

0   20   40   60   80   100

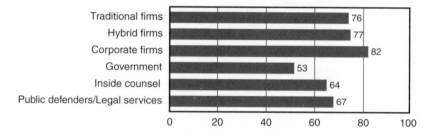

Women and Minorities Have Equal Chance to Advance

Traditional firms 76
Hybrid firms 77
Corporate firms 82
Government 53
Inside counsel 64
Public defenders/Legal services 67

0   20   40   60   80   100

Note: Percentages are those who "agreed" or "strongly agreed" that the characteristic was present in their practice context.
[a] Respondents are those who worked in organizations employing five or more lawyers.

public defenders or legal services lawyers, however, were much less likely to report broad participation in hiring—these practice settings manifest a clear departure from professional self-governance.

As organizations grow larger and more bureaucratic, the locus of collegial relationships may move from the organization as a whole to a subunit. To assess the nature of connections within and among departments and the stature of the respondent's department within the organization, we asked respondents whether they agreed or disagreed with these two statements: "The departments or work groups within my firm operate as relatively autonomous units," and "Access to positions of power within the firm is significantly affected by the department or work group within which one works." Lawyers in traditional firms usually did not report work-group autonomy, probably because those firms lacked formal departments. In other practice contexts, such autonomy appears to have been quite widespread, but there was less agreement with the proposition that departments determined access to positions of power. Lawyers in corporate firms were more than twice as likely as those in other private firms to say that work groups affected access to power, but only among government lawyers did a majority accept that characterization. In government offices, the top positions are often held by political appointees, and the staff jobs are held by career civil servants. In many cases, the civil servants probably do not aspire to the top jobs.

We should note what might be a counterintuitive finding about the opportunities for women and minorities to succeed in their organizations. Lawyers who worked in organizations that were diverse in race or gender were asked to indicate their level of agreement with this statement: "Women and minority lawyers have at least as good a chance as white males of succeeding within this organization, if they are good lawyers." Three-quarters of private firm lawyers agreed with this, which is a significantly higher level of agreement than that of lawyers in employed contexts, where less than two-thirds agreed. Because a larger percentage of the lawyers in government and inside-counsel positions were women and minorities, the lower level of agreement in those settings may reflect greater sensitivity to the operation of bias in the work context rather than an assessment of a difference in actual behavior. But even in those organizations a strong majority of the lawyers said that women and minorities could rise through the ranks. There were strong differences between men and women and between white and African American respondents in their answers to this question. Of men, 81 percent said that white males did not have better opportunities for success than did women and minorities, but only 58 percent of women gave that response.[8] Among white lawyers (male and female), 78 percent perceived that women and minorities enjoyed equality of opportunity (or better), but only 44 percent of black lawyers had the same perception.[9]

Because of perceived conflicts between professional prerogatives and administrative rules, professionals may be less satisfied with contexts that are more bureaucratic. But we found only weak support for this hypothesis. Respondents were asked how satisfied they were with their level of responsibility, their supervisors, their relationships with colleagues, and the policies and administration of their firm or organization. Job satisfaction is considered in more detail in chapter 11, but note that lawyers in all organizational contexts expressed general satisfaction with their degree of responsibility and their colleague relationships. Satisfaction with supervisors was less universal, and supervisors were least popular among lawyers in government and inside-counsel jobs, where the power of nonlawyers may create tensions. The question that elicited the most dissatisfaction, however, was the one dealing with organizational policies and administration. Only a third of government lawyers and fewer than half of lawyers in hybrid and corporate firms were satisfied in that respect. Only in traditional law firms—where a high percentage of the respondents were involved in firm management—did a majority express satisfaction. Thus, this item may reflect the dissatisfaction with bureaucracy that theory would predict.

The interview also sought to explore the more subtle exercise of power in these varying practice contexts by asking whether the organization's management would refuse to consider some issue of concern to the respondent.[10] Overall, only 17 percent of lawyers indicated this to be a problem. The percentage was somewhat higher for inside counsel and for legal services lawyers and public defenders, but the differences across organizational contexts are not statistically significant. Surveys are blunt instruments, no doubt, for learning about the power of organizational leaders to silence the discussion of potentially divisive issues. Nonetheless, our invitation to complain did not reveal deeper currents of discontent.

Professional Autonomy

The degree to which client demands or interests restrict lawyers' exercise of professional judgment may vary systematically with the practice context. As already observed, particular fields of law tend to be concentrated in a limited range of practice settings (see chap. 3, table 3.2)—most of the work for big corporations is done in large law firms and in the offices of inside counsel, most of the legal problems of individuals and small businesses are handled by smaller firms and solo practitioners, and much of the environmental, civil rights, and of course criminal work is done in government offices. Differences in the nature of the work in the various fields shape the relationships between lawyers and clients, including the extent of the lawyers' dependence upon one client or a small set of clients. The number of clients that respondents to the 1995 survey had represented in the past year varies widely by practice setting. In private practice, the number decreases as the size of firm increases.[11]

The percentage of practice time devoted to work for large corporations ranged from an average of 11 percent among solo practitioners, and 21 percent for those in firms with fewer than ten lawyers, to 61 percent for lawyers in firms of one hundred or more. Intermediate-sized firms had intermediate percentages, in the forties. The differences on these variables, then, were linear functions of firm size, but the likelihood that the lawyers had represented their clients for three years or more was not. Firms with ten to thirty lawyers were the most likely to have a stable clientele—on average, they had represented 60 percent of their clients for at least three years. Many of those firms specialized in fields such as personal injury defense, labor relations, or patents, in which they did recurring work for their clients.[12] The 1995 survey also inquired about the percentage of time devoted to the client for whom the respondent had done the most work during the past year. Among solo practitioners and those in firms with fewer than ten lawyers, the most time-consuming client typically received less than a quarter of the lawyers' effort (an average of 22 percent and 24 percent, respectively), but lawyers in larger firms had allocated from 36 percent to 39 percent to one client, on average.[13] These findings are consistent with Nelson's data on four large Chicago firms. He found in 1979–80 that lawyers in those firms devoted an average of 35 percent of their time to their principal client (1988, 251).

In sum, solo practitioners and those in the smallest firms had large numbers of clients, did relatively little work for major corporations, represented fewer than half of their clients for three years, and spent a smaller share of their time on the client for whom they did the most work. Lawyers in larger firms had fewer clients and billed significantly more of their time to their leading client. These findings suggest, of course, that the degree of dependence upon any particular client is likely to be greater in the large firms. But income and prestige are higher in large firm practice than in other practice settings (see chaps. 4 and 7). The superior social position of business lawyers may permit them to exercise considerable professional autonomy even though their clients typically have bargaining power. Indeed, it is quite plausible that the financial and political assets of businesses enhance the power of their lawyers. The bureaucratic tendencies of large organizations, however, are likely to constrain the freedom of action of lawyers in big firms. Large organizations typically create chains of command, rules for the conduct of work, and routine procedures. So it is not clear whether we should expect lawyers in large firms and the inside counsel of corporations to enjoy greater professional autonomy than those who practice elsewhere. The issue is the extent to which lawyers are free to decide what kinds of work they will do and how they will go about that work, characteristics that have been said to be defining traits of the professions (R. Greenwood 1957; R. Hall 1975).

To assess autonomy, the Chicago surveys asked respondents to characterize the nature of their work in relation to pairs of opposite statements. The first set of statements dealt with the extent to which the lawyers had "latitude in selecting clients," and the second concerned the degree to which the lawyers could "do largely whatever they like without having someone . . . directing their work."[14] These two measures were used in both surveys. Figure 5.5 shows the percentage of respondents, in both years, who chose the two positions closest to the end of the scale indicating greater autonomy.

Figure 5.5. Measures of Autonomy by Practice Setting, 1975 and 1995 (percentages)

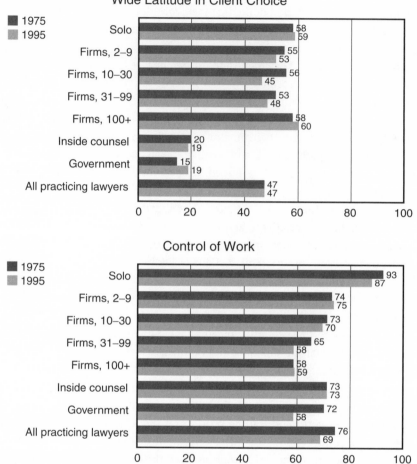

The percentage of all practicing lawyers indicating wide latitude in selecting clients was unchanged from 1975 to 1995 (47 percent). In both years,
solo practitioners and lawyers in the largest firms were the most likely to
report freedom to choose. Inside counsel and government lawyers were at
the other extreme—they are, of course, employees rather than independent
practitioners, but they refer to the various offices within their organizations as their "clients" (see note 10), and their responses appear to indicate that they perceived little control over the assignments. In 1975, there
was little difference on this variable among the private-practice categories.
By 1995, intermediate-sized firms differed from the largest firms and from
solo practitioners, but the principal difference was still that between private

Figure 5.5 *continued*

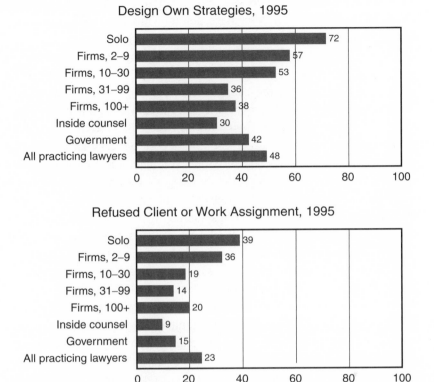

Design Own Strategies, 1995

Refused Client or Work Assignment, 1995

practice and employed positions. Firms of ten to thirty lawyers reported the largest change over the twenty years—the percentage claiming wide latitude dropped from 56 percent (one of the highest in 1975) to 45 percent. In 1975, many firms of that size had a general commercial practice. By 1995, however, Chicago firms with fewer than thirty lawyers received commercial work less often. As suggested above, some of these were specialty "boutiques" with a stable clientele, and perhaps also a more limited range of client choice. The number of potential clients generating a substantial volume of patent work, for example, is probably relatively limited.

Although one might have thought that organizational imperatives and the power of corporate clients impose constraints in large firms, most lawyers in the largest firms indicate a high degree of client choice. If we separate partners from associates in large firms (one hundred or more lawyers), we find that 75 percent of partners in 1975 and 72 percent in 1995 reported autonomy in client choice, while only 41 percent and 45 percent of associates claimed such autonomy. Thus, the difference between partners and associates remained clear, but associates who reported the ability to select their clients increased by a few percentage points, while the percentage among partners declined slightly. The changes, however, are not large.

On the second measure (control of work), although we see some decline in reported autonomy overall, differences among the practice settings are again more striking than the changes from 1975 to 1995. Among private practitioners, lawyers in the larger-firm categories were less likely to report a high degree of control over their work—in 1995, 87 percent of solo practitioners claimed to have great freedom of action, but only 58 percent and 59 percent of those in firms of thirty-one to ninety-nine and one hundred or more, respectively, did so. The only category with a very large decline is government lawyers. This may reflect the increase in size of government law offices (see chap. 1) and a corresponding increase in bureaucratic procedures. In both years, inside counsel were about as likely to report a high degree of control over their work as were lawyers in small firms.

Another set of polar opposites, dealing with the extent to which lawyers design and execute their own strategies in their work, was used in the 1995 survey.[15] As one might expect, the pattern of response is generally similar to that for control of work, but with the notable exception that inside counsel were least likely to report this type of autonomy. Generally, on this measure, lawyers serving a business clientele (those in larger firms and inside counsel), were less likely to report freedom of action—they were far less likely to do so than were solo practitioners or lawyers in the smallest firms.

The 1995 interview also asked whether the respondent "ever had occasion to refuse a potential client, or a work assignment, not because of a formal conflict of interest but because of . . . personal values." The question had been used previously in Nelson's study of four large Chicago law firms (1988) and in a survey of Washington lawyers and lobbyists (Heinz et al. 1993), but there are at least two problems with this measure. First, although respondents were asked to distinguish these reported refusals from occasions when they declined work because they "thought the case was weak or . . . the work would be unprofitable," it is no doubt difficult to separate the influence of the various motivations. Second, lawyers in some types of practice are probably more likely to encounter questionable work or questionable clients, but the question as posed does not distinguish between practitioners who were never asked to do problematic work and those who acceded to such requests. Whether one encounters questionable work, however, is at least in part a matter of perception. Tax returns or bankruptcy work can certainly present ethical problems just as surely as can criminal defense (Regan

2004). Nonetheless, the data show strong differences across the practice settings. Nearly two-fifths of solo practitioners and of lawyers in the smallest firms reported that they had refused a client or work assignment at least once, but only 9 percent of inside counsel and a fifth or less of those in other practice settings had done so. The finding for large firms is similar to Nelson's. In 1980, he found that 16 percent of his sample had refused work (the rate was 11 percent for associates and 28 percent for partners; 1988, 254–56). The Washington study, however, found a much higher rate of refusal among lawyers who represented clients vis-à-vis the federal government—of those working in law firms, 60 percent said that they had refused work. The higher rate may be attributable to the fact that Washington representation much more often presents issues on which political alignment is salient (Heinz et al. 1993, 188).

Solos and small-firm lawyers who refuse clients are less likely to suffer business consequences than are lawyers in big firms. Although Rumpole of the Bailey built a career on the representation of the burglars in the Timson family (Mortimer 1993, 9–13), the clients of solo practitioners and of lawyers in small firms are, on the whole, not likely to be steady customers. Marc Galanter called these clients "one-shot players" (1974). The businesses represented by big law firms, however, are "repeat players"—they generate recurring legal problems. By declining the business of such a client, the firm forgoes not one fee but future fees as well. This is, no doubt, an important part of the reason why lawyers in large firms were less likely to refuse clients than were solo practitioners and those in the smallest firms. The explanation for the low refusal rates of lawyers in government and in inside-counsel offices, however, is somewhat different. For the most part, they know what kind of clients they will have when they take the job. If they go to work in the Pentagon, they will not be surprised to find themselves representing the military. If they discover later that they do not like the clients, their principal alternative is to move to another job. As Nelson observed, "the notion that lawyers struggle with clients over fundamental questions about the common good is simply wrong" (1988, 258–59). They either do the work or walk away.

Examining the responses of lawyers who devoted a quarter or more of their time to each field of law, we find that in most fields the percentage who had refused work was relatively near the overall rate for all practicing lawyers, 23 percent. Three fields, however, stand out as having high refusal rates: personal injury plaintiffs work (44 percent), criminal defense (46 percent), and divorce (48 percent). These three fields serve individual clients and deal primarily with one-shot players (apart from some career criminals and matrimonial recidivists). By contrast, the other side of personal injury work (representing insurance companies) had one of the lowest refusal rates: 13 percent. The rate in employment law on the management side was 10 percent, and environmental defense had the lowest rate—9 percent. These fields serve businesses.

We also did multivariate analyses of the refusal rates. In a logistic regression model using only social background characteristics, we found that women were significantly less likely to have refused an assignment, and that older lawyers, Catholics, and Jews were significantly more likely to have refused.[16] But the total amount of variance explained by this model was small (pseudo R^2 = .06), and the effects of social background disappeared when professional characteristics were added to the model. That is, the social effects could be attributed to systematic differences in the distribution of women, older lawyers, Catholics, and Jews across the practice settings and the income categories. In the full model, we found that, net of the effects of other variables, lawyers with higher incomes were more likely to have refused work. This may reflect the superior social power or professional standing of those lawyers. Although the full multivariate model explained only 14 percent of the total variance in refusal rates, this is more than twice the variance explained by social background alone, and the multivariate model confirmed that solo practitioners were significantly more likely to have refused work, net of the effects of other variables, and that lawyers practicing in business law fields were less likely to have refused.

Determinants of Compensation

A series of questions sought to capture lawyers' perceptions of the factors influencing compensation decisions in the various practice settings (see chap. 7 for the analysis of the distribution of lawyers' income). Each of the factors was rated on a four-point scale: very important, important, little importance, not important at all. Figure 5.6 shows the percentages of respondents in each practice setting rating the item unimportant (either of the latter two ratings). Some of the factors are applicable only in private practice, and others apply only in employed contexts: lawyers in firms were asked to rate the importance of "bringing in new business" and "client ties," while respondents employed by government or as internal counsel were asked to rate "ties to important people in the organization's management."[17]

Lawyers in all three types of private firms were likely to assign great importance to "bringing in new business," but there was more unanimity in those ratings in corporate law firms. Only one of the 210 respondents from

Figure 5.6. Perceived Determinants of Compensation, by Organization Type, 1995

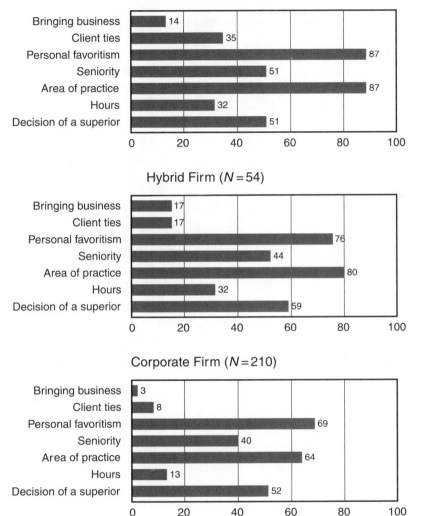

Traditional Firm (N = 56)

Factor	Value
Bringing business	14
Client ties	35
Personal favoritism	87
Seniority	51
Area of practice	87
Hours	32
Decision of a superior	51

Hybrid Firm (N = 54)

Factor	Value
Bringing business	17
Client ties	17
Personal favoritism	76
Seniority	44
Area of practice	80
Hours	32
Decision of a superior	59

Corporate Firm (N = 210)

Factor	Value
Bringing business	3
Client ties	8
Personal favoritism	69
Seniority	40
Area of practice	64
Hours	13
Decision of a superior	52

continued

such firms rated bringing in business as "not important at all." In contrast, 10 percent of those in traditional firms and 9 percent of those in hybrid firms assigned the factor no importance. While 64 percent of lawyers in corporate firms gave this factor the highest rating, "very important," a minority of those in traditional and hybrid firms (45 percent and 46 percent, respectively) did so.

Private practitioners were also likely to perceive client ties as having

Figure 5.6 *continued*

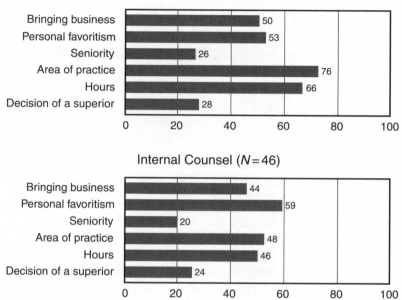

Government (*N* = 42)

Bringing business	50
Personal favoritism	53
Seniority	26
Area of practice	76
Hours	66
Decision of a superior	28

Internal Counsel (*N* = 46)

Bringing business	44
Personal favoritism	59
Seniority	20
Area of practice	48
Hours	46
Decision of a superior	24

Note: Percentages are those rating the factor unimportant.

important influence on compensation. A quarter of those in both traditional and hybrid firms rated that factor "very important," and 36 percent of those in corporate firms assigned it the highest rating. Only 3 percent of the lawyers in corporate firms thought it had no importance, versus 19 percent in traditional and 8 percent in hybrid firms. Thus, both bringing in new business and client ties were nearly uniformly seen as important determinants of compensation in corporate firms, and these factors were also likely to be assigned importance (but less uniformly so) in traditional and hybrid firms.

By contrast, relatively few lawyers in private firms thought that personal favoritism or area of practice influenced individual compensation. There were, however, interesting differences among the firm types. Lawyers in traditional and hybrid firms were less likely than lawyers in corporate firms to see those factors as important: 31 percent in corporate firms, 24 percent in hybrids, and only 13 percent in traditional firms indicated that personal favoritism influenced compensation decisions; and 37 percent of lawyers in corporate firms, 20 percent in hybrids, and 13 percent in traditional firms assigned importance to the lawyers' practice area. Again, then, corporate firms were at one end of the distribution and the traditional firms were at the other.

Seniority and "the decision of a senior partner" elicited a more varied set of responses within each type of firm. On those two variables, the ratings of private practitioners were more evenly divided, and there were not great differences among the three categories of firms. (But lawyers in corporate firms were somewhat more likely to assign importance to seniority than were lawyers in traditional firms, with responses from those in hybrid firms again falling between the two.) There were, however, clear differences between the private practitioners and the two employed settings—both government lawyers and internal counsel were much more likely to perceive seniority and the decision of a single supervisor as important determinants of pay. Indeed, those were the variables most consistently assigned importance by lawyers in those settings. Government lawyers usually saw area of practice and hours worked as unimportant—the latter, perhaps, because there was relatively little variance in the length of the workday of government lawyers.

In summary, the important determinants of compensation were perceived by private practitioners to be bringing in business, client ties, and (especially in corporate firms) hours billed. For employed lawyers, the factors most often identified as important were seniority and the decision of a supervisor. Thus, not surprisingly, the factors emphasized in private practice reflect entrepreneurial values—the most important variables are those that tend to maximize the firm's profits. In the employed contexts, the factors reflect the formal rationality of bureaucracy—an easily measured, "objective" standard (years of service) and a hierarchical decision structure.

Changing Management Policies

In his study of four large Chicago firms, Robert Nelson examined two "traditionally organized" firms (they exhibited weak departmentalization and had relatively informal managerial policies and practices) and two "bureaucratically organized" firms (strong departmentalization and a developed managerial structure) (Nelson 1988). Lawyers at all four firms were asked about contested management issues: should associates specialize intensely and early in their careers? should the firm be organized in departments? should the firm court the clients of other law firms? and should the firm grow to meet client demand, no matter how large the firm became? From these questions, Nelson developed a "rationalization scale" measuring how much the respondents would support those developments in their own firms. On this measure there were clear differences across the four firms: lawyers in the two traditionally organized firms had lower scores on the scale than did those in the bureaucratically organized firms. Associates scored lower than did partners in both types of firms—perhaps because associates perceived themselves to be targets of rationalization, but partners expected to profit from the efficiencies.

In the 1995 survey, we used Nelson's questions to determine whether attitudes had changed in the four firms he studied and to assess professional values in other practice settings. In our typology of firms—traditional, hybrid, and corporate—all four of Nelson's firms, even the two he characterized as "traditional," are corporate firms. The two firms had grown significantly by 1995 and had developed the structural features that differentiate corporate firms from traditional and hybrid firms. Our sample includes from five to thirteen respondents from each of Nelson's firms. Although these are small numbers, the responses generally suggest that the level of support for rationalization had increased since the early 1980s. Scores on the scale rose in three of the four firms. They declined only in the firm that had the highest score in Nelson's 1979 to 1981 data, which nonetheless remained highest in 1995. At the time of Nelson's study, that firm had already pursued a strategy of departmentalization and of early specialization by associates, even though those practices were then relatively unusual. The lawyers in Nelson's other three firms also had relatively high scores on the rationalization scale in 1995—all had mean scores higher than those in traditional and hybrid law firms.[18]

We expected to find greater support for rationalization in corporate firms than in hybrid firms, and the least in traditional firms, but this was not an obvious proposition. Carroll Seron (1996), Jerry Van Hoy (1997), and others have shown that some small-firm attorneys are very entrepreneurial in the organization of their practices—this might suggest little difference in attitudes about rationalization across the categories. But we found that lawyers in corporate firms scored considerably higher (3.49) than those in traditional (3.12) or hybrid firms (3.10).[19] Lawyers' professed preferences tended to correspond to the actual structure of their firms. Whether this is due to selective recruitment, socialization into firms, or selective attrition from the firms, it appears that lawyers endorse the managerial strategies of their organizations. The difference between corporate firms and the others is considerable. There was no professionwide consensus on how law firms should be organized.

We also found, in all three types of firms, that partners were more committed to rationalization than were the associates who worked for them.[20] Consistent with Nelson's finding, associates were "more traditional" than their superiors. Perhaps the associates' future prospects are improved if there is less pressure to specialize early. Or perhaps they simply had not yet learned what it takes to make a law firm profitable. Or they may have been more idealistic—those who went to law school to avoid the business world might be predisposed against a corporate model for running their law firms (see Schleef 2000; Granfield 1992). Indeed, many voices within the legal academy would encourage traditionalism (e.g., Glendon 1994; Kronman 1993; Schiltz 1999). Whatever the reason, there appears to be a tension between the attitudes of associates and partners toward issues of specialization, assignment, departmentalization, and promotion.

We are also able to make limited comparisons with attitudes toward rationalization in the employed practice contexts. Most government lawyers work in bureaucratic contexts, of course, with clear specialization and departmentalization, but perhaps government lawyers might, like associates in law firms, resist those structures. Corporate inside counsel, however, might be expected to embrace rationalization as part of a general ethos that supports businesslike organizational practices. Three items in the rationalization scale addressed these speculations; two dealt with specialization and one dealt with departmentalization.[21] The findings suggest that both inside counsel and government lawyers embraced rationalization. Their scores exceed those of lawyers in traditional and hybrid firms, and fall just below those in corporate firms.[22] Once again, then, we see a congruence between practice and ideology.

Given the increasing number of women and minorities in the legal profession, there has been growing interest in hiring and promotion practices (see, e.g., Wilkins and Gulati 1996; Epstein 1993; Schaafsma 1998; Reeves 2001). We have already noted the significant differences across organizational contexts in the presence of women and minorities (see chaps. 3 and 6). We asked the respondents, therefore, whether their organizations had formal affirmative action plans, and whether lawyers within their organizations had ever taken maternity or paternity leave. Figure 5.7 presents the differences across organization types on all three measures. Some of the variance may be attributable to the size of the practice settings—because traditional firms are smaller, each firm had fewer possible candidates for leaves. Lawyers in traditional firms were, we find, much less likely to report that lawyers had taken a maternity leave than were lawyers in other practice contexts. But even though those firms had a high percentage of men, few reported paternity leaves. Leaves for fathers were relatively rare in all types of organizations except in the public defender/legal services category, which is quite small. Although 96 percent of the government lawyers reported that a maternity leave had occurred in their organizations, only 31 percent of them reported paternity leaves; and only 6 percent of internal counsel reported

Figure 5.7. Parental Leave and Affirmative Action, by Organization Type, 1995

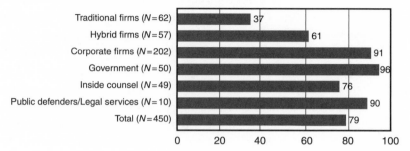

Lawyer in Organization Took Maternity Leave***

Traditional firms (N=62) 37
Hybrid firms (N=57) 61
Corporate firms (N=202) 91
Government (N=50) 96
Inside counsel (N=49) 76
Public defenders/Legal services (N=10) 90
Total (N=450) 79

0   20   40   60   80   100

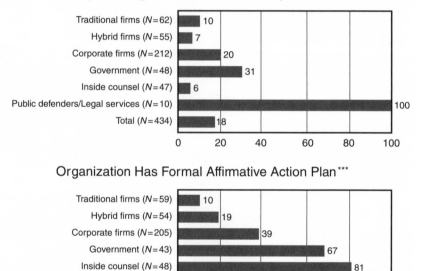

Lawyer in Organization Took Paternity Leave***

Traditional firms (N=62) 10
Hybrid firms (N=55) 7
Corporate firms (N=212) 20
Government (N=48) 31
Inside counsel (N=47) 6
Public defenders/Legal services (N=10) 100
Total (N=434) 18

0   20   40   60   80   100

Organization Has Formal Affirmative Action Plan***

Traditional firms (N=59) 10
Hybrid firms (N=54) 19
Corporate firms (N=205) 39
Government (N=43) 67
Inside counsel (N=48) 81
Public defenders/Legal services (N=9) 67
Total (N=418) 40

0   20   40   60   80   100

Note: Percentages are those respondents answering the question affirmatively.
***$p \leq .001$

paternity leaves, even though 76 percent reported instances of maternity leave in their organizations. Affirmative action policies also varied greatly by organizational context. Smaller, less bureaucratic law firms—traditional firms and hybrid firms—seldom had formal affirmative action plans. Indeed, even in corporate firms, fewer than half the lawyers reported formal policies. Government and corporate law departments, however, typically did have such plans. Thus, the contexts where the largest percentages of women and minorities were employed were, not surprisingly, the most likely to have affirmative action plans. Whether the presence of women and minorities precedes or follows the establishment of the plans, however, is less clear. Traditionally disadvantaged groups may gravitate to these organizational contexts due to the procedural protections offered, the hiring practices may actually recruit more women and minorities to the organizations, or the lobbying power of minorities within these contexts may lead to the adoption of the plans. In any event, several comments made by respondents concerning their experiences with discrimination on the basis of race or sex suggest that they had experienced discrimination in private law firms and then turned to government or corporate jobs to avoid it.

Another significant change in the employment practices of law firms since the 1970s has been the increase in the recruitment of partners from other law firms and from senior government positions (Galanter and Palay 1991; Nelson 1988). New partners have also been acquired through mergers with other firms. These changes are a source of tension in law firm hierarchies, as associates working their way up the ladder to partnership see slots handed to outsiders. Even if the "lateral hires" do not reduce opportunities for associates to make partner (a proposition that is probably not demonstrable at the time of the hiring), they make clear, at the least, that service to the partnership is not the only path to the top. In order to assess the extent of lateral hiring across practice contexts, therefore, we asked respondents what percentage of their partners (in law firms) or supervisors (in employed contexts) were hired from outside the organization. We expected to find more lateral hiring in corporate firms precisely because those firms manifest less support for traditional values. Once again, however, we were surprised by the data. Significantly more lateral hiring was reported in traditional law firms than in hybrid or corporate firms. Of attorneys working in traditional firms, 54 percent reported that more than half of their partners had been hired from outside, compared to only 17 percent in hybrid law firms and only 7 percent in corporate law firms.

In small firms, the addition of partners from outside is common. Small partnerships are assembled and reassembled more often and more dramatically than are larger ones. When large law firms began to depart from their rigid internal promotion policies, the change received great attention in the legal press, and the break from tradition created the impression that lateral hiring was common in large firms. Our findings, however, indicate that it occurred much less often than in smaller partnerships.

Like the larger firms, employed practice contexts did relatively little hiring of supervisors from outside. Some 73 percent of government lawyers, 82 percent of inside counsel, and 67 percent of public defenders and legal services lawyers reported that only a tenth or fewer of their supervisors had been hired laterally. No lawyer in these settings reported that more than half of the supervisors were lateral hires.

There were, then, significant differences across practice contexts in governance structures, managerial policies, and collegial ideology. In these distinct contexts, lawyers confront very different hierarchies and have different possibilities for participation in organizational governance. The contextual differences, in turn, appear to be associated with systematic variance in the race and gender of the lawyers employed in those settings.

Organizing Principles

Large law firms and the offices of counsel within public or private organizations typically organize their work in one or more of three ways—around the needs of a particular client or set of clients (e.g., the IBM division of the Cravath firm, the capital markets group at Shearman and Sterling, and the "installations and logistics" section in the office of the U.S. Air Force general counsel), around substantive legal specialties or particular skills (e.g., tax, estates and trusts, litigation), or around prominent senior partners (e.g., the Solovy group at Jenner and Block). Each of these modes of organization embodies a different logic and reflects different motivations. The first is what Stephan Haeckel calls a "client-centric approach" (1999, 121). The second is doctrinal; it uses the categories and logic of the law itself. The third is personal or political; it reflects the distribution of power within the law firm.

In the 1995 interviews, respondents were asked to indicate which organizing principles were used to define the subdivisions in their offices. As noted in table 5.1, most corporate law firms had departments, three-quarters of traditional firms did not, and hybrid firms were divided equally between those with departments and those without. In government offices, 94 percent of the respondents said their practice was subdivided in some way, as did 83 percent of those in private organizations. In all settings, the subdivisions were most commonly defined by doctrinal categories—that is, by substantive areas of the law or skill types. (Note that respondents could choose more than one organizational mode.) Of respondents reporting subdivisions, 95 percent of those in corporate firms reported departments or practice groups based on areas of the law. They were also reported by 93 percent of lawyers in hybrid firms, 83 percent in traditional firms, 77 percent in government, and 65 percent in inside-counsel offices. It is important to note that doctrinal subdivisions, in a sense the most traditional or "professional" form of organization, were more common in private law firms than in inside-counsel or government offices. Subdivisions organized around partners or clients were not rare in law firms, but they were far less common than subdivisions organized around practice specialties. Only about a fifth of lawyers in private firms reported partner-based groups, and less than one in ten had client-based groups. Not surprisingly, the subdivisions of government and corporate organizations were even less likely to be identified with particular lawyers. In corporate entities, it would seem curious for a work unit to be formally defined by an individual, however prominent. Subdivisions organized around particular clients were much more commonly used in the offices of inside counsel, which was, in fact, the practice setting most likely to report that form of organization. A third of the inside counsel reported that divisions of their company or organization defined the practice groups. Yet, even in those offices and in government, the predominant organizing principle was substantive areas of law.

Because substantive fields of law are not distributed randomly across the practice settings, separating the effects of field and of practice context on lawyers' work is not straightforward. There are, however, significant differences across organization types in levels of field specialization. The most specialized lawyers worked for government. Lawyers in all kinds of organizations were significantly more specialized than solo practitioners. The index of specialization, introduced in chapter 2 (see fig. 2.1), increases as one moves from traditional to hybrid to corporate firms.[23] To some extent, this is attributable to higher levels of specialization among associates, who are more numerous in corporate and hybrid firms. Even if we look only at the work of partners, however, we find greater specialization by those in corporate firms than in traditional and hybrid law firms. Inside counsel had specialization levels similar to those in hybrid law firms.

These findings suggest that substantive specialization is associated with increasing organizational scale. Two distinct processes are probably at work. For government lawyers, specialization is largely dictated by the jurisdiction of their branch of government and, as government has become larger, its agencies have become more differentiated. In private law firms, the larger, more rationalized firms have become, in effect, affiliations of highly specialized substantive experts. Corporate firms are able to assign client work to specialized departments, or to groups designed for a particular transaction, drawing on various specialties. Specialization may not be a cause of law firm growth, but it appears to be a strong correlate of firm size.

Hours Worked

The conventional wisdom is that law firms demand many more work hours than government and internal counsel offices. Indeed, one of the leading speculations about why women are more likely to practice in government and as inside counsel is the hypothesis that they prefer shorter, more predictable workdays. Large firms are commonly thought to make greater time demands. The data, however, show only small differences across organizational types in total hours worked, and again there are surprises. The median number of total hours per week is highest among solo practitioners, where it is 53. Traditional, hybrid, and corporate law firms all have 50-hour medians, and total hours are only modestly lower among government lawyers (49 hours), inside counsel (47.5), and the sixteen public defenders and legal services lawyers (45). We are somewhat skeptical about the validity of these data, however. If respondents were inclined to overstate their hours, 45 to 50 per week might be a plausible-sounding range to choose.

These hours include the respondents' time devoted to remunerative employment in which they did something other than legal work—some solo practitioners, for example, supplement their income by selling insurance or real estate. If we look only at hours devoted to legal work, we find that the median for solos is 50, the same as the medians in the three types of firms, all of which remain at 50.[24] Thus, lawyers who work in firms appear to do little remunerative work apart from the practice of law. Although our attitudinal data on compensation suggest that corporate law firms put great emphasis on hours billed, we find little effect of that emphasis in reported hours. Given the very large differences in compensation, therefore, government lawyers appear to work almost as much as corporate practitioners at a small fraction (from one-half to one-seventh) of the pay (see chap. 7).

The data, if they are to be believed, provide only weak support for the hypothesis that particular subgroups of associates, especially women, are more likely to leave large firms. Working 50 hours per week is no doubt incompatible with any substantial amount of child care responsibility, over the longer term, but other practice settings do not provide less demanding options. The greater workload falls on the junior lawyers. Associates report more hours than partners in both corporate and hybrid firms. The difference is of the same order of magnitude in both: in corporate firms, 54.1 versus 49.9 hours, on average, compared to 51.7 versus 47.4 in hybrid firms. But in traditional firms, partners reported a mean of 50.8 hours, while the mean for associates was only 47.7. This suggests that the role of an associate in a traditional firm is somewhat different than in a corporate or hybrid firm. In the smaller, less formal context of traditional firms, associates are more like employees. They may not aspire to partnership; they may be more likely to come and go.[25] In the up-or-out hierarchies of law firms, however, associates put in the hours in order to have a chance at higher earnings and lower work demands later in their careers. The effects of rank are also visible in government and inside-counsel offices. We find that supervisors in government legal offices report 45.6 hours per week, on average, but lawyers in staff positions report 48.4. In the offices of inside counsel, supervisors report 43.9 and staff report 44.1 hours, a much smaller difference. (In these two practice settings, the mean hours worked are lower than the medians because respondents working relatively few hours pull down the averages.) Thus, rank appears to play varying roles in the work cultures of the different practice settings. Although government offices are not up-or-out hierarchies, and compensation there is pegged to seniority and pay grade, seniors appear to work fewer hours than juniors, as in the more bureaucratic of the private firms.

With respect to pro bono work, solo practitioners report the largest amount, a median of 3.5 hours per month. Respondents in firms with three hundred or more lawyers report a median of only 0.5 hour per month, and the other firm-size categories report medians from 1 to 3 hours. For inside counsel and government lawyers, the median number of hours per month devoted to pro bono work is 0.[26]

Task Structure

Lawyers devote varying amounts of effort to tasks such as drafting wills or contracts, writing legal briefs, doing legal research, meeting with clients, and appearing in court, and there is a status ordering of these tasks within each organization. Partners' tasks typically differ from those of associates. Associates do research, organize records, write memos, and draft documents, all at the behest of partners who incorporate the product into their work. It is largely assumed but relatively undocumented that tasks also differ across practice settings. For example, internal counsel were traditionally thought to do more routine work than did the corporations' outside law firms (Slovak 1979).

In the 1995 survey, respondents were given a long list of tasks and asked how often they did them. (The interview used a five-point scale, from "never" to "very frequently.") The findings indicate that the frequency of some tasks differed little across organizational contexts or rank within organization. Almost all lawyers talked to clients often and regularly engaged in negotiations with lawyers outside their employing organization. But some tasks had distinct organizational profiles. Supervising and reviewing the work of other lawyers was a defining characteristic of the role of partners in large law firms, but not of other lawyers. In corporate firms, 87 percent of partners reported that during the preceding year they had supervised and reviewed the work of other lawyers frequently or very frequently. Fewer partners in the other firm categories (60 percent of those in traditional firms and 58 percent of those in hybrid firms) supervised other lawyers that often, probably because those firms are smaller and have fewer associates. Surprisingly, however, in internal counsel offices, even the supervisors were not especially likely to supervise: less than half reported having done so frequently.[27] Organizational management, as one might expect, was also much more likely to be done by partners than by associates, but there were, again, noteworthy differences among partners in the three law firm categories—62 percent of partners in traditional firms, but only 39 percent of those in hybrid firms and 51 percent of those in corporate firms reported that they frequently made decisions regarding the management of their organizations (the question gave examples: "such as recruitment, assignments, etc."). More than half of the associates in all three kinds of firms reported that they "seldom" or "never" made such decisions.

Interestingly, of partners in the three types of firms, those in corporate firms were the most likely to report "routine paperwork on billing information, client intake forms, employee evaluations, travel reports, and the like,"[28] and were the least likely to do legal research. Of solo practitioners and partners in traditional and hybrid firms, somewhat more than half reported doing routine paperwork frequently—about 10 points less than corporate firm partners.

Only 17 percent of partners in corporate firms did legal research frequently, and more than a third said that they did research seldom or never. In traditional and hybrid firms, partners were much more likely to do some of their own research—half of those in traditional firms and 46 percent of those in hybrid firms did so frequently. In all three kinds of firms, associates did research often.[29]

Solos and internal counsel were the most likely to report that they devoted substantial time to "drafting legal documents, such as contracts, settlement papers, wills, etc."—61 percent to 64 percent did such work frequently, but government lawyers were much less likely to do so.[30] Although partners in corporate firms were relatively unlikely to report substantial effort on legal research, they were toward the high end on drafting chores: 59 percent of partners reported doing it often, but only 49 percent of associates in such firms did so.

Internal counsel and solo practitioners often drafted legal documents, but they were relatively unlikely to write briefs and memoranda: only 22 percent and 33 percent, respectively, reported doing such writing frequently. Briefs and memoranda were most likely to command the attention of associates in private firms—from 61 percent to 80 percent of associates did that work often in the three types of firms. Government lawyers and partners in all types of firms were near the overall percentage (47 percent).

We might expect brief writing to be associated with court appearances, but some types of courtroom work involve little writing. Solo practitioners, who reported relatively little work on briefs or memoranda, went to court more often than most Chicago lawyers—57 percent of solos but only 47 percent of other practicing lawyers reported doing courtroom work frequently. Government staff lawyers, many of whom were prosecutors, were most likely to report frequent court appearances (66 percent). Courtroom work was also common among partners and associates in both traditional law firms and hybrid firms—about three-fifths did it frequently. Lawyers in corporate firms, however, were substantially less likely to report frequent court appearances (37 percent of partners, 49 percent of associates). This reflects both the volume of "transactional" (nonlitigation) work done in corporate firms and the practice of sending associates to court to file routine motions, appear for "status calls," and so on. As might be expected, most internal counsel seldom appeared in court—only about 15 percent said that they did so frequently, while 75 percent of the supervisors and 61 percent of the staff in those offices did courtroom work seldom or never. Participation in alternative dispute resolution, including arbitration, shows a similar pattern.

The hierarchical character of private law firms pervades their division of labor. For internal counsel and government lawyers, however, rank does not produce large differences in task profiles—as was the case in patterns of specialization by field and hours worked, lawyers in inside-counsel positions and in government offices reported smaller differences between the tasks performed by staff and by supervisors. Thus, contrary to the assumption that employed legal settings are more bureaucratic and private law firms are more collegial, we see more effects of hierarchy in law firms than in government or businesses. In law firms, the hierarchies may be governed by professionals rather than by nonlawyers, but they are even more hierarchical.

Given the prominence of theories regarding the alienation of professional workers in bureaucratic employment contexts (Derber 1982; Spangler 1986), we sought to measure the extent to which lawyers in different organizational settings disliked their work. After asking respondents about the frequency of their various tasks, we asked them to rate the degree to which they liked each task. From these ratings, we calculated an aggregate measure of "task dissonance"—that is, the extent to which they did work they disliked. Theoretically, the measure could vary between 0 (no task dissonance) and 36 (all 9 tasks were disliked and all were done very frequently). In the actual responses, the measure varies between 0 and 21, with a mean of 3.8. The overall level of dissonance thus appears to be modest—equivalent to having to do two disliked tasks "sometimes."

We might predict that government lawyers and inside counsel would have high levels of task dissonance. Presumably, those organizations have more rigid rules and procedures, and at least a substantial segment of their lawyers are told what to do. But inside counsel and government lawyers, both supervisors and staff, had the lowest levels of dissonance and partners in all three types of law firms had relatively high scores.[31] In inside-counsel and government offices, only 24 to 28 percent of supervisors and staff had task dissonance scores above the overall mean, about half of what we found among partners in traditional firms (56 percent). Associates in those firms had the highest percentage above the mean, 60 percent. For solo practitioners, it was 41 percent.

The difference between the task dissonance reported by partners and associates is also statistically significant.[32] Associates report greater dissonance than partners only on legal research tasks (which most partners avoid). Many partners report an aversion to tasks concerning management decisions and the supervision of other lawyers; associates do much less of that work. But partners also have higher dissonance scores than do associates on drafting documents, negotiating with other lawyers, talking with clients, and doing routine paperwork. Given the roles and mix of tasks performed by partners and associates, partners appear to be required to do more things that they dislike.

It is hard to find much support in these data for a professional alienation thesis. The dissonance measure may be too blunt an instrument to reveal the dissatisfaction, but we do have additional indices that permit us to address the alienation thesis further. Proponents of the thesis typically make two assertions: professional work has become "deskilled" (transformed from individual craftsmanship into an assembly line), and professionals have lost control of the end product of their work (sometimes referred to as ideological proletarianization) (Derber 1982). In the interviews, we sought to determine whether lawyers perceived their work as having these characteristics. The questions were posed as opposite statements about the nature of the work, and respondents were then asked to indicate, on a five-point scale, whether their work was better characterized by one statement or the other. Figure 5.8 reports the percentage of respondents choosing the two scale positions closest to the description indicated.

Overall, 74 percent of the lawyers said that the law involved in their work was changing rapidly. Only 19 percent reported that a paraprofessional could do their job, but there was considerable variation across the organization types—government lawyers and solo practitioners were the most likely to agree with this characterization, but still only a minority of them did so (32 and 33 percent, respectively). Thus, Chicago lawyers characterized their work as requiring special expertise and adaptation to change—not an image of deskilling.

The findings on control of work are more mixed. As indicated above (at fig. 5.5), a strong majority of lawyers (69 percent) said that they could work independently. Although solo practitioners and those in public defender or legal services offices were the most likely to report that they did so, a majority of respondents in every practice context agreed with that statement. But just less than a majority (48 percent) agreed with the statement that their work strategies were largely their own. For example, although most inside counsel said that no one second-guessed them, they were much less likely to characterize themselves as devising and executing work strategies. Only in solo practice, in smaller law firms, and in public defender and legal services offices did a majority of respondents claim the latter sort of independence. In sum, autonomy was consistently high among solos and public service lawyers, both of whom tend to do less prestigious work for less powerful clients (see chaps. 3 and 4), and was at relatively moderate levels among lawyers in private firms. There appeared to be some trade-off, then, between autonomy and prestige: powerful clients and strong organizations provide status and security but impose constraints.

Two-thirds or more of respondents in all three types of private law firms said that they wanted to have the same job in five years. By contrast, little more than a third of government lawyers and of public defenders/legal services lawyers said that they wanted to remain in their current jobs. Inside counsel were evenly divided on the question. When asked whether they would again choose to become a lawyer, however, more than three-quarters of inside counsel and public service lawyers, and more than 70 percent of government lawyers, said that they would (see chap. 11). Partners in law firms were more likely than associates to prefer job stability, probably because associates did not want to remain associates.[33] These data seem to

Figure 5.8. Characterization of Work by Organization Type, 1995 (percent agreement)

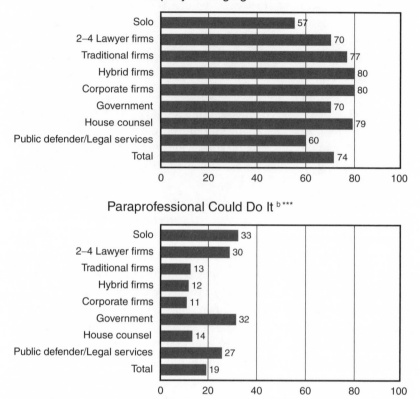

Rapidly Changing [a]*

Solo	57
2–4 Lawyer firms	70
Traditional firms	77
Hybrid firms	80
Corporate firms	80
Government	70
House counsel	79
Public defender/Legal services	60
Total	74

Paraprofessional Could Do It [b]***

Solo	33
2–4 Lawyer firms	30
Traditional firms	13
Hybrid firms	12
Corporate firms	11
Government	32
House counsel	14
Public defender/Legal services	27
Total	19

Note: Percentages given are respondents choosing, on a five-point scale, the two positions closest to the description indicated.
[a] The item read, "My area requires a great deal of reading of legal material in order to keep abreast of new developments." The opposite statement was, "Things don't change too rapidly in my area of law, so there is little need for constant revision of my knowledge and activities."
[b] The item read, "A paraprofessional could be trained to handle many of the procedures and documents in my area of law." The opposite statement was, "The type and content of my practice is such that even an educated layman couldn't really understand or prepare the documents."
Chi-square *$p \leq .05$ ***$p \leq .001$

mirror the hierarchy of income and status among practice settings: lawyers in better paying, more prestigious practice contexts were more likely to commit to staying in them.

The data reviewed here—on specialization, hours worked, and task profiles—make clear that the work of lawyers is shaped by the types of organizations in which they practice and, to varying degrees, by rank within organization. Yet, the fact that lawyers' work is organizationally based and determined does not mean that it is alienating. To be sure, lawyers working in employed contexts (as inside counsel or in government) less consistently characterized themselves as independent, but several measures that were designed to identify deskilling and alienation in lawyers' jobs failed to disclose much evidence of such complaints. Chapter 11 analyzes several additional measures of job satisfaction. Overall, the findings indicate that the lawyers were content.

Change and Continuity

One might argue that the changes we observe are driven by the market rather than by organizations, that organizations are merely the sites in which market effects appear. We have no aversion to market explanations, as is clear from our discussion of the causes for the rise of large law firms, but a market account is necessarily incomplete. The market for legal services is institutionally created. One need not adopt Richard Abel's (1989) theory of market closure to recognize that the supply of and demand for law is determined by a combination of institutional variables—including formal law, business and personal norms about when it is appropriate to invoke law, and the social organization of lawyers. The decisions of corporations about their use of law as an instrument in dealings with government, with their competitors, and with their customers have shaped the demand for legal services (Macaulay 1963). The decisions of the polity about expenditures for legal services have determined both the resources available to low-income populations and the career options of government lawyers. Decisions within the legal profession about indigent defense and contingency fees affect the incentives of lawyers to pursue or avoid particular lines of work, and thus also affect the mechanisms of supply and demand. Law firms and law departments are not passive subjects of market forces, but are strategic actors who actively seek to reshape the market and the institutional processes in their favor. The managers of firms adapt and refine their strategies, making their own judgments about how to organize the firms. These institutional dynamics blur the line between market and organizational processes, and many policies and practices of the organizations are only loosely linked to market demand. The market may punish some strategies and reward others, ultimately reshaping the ecology of law firm structures, but several strategies of organization appear to remain viable.

Even if market forces are the more fundamental determinants of change in law practice, organizations that deliver legal services must deal with the consequences of those forces. Should a smaller law firm merge with a larger one in order to enter a different segment of the market? Should the firm offer somewhat lower starting compensation for associates, but greater chances at partnership? Should inside counsel try to keep a larger share of work in-house, or spread their legal work among several law firms, or secure volume discounts from a smaller number of outside firms, or let the firms compete on price even at the cost of quality? And, if a law firm reacts to sharply growing demand by adding many more lawyers, how should it govern the new, larger organization? The significance of market forces does not lessen the organizational challenges that law firms and law departments face.

Law firms and employed practice contexts remain mixtures of bureaucracy and collegial control. Many of the largest firms retain elements of democratic governance. Even the internal law departments of corporations exhibit important elements of professional self-governance, as in the hiring of lawyers. Personal favoritism may be more important in the management of government law departments than in other contexts. And, there are qualitative differences among organizations that are not neatly summarized by indices of bureaucratization. Collegially governed firms often have a more hierarchical division of labor than do corporate law departments or government law offices, and the up-or-out character of private firms imposes a very different set of expectations about work and careers than do the graded ladders of corporate and government law offices.

There is no clear association between larger, more structured work contexts and the dissatisfaction or alienation of lawyers. On the contrary, we found that organizations were able to shape the professional ideologies of their lawyers in the image of the organization. Corporate firms select and socialize lawyers so that they accept a business model of law firm management. Although there are tensions between partners and associates on these issues, with the associates supporting more traditional modes of organization, this does not appear to pose an obstacle to the further rationalization of the firms. Nor is this new: Nelson found it in his study of four Chicago firms (1988). What little alienation there is seems to derive from relative financial and status deprivation, especially among government lawyers (see chap. 11). The dissatisfaction of these lawyers is not a result of proletarianization so much as of a lack of public investment in government law offices and legal services for the poor. Although lawyers in organizational settings are engaged in a form of team production and they develop their practice strategies in consultation with others, they are not just tightening bolts on a standard model (Lazega 2001, 93).

When we examine the Chicago bar from an organizational perspective, we see profound change, but also elements of continuity with professional traditions. A revised form of law firm—the corporate model—grew from the high-status firms of the past. Corporate firms achieved a new level of economic and demographic power in the market for legal services, but for the most part they continued to be organized around substantive specialties. The practice of law in other contexts was also structured by the forms of organization found there. Managers of the organizations struck compromises with professional tradition as they sought to rationalize the practice of law, but they succeeded in their efforts to build larger, more bureaucratic institutions. Lawyers working in these different organizational contexts espoused varying views of how their organizations should be run, but the organizations remade the ideologies of lawyers, as well as the practice of law. Thus, the transformation of law practice occurred incrementally, without a radical shift in how lawyers viewed their status as professionals.

Chapter 6
Careers
With Kathleen E. Hull

The progress of a career often feels unique to the person who lives through it, but individual stories usually fall into categories of broadly similar transitions shared by others. Many of the regularities observed in work histories reflect the predictable interaction of personal biography with broader market conditions and the employment policies of organizations (Spilerman 1978). Within an occupation, predictability of careers helps to maintain solidarity. Shared experiences—of being an associate in a law firm, of appearing in traffic court repeatedly with the same judges and the same crew of defense attorneys, of working long hours compiling complex briefs— provide an experiential basis for common identity. Shared expectations—of eventual promotion to partnership, of a steady supply of clients with predictable problems, of finally appearing as lead counsel in a trial court— support a culture of common aspiration and a sense of common fate (Carr-Saunders and Wilson 1933; Freidson 1994, 75–91; Parsons 1968). When these expectations are met in one's own life and in the lives of one's peers, occupational culture and identity are affirmed, but when careers become unpredictable or the supply of work becomes unreliable, the sense of identification with work and colleagues can weaken.

In Chicago, paradoxically, lawyers' careers became both less predictable and more strongly characterized by common experience. By 1995, a majority of the respondents had worked as an associate in a private law firm at some point in their careers, but they were less likely to have been promoted to partnership in the first firm in which they worked, and partners became less likely to spend an entire career in a single firm. Some aspects of lawyers' careers remained much the same, however. In both 1975 and 1995, lawyers' work histories seldom spanned the divide of client type. Lawyers who started out in work for individuals usually stayed with that work, and lawyers who started their careers working for businesses generally spent all of their working lives with such clients.

Work History and Careers

To examine changes in the career patterns of Chicago lawyers, we use work-life history data. Respondents were asked to recall specific aspects of each job they had since becoming a lawyer: the job's setting, the date they started work there, the date they left that organization (or stint in solo practice), and their title when they left. In the 1995 survey, lawyers were also asked about changes in position as a result of promotions or lateral moves during their time with a particular organization, and for the dates when these changes occurred. Based upon those data, we constructed complete career histories and calculated measures that describe lawyers' careers, such as rates of promotion to partnership and the probability of moving from one type of job to another. By comparing job histories of lawyers in each survey, we can learn about how lawyers' careers changed over time.

Each survey includes only persons eligible to practice law in the year prior to the survey, and the information we have about attrition from the profession is imperfect. People who were excluded—lawyers who did not maintain their eligibility to practice—may differ in important ways from these respondents.[1] Moreover, patterns of attrition may have changed over time, making comparison of the opportunities in the two periods more complex. In the 1975 survey, retired or unemployed lawyers were not included in the sample, and 6 percent were working in nonlegal jobs. In the 1995 survey, 1 percent of the lawyers were retired, 0.4 percent were unemployed, and 7 percent were working in nonlegal jobs (see fig. 1.1). Studies of variation in attrition across occupations have been done for single points in time (Evans and Laumann 1983), but little information is available about changes in rates and patterns of attrition over time. In interpreting our findings, therefore, we will want to consider how attrition may have affected the data.

In the bar as a whole, rates of mobility between organizations are similar in the two surveys. The average number of jobs per respondent after law school was 2½ at both times. As table 6.1 indicates, job mobility was unchanged for lawyers with similar levels of experience.[2] This stability suggests that careers of Chicago lawyers remained constant for twenty years

Table 6.1. Mean and Median Number of Moves between Organizations, by Years since Entry into the Profession, 1975 and 1995

Years in the profession	1975			1995		
	Mean	Median	N	Mean	Median	N
Fewer than 10	0.9	1.0	292	0.8	1.0	284
10–19	1.6	1.0	194	1.6	1.0	264
20–29	2.0	2.0	143	2.3	2.0	143
30–39	2.6	2.0	70	2.5	2.0	52
40 +	2.0	2.0	75	2.3	2.0	33

Note: In these analyses, a solo practice is treated as an organization. Entry into the profession occurs when the lawyer takes his or her first job after completing law school. Missing data on the start date of the first job leads to the exclusion of three cases in 1975 and twelve cases in 1995. Two-tailed t-tests reveal no statistically significant differences between surveys.

after 1975. The overall stability, however, is produced by counterbalancing changes in different parts of the bar. Some of these offsetting changes are revealed in figure 6.1. In each of thirteen settings—solo practice, four firm-size categories,[3] federal government, state government, local government, public-defender and legal aid offices,[4] house counsel, the judiciary, legal education, and nonlegal jobs[5]—the figure shows the mean number of jobs held after the first job.

Shifts in the structure of the bar are revealed by the distribution of first positions (fig. 6.2). Over time, more lawyers started their careers in private practice largely because more lawyers started in large law firms. While 17 percent of the 1975 lawyers took their first job after law school in a firm with more than ten lawyers, 39 percent of the 1995 lawyers had done so. Hanging out one's own shingle became less common as a way to enter the profession: solo practice accounted for 13 percent of first positions in 1975 but only 6 percent in 1995. Starting out as house counsel also became less common. Fully 14 percent of lawyers in the 1975 survey but only 6 percent of the 1995 sample had first jobs in internal counsel offices. This pattern is consistent with national trends. Between 1950 and 1970, corporate counsel grew more rapidly than the profession as whole, but they declined as a proportion of the profession after 1970 (Sandefur 2004). Nonlegal employment also became less common as a first job: 12 percent of lawyers in the 1975 survey but 9 percent of those in 1995 had started work in nonlegal settings.

Figure 6.3 shows the number of moves per year for lawyers starting in each setting. This quantity is a simple rate that indicates the speed with which lawyers move between jobs. The inverse of this rate is the average number of years lawyers stay in a position before moving. Mobility between

Figure 6.1. Mean Number of Subsequent Jobs, by Setting of First Job, 1975 and 1995

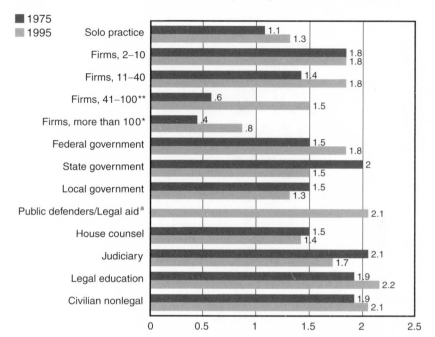

Note: In 1975, 26 lawyers whose first job after entering the profession was in the military are excluded from the table. In 1995, 12 lawyers whose first job after entering the profession was in the military and 2 lawyers who had never held a job are excluded from the table.

[a] In 1975, public defenders and some legal aid lawyers were coded as government lawyers.

$*p < .05$ $**p < .01$, two-tailed t-test of means for difference between surveys.

organizations increased significantly for lawyers who started in private practice (fig. 6.3). In the 1975 survey, lawyers who began in solo practice averaged one move after 16.7 years (1/0.06), but one move after 10 years (1/0.10) in the 1995 survey. Lawyers starting out in firms of eleven to forty lawyers averaged one move after 12.5 years (1/0.08) in the 1975 survey, and one move after 7.7 years (1/0.13) in 1995. Despite increased mobility among private practice organizations, however, lawyers who started their careers as private practitioners were likely to remain in private practice. In 1975, 82 percent of the lawyers who had first worked either as solos or in firms were still in private practice at the time of survey. In 1995, this declined only 3 percentage points.[6] Lawyers who began their careers in government and house counsel offices evidenced small, and not statistically significant, decreases in mobility between organizations.

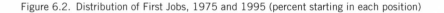

Figure 6.2. Distribution of First Jobs, 1975 and 1995 (percent starting in each position)

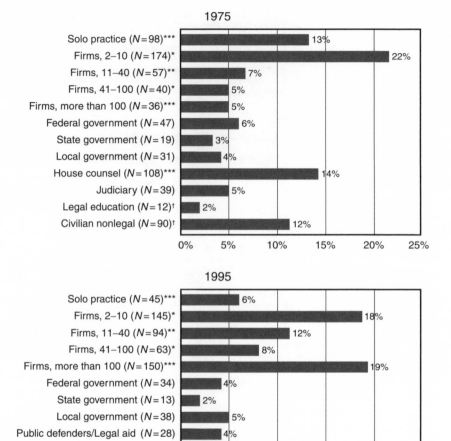

Note: In 1975, 26 lawyers whose first job after entering the profession was in the military are excluded from the table. In 1995, 12 lawyers whose first job after entering the profession was in the military and 2 lawyers who had never held a job are excluded from the table. Percentages will not sum to 100 because of the exclusion of these lawyers. In the 1975 survey, public defenders and some legal aid lawyers were coded as government lawyers.

†p < .10   *p < .05   **p < .01   ***p < .001, chi-square test for difference between surveys.

Figure 6.3. Average Number of Moves per Year in the Bar, by Setting of First Job, 1975 and 1995

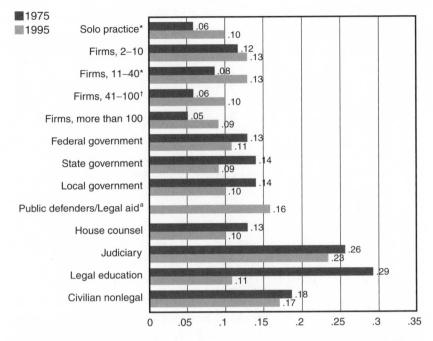

Career Stability

In both 1975 and 1995, lawyers' options were constrained. Lawyers rarely move between the "two hemispheres" of the bar, the personal-service profession and the corporate-service profession. In the 1975 survey, only 8 percent of lawyers working in firms of forty or more—the kinds of organizations in which most corporate legal work was then done—had started their careers in solo practice or in firms of two to ten lawyers, the kinds of organizations in which most personal service lawyers worked. In the 1995 survey, only 3 percent of lawyers working in firms of forty or more had started out in smaller contexts.[7] Lawyers who began their careers in government were also unlikely to move into large-firm practice—9 percent of large-firm lawyers in 1975 and 6 percent in 1995 had started in government practice.[8] In both surveys, those who began their careers in the most prestigious government setting—work for the federal government—accounted for the majority of government lawyers' movement to large-firm practice.[9]

Movement the other way—movement to less remunerative work from positions with higher starting pay, more prestigious work, and the possibility of affluence—was also rare. Because more lawyers in the second survey had started out in large firms, lawyers who left those jobs increasingly supplied the workforce of other settings. But controlling for this compositional change, we found that the relationship between starting out as an associate in a large firm and working for government at the time of the survey remained substantially the same. In the 1975 survey, no lawyer working for an agency of government had started in a large law firm; in the 1995 survey, 8 percent of lawyers in government practice had started in large firms.[10] Large law firms also became a source/supplier of lawyers working alone and in the smallest firms. Although only 2 percent of those in solo practice or in firms of two to ten lawyers at the time of the 1975 survey had begun their careers in large firms, in the 1995 survey 13 percent of solo and small-firm lawyers had started as big-firm associates.[11]

Even among lawyers serving primarily a corporate clientele, there was little movement between private practice and employed practice: 4 percent of large-firm lawyers had started out as inside counsel in 1975, and only 2 percent had done so in 1995.[12] In the 1975 survey, 5 percent of inside counsel had started in firms of forty or more lawyers; in the 1995 survey, 15 percent had done so.[13] In both cases, then, the likelihood of a move between employed and private practice within the corporate bar remained low, controlling for compositional change.

In one important way, lawyers' careers became less regular and predictable after 1975: lawyers who began in larger law firms became more likely to leave them. Of respondents who started their careers in firms of forty or more lawyers, 82 percent in 1975 but only 66 percent in 1995 were working in firms that large when they were interviewed. This apparent weakening of the holding power of large-firm practice persists when changes in distributions by age, gender, and practice setting are taken into account.[14] Women who started their careers in large firms were, however, more likely than men to leave them. Lawyers deserting the large-firm setting were not especially likely to go to any other specific destination, though in both surveys they were *unlikely* to move to government practice: none had done so in the 1975 survey, and only three of the 1995 lawyers had moved to government. The greater attrition from the large-firm setting is consistent with changes, just beginning at the time of the 1975 survey, in the demographic composition of the bar (see chap. 3) and in the organization and management of large law firms (see chap. 5).

These patterns of mobility reflect individual choices and the varying skill requirements of different kinds of legal jobs, but they probably also reflect some degree of labor-market segmentation. Labor markets are said to be segmented when people of similar skill and experience are differentially able to move into particular jobs, or when they receive different levels of pay for substantially similar work (Cain 1976; c.f. Hagan 1990). If corporate legal work as an employee on the staff of a corporation made one unfit to do the work of a large private firm, then the rarity with which lawyers move from internal counsel offices to large firms could be said to reflect real differences in the requirements of the two jobs. But some barriers to movement between practice settings probably reflect an unwillingness of the organizations to consider lawyers who lack a traditional credential, often an educational credential or a particular type of experience.

As we noted in chapter 3, one powerful influence on lawyers' career opportunities is the relative standing within the profession of the law schools they attended. In both surveys, graduates of prestigious schools[15] were overrepresented in larger firms and underrepresented in government and small-firm practice; see table 3.1. Large law firms pay substantial premiums to attract graduates of highly ranked schools because they believe these lawyers are better able to do complex corporate legal work or, perhaps, will have superior networks of association. To the extent that these beliefs are inaccurate—for example, to the extent that graduates of the University of Illinois or John Marshall would be equally productive in work on mergers and acquisitions or initial public offerings—then, the labor market for lawyers is segmented.

The Golden Age and Its Fading

The 1950s and 1960s have been called the Golden Age of the big law firm (Galanter and Palay 1991). A young man—it was then, of course, almost always a man[16]—fortunate enough to be hired as an associate in such a firm could, given ability and hard work, hope for an "orderly procession to unassailable eminence" (Galanter and Palay 1991, 76). After six to eight years as an associate, he would either be promoted to partner in the firm, or, if he somehow did not "fit" with his colleagues, he would be placed as an internal counsel to one of the firm's corporate clients (Hoffman 1973; Smigel 1964). Once a lawyer became a partner in a law firm, he stayed there for the rest of his working life, receiving an income that reflected his seniority in the firm and the economic health of the partnership as a whole, much more than his individual contributions to the bottom line.

In the 1970s, the Golden Age began to fade. As firms grew larger, they increasingly resembled pyramids, with larger classes of associates competing for fewer partnerships in each firm (Galanter and Palay 1991). At the same time, the nature of partnership itself changed. New forms of partnership emerged that granted higher pay than work as an associate, but they did not confer a share of ownership of the firm (Gorman 1999; Heintz and Markham-Bugbee 1986). In the 1975 survey, only one of 220 "partners" in law firms of two or more lawyers held a title indicating that he probably was not an owner of the firm, but the 1995 survey found a number of new statuses, such as "salaried partner" and "contract partner," indicating that these lawyers were not owners (see table 5.1). Of law firm "partners," 13 percent reported these new titles. Partnership itself had changed, no longer representing "unassailable eminence" in all cases. Firms began to expel lawyers judged insufficiently productive (including "real" partners) and began to compete with each other for rainmakers, lawyers with proven ability to attract lucrative work (see chap. 12; Galanter and Palay 1991, 67–68; Hoffman 1982; Menkel-Meadow 1994).

The careers of lawyers in large firms changed substantially, though not quite as much as may be implied by comparing the contemporary bar to the idealized Golden Age. Among Chicago lawyers, Golden Age careers were always a rarity. Figure 6.4 reports the prevalence of two job histories, "Golden Age success" and "Golden Age failure." A Golden Age success is a lawyer whose first job in regular practice[17] after law school was in a law firm, who was then promoted to full, owning partner in that firm, and who was still a partner there at the time of the survey. A Golden Age failure had a first job in a law firm but left that firm to work as internal counsel.[18] There are two analyses in figure 6.4: the first considers only lawyers who started practice in large firms, and the second shows the prevalence of these careers among lawyers starting out in law firms of all sizes. For respondents in the 1975 sample, large firms are defined as those with twenty or more lawyers, which was quite large at the time (only 14 percent of the 1975 lawyers started their careers in firms that large). For lawyers in the 1995 sample, a large firm is defined as a firm with more than forty lawyers (31 percent had started their careers in law firms of that size).

As the figure indicates, Golden Age success was never common, and it became a less likely outcome for lawyers who started their careers in large firms. In each survey, only 5 percent of all lawyers reported careers that

Figure 6.4. The Prevalence of "Golden Age" Careers, 1975 and 1995

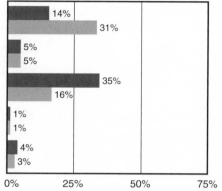

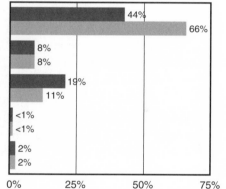

[a] In 1975, $N = 111$; in 1995, $N = 247$.
[b] In 1975, $N = 345$; in 1995, $N = 519$.
$**p < .01$ $***p < .001$, chi-square test of difference between periods.

looked like large-firm success stories. Although starting one's career in a law firm of any size became more common, accounting for 44 percent of first practicing positions in 1975 and 66 percent in 1995, a smaller percentage of the 1995 lawyers reported the stereotypically successful career. Among lawyers starting their careers in firms with two or more lawyers, 19 percent of those interviewed in 1975 became partners and remained in the firm where they started, compared with only 11 percent in 1995. Among lawyers who had started practice in large law firms, 35 percent enjoyed Golden Age success in 1975; in 1995, only 16 percent had that career pattern. And the "failed" Golden Age career was never common; no more than 1 percent of lawyers in either survey could have experienced it.

Two changes contributed to the demise of Golden Age success—associates were less likely to be promoted to partnership in the firm where they started work (Abel 1989, 201; Galanter and Palay 1991, 63; Phillips 2001, fig. 3), and partners were more likely to move from one firm to another. In 1975, 38 percent of the lawyers who began their careers in large firms had become partners in the firms where they started; in 1995, only 26 percent had.[19] Of lawyers who started in law firms of all sizes, 30 percent in 1975 and 22 percent in 1995 held the position of partner in the firm in which they took their first job.[20] In both surveys, among lawyers who did not become partners in their first law firms, less than half worked in other firms later and only about a quarter eventually became partners.[21] Being denied partnership in one's first law firm meant that one was less likely *ever* to attain partnership. Moreover, if lawyers who were not promoted to partner in their first firm simply left the profession, these calculations may understate the true size of the decline. Among lawyers who attained partnership in their first firm, 85 percent in 1975 but only 46 percent in 1995 stayed there until the time of the survey.[22] So, another large part of the demise of the successful Golden Age career was the greater mobility of law firm partners. Lawyers who left partnerships moved to a variety of other jobs, and the pattern of this mobility changed in an important way: careers characterized by multiple partnerships in different firms became more common.

As figure 6.5 shows, 13 percent of the 1975 lawyers who were or had been a partner in one law firm reported having also been a partner in another firm. In 1995, that more than doubled (29 percent). The other jobs held by partners during their careers were largely unchanged. A small minority had been judges, and a larger share had served in government or legal aid. In 1975, 18 percent of partners had practiced at some point as house counsel, as had 13 percent in 1995. Nonlawyer positions were held by 15 percent in 1975 and 13 percent in 1995, and 25 percent of the 1975 and 21 percent of the 1995 partners had also done at least one stint as a solo practitioner. Few had worked in legal education.

In these patterns of job mobility, we see the growing importance of an external labor market within private practice, especially for senior lawyers. Fewer lawyers became partners in their first firms and spent their careers there. Rather, lawyers in private practice became more likely to move between large firms. This could be a positive development from the lawyers' perspective—greater job mobility may permit lawyers to find a job that is a better match for their skills or tastes (Bridges 1995; cf. Leicht and Fennell

Figure 6.5. Mobility by Law Firm Partners, 1975 and 1995

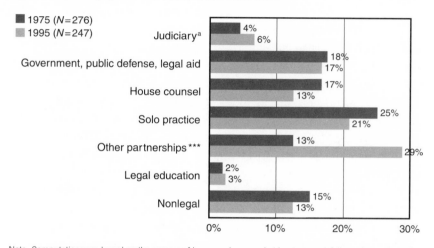

Note: Computations are based on the careers of lawyers who served at least once as full, owning partners in law firms of two or more lawyers. For each job setting, the percentage given is the proportion of such lawyers' careers that include a job in the specified setting.
[a] In this analysis, work in the judiciary does not include judicial clerkships.
[***]$p < .001$, chi-square test of difference between periods.

2001; McBrier 2003; Rogers 2000). Nevertheless, much of the job mobility reflects the lower likelihood of attaining partnership anywhere, because owning partners became a smaller share of private practitioners (Abel 1989, 201; Hagan and Kay 1995, chap. 1; Sandefur 2004). Among partners, greater mobility may reflect the emergence of a "winner-take-all" market, in which the incomes and professional opportunities of a small group of top, "star" lawyers far exceed those of their colleagues (see chap. 7; S. Rosen 1992; R. Frank and Cook 1995; Sandefur and Heinz 1999).

Another factor in the decline of Golden Age careers is the entry of women into large law firms. In 1975, 5 percent of respondents in firms of forty or more were women; by 1995, women made up 22 percent of the lawyers in these firms. But the women were more mobile. In 1995, among lawyers of comparable education and years of experience who started their careers in firms with forty or more lawyers, women's odds of staying in large-firm practice were a bit more than half (56 percent) of men's.[23]

Paths to Eminence in the Profession

For at least the first half of the twentieth century, the elite of the American legal profession discriminated against Jewish lawyers (Auerbach 1976), and law schools and the organized bar erected formal barriers to exclude blacks and women (Abel 1989; Auerbach 1976; Epstein 1993). These barriers persisted until the 1960s. As late as 1971, only 3 percent of lawyers were women (Carson 1999, table 2). In the mid-1970s, the vast majority of law degrees were taken by non-Hispanic whites—92.4 percent in the 1976–77 school year (National Center for Education Statistics 2000a). A quarter of a century later, in the 1997–98 school year, people of color received somewhat more than a fifth of all law degrees: blacks received 7.2 percent, Hispanics 4.6 percent, members of Asian and Pacific Islander groups 10.1 percent, and American Indians 0.7 percent (National Center for Education Statistics 2000a). By 1995, nearly a quarter (24 percent) of America's lawyers were women (Carson 1999, table 2).

Greater access, however, did not mean full integration into the profession for any of these groups of lawyers. As we noted in chapter 3, Jewish lawyers were still overrepresented in certain types of work, such as divorce. Although 23 percent of all law degrees were awarded to people of color in 1997–98, by 2002 only 14 percent of law firm associates and 4 percent of law firm partners were people of color (National Association for Law Placement 2002). In 2002, only 16 percent of law firm partners were women (ibid.), even though women were awarded at least a third of all law degrees in each year between 1982 and 1998 (National Center for Education Statistics 2000b). Women were well represented, however, among law firm associates in 2002 (42 percent; National Association for Law Placement 2002).

Of the new entrants to the profession, the experience of women has been the most extensively studied. Sophisticated quantitative studies of representative samples of elite law firms in major U.S. cities (Chambliss and Uggen 2000), of private practitioners in Ontario (Hagan and Kay 1995; Kay and Hagan 1998, 1999), and of people eligible to practice law in Chicago (Hull and Nelson 2000) have consistently documented women's lower probabilities of partnership in law firms and their greater probability of attrition from the large-law-firm setting (Kay and Hagan 2003). In comparison with men of similar education, social class, ethnoreligious identity, family situation, and career history, women are less likely to be found as full, owning partners in law firms and more likely to be found as supervisors in employed settings, such as internal-counsel offices and agencies of government (Hull and Nelson 2000, table 4). Among law faculty, women move more slowly than men of comparable achievement and family situation out of short-term academic positions into teaching positions in which they are eligible for lifetime job security, often called the tenure track (McBrier 2003).

In part, women's careers differ from men's because they begin differently. Women are more likely than men of comparable education, socioeconomic background, and job preference to start their careers in organizations such as government agencies and business corporations (Hull and Nelson 2000, table 2). As already shown, there is little movement between different kinds of practice organizations and different kinds of clients, so early work experiences are highly consequential for entire careers. Among academic lawyers, women are more likely to take a position at the school where they received their degree, and this academic inbreeding appears to slow movement into the tenure track (McBrier 2003). The magnitude of these early differences between male and female lawyers can be attributed in part to preferences for different kinds of work and for different work settings, but other factors—such as steering by law school mentors and potential employers and the tendency for women to have a greater share of household management and childrearing responsibilities—also play a role. These initial differences grow into larger disparities over the course of lawyers' careers, and early, preference-based choices are thus only part of the story (Hull and Nelson 2000).

Studies of the correlates of professional attainment suggest that certain lifestyle choices and work accomplishments affect men's and women's professional advancement differently. In the "promotion to partnership tournament" within large law firms (Galanter and Palay 1991), high-performing women do at least as well as comparable men. But, "mediocre" men appear to be more likely to get the benefit of the doubt than are mediocre women (Kay and Hagan 1998). Among legal academics, the number of a scholar's publications and whether he or she is married have career effects that differ by gender. Among men, marriage increases the probability of advancement onto the tenure track, but, for women, marriage reduces the likelihood of reaching tenure-track positions, net of their research productivity, the number of their children, and whether they had imposed geographic restrictions on their job search (McBrier 2003; see also Dixon and Seron 1995). On the other hand, "women were rewarded more highly for scholarly productivity than men with respect to movement across the boundary from non-tenure-track to tenure-track employment" (McBreir 2003, 1236–37). Debra Branch McBrier suggests that some choices and achievements are "more important signal[s] of career commitment for women than for men" (2003, 1237).

Women and men report being treated differently by colleagues and employers, who are (still) mostly men. Lawyers who feel that they are not taken seriously by senior colleagues or who feel excluded from important work may well feel less attached to the employing organization (Kay and Hagan 2003). Among lawyers working in law firms, women are more likely than men to report that they were denied assignments to work on important cases or with important clients (Kay and Hagan 2003; Reichman and Sterling 2002), thus depriving them of opportunities both to learn how to do this work and to demonstrate superior performance. Elizabeth Chambliss and Christopher Uggen (2000) found that, in elite urban law firms, women's rates of promotion are higher in firms that already have more women partners. The finding may reflect the greater decision-making power of women in these firms, which may permit them to challenge negative stereotypes and assumptions about what makes a good lawyer or a promising partner (Chambliss and Uggen 2000; Ridgeway 1997).

Much less is known about how racial minorities have fared since the profession began to open to these groups in the 1970s. We do know that black, Hispanic, and American Indian graduates of an elite law school were less likely than their white counterparts to start their careers in private practice (Lempert, Chambers, and Adams 2000, table 10), and that, among partners in large law firms, there are few lawyers of color (National Association for Law Placement 2002; Wilkins and Gulati 1996). Evidence from studies of black lawyers suggests that they experience some of the differential treatment that is reported by women. Like women, black lawyers may be less likely to be given the challenging assignments that both lead to the development of important legal skills and provide young professionals with opportunities to impress the partners evaluating them (Wilkins and Gulati 1996, 1998).

As reported in chapter 3, external social hierarchies appear to have significant effects on the careers of Chicago lawyers. Figure 6.6 summarizes the disparity between the presence in the bar and the presence in senior positions of three groups: female lawyers, black lawyers, and Jewish lawyers. The positions examined are those of at least supervisory authority in offices of internal counsel or agencies of government (top graph) and full, owning partnerships in law firms of two or more lawyers (bottom graph). Women were completely absent from senior positions in employed practice in 1975 but held a third of such positions in 1995, roughly at parity with their presence in the bar. They were substantially and significantly underrepresented among law firm partners in 1995, however, constituting only 7 percent of partners, 22 percentage points less than their presence in the bar. Black lawyers were significantly underrepresented in partnerships in both surveys. The disparity scores of Jewish lawyers show more progress toward inclusion. Jewish lawyers were underrepresented in senior employed positions by 16 percentage points in the 1975 survey, but present in these positions roughly at parity with their presence in the bar in the 1995 survey. Although the analyses reported in chapter 3 show that Jewish lawyers were underrepre-

Figure 6.6. Presence of Female, Black, and Jewish Lawyers in Senior Positions, 1975 and 1995 (disparity scores)

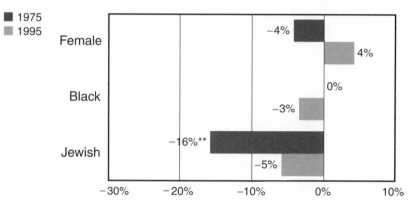

Senior Position, Internal Counsel or Government

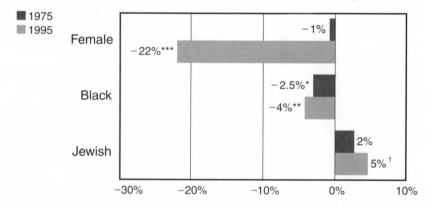

Full, Owning Partner in a Law Firm of Two or More Lawyers

Note: The disparity score is the difference between the percentage of lawyers in the bar and the percentage of lawyers in the senior position who are female, black, or Jewish, respectively.
† $p < .10$ *$p < .05$ **$p < .01$ ***$p < .001$, chi-square test of significant difference from the bar as a whole.

sented among partners in *large* law firms, we see in figure 6.6 that they were slightly overrepresented in 1995 when partners in all firms with two or more lawyers are taken into account.

Many of these disparities in career outcomes persist when we control for other characteristics of the lawyers. We computed a series of logistic regression models[24] predicting the attainment of these two types of senior positions: full, owning partnership in a law firm, and positions of supervisory responsibility in internal counsel offices or agencies of government.[25]

Each model includes the following independent variables: gender, whether the lawyer is black, whether the lawyer is Jewish, the number of years since the lawyer took his or her first job after law school, that quantity squared (to test for curvilinear effects of age), the prestige of the law school attended, whether the lawyer ranked in the top 10 percent of the graduating class or was on the law review, and whether the lawyer's first job was in a firm of fewer than forty lawyers (including solo practice), in a firm of forty or more lawyers, in government or legal aid, or in an internal counsel office. The findings of the analysis reveal changes in both the career paths to senior positions and the access of minorities to positions of organizational power and professional influence. As already seen, in 1975 women were completely absent from senior positions in house counsel and government offices. In 1995, women were more likely than men of the same race, ethnoreligious affiliation, education, years of experience, and starting position—about 76 percent more likely—to be in senior positions in employed practice relative to all other positions (Hull and Nelson 2000), but the difference did not reach statistical significance in this model because of the small numbers in the sample.[26] In both surveys, the few black lawyers were less likely to occupy senior positions in government or as internal counsel, but the differences were not statistically significant.[27] In 1975, Jewish lawyers were only 38 percent as likely as comparable non-Jewish lawyers to be working in senior positions in employed practice,[28] but in 1995 the disparity was no longer statistically significant.[29]

In both years, lawyers who started their careers in internal counsel positions were much more likely than lawyers of comparable experience, race, gender, and education who started in other work settings to reach senior positions in employed practice. Starting out in government work, however, was less strongly linked to reaching a senior employed position in 1975; and, in 1995, lawyers who began their careers in government practice were no more likely than those who started in private practice or in nonpracticing positions to have achieved senior employed positions at the time of the survey. The difference between starting in government, on the one hand, and starting as internal counsel, on the other, suggests that internal counsel offices may have more developed internal labor markets than do government agencies. The greater opportunities open to internal counsel appear to allow lawyers to advance farther, without leaving the active practice of law, than is possible in government. If this is the case, then greater chances for advancement may be added to higher pay (see chap. 7) as a further inducement to choose employment by private business interests over employment in public service.

The likely routes to full partnership in a law firm are different. Lawyers who started out in employed practice were no more likely than lawyers whose first jobs were outside the regular practice of law (e.g., in business) to be a full partner in a law firm at the time of either survey. In 1995, lawyers who started as internal counsel were, in fact, somewhat less likely to be partners than were those who started outside regular practice.[30] In both surveys, lawyers who started in firms of forty or more had the best chance of being a partner in a law firm of any size at the time they were interviewed, and the size of the relative advantage was similar in the two surveys.[31] Women were substantially less likely than men to be partners in law firms at the time of the 1995 survey, controlling for starting position, legal education, years of experience, race, and ethnoreligious affiliation.[32]

Lawyers Not Practicing

At the time of the 1975 survey, 7 percent of lawyers who were working had positions that were not defined by knowledge of law, and 9 percent held such positions in 1995. Some lawyers appear to have made a career of work outside of professional practice. Among lawyers holding nonlegal positions in 1975, 40 percent had never worked in regular practice of any kind, taught law, or served as a judge or judicial clerk. In 1995, 36 percent of those working outside law had never held a law job. In each survey, such lawyers amounted to about 3 percent of all respondents.

The nonlaw jobs held by lawyers were varied. Many were in occupations either affiliated with or competing with the legal profession (Abbott 1988), such as accounting, insurance, banking, real estate (including title companies), and stock trading. These employed about half of the lawyers who had nonlaw jobs (55 percent in 1975 and 48 percent in 1995). In both surveys, some respondents worked as executives in various kinds of corporations, in public administration, and in not-for-profit organizations. In 1975, none were in elected office (except judgeships), but two of the 1995 respondents held such jobs. The social and professional characteristics of lawyers who had never worked in the law did not differ substantially from those of practicing lawyers: men and women, blacks and nonblacks,[33] Jewish and non-Jewish lawyers, graduates of law schools of differing prestige,[34] excellent students and less accomplished scholars were all essentially equally likely to spend their careers outside the practice.

Rather than focus on the small set of respondents who had never practiced law, we used a logistic regression equation to estimate the probability of working in a nonlaw job at the time of the interview, and found that the largest group of new entrants to the bar—women—were also the group most likely to work in such jobs. In 1995, among lawyers of comparable starting position, legal education, years of experience, race, and ethnoreligious affiliation, women were 77 percent more likely than men to be working outside the practice of law.[35]

Conclusion

Though the patterns of Chicago lawyers' careers remained generally stable, some noteworthy changes reflect a partial reorganization of the profession. Private firms came to dominate the labor markets for lawyers—both numerically, in terms of the share of the profession who had worked in such firms, and, as we see in the next chapter, economically, in terms of the incomes they provided. These law firms had long participated in an external labor market for associates, and they came to participate more extensively in an external market for partners. Although Chicago lawyers became more likely to move between firms, more also began their careers in private practice (63 percent in 1995 versus 53 percent in 1975) and lawyers who started in private practice remained likely to stay there. The two changes—greater job mobility and greater predominance of private practice—may have offsetting effects on professional integration. Career instability interferes with the formation of strong professional networks and may weaken identification with the profession. But, at the same time, the increase in the percentage of lawyers employed by organizations owned and controlled by professional colleagues might bolster professional attachment.

Women and members of racial minority groups became better represented in the bar, but in 1995 these groups were not yet fully integrated into the profession. Women became more likely to attain positions of power and authority in organizations not controlled by lawyers—corporations and agencies of government—whereas men were more likely to attain eminence in organizations firmly within professional control: private law firms.

Black lawyers were similarly underrepresented in the leadership of organizations at the core of the profession. Women were more likely to end up working outside law entirely. The exclusion of women and blacks from positions of power in the organizations in which the most remunerative and prestigious work was done resulted in a profession divided not only by where lawyers worked and who they served, but by the clearly visible characteristics of the lawyers themselves.

Chapter 7
Income and Income Inequality

The average American lawyer earns more than twice as much as the average American worker.[1] But lawyers' pay varies greatly from lawyer to lawyer and from job to job. A single opinion letter concerning a corporate tax shelter typically brings $50,000 to $75,000 to the firm that produces it (Johnston 2003, A15), while lawyers serving the indigent receive government-sponsored payments as low as $30 for each hour they spend in court (Fritsch and Rhode 2001, B5). Lawyers' incomes, in fact, are among the most unequal of those in any profession (Sander and Williams 1989, 440).

Some degree of income inequality is functional, of course. Inequality helps to facilitate an efficient social allocation of labor according to taste and ability. The higher rewards received by some compensate for long periods of training or arduous work schedules, and they serve as incentives for people of exceptional talent to take on difficult and important tasks (Becker 1993; Davis and Moore 1945; Lenski 1994). High inequality, however, can also be inefficient and potentially destructive. When necessary work receives very low rewards (e.g., public school teaching, nursing), it may be difficult to attract enough people or enough capable people to do that work, and when inequality is characterized by very high rewards granted to a very few, the lure of a large prize can divert talent toward its pursuit and away from work that might better suit the talent or from which society might gain greater benefit (R. Frank and Cook 1995; Sandefur and Heinz 1999; Tumin 1953).

In the legal profession, income inequality tends to reinforce other differences. Lawyers who make more money report greater overall satisfaction

159

with their jobs (see chap. 11), even after such factors as where they work and the kind of work they do are taken into account (Dau-Schmidt and Mukhopadhaya 1999). Important, complex and intellectually rewarding legal work is most often generated by large private corporations, is done in large law firms, and tends to be the most lucrative work in the bar (Sandefur 2001). The lower the absolute rewards of public service and individual client work, or the greater the disparity between corporate work and other work, the stronger the pull of large-firm, corporate practice. A lawyer entering the profession or hoping to change jobs faces a choice. Within the range of possible opportunities, given educational credentials and past performance, should one opt for lower-paid service to individuals or government, or for higher-paid service to corporations? Because the distribution of justice depends upon the availability of legal services that permit potential clients either to advance claims or to defend themselves, very high inequality in lawyers' incomes presents a special problem.

During the 1970s and 1980s, the disparity between the incomes of lawyers working in government or in the service of individuals and those of lawyers working for the large law firms that tend to serve business clients increased substantially (Kornhauser and Revesz 1995; Sander and Williams 1989). Those decades saw both an absolute decline in the real incomes of government lawyers and solo practitioners and an absolute increase in the real incomes of lawyers working in large law firms. The types of practice suffering the greatest declines in pay tended to be the areas in which new entrants to the bar—especially women and blacks—made the greatest inroads.

In Chicago, the dynamics of income inequality mirror those in the profession nationally. The city's best-paid lawyers were even better off in 1995 than in 1975, while the lawyers who received relatively low (for lawyers) incomes in 1975 received even less in 1995. Thus, the most affluent lawyers captured an increasing share of the total income received by the practicing bar. Figure 7.1 illustrates this growing concentration. In 1975, lawyers whose incomes were in the bottom 25 percent of the profession, sometimes called the first quartile of the income distribution, made an average of $43,231 each in constant (1995) dollars. Together, these lawyers collected an estimated 9 percent of the total income received by all practicing lawyers. By 1995, the incomes of lawyers in the first quartile averaged about $10,000 less in real terms, $33,816, and this group of lawyers captured only 6 percent of total income. Lawyers in the middle two quartiles of the income distribution collected an estimated 37 percent of all earnings of Chicago lawyers in 1975. Their incomes were $73,938 and $112,357, respectively, in 1995 dollars. In 1995,

Figure 7.1. Distribution of Total Income from Practice, by Quartiles, 1975 and 1995

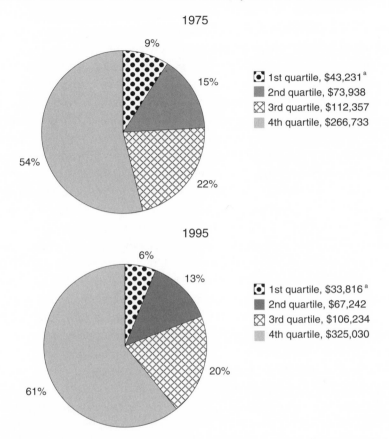

1975

9%

15%

☉ 1st quartile, $43,231 [a]
■ 2nd quartile, $73,938
⊠ 3rd quartile, $112,357
▓ 4th quartile, $266,733

54%

22%

1995

6%

13%

☉ 1st quartile, $33,816 [a]
■ 2nd quartile, $67,242
⊠ 3rd quartile, $106,234
▓ 4th quartile, $325,030

61%

20%

Note: In 1975, *n* = 656, in 1995, *n* = 633. In each survey, income information was collected by asking the lawyer to report his or her income in one of a series of intervals. The top interval was open-ended ("more than $500,000"). Lawyers' responses were recoded to the midpoint of the interval they indicated. The midpoint of the top interval in each survey was estimated assuming that the income distribution for practicing lawyers in that survey followed a Pareto distribution of the first type (Quandt 1966). Income figures for 1975 are converted to 1995 dollars by use of the Consumer Price Index (CPI-UX).
[a] Average income, in constant (1995) dollars, of lawyers in the designated quartile.

the middle quartiles collected somewhat less of the total income received by the bar (33 percent), and their average incomes were also lower—$67,242 and $106,234, respectively, in the year prior to the survey. By contrast, the most highly paid lawyers captured a larger share of all income. In 1975, the fourth quartile earned $266,733 (1995 dollars), on average, and collected an estimated 54 percent of all lawyer income. In 1995, their average income was 22 percent higher, $325,050, and they collected 61 percent of the earnings of Chicago lawyers.

Structural Sources of Inequality

Lawyers and law firms have good years and bad years—variations in luck, as well as industry and talent, are reflected in their earnings. Thus, lawyers who do the same type of work often take home very different pay. This inequality is to be expected in a profession where demand for services can fluctuate considerably and where several years of work may be invested in a single case. While fluctuation and inequality are always present, however, between 1975 and 1995 the economic viability of some kinds of legal work became more uncertain. The organizations in which lawyers worked and their client bases became increasingly important factors determining their incomes.

Table 7.1 reports the distribution of income among practicing lawyers, with the lawyers classified in two ways. The first comparison is based on types of clients served. Three categories include lawyers who devoted 75 percent or more of their work to a single type of client, and the fourth includes those whose client base was not dominated by a particular type of client (identified as a mixed practice).[2] The second analysis classifies lawyers according to the kind of organization in which they worked—solo practice, firms of 2 to 5 lawyers, firms of 6 to 25, firms of 26 to 100, firms of 101 to 299, firms of 300 or more, inside counsel, and government, legal services, and legal aid.

The variability in lawyers' incomes that was associated with differences in client base rose modestly, from 7 percent in 1975 to 9 percent in 1995. Among lawyers concentrating in the service of business, mean income was higher by 6 percent in 1995 ($151,398, versus $142,602 in 1975) and median income was 14 percent higher ($112,500, versus $99,159 in 1975), suggesting not only a general rise in these lawyers' incomes, but also a decrease in the spread, or inequality, of their incomes. (The ratio of the mean to the median of an income distribution is a conventional summary measure of inequality, useful for indicating how distant the highest earners are from those at the middle of the distribution; Allison 1978; Coulter 1989.) The fortunes of lawyers devoting themselves largely to the service of individuals appear very different. That category was 39 percent smaller in the second survey (89 lawyers in 1995, as compared with 146 in 1975). The average income of such lawyers decreased by 9 percent in the second period ($105,955 in 1995, $116,348 in 1975) and their median income was lower by 34 percent ($65,000 in 1995 as compared with $99,159 in 1975). This suggests both that real incomes in the personal client sector of the profession were falling and that income inequality was increasing. Among lawyers concentrating in service to not-for-profit organizations, average salaries were higher in the second

Table 7.1. Income and Income Inequality, by Practice Setting and Client Type, 1975 and 1995

	1975			1995		
	Mean	Median[a]	N	Mean	Median[a]	N
Client concentration						
Businesses	$142,602	$99,159	321	$151,398	$112,500	345
People	$116,348	$99,159	146	$105,955	$65,000	89
Not-for-profit organizations	$63,458	$70,828	74	$81,378	$55,000	78
Mixed	$125,144	$99,159	115	$135,248	$75,000	121
Portion of total inequality between client concentrations[b]	7%			9%		
Practice setting[c]						
Solo practice	$115,694	$99,159	132	$80,075	$55,000	100
Firms 2–5 lawyers	$143,313	$99,159	130	$150,434	$75,000	69
Firms 6–25	$140,258	$99,159	109	$155,312	$90,000	96
Firms 26–100	$166,216	$99,159	75	$126,884	$95,000	73
Firms 101–299	$144,985	$99,159	42	$156,178	$112,500	70
Firms 300 +[d]				$271,706	$112,500	82
House counsel	$103,069	$70,828	88	$105,139	$95,000	72
Government	$63,458	$70,828	74	$49,190	$45,000	71
Portion of total inequality between practice settings[b]	8%			19%		

[a] In each survey, lawyers were asked to report their income from the practice of law in intervals of $10,000, with open-ended intervals at the top and bottom of the scale. For the analyses, we recoded each lawyer's response to the midpoint of the bounded interval into which it fell. The midpoint of the bottom interval "less than $10,000" was estimated as $5,000. For each survey, we estimated the midpoint of the top interval under the assumption that the data followed a Pareto distribution of the first type. We converted the 1975 data into 1995 dollars using the Consumer Price Index, which accounts for the apparent greater precision of the 1975 medians.

[b] The share of variance in the natural logarithm of income that is accounted for by client concentration or practice setting.

[c] Five cases in which firm size data were missing are excluded from the 1975 findings.

[d] Because only one 1975 respondent who reported income data worked in a firm of 300 or more, that category is blank here.

period, but so was the disparity between lawyers at the top and lawyers at the median. The mean income of these lawyers rose from 89 percent of median income ($63,458 and $70,828) in 1975 to 150 percent of median income in 1995 ($81,378 and $55,000).[3] Lawyers with mixed-client portfolios, like those in the not-for-profit sector, received higher average incomes in 1995 than in 1975 ($135,248 and $125,144, respectively) and also exhibited increasing inequality—their average income rose to 1.8 times ($135,248 and $75,000) median income in 1995 from a ratio of 1.3 ($125,144 and 99,159) in 1975.

The overall increase in income inequality reflects substantial and growing disparities among the practice settings. The kinds of organizations in which lawyers worked became more important in determining their immediate professional opportunities. The bottom portion of table 7.1 presents information about the distribution of income among lawyers classified by type of organization. In 1975, differences between practice settings explained about 8 percent of income variation; in 1995, the portion of inequality explained by practice setting more than doubled, to 19 percent. The greatest income growth was in private practice partnerships. In law firms of all sizes, average incomes were higher in 1995 than in 1975, with lawyers in the smallest firms reporting the smallest increases and lawyers in the largest firms reporting the largest.[4]

Solo practitioners experienced both substantial decreases in average income and growing income inequality. The average incomes of lawyers in solo practice were 31 percent lower in the second period ($80,075 in 1995 as compared with $115,694 in 1975), while the ratio of the mean to the median rose from 1.2 ($115,694 and $99,159) to 1.5 ($80,075 and $55,000).

National studies of the legal profession suggest that the decline in solo practitioners' fortunes began in the early 1970s (Sander and Williams 1989, table 11). The incomes of solo practitioners peaked in 1972 and declined by 28 percent in real terms between 1975 and 1995 (Sandefur 2004, fig. 1). A variety of factors probably played a role. First, the needs of private individuals for legal services and their ability to pay for them failed to keep pace with the increasing supply of lawyers. As noted in chapter 1, the United States had one lawyer for every 572 people in 1971, but by 2001 there was one for every 264 people (Carson 2004),[5] and the number of Chicago lawyers approximately doubled from 1975 to 1995. Perhaps in response to a growing imbalance between the supply of personal client lawyers and the demand for their services, Chicago's solo practitioners diversified both their practice portfolios and their participation in other occupations. Solos reported in 1995 that an average of 56 percent of their clients were individuals, down from 63 percent in 1975.[6] At the same time, lawyers working alone derived a decreasing share of their income from the practice of law. In 1975, they received an average of 83 percent of their total income from legal work, and only 2 percent did work other than their practice. In 1995, 32 percent of lawyers in solo practice reported second jobs, and they derived somewhat less of their total income from the practice of law, an average of 76 percent.[7]

Inequality, as measured by the disparity between mean and median income, was highest in 1995 at the top and at the bottom of the firm size distribution. Among respondents in firms with two to five lawyers, the ratio of the mean to the median was 2.01 to 1, and in firms of three hundred or more lawyers it was 2.42 to 1. The highest ratio in any of the other firm size categories was 1.73 to 1. Why would the greatest inequality be found in the smallest and the largest firms? One plausible hypothesis is that senior lawyers, the elites of the firms, enjoy greater power in those practice settings and are therefore able to take home bigger pieces of the pie. Very small firms are commonly built around one principal. The senior partner, often the founder of the firm, holds the brand name and is therefore in a position to control decisions, including decisions about the distribution of earnings. Small firms are also more vulnerable to fluctuation in demand or in fortune from year to year. Their portfolios are smaller, and they are therefore less able to spread the risk (and rewards). Personal injury plaintiffs lawyers, for example, may win a very large verdict in one year and then not hit it big again for some years thereafter. Small firms are also, perhaps, more variable in quality than are larger ones—some small firms are excellent; others are distinctly not. This will, of course, also contribute to income inequality within the small-firm category.

In the largest firms, we hypothesize a different sort of process contributing to inequality, but again it may have to do with the power of seniors. The largest firms have lawyers employed in the full scale of gradations of position. Smaller firms often have more truncated distributions. Large firms are, therefore, likely to distribute a greater range of compensation, from the most meager to the most munificent. Moreover, as firms become larger, the elites within the firm become more distant from most of the lawyers. A firm of thirty or fifty lawyers can maintain strong norms that constrain seniors from grabbing an inordinate share, norms that support equality in the distribution of earnings. When firms have three hundred or a thousand or two thousand lawyers, however, the chairman of the firm becomes more akin to a corporate CEO. Leaders of firms of that size are remote, even exalted. They are seen as responsible for the fate of a large enterprise, and they are handsomely rewarded for bearing the responsibility. In this, the biggest firms may emulate the practices of their corporate clients (DiMaggio and Powell 1983): "In the late eighties, a seven-figure salary was a lot to pay a C.E.O.; by the late nineties nine-figure fortunes were routine. The chairman of General Motors, for example, made five hundred and seventy-five thousand dollars in base salary in 1991 and just over two million in 2000. Michael Ovitz, at Disney, got a severance package worth somewhere between ninety and a hundred and thirty million dollars" (Toobin 2004, 60). Thus, some of the income inequality in the largest firms may be attributable to yet another manifestation of winner-take-all markets (R. Frank and Cook 1995; S. Rosen

1992). But we should recall that a full half of the equity partners (owners) in these firms earned at least $350,000 in the year before the 1995 survey (see fig. 7.2). If elites grab a larger share but, at the same time, the whole pie is growing so much that the juniors nonetheless receive increases, the inequality may be easier to bear.

Figure 7.2 provides more detail about the earnings of lawyers in firms of different sizes. The median income of lawyers who were not full, owning partners in their firms held steady or fell in smaller firms and rose in larger firms. Median income of associates and other lawyers who were not part owners of the firm was the same in all firm size categories in 1975, $70,828. By 1995, median income of associates and other lawyers employed by firms had risen by 20 percent in the two largest categories, to $85,000. In firms of twenty-six to one hundred lawyers, median nonowner income was modestly higher in the second survey, $75,000, but in firms of six to twenty-five lawyers it was 8 percent lower, $65,000. In the smallest firms, those with two to five lawyers, the median income of nonowners was equivalent in the two surveys ($70,828 in 1975 and $70,000 in 1995).

The salaries of equity partners (owners of the firms) followed a more pronounced pattern of decline in the smallest firms and growth in the largest. Real median income of the owners of the smallest law firms fell by 25 percent, from $127,490 in 1975 to $95,000 in 1995. Owners in firms of 6 to 25 lawyers saw more modest decreases, on the order of 12 percent in real terms, from $155,821 in 1975 to $137,500 in 1995. Owners in firms of 26 to 100 lawyers saw declines of 24 percent, with their median income falling from $212,484 in 1975 to $162,500 in 1995. But equity partners in firms of 101 to 299 lawyers reported incomes 44 percent higher in 1995, with median income rising from $155,821 in 1975 to $225,000 in 1995, and owners in the largest firms reported the highest incomes of all, a median of $350,000 in the previous year.

Among lawyers employed as internal counsel of businesses, private not-for-profit organizations, and government agencies, a pattern of increasing disparity emerges between service to private organizations and public service. As reported in table 7.1, the average income of lawyers working as internal counsel held steady ($103,069 in 1975 and $105,139 in 1995), while their median rose by 34 percent (from $70,828 in 1975 to $95,000 in 1995). In contrast, the average incomes of lawyers working in government fell by 23 percent, (from $63,458 in 1975 to $49,190 in 1995), and the median income of government lawyers fell even more, by 37 percent, (from $70,828 to $45,000, see fig. 7.3). The median income of Chicago lawyers employed by federal agencies in 1995 was more than $20,000 less in real terms than that

Figure 7.2. Median Income in Constant (1995) Dollars, by Ownership and Firm Size, 1975 and 1995

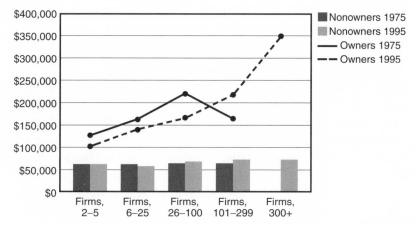

Figure 7.3. Median Income in Government and Legal Aid in Constant (1995) Dollars, 1975 and 1995

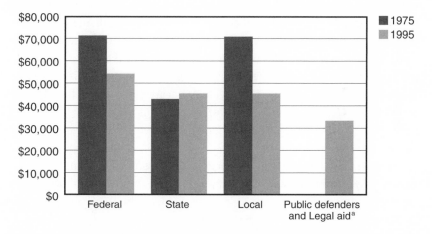

[a] In the 1975 data, public defenders and government-funded legal services lawyers are not distinguishable from government lawyers.

of their counterparts twenty years before ($55,000 in 1995 versus $70,828 in 1975). Those working for local government in 1995 reported median incomes averaging roughly $25,000 lower than in 1975 ($45,000 in 1995 versus $70,828 in 1975). In state government, lawyers' income was about the same in the two surveys ($42,497 in 1975 versus $45,000 in 1995). Legal aid lawyers and public defenders reported the lowest 1995 incomes, with a median of $35,000. As we will see below, the growing disparity between government practice and other work settings is not explained by changes in the characteristics of the lawyers, such as their years of experience, the prestige of their educational credentials, and their performance in law school.

Nonpracticing Lawyers

Lawyers not engaged in active practice range from people whose work is clearly identified with the profession—law teachers, and judges and their clerks—to lawyers who work in other jobs where they draw upon their legal expertise, to those who do work that has little or nothing to do with law. In both surveys, these nonpracticing lawyers are a small proportion of the bar. As noted in chapter 1, about 3 percent of both the 1975 and 1995 respondents were judges or judicial clerks. Law teachers were 1.3 percent of each sample. The largest number of nonpracticing lawyers worked outside the profession—6 percent of the 1975 sample and 7 percent in 1995.

Because of the small numbers of respondents in these categories, conclusions regarding the incomes of such lawyers must be tentative. The salaries reported by judges and clerks bear out our earlier observations about the growing disparity between public service and work for business. When all levels of government are combined, median judicial incomes decreased from $99,159 in 1975 to $85,000 in 1995. As compared to the pay of lawyers in private practice, judicial pay fell even further: in 1975, the median income of judges was 64 percent of that received by partners in firms with 101 to 299 lawyers and 47 percent of that of partners in firms with 26 to 100 lawyers. In 1995, however, judges' median income was only 24 percent of that of partners in the largest firms. Lawyers working in nonlegal positions who maintained their eligibility to practice—a heterogeneous group, as we saw in chapter 6—fared better in 1995 than in 1975. Their median income was higher by almost $22,000, or 77 percent ($28,331 in 1975 versus $50,000 in 1995).

Individual-Level Correlates of Income

While the kinds of clients a lawyer served and the type of organization in which she worked became more important in determining how much money a lawyer was likely to make, considerable inequality remained among lawyers doing broadly similar jobs. Among practicing lawyers, work setting explained 19 percent of observed income inequality in 1995 (see table 7.1), which means that the other 81 percent of the observed inequality was found among lawyers working in similar types of organizations.

Table 7.2 presents an analysis of the individual-level correlates of practicing lawyers' income. These regression analyses relate lawyers' incomes to information about their demographic characteristics, legal education, years of work experience, practice setting, law firm ownership, rank in other kinds of organizations, and client base. Client base is indicated by whether or not the lawyer concentrates in the service of business clients, as defined in table 7.1. The effect of business concentration is estimated in reference to all other client combinations. Practice setting is measured using the classification of table 7.1.[8] Work experience is measured by the number of years since the lawyer took a first job in law after law school. A quadratic term is included in the model to permit the effect of experience to taper off over time (Becker 1993; Stolzenberg 1980). Organizational rank is measured by whether or not the lawyer is an owning partner in a law firm or has supervisory responsibilities in an organization not controlled by lawyers.[9] Law school prestige is indicated by whether the respondent graduated from an elite law school, such as Harvard, a school in the "prestige" category, such as Northwestern, a regional law school, such as Notre Dame, or a local law school, such as John Marshall (see chap. 1).[10] Law school class rank distinguishes respondents who graduated in the top 10 percent of the class or were law review editors from those in the top 11 to 25 percent of the class, as compared to lawyers who did not graduate in the top quarter. The gender, race, and ethnoreligious categories are familiar.[11]

Model 1 in table 7.2 presents the results of regressions of income on practice setting and client base, for each year.[12] Client base and practice setting together explain more of the variation in lawyers' incomes in 1995 than in 1975 (18 percent in 1995 versus 8 percent in 1975). Net of client base, the average 1975 incomes of lawyers in private practice did not differ significantly across the firm size categories. Incomes of internal counsel averaged 34 percent lower than those of lawyers in the smallest firms, controlling for differences in client base. Incomes of government, legal services, and public defenders averaged 49 percent lower than those of lawyers in firms of 2 to 5 lawyers.

In 1995, differentiation in the average incomes of lawyers working in different practice settings is more pronounced. When client base is controlled, solo practitioners' incomes average 42 percent lower than those in the firms of 2 to 5 lawyers, while the incomes of lawyers in firms of 101 to 299 lawyers averaged 29 percent larger and those of lawyers in the largest firms were 47 percent larger. Controlling for client base, internal counsel no longer had lower incomes than lawyers in the smallest firms in 1995, but the disparity between government lawyers' salaries and the pay of lawyers in the smallest

Table 7.2. Regression Analyses of Correlates of Income of Practicing Lawyers, 1975 and 1995

| | Model 1 | | | | Model 2 | | | | Model 3 | | | |
| | 1975 | | 1995 | | 1975 | | 1995 | | 1975 | | 1995 | |
	B	SE	B	SE	B	SE	B	SE	B	SE	B	SE
Intercept	11.486***	.060	11.322***	.097	10.693***	.070	10.391***	.091	10.564***	.087	10.216***	.113
Client type[a]												
Concentrates in service to business	.227***	.066	.138	.080					.112*	.054	.193**	.062
Practice setting[b]												
Solo practice	-.076	.080	-.424***	.122					.202*	.081	-.491***	.099
Firm 6–25 lawyers	-.057	.086	.047	.126					.047	.071	-.109	.096
Firm 26–100 lawyers	.010	.098	.072	.137					.201*	.085	.105	.105
Firm 101–299 lawyers	-.139	.121	.291*	.140					.163	.107	.178	.109
Firm 300 or more lawyers			.472***	.135							.337**	.108
Government, legal aid, public defenders	-.490***	.097	-.604***	.134					-.014	.090	-.253*	.111
Internal counsel	-.339***	.100	-.013	.139					.087	.094	-.081	.126
Experience												
Years since starting first legal job					.063***	.006	.080***	.008	.060***	.006	.100***	.008
Years since starting first legal job squared					-.001***	.000	-.001***	.000	-.001***	.000	-.002***	.000
Organizational rank[c]												
Partner					.475***	.049	.607***	.069	.528***	.064	.333***	.072
Supervising attorney					-.106	.093	.105	.093	-.048	.098	.063	.109
Law school[d]												
Elite					.118	.070	.333***	.086	.082	.071	.218**	.080
Prestige					-.024	.072	.170*	.085	-.030	.072	.076	.079
Local					-.004	.060	-.138*	.061	.029	.060	-.020	.058

Law school class rank[e]						
Top 10% or law review			.147** (.051)	.358*** (.065)	.105* (.053)	.228*** (.062)
Top 11–25%			.078 (.052)	.288*** (.062)	.057* (.052)	.183** (.058)
Gender[f]						
Female			−.271* (.106)	−.131* (.062)	−.231* (.105)	−.100 (.059)
Adjusted R^2	.08	.18	.39	.44	.40	.53
N	654	631	654	631	654	631

Note: The dependent variable is the natural logarithm of income in constant (1995) dollars.

[a] Omitted category is lawyers whose client base was less than 75 percent businesses.

[b] Omitted category is lawyers in firms of 2–5 lawyers.

[c] Omitted category is lawyers who were associates in law firms or who held positions, in government or in offices of internal counsel, that did not involve supervision of other lawyers.

[d] Omitted category is lawyers graduated from regional law schools.

[e] Omitted category is lawyers graduating in the bottom 75 percent of their class in law school.

[f] Omitted category is male lawyers.

*** $p < .001$ ** $p < .01$ * $p < .05$ + $p < .10$

firms had grown even larger, net of client base. In 1995, government lawyers earned incomes that averaged 60 percent lower than those of lawyers in the smallest firms.

Models 2 and 3 in table 7.2 control for racial and ethnoreligious group membership,[13] but these coefficients do not appear in the table. Our random samples include only small numbers of members of most racial and ethnic minority groups, reflecting the composition of the bar (see chap. 1). The coefficients for race and ethnicity are therefore estimated based on small subsamples; because the small number of observations in the minority categories may lead to unreliable point estimates, we elected not to present the coefficients for these variables. We discuss some of these variables below.

Model 2 in table 7.2 reports regressions of income on lawyers' individual characteristics. Lawyers' years of work experience, legal education, organizational rank, gender, and race and ethnicity account for 39 percent of the variance of income in 1975 and 44 percent in 1995. Net of legal work experience, race, gender and education, there was a higher premium for partnership in 1995, in comparison with nonowning positions in law firms and staff positions in government and internal counsel (48 percent in 1975; 61 percent in 1995). Where lawyers were educated and their performance in law school were also more strongly associated with income in 1995 than twenty years previously. In the 1975 survey, lawyers who graduated in the top 10 percent of their class or who were on law review reported incomes that averaged 15 percent higher than lower-ranked lawyers of comparable experience, prestige of law school, gender, and race and ethnicity, but no other educational credentials were statistically significant in 1975, ceteris paribus. In 1995, in contrast, law school reputation was also significantly associated with income, net of other lawyer characteristics. Graduates of elite schools earned incomes that averaged a third higher than the graduates of regional schools, and graduates of prestige law schools enjoyed an average premium of 17 percent, both ceteris paribus. But graduates of local schools experienced a net penalty of about 14 percent in comparison with lawyers from regional schools. The 1995 premium for graduating in the top 10 percent or being on law review (36 percent) was more than double that of 1975, and graduates in the next tier, those in the top 11 to 25 percent of their graduating class, averaged 29 percent higher incomes than comparable graduates in the bottom three quarters. In both surveys, when years of experience, law school prestige, law school performance, organizational rank, and race and ethnicity are controlled, women's incomes averaged significantly lower than men's—by 27 percent in 1975 and by 13 percent in 1995.

Model 3 in table 7.2 combines the variables in models 1 and 2, and accounts for 40 percent of the variation in income in 1975 and 53 percent in 1995. In both years, lawyers who concentrated in service to business earned significantly more than lawyers who did not (11 percent more in 1975; 19 percent more in 1995), net of all other factors—practice setting, years of experience, organizational rank, law school prestige and performance, gender, and race and ethnicity. Differing practice settings were also associated with growing disparities in income, disparities that persist when lawyers' characteristics are controlled. Net of other factors, solo practitioners in 1975 earned incomes 20 percent higher than lawyers in firms of two to five lawyers, as did lawyers in firms of twenty-six to one hundred lawyers, but there were no other significant differences between the smallest firms and other practice settings in 1975. By contrast, solo practitioners' 1995 incomes were 49 percent lower than those of lawyers in the smallest firms, ceteris paribus, and the incomes of lawyers in government, legal aid, and public defender offices were 25 percent lower, while lawyers in the largest firms earned incomes 34 percent higher than those of comparable lawyers in the firms of two to five lawyers.

Thus, the type of practice organization appears to have had increasing impact on lawyers' incomes, while lawyers' positions within their organizations had less. The relative premium paid to partners was smaller in 1995 than in 1975 (33 percent in 1995 versus 53 percent in 1975) when the other variables are controlled. Net of practice setting, client base, and personal characteristics, the small income penalty experienced in 1975 by supervisory lawyers (minus 5 percent) had disappeared by 1995. Elite law school graduates did not command a premium in 1975, when other lawyer characteristics, work setting, and client base are taken into account, but in 1995 they earned 22 percent more than comparable lawyers who had attended regional schools. The increasing premium for class rank observed in model 2 persists when client base and work setting are controlled—graduating in the top 10 percent or on law review added 11 percent in 1975 and 23 percent in 1995 in comparison with the bottom 75 percent of the graduating class. Graduates in the second tier, the top 11 to 25 percent, earned a 6 percent premium in 1975 and an 18 percent premium in 1995.

The pattern of income differentiation between men and women also changed in notable ways. Controlling for where lawyers worked, their positions in those organizations, the kinds of clients they served, their years of experience, and their legal education, women's incomes averaged 23 percent lower than men's in 1975. In 1995, the difference drops below conventional levels of statistical significance. Because we do not have enough cases for the computation of interaction effects, however, we cannot say whether women earn as much as men who have the same attributes. We know that women are unlikely to possess the most advantageous attribute, partnership in a large firm, and so women relatively seldom reach the positions that generate the largest incomes. As we see in the regression models, in 1975 a position as an equity-holding partner in a law firm accounts for the largest share of the explained variance in income, apart from experience, and in 1995 partnership combined with organizational setting (and law school grades) explains most of it. In other words, once we know whether someone has achieved partnership in the right sort of organization (i.e., a profitable one), we know most of what is important in predicting income, given these data. Of the 181 equity-holding partners in the 1995 sample, only fifteen are women—one in a firm of 2 to 5 lawyers, three in firms of 6 to 25, none in firms of 26 to 100, eight in firms of 101 to 299, and three in firms of 300 or more lawyers. Given a random sample with substantially larger numbers of women partners, we could assess whether they do as well as their male counterparts. But the overwhelming fact here is that there are not many female partners (see chaps. 3 and 6).

This pattern is even more extreme for minorities. Of the 181 law firm owners in the 1995 random sample, only three are African American and two are Hispanic. Three of these five partners were in firms with fewer than one hundred lawyers, and only one was in a firm with three hundred or more lawyers (one of the two Hispanics).[14]

In sum, the types of organizations in which lawyers worked came to have greater effects on their pay, even after the differences between organizations in lawyers' work experience and performance in legal education were taken into account. In particular, solo practice and government employment came to pay substantially less than work in small and medium-sized firms, while practice in the largest firms came to pay substantially more.

Our findings here reveal a second pattern of note: Two groups relatively new to the profession, women and blacks, were especially concentrated in the work settings where pay fell the most, in both relative and absolute terms. External social hierarchies penetrate the bar, as they did when Jewish lawyers were segregated in the lowest-paid, least prestigious kinds of legal practice.

Equal Justice

Institutionalized pay inequality can affect legal services in two ways. First, some populations and social purposes may be underserved because low-paid work does not attract enough lawyers. Certainly, critiques of our nation's system of public defense describe perfunctory or otherwise inadequate service to clients, as a result of overwork (Fritsch and Rhode 2001; Reiman 2001). Second, when work is relatively poorly paid, the quality as well as the quantity of the lawyers may suffer: it may be difficult to recruit good lawyers to do that work. In recent cases, capital sentences were imposed on defendants whose lawyers were inexperienced, ignorant of relevant law, drunk in court, or asleep during proceedings (Dieter 1995). The evidence from the Chicago survey suggests that large law firms continue to capture a disproportionate share of the graduates of the more prestigious law schools. What is perhaps surprising is the finding that, despite the growing premium paid by these organizations, their power to attract graduates of top law schools did not significantly increase (see chap. 3, table 3.1).

The ideal of equality under the law—of equal treatment of rich and poor, powerful and oppressed—is often proclaimed,[15] and courts and other legal institutions sometimes proceed as if it is a reality. The formalism of equality commonly extends to the treatment of parties at law as if they possess equal resources, as if each contestant is armed with only the merits of his or her case. But if the pursuit of justice requires resort to law, it will usually be necessary to employ lawyers in that pursuit, and the ability to secure the services of competent and effective counsel often determines who will win and who will lose. Clients with superior resources—money, experience, information—have greater access to lawyers and to well-trained lawyers, and the varying wealth and power of identifiable types of clients result in systematic inequities in the allocation of legal remedies (Auerbach 1976; Galanter 1974; Hadfield 2000; Reiman 2001; R. Smith 1919).

PART III
Lawyers' Lives

Chapter 8
Divided Opinions
With Monique R. Payne

Legal education is said to be formative, training the student to "think like a lawyer" (Blaustein and Porter 1954, 98–100; Miller 1995, 172). The socialization of lawyers into the profession—whether that socialization is carried out in law schools, in work settings, in the courts and other legal institutions, or in the organizations of the bar—might, perhaps, lead lawyers to endorse a distinct set of norms and values. If lawyers do in fact think alike (or even substantially alike), that could facilitate the process of conflict resolution. Lawyers who share basic values and common understandings about the legitimate processes of government might be more likely to resolve their clients' differences. Conversely, dissensus on fundamental assumptions would probably reduce the likelihood of finding a mutually acceptable result.

The probability that the bar would mobilize for collective action to achieve specific goals would also be enhanced by a common viewpoint. That is, if lawyers agree on social issues, bar associations may be more likely to formulate legislative agendas or to evaluate candidates for the bench definitively (Auerbach 1976; Halliday 1987; Powell 1988). Whether effective collective action by the bar is to be desired, however, is another matter. In 2001, officials in the White House decided that the American Bar Association had a pronounced liberal bias, and the president therefore terminated cooperation with the ABA in the review of proposed appointments of federal judges, a role that the ABA had played for decades (Lewis 2001; Goldstein

2001). In the view of the administration, the ABA had a position on the issues that, if not monolithic, was at least clearly identifiable.[1] The question of whether the legal profession has a distinct, identifiable point of view on public issues was, then, a question of some moment.

Louis Brandeis urged lawyers to assert their independence and to take into account the public interest (Brandeis 1905; J. Frank 1965; Spillenger 1996), but he believed that too few did so:

> [I]nstead of holding a position of independence, between the wealthy and the people, prepared to curb the excesses of either, able lawyers have, to a great extent, allowed themselves to become adjuncts of great corporations and have neglected the obligation to use their powers for the protection of the people. We hear much of the "corporation lawyer" and far too little of the "people's lawyer." (Brandeis 1905, as quoted in Auerbach 1976, 34–35)

Lawyers are, of course, heavily represented among professional politicians and public officeholders, but it is less clear whether they serve their own interests or those of their clients or constituents in such positions (Eulau and Sprague 1964). In relatively rare cases, lawyers dedicate their careers to specific political goals and thus become "cause lawyers" (Sarat and Scheingold 1998, 2001; Southworth 1993, 1996, 1999). But most lawyers probably do not see themselves as political actors, even if their work has important political and social consequences (Gordon 1988, 1990; Luban 1988; Macaulay 1979; R. Rosen 1984).

In their daily work, lawyers serve particular interests, and there are usually opposing interests. There are good guys and bad guys, and which are which depends upon one's point of view. How lawyers feel about the distribution of wealth and power might, therefore, affect their choice of clients and their attitudes toward the work. The causal arrow (if there is one) could even point in both directions: while lawyers may choose a clientele that suits their predispositions, the choice of clients may also come to influence the lawyer's worldview. It is probably difficult to continue working for someone over the longer term while regarding them as abhorrent. (Difficult work, however, is sometimes highly compensated.) In constructing arguments designed to support client interests, the lawyer may find it comfortable to identify with those arguments. It may also be functional—that is, it may make the lawyer's presentation of the case more effective. So it is plausible to hypothesize that lawyers adapt their own views on social issues to those of their clients, but "professional independence" is also highly valued.

The Chicago Data

The 1975 and 1995 Chicago surveys included questions about the lawyers' social and political values, and several of the questions were used in both surveys. We are, therefore, able to assess changes over the two decades. Given the entry into the profession during that period of large numbers of women and minorities, groups strongly identified with liberal political values (Manza and Brooks 1999), we might expect a shift toward more liberal positions. But, as we saw in chapter 2, a larger share of Chicago lawyers worked for businesses in 1995 than in 1975, which would tend to move their values in the opposite, more conservative direction, especially on issues of economic regulation.

Figure 8.1 indicates the political affiliations of the 1975 and 1995 samples. Note that, if independents leaning toward one party or the other are grouped with the partisans, there is virtually no change in the total preference for either party—57 percent preferred the Democrats in 1975 and 55 percent in 1995, while 30 percent and 28 percent, respectively, favored Republicans. Given Chicago politics, it is probably not surprising that Democrats outnumbered Republicans by almost two to one. If we focus on independents of various stripes, however, we see a more nuanced picture. The number of independents leaning Democratic declines substantially, from 20 percent of the 1975 sample to only 12 percent in 1995. The first Mayor Daley, who was unpopular with many liberals, including elements within the bar (Powell 1979), was still in office at the time of the 1975 survey. Many Chicago lawyers at that time characterized themselves as independents locally, while tending to prefer Democrats for national and statewide office (Heinz and Laumann 1982, 11–14). The other two independent categories shown in figure 8.1 remained stable, while the total of those identifying themselves as either Democrats or strong Democrats increased from 37 percent in 1975 to 43 percent in 1995, suggesting that with the passing of the first Mayor Daley the liberal independents became Democrats.

Although this tabulation of party preference suggests relatively little movement, and such movement as there was appears to be primarily a change in the choice of label by some of the liberals, our questions regarding particular social and economic values disclose more substantive changes. In addition to the amount and direction of change from 1975 to 1995, however, we are interested in the degree of consensus within the profession. We want to explore the extent to which lawyers agree or disagree on matters in which the law plays a major role.

Figure 8.1. Political Party Preferences, 1975 and 1995

1975

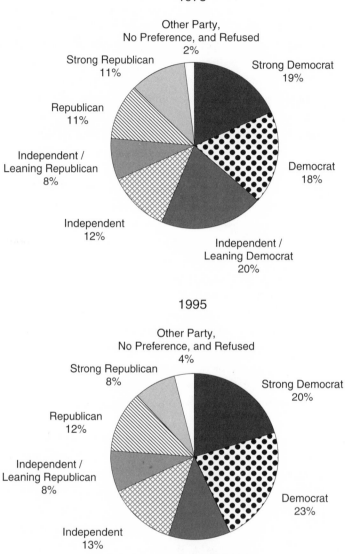

Other Party,
No Preference, and Refused
2%

Strong Republican
11%

Strong Democrat
19%

Republican
11%

Independent /
Leaning Republican
8%

Democrat
18%

Independent
12%

Independent /
Leaning Democrat
20%

1995

Other Party,
No Preference, and Refused
4%

Strong Republican
8%

Strong Democrat
20%

Republican
12%

Independent /
Leaning Republican
8%

Democrat
23%

Independent
13%

Independent /
Leaning Democrat
12%

Figure 8.2 summarizes data derived from questions dealing with economic values, the distribution of wealth, and the regulation of economic enterprise. These items were used in both surveys. (A second set of items, presented in fig. 8.3, deals with social values and was used only in the 1995 survey.) The statements are numbered in the figures for ease of reference.

On the first statement, "differences in income among occupations should be reduced," there was little disagreement in either year. Only 14 percent agreed in 1975 and only 16 percent in 1995. Chicago lawyers did not appear to be inclined to bite the hand that feeds them. They knew they were relatively well-to-do, despite income differences within the legal profession. On the distribution of wealth more generally, however, we see a much different pattern. Majorities in both years disagreed with the second statement, "economic profits are by and large justly distributed in the U.S. today," and only about a quarter agreed. This appears to be a striking condemnation of the "justice" of the U.S. economic system. On neither of these first two items was there appreciable change in the distribution of responses from 1975 to 1995.

A strong majority endorsed the third statement, on government's role in assisting the poor ("one of the most important roles of government is to help those who cannot help themselves, such as the poor, the disadvantaged, and the unemployed"), but the total percentage agreeing or strongly agreeing with the proposition declined by a full ten percentage points, from 78 percent in 1975 to 68 percent in 1995. On this item, therefore, there was clear movement in a more conservative direction. That was also true on the fourth statement—"all Americans should have equal access to quality medical care regardless of ability to pay." Again, strong majorities endorsed the proposition in both years, but the majority decreased by 19 percentage points, from 87 percent in 1975 to 68 percent in 1995. This decline may be attributable to the fact that the 1995 survey came in the wake of the Clinton administration's unsuccessful legislative initiatives on health care, which raised the political visibility of the issue. Still, even in 1995, more than two-thirds of the lawyers endorsed universal medical care and less than a fifth disagreed.

On the clearest test of support for the free market (statement 5 in fig. 8.2), however, Chicago lawyers were quite evenly divided. When asked whether "the protection of consumer interests is best insured by vigorous competition among sellers rather than by federal government intervention and regulation on behalf of consumers," 46 percent of the respondents endorsed the proposition in both years, while 44 percent and 43 percent, respectively, disagreed. Thus, this question split the profession down the middle. The

Figure 8.2. Economic Values, 1975 and 1995 (percentages)

1. Differences in income among occupations should be reduced.

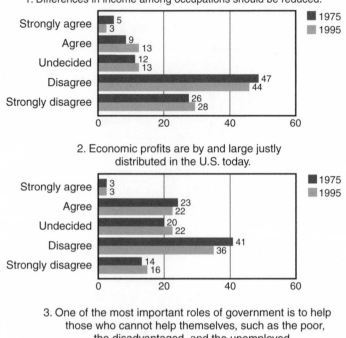

2. Economic profits are by and large justly distributed in the U.S. today.

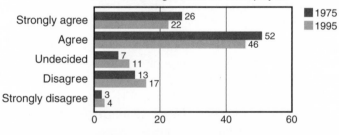

3. One of the most important roles of government is to help those who cannot help themselves, such as the poor, the disadvantaged, and the unemployed.

4. All Americans should have equal access to quality medical care regardless of ability to pay.

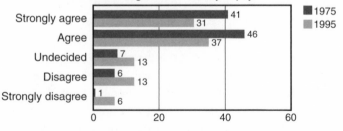

Figure 8.2 *continued*

5. The protection of consumer interests is best insured by vigorous competition among sellers rather than by federal government intervention and regulation on behalf of consumers.

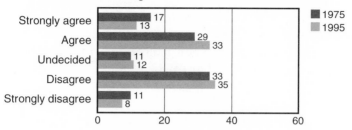

6. The gains that labor unions make for their members help to make the country more prosperous.

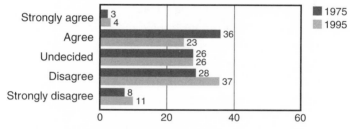

7. There is too much power concentrated in the hands of a few large companies for the good of the country.

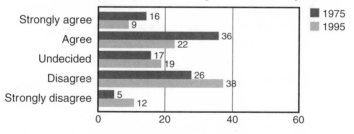

responses in 1995, however, did moderate a bit—there was some movement away from the ends of the scale (the "strongly agree" and "strongly disagree" positions). The profession was also split on statement 6, that "the gains that labor unions make for their members help to make the country more prosperous." In 1975, the division was quite even, with 39 percent endorsing the pro-union position and 36 percent disagreeing. In 1995, however, there was a clear shift to a more negative view of unions, with only 27 percent agreeing and 48 percent disagreeing with the statement. Moreover, on statement 7, the last of the economic items, we again see a conservative shift. In 1975, a majority of the lawyers thought that "there is too much power concentrated in the hands of a few large companies for the good of the country"—a total of 52 percent agreed with the statement, while 31 percent disagreed. In 1995, that reversed—31 percent agreed and 50 percent disagreed.[2] Thus, an increasing share of Chicago lawyers were inclined to be supportive of big business, while fewer supported unions. Recall that in 1995 a considerably larger share of the effort of Chicago lawyers was devoted to the representation of big business than was the case in 1975 (see chap. 2). The shift of political views in a more conservative direction tended to produce greater disagreement within the profession on issues such as health care, but the principal finding here is that, despite substantial (and continuing) agreement on issues concerning the distribution of wealth and the role of the state in providing for the poor, the Chicago bar was deeply split on questions concerning government regulation of business enterprise.

In 1995, they were also divided on whether "affirmative action programs have excessively restricted freedom to hire and promote the best qualified individuals" (see statement 8 in fig. 8.3). Equal numbers strongly agreed and strongly disagreed. There was also a split within the bar as to whether lawyers "should be required" to provide "uncompensated public service" (pro bono work), statement 11; half of all respondents rejected the proposition while only 35 percent supported it. A similar plurality within the profession disagreed with proposition 9, that record albums should have warning labels if the song lyrics include "offensive references to sex, drugs, or violence"—49 percent rejected this, while 34 percent supported it. The remaining item, dealing with parental notification before an abortion is performed on a minor, was rejected by a margin of more than two to one, 59 percent to 25 percent. On these social issues, as on economic values, lawyers certainly did not speak with one voice. The next question, then, is where the lines of division occur.

Differences among Types of Lawyers

Lawyers' positions on social and political values might, of course, be influenced both by their professional allegiances and by their personal backgrounds. Hypothetically, two lawyers who work for General Motors, one an Episcopalian who grew up in a staunchly Republican suburb and was then educated at Choate and Princeton, and the other an Irish Catholic who was raised in the inner city and then studied at Notre Dame, might or might not agree. Age, gender, race, family background, clientele, and practice setting could all plausibly be thought to be associated with positions on these political and social issues.

Figure 8.3. Social Values, 1995 (percentages)

8. Affirmative action programs have excessively restricted freedom
to hire and promote the best qualified individuals.

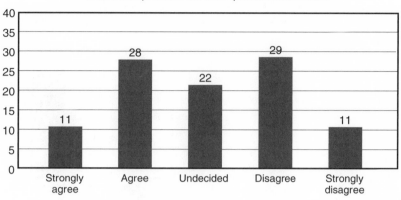

9. The law should require warning labels on record albums informing potential
purchasers (and/or their parents) that the lyrics of the songs
include offensive references to sex, drugs, or violence.

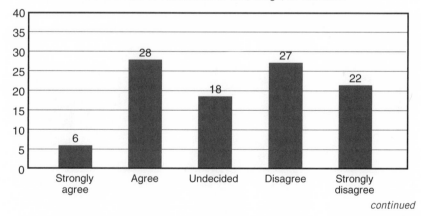

continued

To explore the differences among lawyers and to identify correlates of
those differences, we constructed an "economic liberalism" scale using the
seven economic values questions in figure 8.2. The five agree-disagree positions on each question were coded with a score of one for the most conservative position and a score of five for the most liberal position (in conventional
U.S. political terms).[3] From 1975 to 1995, the overall mean score on this scale
declined from 3.27 to 3.06, moving from a position that was (moderately, but
distinctly) toward the liberal side to one that was nearly in the center. As a
higher percentage of Chicago lawyers became Democrats, as women entered
the profession in large numbers, and as the rapid growth of the bar reduced

Figure 8.3 *continued*

10. The law should require that physicians and hospitals, at least seven days prior to performing an abortion on a patient under the age of 18 years, inform the parents of the patient about the proposed abortion.

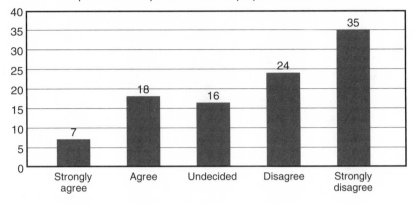

11. All lawyers should be required to spend a specified number of hours doing uncompensated public service (pro bono work) or to hire some other lawyer to perform that service for them (i.e., by buying "pro bono credits").

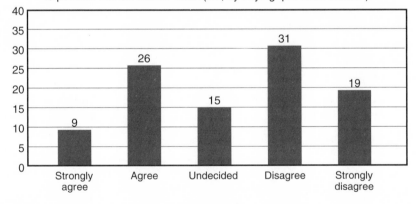

the mean age, lawyers overall nonetheless became more conservative—at least, as measured by this economic liberalism scale. Let us explore that.

In 1975, the youngest lawyers had the most liberal scores on the economic liberalism scale (ages 25 to 29 = 3.50 mean, 30 to 34 = 3.47); older lawyers were more conservative (55 to 59 = 3.04 and 60 to 64 = 3.09). Scores declined with age in a rather orderly fashion. But in 1995 the youngest lawyers were among the most conservative—the scores of those age 25 to 29 were much the same as those of the 55-to-64 group, while those in their mid-to-late 40s were the most liberal.[4] Thus, the same cohort that was liberal in 1975 (those who went to college and law school during the Vietnam War years of the late 1960s and early 1970s) was still distinctly liberal twenty years later.

Women were significantly more liberal than men in both years, but recall that there were only 30 women in the 1975 sample. Their 1975 mean score was 3.67, which fell to 3.31 for the 213 women in the 1995 sample, a decline of .36. The scores of men also declined—from 3.26 to 2.95, a decline of .31. Thus, despite the women's move in a more conservative direction, the 1995 women were much more liberal than the men. The substantial numbers of women in the later sample moderate what would otherwise have been a more dramatic shift toward conservative positions by the bar overall.

Not surprisingly, minorities have more liberal scores than do whites, by a margin of about .5 in 1975 and .3 in 1995. Some of the narrowing of the gap between whites and minorities is attributable to the presence in the 1995 sample of Asians and Hispanics, whose views on economic issues are more similar to those of whites than are the views of African Americans. Of the ethnoreligious groups, type I Protestants (Episcopalians, Presbyterians, and Congregationalists, see chap. 3) had the most conservative scores in both surveys (2.98 in 1975 and 2.80 in 1995). This is somewhat at odds with national findings that old-line Protestants have moved toward support of Democratic presidential candidates, while fundamentalist Protestants have become Republican stalwarts (Manza and Brooks 1999). Type II Protestants (all other Protestant denominations) were also near the conservative end of the scale (at 3.06) in 1975, while Catholics were then more liberal (3.24). In 1995, however, Catholics were more conservative (2.98) than type II Protestants (3.09). Jewish respondents, like Catholics, had liberal scores in 1975 (3.39) but moderated in 1995 (3.11). This may reflect the movement of both Jewish and Catholic lawyers into large-firm, corporate practice. Lawyers with no religious affiliation were the most liberal in both years, probably indicating a generally antiestablishment stance (see chap. 9).

In both years, lawyers who came from more privileged family backgrounds tended to have lower, more conservative scores, though not by a large amount. The most conservative were those whose fathers were lawyers (3.13 in 1975, 2.92 in 1995), followed by those who had fathers in other professional, technical, or managerial positions (3.28 in 1975, 3.04 in 1995), while those whose fathers pursued occupations of lower socioeconomic status were the most liberal in both years (3.33 and 3.17).

The type of organization in which the lawyers worked was also significantly associated with their views. Apart from categories with very few respondents (judges, law professors, legal services lawyers), the most liberal scores in both years were those of government-employed lawyers and solo practitioners. Government lawyers were the only category that did not move in a clearly conservative direction over the twenty years—their mean scores were 3.36 and 3.34, an insignificant difference. Lawyers in large firms moved from near the middle of the distribution to the most conservative position. In 1975, their mean (3.24) was just below the overall mean for the full sample (3.27). By 1995, however, the score of large-firm lawyers had dropped by 0.42 (to 2.82). Internal counsel, who anchored the conservative end of the scale in 1975 (3.14), were nearly as conservative as those in large firms in 1995 (2.86). Thus, the views of Chicago lawyers became more closely aligned with those of their clients, and the gap between those in government and those in corporate practice became a gulf.

If we examine the scores of lawyers who devoted a quarter or more of their time to particular fields of practice, we again observe the congruence between economic values and type of practice.[5] For example, on the question regarding whether consumer interests were more effectively protected by competition or by government regulation, 77 percent of the respondents who devoted a quarter or more of their time to trademarks and copyrights preferred competition, as did 74 percent of the patent lawyers and 72 percent of those in state and local tax work, while only 26 percent of the divorce practitioners and 25 percent of the civil rights/civil liberties lawyers took that position. Fields with notably conservative scores in one or both years include public utilities, patents, antitrust defense, securities, business litigation, banking, and general corporate practice. Those with especially liberal scores are civil rights, employment law on the employee or union side, general family practice, and criminal defense.

The influence of client type can also be seen if we compare scores in fields where lawyers representing plaintiffs are separated from those representing defendants. In the 1995 data, lawyers on the plaintiff side of environmental law (those who pursued complaints against alleged polluters) scored 3.35 on the economic liberalism scale, while those who worked for defendants in environmental cases scored 2.92. In employment law, lawyers on the management side had a mean of 3.06, while those who represented employees or unions had a mean of 3.66. The difference between the plaintiff and defense sides of antitrust work is huge (3.52 versus 2.62), but only a few lawyers devoted 25 percent or more of their time to those fields, so the scores may not be reliable. The differences in personal injury work and criminal law are less extreme, but still discernable—personal injury lawyers representing plaintiffs scored 3.07 and defense lawyers 2.89, while prosecutors scored 3.23 (substantially more liberal than the mean of the bar overall) and criminal defense lawyers scored 3.36. In real estate practice, although the two types of clients are not necessarily antagonistic, lawyers handling real estate transactions for businesses had a mean of 3.05 and those representing individuals scored 3.35.

Adaptation to Client Values?

The data thus show clear differences in the values of lawyers engaged in particular types of legal work, and those differences indicate alignment between the lawyers and the positions of their clients. The structure is evident, but what is the process by which it comes about? Do lawyers choose to work for clients with whom they already have sympathy or some sense of identity, or do the lawyers take the work they can get (perhaps the most remunerative work) and then develop affinity with the clients after having advocated their interests? Selective attrition from the fields would also produce the appearance of adaptation—that is, lawyers who are uncomfortable representing a particular clientele might move into a different specialty. Differences among the fields over time could be affected, of course, by generational differences in social values, the occurrence of historical events, or the strength of the markets for varying types of legal work. If demand for intellectual property work, for example, increased greatly, some lawyers would be likely to move into that field (perhaps without much regard for their social or political values). Conversely, one cannot do work for which there is no demand. Opportunities in fields may be time specific, so that lawyers who graduated from law school in the 1980s may have had a different menu of choices than did those who entered practice earlier and then became locked in by institutional investment or personal circumstances. Therefore, cross-sectional data, even from different times, are not adequate for the evaluation of all the possibilities.

We can, however, look at whether the values of practitioners in contrasting fields vary with the age of the lawyers. Although this is an imperfect measure of adaptation to client interests, it can tell us whether the difference between the fields is large even among the youngest lawyers, who have not been in practice long, thus suggesting that lawyers select a clientele to which they are favorably predisposed. Or, in the alternative, if the difference between the fields is small in the youngest age group but greater among older lawyers, that could suggest either selective attrition from the fields or adaptation to the views of clients over time. To explore these possibilities, we identified respondents who devoted a quarter or more of their time to a set of fields representing business interests—antitrust defense, banking, patents, public utilities, securities, business litigation, and general corporate practice.

We then divided the respondents into four age groups and compared the economic liberalism scores of respondents practicing in the business fields with those in other fields. The findings are presented in figure 8.4.

In each age group, lawyers working in the business fields have more conservative scores on the economic values questions than do those practicing in other fields (see the Difference, Business vs. Other Fields graph in the figure), and that the oldest and youngest age groups are, in both sets of fields, the most conservative. The difference between business fields and other fields is almost as large in the youngest age group as it is in the oldest groups, suggesting that ideology influences recruitment to the fields. In three of the four age groups, the difference between the two sets of fields is 0.38 or more, a considerable average difference on a five-point scale. The exception is the 32–39 category, where the difference is only 0.11. Almost all the lawyers in that age group entered the bar in 1982 to 1989, a period of very rapid growth in corporate law practice and of consequent high demand for personnel in large firms. The opportunities in corporate work at that time and a growing gap between earnings in corporate practice and in other fields (see chap. 7) appear to have offset the ideological preferences of lawyers seeking employment during the 1980s.[6] Thus, the difference between the fields is large even among the youngest lawyers and remains at about the same order of magnitude in the older groups, but it may be affected by fluctuations in demand for lawyers in the various fields.

As we saw in chapter 3, the organizational settings in which law is practiced serve different clienteles and recruit their lawyers disproportionately from distinct social groups. When we observe correspondence between lawyers' social values and those of their clients, therefore, the affinity might be attributed either to the lawyers' professional roles or to selective recruitment of lawyers known to be sympathetic to the views of a particular clientele. If a law firm or other employer knows that its clients will feel more comfortable working with conservative Republicans, it would be rational for the organization to hire job candidates of that persuasion. Because social and political characteristics of the lawyers are associated with types of practice settings, then, it may be difficult to sort out the effects.

To address that task, we computed multiple regression models using both personal background characteristics and practice characteristics to predict economic liberalism scores.[7] In one model, we used only personal characteristics; in another, we added legal profession variables (law school, law practice income, practice setting, organizational position, and practice in a "wealth-conserving"[8] field). The models account for significant but quite modest percentages of the total variance in economic values in both years.

Figure 8.4. Economic Liberalism Scores of Business Fields versus Other Fields, by Four Age Groups, 1995

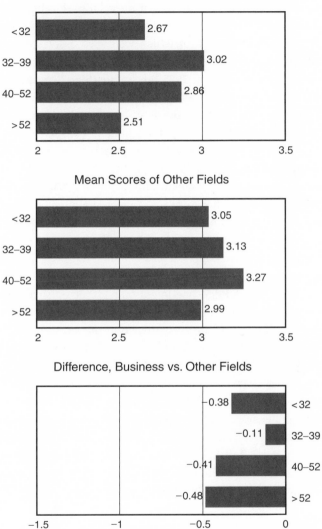

In 1975, personal characteristics alone explain 14 percent of the variance and the law practice variables add another 7 percent. In 1995, personal characteristics predict somewhat less well (11 percent) and the practice characteristics again contribute an additional 7 percent. In both years, in both models, gender, race, and age are significant, but the direction of the age effect changes. In 1975, older lawyers had lower, more conservative scores, and in 1995 older lawyers were more liberal. As might be expected, women and African American lawyers had more liberal scores in both years, controlling for the other variables. Three other personal characteristics are also significant in both years—age squared, indicating that the relationship between age and economic liberalism is curvilinear, and two of the ethnoreligious categories, Jewish and nonreligious, both of which were also associated with liberal views. Catholic lawyers were significantly more liberal than the reference category (type I Protestants) in 1975 but not in 1995. Relatively few of the other variables are significant—having a father employed in a lower-status occupation was associated with more liberal scores in both years, while graduates of local law schools were significantly more conservative in 1975 but not in 1995, and higher income was strongly associated with more conservative scores in both years, as was employment in a wealth-oriented field. In 1975, employment in government and in the judge/law professor/legal services category were both significant in the liberal direction, and a nonlegal job was significantly conservative. In 1995, the only practice setting that was significant, controlling for other variables, was internal counsel, and it was associated with conservative scores.

Given the numbers of women and minorities entering the legal profession between 1975 and 1995, one might have expected social background variables to make a larger contribution to the prediction of responses in the second survey. (There was greater variance in the social background data in 1995 as a result of the increasing diversity.) But we found the opposite. This finding probably reflects the fact that, in 1995, lawyers with distinct social background characteristics were less systematically spread across the various practice settings and political types of clients. Thus, for example, as the economic views of inside counsel became more consistent (as noted above, this variable became significant in 1995), their social characteristics became more diverse. In 1975, only 3 percent of inside counsel were female; in 1995, 46 percent were. In 1975, only 1 percent of inside counsel were members of minority groups; in 1995, 10 percent were.

Social Values

Unlike the economic values items, the four social values questions (see fig. 8.3) cannot validly be combined into a single index. They do not satisfy the statistical criterion for "scaling," which means that opinions on these issues vary independently of each other. We have, therefore, examined differences within the bar on each of the questions.

Personal background characteristics are clearly stronger predictors of the lawyers' positions on the social issues than are practice characteristics. On all four questions, for example, Catholics had significantly conservative scores: they were more likely to believe that affirmative action programs have been excessive, more likely to favor requiring warning labels on record albums and parental notification of proposed abortions, and more likely to oppose mandatory provision of pro bono services. On three of the four questions, women were disproportionately likely to take the opposite, liberal position. The only issue on which women did not differ significantly from male lawyers was record warning labels. There was, however, an age difference on that question. Older lawyers were more likely to favor requiring warnings on albums with offensive content.

Race was significant on affirmative action and the pro bono service issue, but not on warning labels or abortion. More specifically, 36 percent of white lawyers but 64 percent of Hispanics and 91 percent of African Americans disagreed or strongly disagreed with the proposition that affirmative action programs had excessively restricted freedom to hire and promote. A majority of female lawyers (54 percent), but only 35 percent of men, disagreed with the proposition condemning affirmative action. In the ethnoreligious categories, 47 percent of nonreligious respondents and 45 percent and 49 percent of types I and II Protestants, respectively, supported affirmative action programs, as compared to 34 percent of Catholics and 35 percent of Jewish respondents. On the parental notification of abortion issue, only 12 percent of women but 31 percent of men favored notification. It was supported by 41 percent of Catholics but only 12 percent of nonreligious respondents. On the proposal to require warning labels on records, lawyers under age thirty-five were about half as likely to support the proposal (25 percent) as were those fifty-five or older (49 percent). Of Jewish and nonreligious respondents, 30 percent and 26 percent, respectively, supported the proposal, but 42 percent of Catholics thought it was a good idea. The proposal that pro bono service be required was endorsed by 61 percent of those in racial minority groups, but by only 31 percent of white respondents. It was supported by 47 percent of women, 40 percent and 41 percent of types I and II Protestants, but only 28 percent of Catholics and 30 percent of men. Thus, race, gender, and ethnoreligious categories manifest strong differences on social issues. These differences, of course, may be affected by their differential distribution across practice settings.

As in the analysis of the economic liberalism scores, it is important to assess the relative contributions of these variables when they are considered simultaneously. Since the items do not "scale," we cannot use models pre-dicting a combined social values score. As a diagnostic tool, therefore, we computed two regression models analyzing responses to the affirmative ac-tion item, the question on which the profession was most evenly divided. We used the same procedure as that employed for the economic liberalism scores—that is, the first model included only personal characteristics, and the second added legal profession variables.

The regression analyses indicate that social background variables have the larger share of the explanatory power. The model including only those variables explains 11.5 percent of the total variance, and the addition of le-gal profession variables increases the amount of explained variance by only 2.5 percent. Law school category, income, firm size, practice setting, and the organizational position of the respondents are all nonsignificant. Of the profession variables, only the one indicating that the respondent was retired or unemployed was systematically related to affirmative action responses (at the .05 level or better), controlling for the other variables. It was associated with rejection of the proposition that affirmative action programs "have ex-cessively restricted freedom to hire and promote" (note that this is net of age and race effects). The variables of principal importance here are clearly gender and race, both of which are highly significant. The interpretation of this finding would seem to be straightforward: social groups that have benefited directly from affirmative action were more likely to favor it. Un-like economic values, where lawyers' views appear to have been associated with client interests, social values were little affected by practice setting or the lawyers' work.[9]

We hypothesize mutually reinforcing processes. Lawyers choose practice settings with which they have affinity, and the organizations select lawyers who will fit in. Law firms specialize in a particular clientele and achieve efficiencies by developing a "brand identity" among those clients (see chap. 12), the firms then recruit lawyers who will be comfortable with the clientele and with whom the clients will in turn be comfortable, and the increasing identification of the organization with a limited set of interests creates de-mand (both within the organization and among the clientele) for adherence to a distinct ideological stance. When there is a clearly defined party line, there may well be pressure to hew to that line. In practice settings where the clients are more diverse, however, we would not expect to see such strong incentives for conformity to client views. Similarly, the degree of pressure to conform will probably be shaped by power relationships between lawyers and clients. If the clients are powerful and the lawyers are dependent upon them, we would expect the lawyers to be more likely to adhere to client positions. If the clients are of lower socioeconomic status or the demand for the lawyers' services is strong and secure, then the lawyers may feel more free to express contrary views and to act independently.

Conclusion

Why do we care what patent lawyers think about abortion? Does it make any difference what a lawyer's views are if the issue never arises in the lawyer's own work? We think it does matter, for two reasons. First, the degree to which lawyers are of one mind on questions of public policy affects the social integration of the profession, one of the major themes of this book. The patterns of consensus or dissensus identify lines of affinity and division—by gender, race, age, religion, type of practice, or type of clientele. Second, given the positions of community leadership held by lawyers (see chap. 9) and their access to officeholders, a unified profession might be able to wield considerable power, for good or ill. Lawyers, if united, could be a moral force as well as a more narrowly instrumental one on issues such as abortion or affirmative action or the distribution of wealth, in one direction or the other. Whether one thinks that lawyer solidarity would be desirable, however, probably depends upon whether one predicts that the profession's position would be aligned with one's own.

We found a high level of agreement among Chicago lawyers on some issues. On the proposition endorsing "equal access to quality medical care regardless of ability to pay," 87 percent of the respondents agreed or strongly agreed and only 7 percent disagreed in 1975; in 1995, although there was an increase in dissensus, those in agreement still outnumbered the dissenters by more than three to one. On the question concerning parental notification of abortion, the opponents of notification outnumbered the supporters by more than two to one. But on most of the issues presented—including affirmative action, warning labels on record albums, mandatory pro bono work, and issues concerning support for large companies and the free market versus government regulation—Chicago lawyers were sharply divided.

If more lawyers represented clients who had a stake in the two issues on which there was a high level of agreement, abortion and access to medical care, perhaps the lawyers would align themselves with their clients and would then become divided by the conflicting interests. The lack of client interest or sponsorship may also explain why the organized bar has not been politically active on these issues, even though most lawyers (in Chicago, at least) appear to be in agreement on them. In the twenty years between 1975 and 1995, the Chicago Bar Association did not lobby on abortion or file amicus briefs in related cases. Individual lawyers did, of course, play important roles, some on each side, but the bar as a whole did not. When lawyers represent the National Abortion Rights Action League or Americans United for Life, they have the potential to influence both the councils of the organization and its external political activities. But note that it is the group affiliation that makes the lawyers influential. Groups are the principal actors in politics (Bentley 1908; Truman 1951). If the internal politics of the organized bar were different, it might more often choose to act as an interest group, but it has picked its fights very selectively and cautiously. It seldom engages when it is not directly affected.

The difference in motivation between lawyers engaged in religious issues and those serving businesses is sometimes characterized as one of ideological commitment versus professionalism. Business lawyers are seen as more detached from their clients, "just doing their job," and no doubt many of them are. A few of these lawyers represent the National Association of Manufacturers or the Chamber of Commerce, and more represent particular trade associations, but most business lawyers simply do the legal work of some set of companies. Lawyers representing religious groups, however, are often seen as ideologues, and they may in fact embrace a more distinctive range of views (Heinz, Paik, and Southworth 2003). When ideological motivation is salient, the usual assumption is that the lawyer's position on the issue is formed first, and that affiliation with a group then follows. But organizations are important not only because they aggregate individual sentiment, marshal opinion, and make political activity more efficient and effective, but because they transform and redirect individual preferences. Association with others of a similar bent assures the group member that his own views are not idiosyncratic, it validates his perceptions of the world, and it encourages him to believe that, by making common cause, his own positions may be advanced. Indeed, association does even more than that: communication within organizations corrects deviation and it rewards conformity and purity. True believers are admitted to the inner circle, the core. Revisionists are criticized or shunned. Thus, as ideological uncertainty and inconsistency are constrained, group positions become increasingly polarized (Haslam 2001; Friedkin 1999; Moscovici and Zavalloni 1969). The interest group is different than the sum of its parts.

But perhaps there is something distinctive about lawyers as lawyers, a habit of mind, that gives them a particular political valence. Some commentators believe that lawyers, in their political roles at least, behave in distinct, identifiable ways. This proposition has been referred to as a thesis of "lawyer exceptionalism" (Heinz, Paik, and Southworth 2003). In *The High Priests of*

American Politics (1995), Mark Miller includes a chapter titled "Are Lawyers Really Different from Nonlawyers?" and he answers the question "yes." He concludes:

> Thinking like a lawyer involves accepting a narrow legal ideology, and this legal ideology pervades our American political institutions because these institutions are dominated, and have long been dominated, by lawyer members. This legal ideology is internalized by law students during law school, and stays with the lawyers throughout their professional careers . . . The effects of having so many lawyer-politicians are widespread; the American legal ideology is pervasive in the American public policy process. (172)

What is the content of this "legal ideology"? Miller argues that it is a "preference for procedure and rights-oriented decision-making processes" (172), and "produces a government that is preoccupied with the procedurally oriented, incrementalist myth of rights, instead of with broader substantive questions of public policy" (174). But lawyers do take positions on pressing issues. As political participants, lawyers advocate for and against building airports, reforming schools, harvesting old-growth timber, and imposing a moratorium on the death penalty. If they can use procedural arguments to advance their goals, they do so—but they have substantive goals, whether their own or those of their clients. In answer to the questions in the Chicago surveys, lawyers did not for the most part choose the middle, neutral position (see figs. 8.2 and 8.3). They did not say they were indifferent, or that they would be satisfied with whatever outcome might be produced by the process (legal or political). Indeed, lawyers are often accused of just the opposite failing—that they are contentious and litigate every issue to the bitter end. Chicago lawyers did not hesitate to endorse stands on the issues, but their stands were often at odds.

If the lawyers' views, and the divisions among them, merely reproduce the prevailing public opinion, then perhaps lawyers serve only to reinforce the existing division of interests. But there is some evidence that the positions of Chicago lawyers diverge from those of the general population.[10] In 1975, the Opinion Research Corporation conducted a telephone survey of a national sample of 1,077 adults and asked whether they agreed or disagreed with the statement, "There is too much power concentrated in the hands of a few large companies for the good of the nation"[11] (Roper Center). Fully 78 percent of the national sample agreed, as compared to 52 percent of Chicago lawyers in 1975 (see fig. 8.2). In 1995, Princeton Survey Research Associates used a variant of this question in a national telephone survey of 1,800 adults

(Roper Center). They posed it as a pair of alternative views: "Too much power is concentrated in the hands of a few large companies, or the largest companies do not have too much power." Three-quarters of the national sample adopted the position that large companies had too much power—nearly the same percentage as in 1975—but only 31 percent of Chicago lawyers held that view in 1995. Thus, at both times, lawyers were considerably more supportive of big business than was the general population, and by 1995 the percentage of the public that was critical of the power of large companies was more than twice the percentage among the lawyers. The increase in the lawyers' expression of support for big business may correspond to the change in their clientele. In 1975, 53 percent of the effort of Chicago lawyers was devoted to business but almost two-thirds was devoted to the corporate client sector in 1995 (see chap. 2, table 2.1).

As we have seen, Chicago lawyers were evenly divided in 1975 on the proposition that "the protection of consumer interests is best insured by vigorous competition among sellers rather than by federal government intervention and regulation on behalf of consumers," and in 1995 the split within the profession was essentially unchanged (see fig. 8.2). The stability of the division within the bar is especially noteworthy in light of data suggesting a large shift of public opinion in a more conservative direction from 1975 to 1995, perhaps attributable to the "Reagan revolution." In 1975, the Opinion Research Corporation asked a national sample of 1,209 adults whether they agreed with the following statement: "Government regulation is a good way of making business more responsive to people's needs" (Roper Center). The sample endorsed that view by a margin of more than two to one—60 percent agreed with it and only 27 percent disagreed. In 1995, Princeton Survey Research Associates used a related but not directly comparable question in a telephone survey of 2,000 adults: "Tell me whether the first statement or the second statement comes closer to your own views—even if neither is exactly right. The pair is . . . government regulation of business is necessary to protect the public interest, or government regulation of business usually does more harm than good" (Roper Center). In the political climate of that time, 45 percent of the sample endorsed the pro-regulation position and 50 percent said that the antigovernment view was closer to their own. Recall that in the 1994 midterm elections Republicans took control of both the Senate and the House (that was the election featuring Newt Gingrich's Contract with America). Thus, there is some evidence that lawyers' views, on the whole, may be more consistently sympathetic to big business than those of the general public, which may be more volatile. The lawyers' views, sharply divided even on fundamental issues concerning the virtues of the free market, appear to be generally congruent with those of their clients.

On social issues, however, lawyers tend to be more liberal than the public at large. On affirmative action, for example, Chicago lawyers were evenly split (see fig. 8.3), but a national sample of the general public, interviewed for the Associated Press Poll in 1995, was more likely to oppose it (Roper Center). In response to the question, "Do you think affirmative action programs make hiring and promotions more or less fair overall?," 48 percent of the national sample said "less fair" and 39 percent said "more fair." On abortion, the Wirthlin Group did a telephone survey in 1995 of 1,001 adults concerning "actions the federal government might take to try to strengthen families and family values" and asked "how effective . . . each one would be—one of the items was, "Requiring parental consent before girls under age 18 can have an abortion" (Roper Center). A strong majority of the respondents said that such a requirement would be effective in strengthening family values (48 percent said "very effective" and another 25 percent said "somewhat effective"). A rating of "effectiveness" is not the same thing, of course, as an expression of approval or disapproval. One might think that the requirement would be effective but disastrous. Chicago lawyers, however, rejected parental notification of abortion by more than two to one—59 percent disagreed with the proposition and only 25 percent supported it—even though notification would be less restrictive than a consent requirement. Moreover, while only 34 percent of Chicago lawyers agreed with the proposition that warning labels should be required on record albums with offensive content, a sample of the general public was more closely divided on a similar question (Roper Center). In 1995, a national telephone survey by the *Los Angeles Times* found that 44 percent of the sample favored "establishing formal government guidelines to limit the amount of sex and violence in movies, television entertainment shows or popular music" (Roper Center).

Chicago lawyers tend to be, overall, somewhat more conservative than the general population on issues concerning free markets and support for large companies, but somewhat more liberal than the public at large on social issues. The latter may be an example of the "Stouffer effect"—that is, that social elites, especially those that are highly educated, manifest greater support for civil liberties (Stouffer 1955). Thus, the relative liberality of lawyers on social issues may be primarily a social class phenomenon. But perhaps some of the difference between the Chicago findings on economic and social issues is attributable to the fact that most lawyers have clients that are directly concerned with economic issues—many of their clients are actively opposed to government regulation—while social issues are the professional concern of only a narrow segment of the bar. Few lawyers represent clients seeking legal abortions or protesting the content of record albums. More lawyers, but still a small share, have clients either making or defending claims of discrimination in employment. This, we believe, is the reason why regression analyses of the lawyers' responses to the affirmative action question indicate that professional characteristics have very little explanatory power, and that gender and race are the principal variables associated with those responses. When lawyers are free to pursue their own inclinations, they are, perhaps, likely to divide along lines much like those that divide other highly educated elites.[12] When their clients' interests are at stake, however, lawyers can usually be counted upon to identify with those interests.

Chapter 9
Community Roles
With Paul S. Schnorr

Chief Justice Rehnquist observed that lawyers have become less likely to serve their communities:

> [A]t the time I practiced law, there was a public aspect to the profession, and most lawyers did not regard themselves as totally discharging their obligation by simply putting in a given number of hours that could be billed to clients. Whether it was pro bono work of some sort, or a more generalized discharge of community obligation by serving on zoning boards, charity boards, and the like, lawyers felt that they could contribute something to the community in which they lived, and that they as well as the community would benefit from that contribution. As law firms focus on the proverbial bottom line, with predictable pressure on associates to increase billable hours, little time remains for public service. (Rehnquist 1994)

If there has been a decline in the community activities of lawyers, this might be expected to produce two consequences—communities would be deprived of the benefit of the skills and expertise that lawyers could provide, and the legal profession would be deprived of the influence acquired through community leadership roles.

It is certainly plausible that the time and energy lawyers voluntarily devote to extramural activities may have been diminished by changes in the nature and structure of law practice. The Chief Justice referred to the pressures of the "bottom line" and, in another speech, again emphasized the widely perceived (but poorly documented) increase in lawyers' hours, citing an estimate that billable hours had increased from an average of 1,450 per year in the 1960s to 2,000 or more in the late 1990s (Rehnquist 1997, 3–4). The demise of the tenure system in large law firms, the creation of multiple classes of partners (equity partners, nonequity partners, counsel, etc.), the increase in lateral movement among firms, the use of contract lawyers employed only for a term or a particular case, the adoption of "eat-what-you-kill" compensation rules (replacing seniority or less quantifiable evaluations), and the increased accessibility of lawyers to their clients through electronic communication technology, with the consequent escalation of expectations regarding the speed of answers, might well have made lawyers' professional lives less secure, less comfortable, and less contemplative, and have meant that lawyers have less time to devote to their own pursuits.

Nonetheless, there are at least four reasons why lawyers might want to continue to participate in their communities. First, they could believe that participation in the broader social contexts that surround them will bring them into contact with potential clients or with officeholders who are in a position to advance their interests. Some roles in community organizations, thus, may serve to enhance the lawyers' visibility or their professional reputations, or to advance their aspirations for elective or appointive office, including judgeships, and some motivations for participation may be consciously economic or careerist. Second, lawyers (like many other people) join organizations in order to pursue ideological or public-policy agendas. The goals may reflect their personal positions and values—regarding religion or civil liberties, for example—or may be objectives of their clients, often pursued through participation in business organizations or trade associations (Heinz, Paik, and Southworth 2003). Third, one motivation for participation is surely the simple desire for social interaction, and especially for interaction with those having similar interests, beliefs, or tastes. Such activity may be diverting, pleasurable, or satisfying for its own sake.[1] Fourth, lawyers may believe that they have an obligation to participate in community or charitable activities because it is the responsible, correct, or moral thing to do. This sort of activity may be distinct from their pursuit of personal ideological preferences.

Whatever changes occurred in the organizational arrangements of law practice or in the degree of pressure imposed by the bottom line, many of these motivations for participation in community activities will not have changed. Indeed, the pressures noted by the Chief Justice and others might conceivably have increased the value to lawyers of such activity, both for the recruitment of clients and for the acquisition of contacts that permit them to achieve their goals more effectively or efficiently. Thus, it remains an open question whether lawyers have in fact reduced the extent or degree of their involvement in voluntary associations or in public service.

Even if the overall level of their associational activity remained constant, however, its distribution might have changed. A stronger emphasis on the financial bottom line, for example, might move their activity toward greater involvement in business-related organizations, with perhaps a corresponding decrease in time devoted to religious organizations or to more purely social activity. Broader changes in the public taste could also alter participation patterns—if physical fitness takes on greater importance in the public consciousness while the salience of ethnic group identification diminishes, for example, lawyers might increase their involvement in athletic clubs and decrease their participation in the Sons of Italy. Thus, changes in societal norms and values are likely to be reflected in lawyers' activities. Changes in the composition of the bar may also alter the activity mix; for example, if female lawyers have different interests or preferences for associational activity than do males, the entry into the bar of substantial numbers of women should produce a shift in the community participation patterns of the profession.

The extent of lawyers' participation in American civic life and the nature and loci of their involvement may affect both the character of the community's initiatives and the outcomes. Lawyers are experienced in maneuvering within bureaucracies and formal systems of regulation. By training, they are better equipped to deal with governmental processes than are most of their neighbors, and they should thus be better able to act as mediators between government and private interests (Horsky 1952). The social networks maintained by lawyers are also likely to differ from those of persons in other occupations—they may be more diversely connected than some and perhaps more narrowly connected than others, but their networks will probably have a distinct character (see chap. 10). Therefore, where and how lawyers participate in voluntary associations may influence the ability of those organizations to function within the larger structure of American institutions. Tocqueville famously observed that

> The government of democracy is favorable to the political power of lawyers; for when the wealthy, the noble, and the prince are excluded from the government, the lawyers take possession of it. . . .
>
>   . . . As the lawyers form the only enlightened class whom the people do not mistrust, they are naturally called upon to occupy most of the public stations. (1945, 275, 279)

An absolute decline in the public-service activities of lawyers would constitute a major change in what has been thought to be one of the identifying characteristics of American politics.

Robert Putnam argued that there has been a serious erosion of civic institutions in the United States—that PTAs, bowling leagues, and Elks clubs are all languishing due to disengagement (Putnam 1995, 2000).[2] Declining participation in such activities and organizations is said to have depleted America's stock of what Putnam and James Coleman (among others) call *social capital* (Coleman 1998). Putnam worried about a loss of the social connections created by participation in voluntary associations, connections that bind together a large, diverse, "pluralist" polity. In the absence of such social capital, the argument goes, the polity will not function efficiently.[3] The thesis focuses not only on altruistic associations, civic boards, and pro bono activities, but on participation in dining clubs, religious congregations, and athletic teams as well, activities in which the requisite social connection may occur and social capital may be created. But the Putnam thesis is controversial, and other scholars have offered contrary data and opposing interpretations (e.g., Greeley 1997; Ladd 1996; Lemann 1996). In any event, lawyers might well diverge from the general pattern of declining participation—and indeed the circumstances of lawyers might give them particular reasons for participation.

The Chicago Data

In the 1975 Chicago survey, 777 lawyers were asked to name specific organizations in several categories (religious, political, business, veterans, fraternal, ethnic, civic, and charitable organizations, dining, athletic, and country clubs) in which they were either an inactive member, active, or in a leadership position. In response, they named more than 1,100 organizations. The data were voluminous, complex, and messy. For example, the ACLU was sometimes listed by respondents in the "political" category and sometimes as a "civic" organization. The nominal categories could not be taken at face value.

Because of the cost of the analysis, these data were not used in the earlier book or in other reports of the 1975 findings. In planning the 1994–95 survey, therefore, we reviewed the 1975 experience and considered whether to repeat the questions. We observed that some of the inactive member responses seemed frivolous (e.g., the American Airlines Admirals Club) and others were organizations where the only discernible participation was sending in a check for membership dues—that is, a contribution—once a year. Moreover, we thought that asking respondents to the new survey to compile a complete list of the organizations in which they were members by virtue of a monetary contribution would consume a large amount of interview time and, probably, produce inaccurate data because of failures of recollection. Active participation and leadership positions, however, were of considerable interest. Consequently, the second survey inquired only about organizations in which the respondents were active or leaders, thereby reducing the volume of data and conserving scarce interview time. But this change may make it problematic to compare responses from the two surveys. For example, suppose a respondent is a member of a synagogue but seldom attends services: if we do not provide the inactive member category and the respondent feels that the religious affiliation is important, he or she might then be more likely to report being "active" in the synagogue.

As indicated above, different respondents sometimes placed the same organization in different categories. We have recoded the data, therefore, in order to achieve consistency of classification. In this coding scheme, the categories are as follows:

- "Religious associations" include churches, synagogues, other religious congregations, and fellowships, societies, or youth organizations affiliated with religious institutions.
- "Business organizations" include trade associations, professional associations (in fields other than law), chambers of commerce, investment groups, business advisory groups, and geographical/community development organizations.[4]
- "Dining and athletic clubs" include country clubs, tennis or yacht clubs, and traditional "men's clubs" with dining and athletic facilities, such as the Union League Club and the University Club.
- "Social clubs" include book clubs, bridge clubs, dance groups, discussion forums, and similar groups.
- "Educational associations" include PTAs, school boards, local school councils, university or school alumni organizations, scholarship funds, and academic honor societies.
- "Civic associations" include charitable organizations, such as not-for-profit hospital boards and the Crusade of Mercy, museums, historical societies, and youth groups such as Boy Scouts and Little League.
- "Veterans associations" include the American Legion, the Jewish War Veterans, and the Retired Officers Association.

- "Ethnic associations" were defined as those made up of people with a shared racial, nationality, or ethnic identification, such as the Japanese-American Citizens' League and B'nai B'rith.
- "Fraternal organizations" include the Elks, Lions, Knights of Columbus, Masons, Greek-letter fraternities or sororities, and similar organizations.
- "Fitness clubs" include health clubs and other organizations providing athletic facilities, and, in some cases, dining rooms.[5]

Although respondents in both 1975 and 1995 were asked to name specific organizations, there were some differences in the prompts used to elicit those responses. That is, categories of organizations were suggested to the lawyers and they were then asked to report participation in such organizations. A "school or educational organizations" category was included in the 1995 interview but not in 1975. Because of this difference in the prompts, we exclude the educational organizations from comparisons of 1975 and 1995 responses in analyses that aggregate types of organizations. Another difference is that the 1995 interview included a category labeled "social clubs (including fraternal organizations, women's clubs, and other social or service organizations)," while the most comparable 1975 category was "fraternal organizations or lodges." (Only thirty of the 1975 respondents were women, and women lawyers do not appear to have been foremost in the consciousness of the drafters of the 1975 instrument.) Because the entry of women into the profession in large numbers is one of the major changes during these years, and because the activity patterns of female respondents are observed to be somewhat different from those of males with respect to these types of organizations, we will not exclude these data from our analyses. Although the measure is not ideal, we believe that the available data are of value and that they reflect a real change in the social composition of the bar.

Most of the categories, however, are clearly comparable, and the specific organizations named have been classified consistently (so that the same organization is always placed in the same category.) Categories that were used in both of the surveys (sometimes with small differences in wording) were religious, business, political, veterans, civic, charitable, and ethnic organizations, and dining and athletic clubs.[6]

Overall Participation

In 1995, 70 percent of all respondents said that they were either "active" or a "leader" in at least one voluntary association (excluding educational organizations).[7] The remaining 30 percent, apparently, had no active role in any of these kinds of organizations. In 1975, 77 percent of the respondents reported participation in at least one voluntary association, but those responses included membership characterized as inactive. The percentage of 1975 respondents indicating that they were active or leaders in the organizations was 59 percent (11 points lower than the percentage in those two categories in 1995). Perhaps some participation of the kind reported as inactive in 1975 might plausibly have been characterized as active in 1995, as we suggested above. Nonetheless, even though the inactive category was dropped in 1995, total participation declines only modestly (from 77 percent to 70 percent).

The most straightforward comparison between the two data sets is the percentage of respondents reporting leadership roles. In 1975, 32 percent of the lawyers claimed at least one such role; that declined substantially in 1995, to 17 percent.[8] Moreover, fewer of the 1995 Chicago lawyers held leadership positions in more than one organization. The mean number of organizations in which the 1975 respondents were leaders was .61 per lawyer; in 1995, it was .26.[9] Thus, although the overall participation rate may have declined little, if at all, from 1975 to 1995, the rate of participation at the more intensive (and, perhaps, more influential) leadership level decreased greatly.

The leadership decrease, however, may be an ecological phenomenon, in whole or in part. As noted in chapter 1, during the 1970s, 1980s, and 1990s, the size of the Chicago bar approximately doubled, from about 15,000 lawyers in 1975 to about 30,000 in 1995. If the total number of leadership positions available in voluntary associations does not increase at a rate equal to or greater than the expansion of the bar, then the number of positions per lawyer will decrease unless lawyers come to occupy a larger share of the available positions. As a measure of change in the number of such positions in the Chicago area, we counted the number of associations listed in the *Encyclopedia of Associations* in 1975 and 1995. While the total number of associations with Illinois addresses increased by 37 percent from 1975 to 1995, the number of associations with Chicago addresses actually decreased by 7 percent during that period.[10] Thus, the number of Chicago area associations in which lawyers might have held leadership positions appears, by this measure, to have lagged far behind the growth of the bar.

Since the percentage of leaders in our samples decreased by less than half from 1975 to 1995 while the number of lawyers approximately doubled, our best estimate is that more Chicago lawyers held leadership positions in 1995 than in 1975. On the other hand, the number of such positions per lawyer declined by more than half, so we would estimate that the total number of leadership positions held by lawyers decreased, but not much. The rapid growth of the bar between 1975 and 1995 created a younger age profile in the profession—in 1975, 40.4 percent of the respondents were over age forty-five; in 1995, only 32.6 percent were.[11] Since younger lawyers are less likely to hold leadership positions, this change in the age distribution within the profession also contributes to the decrease in leadership rates in the 1995 sample data.[12] Other characteristics that are associated with higher leadership rates—education at elite law schools and privileged social origins—were also in shorter supply in the 1995 bar, and these may account for some decline in the rate. We will revisit this point.

Correlates of Overall Participation

Several variables appear to affect activity rates. In 1995, for example, only 61 percent and 66 percent of the respondents in the two lowest annual income categories (the categories below $50,000) were either active or leaders in voluntary associations, while the comparable percentage in the highest income category ($175,000 or more) was 81 percent,[13] but we cannot be certain which way the causal arrow points. It is possible that winning big verdicts or earning big fees attracts notice, which in turn brings invitations to serve on committees or join boards of directors, but it is also possible that contacts acquired through participation enhance one's opportunities to be retained by lucrative clients.

As we might expect, there is also an age effect, but it is primarily a difference between the youngest age category (under thirty-five), where only 59 percent of respondents are active, and the other three categories, where the comparable percentages fall in the narrow range of 74 percent to 77 percent.[14] Thus, once a lawyer gets beyond thirty-five, aging no longer appears to have an effect on the 1995 activity rate.

If we examine religious affiliation, we see that type I Protestants (Episcopalians, Presbyterians, and Congregationalists; see chap. 3 at fig. 3.1) have the highest activity rate (83 percent), while the rates of type II Protestants (all other Protestant denominations; 75 percent) and Catholics (73 percent) are somewhat higher than that of Jews (69 percent), but the biggest difference is the very low activity rate of nonreligious lawyers (55 percent).[15] Since the nonreligious are unlikely to participate in religious organizations, this might depress their overall activity rate (although they could, of course, substitute other sorts of activities). If we exclude religious organizations from the analysis, however, we find that 70 percent of the religious respondents but only 57 percent of the nonreligious were active in secular organizations.[16]

When we analyze differences in activity rates across the various practice settings, we find corporate inside counsel at the high end (77 percent) and government lawyers (61 percent) at the bottom, but the differences across seven practice-setting categories are not statistically significant.[17] Activity rates for men (70 percent) and women (72 percent) also did not differ significantly.

In the 1975 data, although the overall activity rate is somewhat lower, the pattern of differences is quite similar. The activity rates of lawyers in the two lowest income categories[18] were markedly lower than those of lawyers in the two highest categories[19] and, as in 1995, the age difference in activity rates was between lawyers in the youngest category and those in the three older categories.[20] Unlike the 1995 findings, however, in 1975 Catholics and Jews had much lower activity rates (58 percent each) than did the two types of Protestants (73 percent and 75 percent). Thus, over time, the extent of participation in voluntary associations by Catholics and Jews became more similar to that of Protestants. As in the more recent survey, however, nonreligious respondents had by far the lowest activity rate (40 percent) in 1975, and the difference between religious and nonreligious lawyers was significant even when religious organizations were omitted.[21] Practice setting was not associated with statistically significant differences in the 1975 activity rates, but there was a marginally significant association between the category of law school attended and the rate of activity.[22] Of the lawyers who had gone to elite law schools, 68 percent were active or leaders in voluntary associations, while the other law school categories had rates of 60 percent to 55 percent. As in 1995, the difference in the activity rates of men (63 percent) and women (53 percent) was not statistically significant.[23]

Many of the lawyer characteristics that we have considered here are interrelated. As we noted in chapter 7, for example, lawyers who practice in large firms tend to have higher incomes, and lawyers who work for government agencies have relatively low earnings. To identify the effects of the several variables, we did multivariate analyses for both 1975 and 1995. The dependent variable was the number of activities (at the active or leader level), excluding activities in educational organizations in both years. Regression models using both personal background and legal profession variables account for 17 percent of the total variance in 1975 and 18 percent in 1995.[24]

We included both age and age squared in the models to determine whether the relationship between age and activity was curvilinear—that is, whether the rate of activity, after increasing with age, then decreased as respondents reached an advanced age. In 1975, the coefficient for age was significantly positive,[25] while age squared was strongly negative,[26] indicating a curvilinear effect. In 1995, however, age was only of marginal significance[27] and age squared (although still negative) was not significant. Gender was not significant in either year, nor was a variable indicating whether the respondent spent his or her high school years in the Chicago metropolitan area.[28] Some research on volunteer participation has found that married persons are more likely to be active and that participation increases with the number of children in the household (D. H. Smith 1994, 249). In the Chicago data, we found that marriage had only a marginally significant effect, and only in 1975. A question about the presence of children in the home was asked in 1995, but the variable was not significant.

While lawyers who had attended "elite" law schools were significantly more likely than those who had gone to "local" schools to be active in 1975, in 1995 none of the law school categories was significant.[29] Of the practice settings, none differed from the activity rates of solo practitioners at the .05 level of statistical significance. In 1975, lawyers with low income had low rates of activity and lawyers with higher incomes had higher rates of activity[30]—but in 1995 this variable, like several others, became insignificant.

The most persistent findings were in the religion categories. As compared to nonreligious respondents (the reference category), Catholics and both types of Protestants had significantly higher rates of activity.[31] Jewish respondents, however, did not differ significantly from the nonreligious in either year. It is noteworthy that although the effects of age, income, and law school became weaker in 1995, religion continued to be associated with the likelihood of participation in voluntary associations.

Much of the research on volunteer participation supports what has been called a *dominant status model* (D. H. Smith 1994, 246–50). Summarizing a review of that literature, Smith concluded that "participation is generally greater for individuals who are characterized by a more dominant set of social positions and roles, both ascribed and achieved" (D. H. Smith 1983, 86; reiterated in D. H. Smith 1994, 246). Our findings for 1975 are largely consistent with this model—high income, attendance at an elite law school, middle age, and Protestant religious identification all enhanced the likelihood that the lawyer would be active in voluntary associations. In 1995, however, the income and law school effects disappeared and the age effect diminished, leaving only religion with strong significance.

Who Participates Where?

More respondents were active in religious organizations in 1995 than in any other category, followed by dining and athletic clubs, civic organizations, and educational organizations (fig. 9.1.) By contrast, only one percent of the respondents were active in veterans organizations, 3 percent in fraternal organizations, 7 percent in social clubs, 8 percent in ethnic organizations, and 10 percent in fitness clubs. Activity in business and political organizations fell between these extremes. The categories that show the largest

Figure 9.1. Participation by Type of Organization, 1975 and 1995 (percentages)

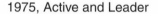

1975, All Membership[a]

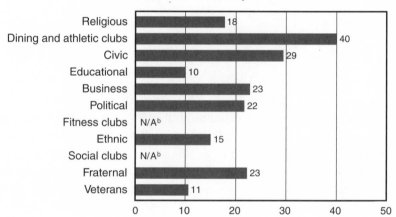

1975, Active and Leader

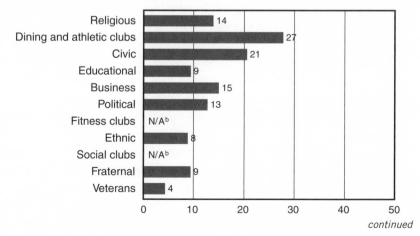

continued

Figure 9.1 *continued*

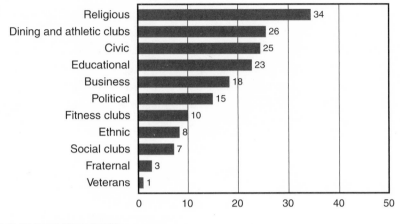

1995, Active and Leader

Religious	34
Dining and athletic clubs	26
Civic	25
Educational	23
Business	18
Political	15
Fitness clubs	10
Ethnic	8
Social clubs	7
Fraternal	3
Veterans	1

[a] Includes "inactive" membership.
[b] These categories were not used in 1975.

increases in rates of activity from 1975 to 1995 are religious organizations and educational organizations, but recall that the latter category was used as a specific stimulus in the 1995 interviews.[32] Activity rates appear to be relatively stable in business, political, and ethnic organizations, and in dining and athletic clubs, while fraternal and veterans organizations show a decline.[33] Thus, pressure on lawyers to maximize profits does not appear to have had the effect of increasing their rates of participation in business organizations at the expense of civic and religious activities. Of the 787 respondents to the 1995 survey, only 54 (7 percent) were active in dining and athletic clubs or in fitness clubs and in no other type of organization. Most Chicago lawyers were active in organizations that had a broader community role.[34]

Examining the specific associations that attracted the participation of the largest number of respondents in the two years, we find that several organizations appear on both lists. These include the Democratic Party and three downtown, traditional, historically men's clubs (the University Club, the Union League Club, and the Chicago Athletic Association). In 1995, two additional dining clubs appear among the organizations in which ten or more respondents report that they are active or leaders—the Standard Club (historically, and still predominately, a Jewish men's club) and the Monroe Club (a luncheon club). The only organizations that commanded a comparable level of participation in 1995 were the Democratic Party and the Catholic

Church. In 1975, by contrast, the list of most popular organizations (at the active or leader level of participation) included B'nai B'rith, the Masons, the Knights of Columbus, the YMCA, and the American Legion. Thus, the character of the most popular choices changed somewhat. The decline in activity in B'nai B'rith, the Masons, and the Knights of Columbus reflects the declining membership of fraternal and ethnic organizations, generally.[35] Dining clubs, however, remained popular. Calvin Trillin observed: "The one generalization that it may be safe to make about lawyers—except, of course, for the statistically incontrovertible one that this country has quite a few more of them than it has any need for—is that the profession includes a large number of serious eaters" (1978, 119).

Correlates of Participation by Organization Type

Lawyers who possessed socially advantaged characteristics—those who were older, had higher incomes, were Protestants, and who attended elite law schools—were more likely to be active in some types of organizations.[36] Privileged lawyers were especially likely to have higher rates of activity in civic and educational organizations. Whether this was the case because of a sense of noblesse oblige, because their economic surplus permitted them to devote uncompensated effort to these causes, or because more opportunities were open to them cannot be resolved with these data. Organizations may perceive that these lawyers possess special competence, or the organizations may hope to draw on the social power held by privileged persons (Wilson and Musick 1997, 698, 710). In ethnic organizations and fitness clubs, however, such lawyers had low participation rates, suggesting that those organizations did not rank high in the social hierarchy.

To make these findings more concrete, let us examine specific examples from the 1995 interviews. The two respondents reporting the most extensive participation in voluntary associations were both white, male, senior partners in major downtown firms, and both had high incomes. One was fifty-nine years old; the other was sixty-five. Both were Episcopalians. One did undergraduate work at the University of Chicago and then law school at Yale, while the other went to Yale first and then the University of Michigan Law School. Both did corporate litigation. One reported activity in the Episcopal Church; the Republican National Committee; three country clubs; two traditional, downtown "men's clubs"; the boards of two private secondary schools; and the board of a major museum (of which he had formerly been the chairman). The other reported activity in the Democratic Party of Cook County, five downtown social clubs, his law school's alumni association, two civic organizations, and four major cultural and arts institutions. These are, of course, exceptional cases.

Another respondent with a high level of activity presents a different profile: a solo practitioner with a relatively low income, male, age forty-six, he attended De Paul Law School, represented individuals and a few small businesses, and did primarily criminal defense, consumer bankruptcy, landlord/tenant, probate, and general family practice. He reported activity as an officer of an independent political organization, an adviser to a Hispanic community group, past president of the local Kiwanis club, a member of the local public school council, a member of a school reform organization, and a member of a Methodist congregation. Another example is a practitioner in a small firm, male, age forty-three, who attended Chicago-Kent Law School, had a moderate income, and reported doing a mixture of personal and business litigation, including criminal defense, probate, some personal injury plaintiffs work, and residential real estate transactions. He said that only a quarter of his clients were businesses and that 90 percent of those businesses were small. His activities were in his parish of the Catholic church, the Holy Name Society (of which he had been an officer), the Democratic Party ward organization, the nominating committee of his children's parochial school, an organization assisting the disabled, and the Irish Fellowship Club. While the character of the patterns of participation of these respondents differ, all of them had unusually high levels of activity.

The following cases are more typical: A lawyer in solo practice, female, age thirty-two, a University of Florida Law School graduate with a moderately high income, did litigation on behalf of individuals, including criminal defense and civil rights work. She reported that about half of the persons she represented were unemployed. Her activities were the East Bank Club (an expensive fitness club), the Jewish United Fund, and service as a coach for the trial advocacy team at a local law school. Another lawyer practicing in a small firm, male, age forty-one, a DePaul Law School graduate, was active in two trade associations and in the Chicago Health Clubs (fitness) and the Monroe Club. He had a low-to-moderate income and did both personal client and business litigation. He reported that 60 percent of his clients were businesses, mostly small businesses. A house counsel working in the trust department of a bank, male, age fifty-two, a graduate of Duke Law School, had a moderately high income and did estate planning. He reported that he was active in the United Church of Christ (Congregational), a business organization, the local public school caucus in his suburb, and as a member of the board of a community soccer club.

Leaders

There were changes from 1975 to 1995 in the kinds of organizations in which lawyers were most likely to hold leadership positions. So let us examine the distribution of the leadership roles across the several types of organizations, bearing in mind that there was an overall decrease in the percentage of respondents reporting leadership positions.

In both years, the largest percentage of leadership was devoted to civic organizations, and those organizations also had the largest increase in lawyer leadership over the two decades. In 1975, 27 percent of the leader positions were in civic organizations, but by 1995 this increased to 39 percent. Religious organizations also showed a substantial increase, from 12 percent to 16 percent of leadership positions, as did educational organizations (but recall our caution about the comparability of the 1975 and 1995 data in that category). The biggest decrease occurred in the dining and athletic club category, where the percentage of leadership positions reported declined from 9 percent in 1975 to only 1 percent in 1995. Other decreases occurred in political organizations (from 11 percent to 6 percent) and fraternal organizations (6 percent to 1 percent). The percentage of leadership positions devoted to business organizations remained constant—13 percent at each time—and that devoted to ethnic organizations was essentially constant (5 percent and 4 percent). Thus, the lawyers who had leadership roles in 1995 were more likely to lead civic or religious organizations, and less likely to lead social, political, or fraternal activities.

It may be instructive to give particular attention to the lawyers who had active roles in the types of organizations that are more likely to take positions on public policy issues or to be concerned with social reform. For this purpose, we will define such organizations as those in the religious, business, civic, and political categories.[37] To determine whether the lawyers who were especially likely to be leaders in these more community-oriented organizations shared any social or professional characteristics, we first constructed a "community participation index" that weighs both the intensity of the activity in these sorts of organizations and the number of such organizations in which the lawyer was active. A respondent was given two points for each organization in which he or she was a leader and one point for each in which he or she was active. Only a fifth of the respondents have a score of three or more on this index; this is true in both 1975 and 1995 (fig. 9.2). Analyzing the characteristics of the lawyers who rank in this top fifth, we found that those who have higher incomes, are older (but not too old), and

Figure 9.2. Distribution of Community Participation Index, 1975 and 1995

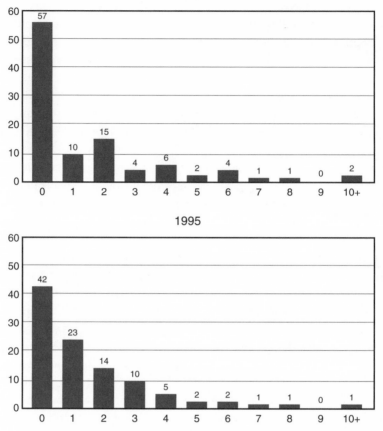

Note: Index scores reflect participation in religious, business, civic, and political organizations. Each active participation = 1 point; each leadership position = 2 points.

are Protestants were significantly more likely to participate in community-oriented organizations to this degree in one or both of the years. Lawyers who are young, have low incomes, and are not religious were least likely to be in this most active group.[38]

We did not find that minorities had significantly higher scores on this index than did whites. Of the thirty-nine African Americans in the 1995 random sample, 21 percent had scores of 3 or more, versus 19 percent of whites. Of the ten Hispanics, only one had a score of 3 or more. But Richard Lempert, David Chambers, and Terry Adams found that minority graduates of the University of Michigan Law School were more likely to have done unremunerated public service than were white graduates (2000, 485–87). In their two older cohorts, minority alumni were significantly more likely than whites to "serve on the board of at least one civil rights, charitable, religious, or other nonprofit organization" (455; see also Bowen and Bok 1998). Michigan is an elite law school, and the types of public service opportunities open to its minority graduates may differ from those available to most minority lawyers in Chicago. A relatively high percentage of the African American and Hispanic lawyers in Chicago are government employees, and that may impose restrictions on their political and fund-raising activity. Moreover, a minority lawyer working in the state's attorney's or public defender's office, who had studied at one of Chicago's "local" law schools, may be less likely than the Michigan graduate to receive invitations to serve on boards of directors. The affirmative action program at Michigan reportedly tries to select candidates for admission who are motivated to engage in public service (Lempert, Chambers, and Adams 2000). It may be that it succeeds.

There is a somewhat larger number of respondents with scores at the high end of the distribution in 1975—sixteen respondents with index scores of 10 or more in 1975, and only six respondents in 1995.[39] But such lawyers amount to a very small percentage of the total in both years. The perception of a decrease in the public service activities of lawyers, therefore, may be based on a real change, but a change affecting only a small number of lawyers.

This change could be not so much a change in behavior as a change in the lawyers' characteristics. Given the doubling of the size of the Chicago bar, a smaller proportion of the 1995 lawyers had long experience. Acquaintances and connections accumulate over the course of our lives, and such contacts open options for activity and lead to invitations to accept leadership roles. The potential for leadership is therefore greater among older lawyers. Moreover, because the number of lawyers produced by elite law schools increased relatively little while the bar was doubling in size, the percentage with elite school credentials decreased from 20 percent in 1975 to 13 percent in 1995. Thus, again, an attribute that tends to enhance the likelihood of selection for positions of leadership became more scarce.

Similarly, analyses of acquaintance with elites of the bar (i.e., "notable" Chicago lawyers; see chap. 10) find that such connections were in shorter supply in 1995 than they had been in 1975, and that those connections are a form of social capital (Sandefur, Laumann, and Heinz 1999). While 38 percent of the 1975 sample lacked instrumental ties to the set of notables, fully 53 percent lacked any connection in 1995 even though the list of notables used in the latter survey included more names and was more diverse (chap. 10). As the bar doubled in size, a smaller percentage of rank-and-file members of the bar had ties to elites within the profession, an asset that increases the probability of being tapped for a position of leadership.[40] Like the increasing scarcity of elite school credentials and the changes in the age distribution, this was an almost inevitable consequence of growth in the size of the bar.

To evaluate these possible effects more formally, we computed a number of multiple regression equations based on varying assumptions. The independent variables were characteristics of the respondents that might plausibly be thought to be associated with leadership—age, law school, income, religion, gender, number of notables known, and so on. When the dependent variable is simply the number of leadership positions held, the period (year) effect is highly significant (even after the other independent variables have been taken into account). Changes in the age, elite law school, gender, and notable acquaintance distributions are therefore insufficient to explain the full extent of the decline in the number of leadership positions. But this finding does not tell us *why* the period effect is significant. Most importantly, it does not indicate whether the decline in leadership is attributable to a change in the motivations of the lawyers—that is, in their preferences with regard to use of their time—or to a change in the opportunities available to them. (See the appendix to this chapter.)

As we have noted, the number of voluntary associations with Chicago addresses, as listed in a standard directory, declined somewhat over the twenty years. Therefore, we did an analysis in which the dependent variable reflected the decline in the number of associations. This was accomplished by making the dependent variable the ratio of the number of positions held by each respondent to the number of Chicago associations listed in the year in which the respondent was interviewed (e.g., 3/722 in 1975 versus 3/672 in 1995). In those analyses, although the period effect declined, it remained strongly significant. But, at the same time that the number of associations declined, the number of Chicago lawyers doubled. Therefore, unless lawyers displaced nonlawyers from leadership positions and thus came to hold a larger share of the total number of such posts, the additional lawyers competed for the available positions. Each organization has only one president, and only one person can hold that position at a given time. Viewed from the perspective of any individual, opportunities for leadership are a function not only of the number of positions but of the number of candidates. We therefore computed another model in which the dependent variable also reflected the change in the lawyer population.[41] In this model, when the dependent variable reflects the doubling of the number of lawyers (or, the halving of the opportunities open to any one lawyer within the population), the period effect disappears. Thus, the decline in the number of positions per lawyer may be accounted for without the need to look to motivation.

Conclusion

If our findings suggest that the extent of the community activities of lawyers changed relatively little and that such change as there was tended to be in socially approved directions, then why is it that the bar is so often accused of desertion from the ranks of public servants, of abandoning the ideal of the "lawyer-statesman" (Kronman 1993)? One of the things to note about this criticism is that it almost always comes from within the profession. The most frequent, compelling, and sometimes strident critics of lawyers tend to be lawyers (Glendon 1994; Schiltz 1999), and the criticism carries special weight, of course, when it comes from the Chief Justice (Burger 1995, 953, 958; Rehnquist 1994), the Dean of the Yale Law School (Kronman 1993), or leaders of the organized bar (Yanas 1990, 3).

When doctors call for other doctors to devote more time and energy to public service, they are talking about providing medical services to the poor. They are not calling upon their colleagues to serve on the board of the YMCA or the Art Institute. This probably reflects a fundamental difference in the way that the two professions conceive of (or would like to conceive of) their societal roles. Doctors claim to be able to treat diseases and injuries; they do not claim to be omnicompetent problem solvers. The elites of the legal profession, however, believe that they and their fellows have a broader societal role, a duty to provide leadership and wise counsel in a wide range of public and private activities. They call upon their colleagues to become "statesmen." This is, of course, a self-serving claim. It asserts that lawyers have a special office—a special ability and, therefore, a special duty to lead society toward desirable social and political outcomes. In the view of the more enthusiastic advocates of the lawyer-statesman ideal, this competence is not attributable solely to lawyers' expertise in matters of legal doctrine or to skill in negotiation or dispute resolution, but to attributes of character and personality that are engendered through pursuit of the ideal:

> The lawyer-statesman ideal is an ideal of character. It calls upon the lawyer who adopts it not just to acquire a set of intellectual skills, but to develop certain character traits as well. It engages his affects along with his intellect and forces him to feel as well as think in certain ways. The lawyer-statesman ideal poses a challenge to the whole person, and this helps to explain why

> it is capable of offering such deep personal meaning to those who view
> their professional responsibilities in its light. . . . [A]n understanding of even
> the most complex intellectual discipline cannot by itself convey the deeper
> satisfaction that comes with the attainment of a valued trait of character like
> practical wisdom. For this does more than increase a person's knowledge of
> the world. It alters one's dispositional attitude toward it and thereby modifies
> one's personality in an essential way. (Kronman 1993, 363–64)

Thus, these attributes will equip lawyers not only to serve in political office but to hold positions of leadership in schools, churches, charitable foundations, businesses, and civic organizations. In short, lawyers will be especially valuable people to have in positions of social power. The "practical wisdom" of lawyers will produce better decisions than we could expect from persons who lack lawyers' advantages of training and character. (At least, this will be so if lawyers will choose to pursue the statesman role). This ideology, obviously, tends to enhance the prestige of the profession and to support lawyers' claims to positions of leadership. It is easy to see why the ideology would be popular with the elites of the profession.

One of the most striking differences between the 1975 and 1995 findings is the considerable increase in activity in religious organizations. This is probably part of a more general resurgence of religion in American society. Several scholars have noted that the United States has high rates of religious affiliation and church attendance, compared with other industrialized nations, and that these rates are growing (Finke and Stark 1992; Gallup 1996; Greeley 1989; Olson 1992). In the general U.S. population, about 92 percent of adults state a religious preference and 69 percent are estimated to be members of some religious congregation (Gallup 1996, 40).[42] Of the respondents to the two surveys of Chicago lawyers, only 12 percent in 1975 and 15 percent in 1995 indicated no religious affiliation. The extent of religious adherence among Chicago lawyers is, then, similar to that of other Americans.[43]

The several functions of religious organizations in contemporary American society have been aptly summarized by Stephen Warner:

> Although religion's public face is less visible and less unifying at the national
> level today than a generation ago, local religious communities . . . still
> make themselves felt to their neighbors. They promote charitable causes,
> from providing meals to elderly shut-ins to housing the homeless. They
> provide services, including resale shops, family counseling, after-school
> tutoring and courses in English as a second language. They host concerts

and community meetings. They lobby city hall to collect the garbage, close
down crack houses, and award development contracts to socially responsive
builders. Perhaps the most important way local religious communities—
"congregations"—contribute to the social order is through the development of
"social capital," the "network of skill and trust that makes civic life possible"
(Warner 1999, 229, 237, quoting Ammerman)

The increase in Chicago lawyers' activity in religious organizations may
therefore have broad community significance. In addition to the roles mentioned by Warner, which tend toward ameliorative activities and the liberal
side of the political spectrum, religious groups have, of course, been active on
both sides of issues such as abortion, school prayer, and gay marriage, and
lawyers have certainly participated in the debates concerning those issues
(Heinz, Paik, and Southworth 2003).

Although research on the public at large found support for a "dominant
status model" of volunteer participation—that is, that persons with socially
advantaged characteristics had higher rates of participation—we might have
speculated that such differences would not be significant within a relatively
narrow occupational stratum such as the legal profession. Certainly, one of
the important predictors of volunteer activity in the general population, educational level, was expected to be less determinative within the bar, simply
because there is less variance. All contemporary lawyers have law degrees.
Nonetheless, although all or most lawyers are, in a sense, elites—with high
educational attainment, earnings that are well above average, and occupational status that is traditionally (if inconsistently) accorded prestige—there
was sufficient variance among Chicago lawyers in age, income, practice type,
and, especially, religion to produce significant differences in the overall rates
of activity in one or both of the surveys, as well as differences in the levels
of activation in several of the particular types of organizations. Status hierarchies within the broader community, as well as social differences in taste,
preference, or "culture," clearly penetrate the bar. Networks of relationships
among lawyers and laymen lead some to serve on the ACLU board, while others serve on the finance committee of the Art Institute, and yet others serve
as scoutmasters. Opportunity for selection to these positions appears to be
determined, in important part, by characteristics that are associated with criteria of status or prestige prevalent in the community. Voluntary associations
outside the bar thus provide lawyers with opportunities for the acquisition
of social capital, but the opportunities are provided differentially, to different
types of lawyers. These associations do not contribute to the integration of
the profession.

Appendix: Period, Age, and Cohort Effects

Because the 1995 sample was significantly younger, on average, than the 1975 sample, and because age is associated with the probability of holding a leadership position, it is important to assess the extent to which the decrease in the leadership rate may be attributed to the age difference. In addition to the age effect, however, it is possible that people in different birth cohorts (e.g., the immediate post-WWII baby boom) may have different leadership rates. Birth year will, of course, be equivalent to age at the time of any one survey, but age and cohort are independent when data from the two surveys are pooled—a person born in 1935 will be forty at the time of the 1975 survey and sixty in 1995. If period (survey year) is included as a variable in the same analysis, however, these variables become linearly dependent—that is, given the 1995 survey year, the 1935 birth date necessarily means age sixty. Thus, the three variables cannot be included in the same equation because of this linear dependency, but any two of them can be.

What we have, then, is a classic problem, familiar to data analysts, of trying to sort out period, age, and cohort effects. Our analyses addressed to this problem are presented in more detail in *Law and Social Inquiry* (26 [2001]: 627). In summary, we found that cohort appeared to have stronger effects than either period or age. Indeed, when cohort was taken into account, age and period became insignificant.

Given the structure of these data, the "cohort effect" is to be expected. That is, people who are older have higher leadership rates, and the overall leadership rate is observed to be higher at the earlier time (1975). Thus, the probability is that the interaction of age and period will produce high leadership rates in the earlier birth cohorts—because cohort combines the age and period effects, it produces a stronger coefficient than either of the other two effects alone.

What the analyses do not tell us is *why* there is a strong cohort effect. The principal competing hypotheses are, first, that there is a difference among the cohorts in the value or utility that they attach to leadership positions (perhaps, for example, because lawyers born during the 1930s were socialized differently than lawyers born during the 1960s), and, second, that the birth cohorts were confronted with differing opportunities for leadership (perhaps, e.g., a smaller number of vacancies in leadership positions per capita were available to be filled by members of the 1950s cohort than by lawyers in the 1930s cohort, which was a much smaller birth cohort). Or, of course, it is possible that the cohort effect could be produced by a combination of these two factors.

Chapter 10
Connections within the Bar

Lawyers develop distinct networks of association and communication in the process of settling cases, referring clients to specialists, recruiting new lawyers for their firms, seeking public office, resolving matters of common concern within the profession, and generally getting things done. These networks are shaped by the variables that differentiate types of lawyers. Segments of the profession that are characterized by strong, reliable, stable, and well-defined ties are "tightly coupled" social systems (March and Simon 1958; Weick 1976). Those where the ties are weaker or shifting are "loosely coupled." In tightly coupled systems, outcomes are relatively predictable—the application of pressure of a certain type and intensity at a particular point in the system may be expected to have consequences, foreseeable within a range, at other points within the system. In loosely coupled systems, the effects of similar pressures are less foreseeable—indeed, there may be no movement at all because essential linkages are lacking. To the extent that communication among contending groups occurs, then, it will provide connections that may facilitate the resolution of issues. The places where ties are absent are, of course, at least as important as those where they are present (Burt 1992). The divisions in the network constitute structural barriers or gaps that can be difficult to cross.

The first step in any analysis of such phenomena is to associate prominent lawyers with the constituencies they represent. Their constituencies constitute bases of power or influence, and the nature of the constituencies reflect the arenas within which the lawyers are active and, perhaps, the types of resources they are able to mobilize. Constituencies might form around any or all of several sources of association. Some kinds of lawyers, for example, will be brought together by their clients. This occurs often in the business world, where trade associations and other industry groups pursue common agendas. Other lawyers meet in courthouses when and where their cases are tried or settled. Some form ties through partisan political activity or through participation in civic enterprises or charitable causes. Still others are recruited for leadership roles through ethnoreligious or fraternal groups, veterans organizations, school alumni groups, and so on (see chap. 9). Then, too, there are the bar associations—national, state, and local, representing the profession as a whole as well as many specialty groups (see chap. 3)—all of which provide opportunities for recognition as a leader of the bar. But the term "leader of the bar" has several meanings. It can be applied to an especially skilled practitioner who drafts a sound debenture or impresses juries, or it may refer to lawyers who are more broadly influential and who function as brokers or advisors. It is the latter who concern us here.

The 1975 Networks

In both Chicago surveys, respondents were asked about their connections with prominent attorneys of varying types. We will not recount the published 1975 findings (Heinz and Laumann 1982, 274–315) here, but it will be useful to summarize the broad outlines of those findings so we can see how the networks changed over the twenty years.

Figure 10.1 is a three-dimensional smallest space analysis in which notable lawyers who have more similar circles of acquaintance are closer together (Guttman 1968). (The lawyers are given pseudonyms.) The third dimension is indicated by down-pointing arrows next to four points, indicating that those points lie substantially below the plane of the page—all of the others are relatively near the plane (Heinz and Laumann 1982; 291). Points that are more similar are more proximate. Here, similarity means that the lawyers represented by the points share circles of acquaintance among the respondents: if the same set of respondents has connections to each of two notables, that pair of notables will be in the same region of the space. By contrast, if the respondents who choose them are disparate, the two notables will be widely separated. The locations of those points will also be determined, however, by the degree of similarity of their circles of acquaintance to those of every other notable in the space. Thus, the solution seeks to optimize the representation of the relationships among all of the pairwise comparisons, considered simultaneously.

Figure 10.1. Patterns of Acquaintance with 43 Notable Chicago Lawyers, 1975

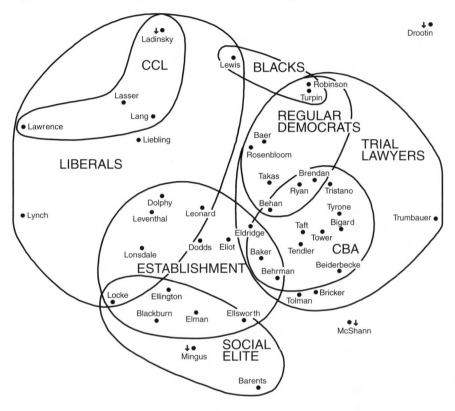

To represent all these relationships with complete accuracy might well require several dimensions; in fact, it could require as many dimensions as the number of points in the space, minus one. The degree to which the solution fits the full complexity of the data is indicated by statistics referred to as measures of "stress." That is, the degree of stress in the solution indicates the amount of error in the representation—the degree to which the distances among the points fail to capture the full extent of the similarities and differences among the cases.

The labels placed on some of the areas in the figure are intended to indicate characteristics of the notables located within those regions. The boundaries and labels are based on inspection of the notables' characteristics rather than on more formal statistical procedures, but there is not much ambiguity in the classifications. CBA and CCL refer to the Chicago Bar Association and the Chicago Council of Lawyers, respectively. Many of the notables found within those areas had served as presidents of the organizations. The CCL was founded in 1969 as a liberal, reformist alternative to the established CBA (Powell 1979).

The overall structure of the space is organized into three sectors, roughly in the form of a Mercedes emblem. The characteristics identified in figure 10.2 primarily describe the constituencies rather than the notables—that is, they describe attributes of the respondents who indicated connections to the notables located within those regions (Heinz and Laumann 1982; 299–309). Nonetheless, most notables shared the characteristics of their constituencies. As figure 10.2 makes clear, political preference, religious identification, and type of law practice tended to be conterminous. Thus, the constituencies had multiple bases of affinity, and this no doubt enhanced the cohesion within them. Notables who were more centrally located in their constituencies were especially likely to exemplify the defining traits of the constituency—that is, they were likely to be more homogeneous types than those located near the boundaries of the constituency.

The three African American notables—Lewis, Robinson, and Turpin (upper center in fig. 10.1)—were exceptions. Although they had the political and law practice characteristics of their respective constituencies, they were located at the boundary between the Liberal/Jewish/Mixed Practice sector and the Daley Democrat/Catholic/Trial Practice sector. In 1975, Robinson was closely aligned with the first Mayor Daley and Lewis was aligned with Jesse Jackson and Operation PUSH (People United to Save Humanity). Despite what amounted to a political chasm in 1970s Chicago, they were drawn into close proximity in the space—and, thus, each was pulled toward the boundary. Quite clearly, the circles of acquaintance of Chicago lawyers in the mid-1970s were importantly defined by race, and the strength of these racial ties appears to have been sufficient to overcome political and professional affinities. Note, also, that the location of the three blacks is diametrically opposite to the region occupied by the social elite. In analyzing the 1995 data, therefore, we try to assess the salience of race in the relationships among Chicago lawyers, to determine whether it diminished over the twenty years or whether it remained strong.

Given the growth in the bar from 1975 to 1995, it will surely have become more difficult for the elites to keep in close touch with any broad segment of the profession. As the population increases, the number of possible dyadic ties increases exponentially. When the number (n) doubles, as it did here,[1] the resulting number of dyads will be four times the original number of dyads plus n. It is highly unlikely that individuals will even attempt to increase their personal ties in proportion to that amount of growth. Consequently, the network structure might become more diffuse or, perhaps,

Figure 10.2. General Structure of the Notables Network, 1975

more specialized. The notable lawyers would, then, tend to represent more narrowly defined constituencies, thus exacerbating the difficulty of bridging those constituencies or of mediating among them.

The 1995 Networks

During the 1994–95 interviews, respondents were given a list of sixty-eight notable lawyers. The names had been selected after extensive consultation with informants familiar with various segments of the Chicago bar. An effort was made to list prominent lawyers representing a wide range of social and professional categories: bar association leaders, Democrats, Republicans, academics, lawyers in very small firms or solo practice, corporate inside counsel, corporate outside counsel, criminal defense lawyers, lawyers engaged in personal injury litigation (both plaintiff and defense sides), labor lawyers (both union and management sides), tax, divorce, real estate, antitrust, and municipal bond lawyers, lawyers engaged in legal services work ("poverty law") and those representing public interest or not-for-profit organizations, women, WASPs, Irish Catholics, persons of southern and eastern European descent, and Latino, Asian and African Americans. Government officials were not included because we did not want to conflate personal or professional notability with the powers of a public office. Care was also taken to avoid the inclusion of more than three lawyers from any one law firm or an excessive number of the alumni of any one law school—though some schools are, in fact, more likely to produce prominent Chicago lawyers.[2]

We did not attempt to create a list of the *most* notable, successful, or influential lawyers. Rather, the list included a selection of lawyers, of varying types, who were prominent in one respect or another but not necessarily more prominent than others. It would, in any event, have been problematic to attempt to specify "notability" with precision. What criteria should be used? Breadth of acquaintance is one possible measure, and it is probably associated with the sort of notability that concerns us. A prominent artist or poet may be able to succeed as a recluse, but it is hard to imagine a lawyer who could achieve great prominence without associating with his or her professional colleagues. To measure breadth of acquaintance, however, one must do a survey of some sort—similar to the one done here—and the list had to precede the survey.

In the interview, respondents were asked to review the list, marking the names of the persons with whom they were personally acquainted. They were then asked to place a second mark by the names of lawyers with whom they had stronger ties.[3] This provides two measures of the connections between the random sample of respondents and the selected list of elites.

The first thing to note about the responses is that most Chicago lawyers did not know most of the notables. In answer to the first question, which asked the lawyers merely to indicate personal acquaintance, 245 respondents (31 percent) said that they knew none of the notables. Another 35 percent knew from one to three, and only 9 percent of the respondents knew more than ten of the notables. When asked about the stronger type of connection, a majority of the respondents indicated that they had no such ties to the notables—420 respondents (53 percent) indicated no strong ties, 24 percent indicated such ties to one or two notables, and 23 percent indicated strong ties to three or more. Only two respondents claimed to have strong ties to as many as twenty-five of the sixty-eight notables.[4]

Respondents who knew more notables were, in some respects, systematically different from those who knew fewer. There was a strong correlation between the income level reported by respondents and the number of notables with whom they had ties (on both measures of acquaintance).[5] Thus, as one might anticipate, respondents who were more financially successful were more likely to move in circles of acquaintance that included notables. Because people acquire acquaintances during the course of their lives, older respondents were likely to know more notables than did younger lawyers.[6] When we control for age, there is not a significant association between gender and the number of notables known—women knew somewhat fewer notables than did males, but the female respondents were younger, on the average. Also, contrary to some expectations, lawyers who practiced in large firms were not more widely connected among the notables. The size of the law firm or other organization the respondent worked in is not significantly correlated with the likelihood of knowing notables.

As noted above, it is difficult at best to determine the extent of a notable's acquaintance before doing the survey, especially when one is striving to include notables of widely varying types. Consequently, three of the persons on our list of sixty-eight proved to be only narrowly acquainted within the bar—these three had fewer than fifteen connections each at the weaker level and only three connections each at the stronger level. In a sense, then, these persons were poor choices, and they were therefore dropped from the network analyses. Surprisingly, two of these three lawyers were vice presidents and general counsel (i.e., the top inside lawyers) of major corporations headquartered in Chicago. Apparently, some of the persons who run the legal departments of the largest corporations do not find it necessary to be widely acquainted within the bar. The other narrowly acquainted person was an African American lawyer in a very small firm.

The Structure of the Networks

Figure 10.3 presents a smallest space analysis of the structure of the 1995 notables' networks. The analytic technique used here is the same as that used with the 1975 data:[7] the degree of proximity in the figure indicates the degree of overlap among the sets of respondents acquainted with each pair of notables. If two notables share few acquaintances, they will be farther apart. As was true of figure 10.1, this is a three-dimensional solution, and the third dimension is, again, indicated by arrows. The six points with arrows are located substantially above or substantially below the plane of the page; the other points are relatively near it.[8]

We again assign pseudonyms to the notables, though not for reasons of confidentiality. The data used to compute the locations of the notables in the network were gathered in interviews with the random sample of Chicago lawyers, not through interviews with the notables themselves. An appendix to this chapter includes brief biographies of each notable, based on public sources such as directory listings and newspaper articles, and those biographies often permit the notable to be identified.[9] The pseudonyms, however, give the names initial letters that indicate some of the categories of notables. We hope that this device may serve to clarify the depiction of the network structure and to make the relationships among the categories more comprehensible.

In this presentation, names beginning with the letter B (bar) are assigned

Figure 10.3. Patterns of Acquaintance with 65 Notable Chicago Lawyers, 1995

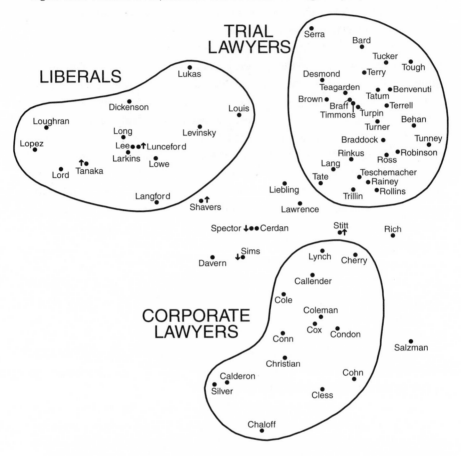

to notables who had served as president of one of the general-membership bar associations—that is, either the Chicago Bar Association (CBA) or the Illinois State Bar Association (ISBA). Names beginning with C are given to corporate lawyers, both those inside the corporation and those in law firms. The deans of three law schools have names beginning with D. Liberals of various stripes are assigned the initial L, and a subcategory of these, former presidents of the Chicago Council of Lawyers (a liberal organization), were given names beginning with La. Names beginning with R are used for both Republicans and "Regular" Democrats (Democrats of a less liberal stripe, especially those who were affiliated with the late Mayor Daley's Regular Democratic Organization). S identifies specialists in particular areas of law, and T identifies trial lawyers (when they serve a corporate clientele, these lawyers are often called litigators). The B, D, L, La, R, and T designations were also used in the presentation on the 1975 notables. Behan, Lang, Lawrence, Liebling, Lynch, Robinson, and Turpin were included on both lists, and we are thus able to compare their positions in the two networks and to observe how their constituencies changed during the intervening twenty years.

The basic structure of the 1995 network is similar to that of the 1975 network. Once again, the analysis indicates three principal regions—a set of trial lawyers (overlapping with bar leaders and political figures) located at the upper right of figure 10.3, a group of liberals (less tightly clustered) located at the upper left, and a set of corporate lawyers (including both house counsel and lawyers in large firms) located in the lower half of the space, toward the middle. In the 1975 network, these categories corresponded to the predominant religious and political affiliations of notables' constituencies. We present, below, analyses that assess the extent to which this was the case in 1995. Given the dramatic changes in the profession over the twenty years—the rapid increase in the size of the bar, the entry of women into the profession in large numbers, the "litigation explosion," the expansion and branching of large law firms, the great growth of the corporate sector of practice, the continuing attrition among solo practitioners—it is perhaps surprising that the network structure does not exhibit greater change.

Figure 10.4 identifies the locations in the structure of the thirteen notables who are women and the eleven who are members of minority groups (African Americans, Latinos, and an Asian American). In the 1975 data, only two women were included in the notables set (reflecting their percentage among Chicago lawyers). Both were located in the top half of the network structure, not in the more conservative, corporate area; in 1995, women were predominantly located in the top half. Of the thirteen women, seven are in the trial lawyers sector, three are among the liberals, two are in the corporate sector, and one is near the center. Several of the women who served a corporate clientele did not have their principal constituencies within the corporate region of the network—Lunceford, for example, was employed by a corporate law firm and handled the work of corporate clients, but she is an African American and was active in issues concerning minority lawyers (see chapter appendix), and the latter appears to determine her position in the network; Tate and Teschemacher were both partners in major law firms that served a corporate clientele, but they were litigators and had political connections that drew them into close proximity to notables who formerly held political office (Lang, Rinkus, Ross, Rainey, and Rollins); Cerdan was employed by the Motorola Corporation but formerly had been the executive director of the American Bar Association, which brought her into contact with broader constituencies. Thus, many of the women with a corporate law practice were not well integrated into the corporate network. It appears that women had greater opportunities to achieve prominence in bar association work or in political activity.

The eleven notables who are members of minority groups are all located in the top half of the space.[10] The two who are lowest on the vertical dimension of the two-dimensional representation (fig. 10.3) both have arrows indicating that they are substantially above the plane. In fact, the four notables who are high in the third dimension are all minorities: three blacks and one Asian. (The two points that are low in the third dimension are both white, male labor lawyers.) Thus, the third dimension of the space appears to have a racial component. The minority notables are almost evenly divided between the liberal sector (with five) and the trial lawyer area (with four), the two specialists (Shavers and Stitt) being outside any of the designated regions.

In the 1975 data, only three members of minority groups—all of them African American—were included among the notables. Two of the three, Robinson and Turpin, are also in the 1995 set. As already noted, in 1975 the three were tightly clustered, which was remarkable because of the differences in their political allegiances. The more general spread of the minorities across the top half of the 1995 network suggests that race was less salient in professional relationships among Chicago lawyers in 1995 than it had been in 1975. But the 1995 set of minority notables was larger and more diverse, and this may affect their dispersion. The increase in the percentage of minorities on the notables list somewhat exceeded the growth of the minority bar—which increased from 3 percent of the 1975 random sample to 8 percent in 1995—but was not greatly out of proportion to it. Arguably, many more minority lawyers achieved positions of prominence during the twenty years. But more significantly, perhaps, the 1995 minority notables were drawn from a more diverse range of practice settings than were the three included in 1975.[11] Like the women among the notables, then, lawyers who are African American, Latino, or Asian American were more likely to acquire visibility through politics or bar association activity—perhaps especially through politics—than in the precincts of the corporate bar (see Wilkins and Gulati 1996).

Of the other five notables included on both the 1995 and the 1975 lists (Behan, Lang, Lawrence, Liebling, and Lynch), only Behan remained in much the same location in the network. He is a prominent personal injury lawyer, was president of the CBA decades ago, and is clearly within the trial lawyers sector, near other past presidents of the CBA and ISBA, but not as close to the center of the network as he was in 1975. This may be attributable,

Figure 10.4. Locations within the Network of Women and Minorities, 1995

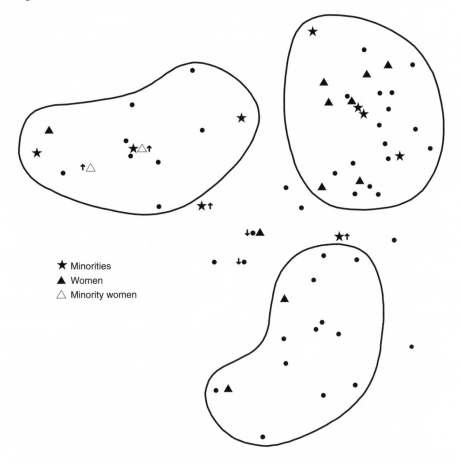

in part, to his age—fifty in 1975 and seventy in 1995. But Liebling was only three years younger than Behan, and he moved from a much less central location in the 1975 network, at the upper left, to a quite central position in 1995. In this respect, Liebling's movement over the two decades is similar to that of Lang, Lawrence, and Lynch. As indicated by their names, all four are liberals; all were located at the upper left in 1975, and Lawrence and Lynch, especially, were near the left margin (see fig. 10.1). In the 1995 data, all are much closer to the center.

Lawrence and Lang were presidents of the Chicago Council of Lawyers in the early 1970s, and both were still in their midthirties at the time of the 1975 survey. In the ensuing twenty years, both acquired considerable additional prominence: Lawrence became dean of the Northwestern University Law School and Lang became corporation counsel (chief counsel) of the

City of Chicago. Thus, both came into contact with broader constituencies. Lang, especially, moved into closer proximity to the city's political elites, and Lawrence was brought into contact with a diverse set of Northwestern law alumni, including the corporate lawyers and firms that were important contributors to the school. The other notable in this set, Lynch, had achieved prominence in 1972 as one of the principal lawyers for the delegation of reform-minded Democrats that successfully challenged the seating of the Regular Democratic delegation, headed by the first Mayor Daley, at that year's presidential nominating convention. In 1984, he was one of the principals in the founding of the Chicago office of a major New York law firm, and he subsequently became the leading partner in that office. Thus, Lynch moved from a position of prominence as a political maverick in 1975 to an established and powerful position in corporate law practice.

The seven specialists (names beginning with S) are all located in relatively marginal positions in the network. Although the specialties of these seven lawyers vary widely—labor law, municipal bonds, antitrust, personal injury defense, commercial real estate, constitutional law (see chapter appendix)—the narrowness of their work appears to bring them into contact with a more restricted set of professional colleagues, which in turn tends to make them more peripheral in the network. Three are found in the outermost ring of points, and the four who appear to be closer to the center in figure 10.1 all have either up or down arrows, indicating that they are distant from the center in the third dimension. While the median number of respondents acquainted with each of the sixty-five notables is forty, the median number acquainted with the seven specialists is only twenty. Only one of the specialists was known by more than twenty-five respondents. The specialists, then, are in a real sense structurally disadvantaged with respect to power or influence. Their locations and limited acquaintance indicate that they would be unlikely either to mobilize large constituencies or to mediate among conflicting sectors of the network.

Notables who possess characteristics associated with more than one region of the space tend to be located between those parts of the network, and they may thus be in a position to convey information from one sector to another and perhaps to mediate conflicts or controversies between the sectors. For example, Davern, the dean of the University of Chicago Law School, was in touch with corporate lawyers and law firms who were important donors to the school, but he was also a member of the board of the American Civil Liberties Union (ACLU) and a former clerk to Justice Brennan. His position in the network is almost equidistant between two other members of the Chicago law school faculty—Silver, who is at the lower left boundary of the corporate sector, and Louis, who is at the upper right boundary of the liberal region. Louis, in turn, was probably drawn toward the trial lawyers because he was the director of the school's legal clinic and had been the public defender for Cook County. Thus, whether notables are in the center of their sectors or near a boundary is affected by the degree of affinity between their personal or practice characteristics and those of another region. Accordingly, most of the notables located in the lower quarter of the trial lawyers sector—from Rinkus and Ross on down—are corporate litigators who are partners in large firms.

The principle that notables with multiple affinities will be placed in an intermediate position, between constituencies, is demonstrated most clearly by the cases of the notables who are in the center. We have already observed that Lawrence and Lynch had backgrounds in liberal politics but subsequently came into greater contact with the corporate bar and with politicians aligned with the Republican and Regular Democratic organizations, and thus moved into positions between those constituencies. Similarly, Liebling was formerly a partner in a major law firm serving a corporate clientele, but for more than two decades before the 1995 survey he headed a "public interest law" organization and was active in reform litigation. He had affinities, therefore, with all three of the major sectors: liberals, trial lawyers, and corporate lawyers. Cerdan also had an unusually varied set of credentials and experiences. In 1995 she was an officer of a major corporation, but she was formerly a litigator, public official, and executive director of the American Bar Association. Consequently, her various roles brought her into contact with a wide range of different types of lawyers.

Because they are in touch with the broadest range of constituencies, these central actors have the potential to act as mediators among the interest groups in the network. But they are probably more likely to be called upon to mediate between or among the several sectors, not within a sector. A problem occurring within the corporate sector, for example, would probably be handled by someone in that region—for example, by Cox, Condon, or Coleman. The most central actors are not necessarily useful as all-purpose mediators or message carriers, good at all times and places. Rather, their utility will be limited by the particulars of a given controversy or problem, as will that of other actors.

Similar research on networks of relationships among political actors in Washington, D.C., and in the Cook County criminal justice system found no central actors (Heinz et al. 1993; Heinz and Manikas 1992). Those political networks were structured as rough spheres, but they had "hollow cores" or empty centers. The reports of those studies include a modest amount of theorizing about possible reasons for the absence of central mediators in the networks. In essence, they argue that in a political network, where the principal activity is competitive, the central position in the network is unstable. Actors in the center may be able to control the flow of information from one side of the network to the other and, perhaps, be able to determine outcomes (winners and losers) through that information control or by shifting their weight to one side or the other. Any actor would probably be happy to occupy the central position but might be uncomfortable with having someone else there. If one actor or a small set were permitted to occupy the central position consistently, across a range of issues, the others would tend to be subordinated. Competitors would, therefore, have an incentive to keep the center open or to keep the situation in flux; they would not want other actors to acquire the power derived from the center position.

In a more cooperative system, however, central actors might be seen as facilitators. Thus, if the networks among Chicago lawyers primarily serve to expedite referral of cases, transmission of professional information, management of firm business, and rationalization of court procedures, the interaction might be more often characterized by cooperation than by competition. And if this is so, then the presence of central actors might be valued rather than feared. Note that central notables were found in the networks in both 1975 and 1995. This basic characteristic, apparently, did not change.

Ethnoreligious and Political Divisions

As we saw in figures 10.1 and 10.2, in 1975 the structure of relationships was organized not only by practice setting and type of clientele but by the religious affiliations and ideological allegiances of the notables and their acquaintances. *Chicago Lawyers* includes a set of figures presenting analyses of the extent to which the acquaintances of each of the notables were drawn from particular religious and political categories (Heinz and Laumann 1982, 299–309). The patterns were very clear. Thus, for example, a figure presenting the percentage of Catholics among the acquaintances of the 1975 notables showed a substantial overrepresentation in the constituencies of notables located at the right side of the space, and these percentages then decreased in a very orderly fashion across the space, from right to left, culminating in a marked underrepresentation of Catholics among the acquaintances of the notables at the left margin (ibid., 306, fig. 9.5).

Figures 10.5 and 10.6 use this same technique to analyze the degree to which the 1995 network is organized by religious affiliations. The figures present the difference from the percentage in the random sample—that is,

Figure 10.5. Characteristics of the Respondents Acquainted with Each of the Notables: Difference from Total Percentage of Catholics, 1995

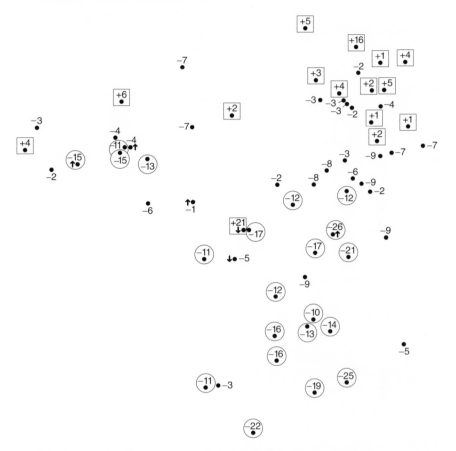

Note: Squares enclose all positive numbers; circles indicate 10 or more points negative.

the degree of either overrepresentation or underrepresentation among the acquaintances of each of the notables. Figure 10.5 indicates the number of percentage points (rounded to the nearest whole point) of divergence from the percentage of Catholics in the random sample, which is 33 percent. The −22 next to the point at the bottom of the space, therefore, indicates that only 11 percent of the respondents who reported acquaintance with that notable were Catholics.

This analysis of the percentage of Catholics among the constituencies of the notables in 1995 again shows a definite pattern, though it is not as sharp as in 1975. Most of the points with positive numbers are clustered at the upper right. The exceptions are three points in the liberal sector and the point

near the middle of the figure that is very low on the third dimension (+ 21).
Note that, of the 65 notables, only 15 have positive percentages—indicating
that Catholic lawyers are less likely to be included among the acquaintances
of the notables. The large negatives are, in turn, predominately found in
the corporate sector, with another small cluster at the center of the liberal
region. Thus, it appears that the trial lawyers and bar association leaders
found at the upper right were more likely to move in circles of acquaintance
that included substantial numbers of Catholics, while the constituencies of
notable corporate lawyers underrepresented Catholics, as did those of some
(but not all) liberals. The salience of religion is especially striking since this is
not an analysis of the social circles or residential neighbors of these lawyers,
but of their professional acquaintances. Some of their professional associates
may also be social friends, of course, but work context is surely an important
determinant of these patterns.

Figure 10.6 shows the percentage of the notables' acquaintances who are
Jewish. The first thing to note is that far more of the numbers are positive, indicating that Jewish respondents were more likely to be included in notables'
circles of acquaintance. The pattern of distribution in the space, if there is a
pattern, is much less distinct. All sectors include both overrepresentation and
underrepresentation of Jewish acquaintances, without marked regionaliza-
tion. If we wished to be somewhat more speculative, we might suggest that
there is a rim or center/periphery effect in the corporate sector. The points
around the outside rim of the sector exhibit a substantial overrepresentation
of Jews, while the points closer to the center have lower percentages. But,
overall, Jewish respondents were acquainted with notables in all regions, in
more or less equal measure.

When we do the same sort of analysis on the partisan political affiliations of the respondents, we find some distinct tendencies, but the divisions are not rigid. As one might anticipate, Republicans are overrepresented
in the corporate sector (especially at its center) and are underrepresented
among the acquaintances of almost all notables in the liberal sector. More
surprising, however, is the fact that Republicans are also overrepresented
in the constituencies of most of the notables in the trial lawyers region.
This is a striking change from the 1975 findings, where Regular Democrats
clearly predominated among the trial lawyers' professional associates. We
explore possible reasons for this change below. Analyses of identification as
Democrats and independents exhibit less distinct patterns. Apart from the
overrepresentation of Democrats among many (but not all) of the notables
in the liberal sector, the distribution of both independents and Democrats
throughout the space appears to be essentially random.

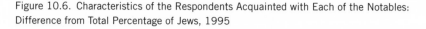

Figure 10.6. Characteristics of the Respondents Acquainted with Each of the Notables: Difference from Total Percentage of Jews, 1995

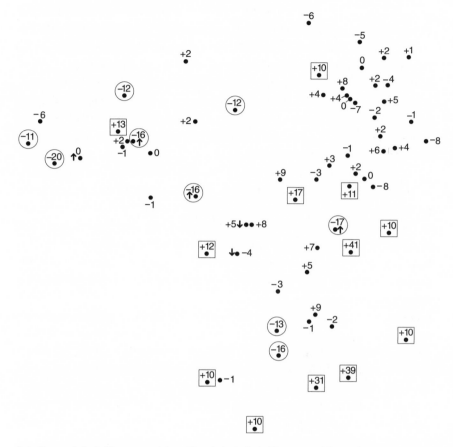

Note: Squares indicate 10 or more points positive; circles indicate 10 or more points negative.

Conclusion

Although the networks had three basic sectors in both 1975 and 1995, and the bases of those sectors were similar, the positions of individual notables often changed. Of the seven notables included in both sets, four moved into a more central position in the network as they matured and gained prominence, while one became somewhat more peripheral. This suggests that, although the roles of individual actors within the networks evolve, the central principles organizing the relationships among elite lawyers and their several constituencies remained constant during this twenty-year period.

But in spite of the similarity in the broad outlines of the structure at the two points in time, the dynamics of the networks differ in important respects. First, the number of respondents knowing each of the notables declined. In part, this might be attributable to the use of a larger and more diverse list of notables in the 1995 study, but it is probably also attributable to the increase in the number of Chicago lawyers and the consequent decrease in the probability that any given lawyer would, through happenstance, come into contact with one of the notables. Each lawyer will have ties to narrow slices of the whole—and, indeed, these slices might be increasingly defined by the lawyers' work settings and by the clientele that they serve. Thus, religious affiliations and partisan political allegiances appear to be less salient in organizing the network in 1995.

But we should not overstate this. Work is clearly not the whole story. That is, it is not the only variable generating the structure of the network, as the distinct identity of a liberal sector makes clear. Political issues appear to be the principal force defining that constituency, including issues such as civil rights and abortion, although legal services to the poor may also have brought some of these lawyers together. The small cluster of politicians near the bottom of the trial lawyers sector, by contrast, is defined principally by work and client type rather than by ideology. These politicians are a mixture of Republicans and regular organization Democrats. Apparently, for these purposes, the difference between those two categories is not important. What these notables (and perhaps their constituencies) have in common is that they served governmental clients (chiefly state and local) and that they worked on projects in which superior access to government agencies and public officials was important—matters such as bond issues, real estate development, zoning, and the defense of governmental agencies in litigation. Many of these notables were former political officeholders.

One of the more remarkable changes in the nature of the networks is the movement of Republicans into the trial lawyers sector. As noted above, in 1975 that region was dominated by Regular Democrats. *Chicago Lawyers* said (Heinz and Laumann 1982, 314):

> The trial lawyers/CBA sphere has clear political ties to the Regular Democrats. It is probable that one of the principal sources of the influence of this sphere within the profession is its ability to mobilize the resources of the city and county governments, to secure the benefits that it is within the power of City Hall to confer.

The change in 1995 was perhaps attributable to a decline in the fortunes of the regular Democratic organization in Chicago and to the Republicans' control of the governor's office. The first Mayor Daley died in 1976, and during the late 1970s and 1980s the organization suffered a series of electoral losses. A challenger (Jane Byrne) defeated the organization candidate for mayor; Chicago elected its first black mayor (Harold Washington); and the second Mayor Daley (Richard M., the late mayor's son) was then elected with liberal support after a split within the black political forces. During the same period, the Republicans continuously controlled the governorship. The lawyer labeled "Rainey" in figure 10.3 was governor from 1977 to 1991, and he and several of his protégés are found near the bottom of the trial lawyers sector. As the power of the old Democratic organization waned, the Republican Party reasserted its traditional position among the downtown business interests, which had always been strong within the legal profession.

The principal changes in the network, then, appear to have been generated by differences in the political context and by changes in the market for lawyers' services. The 1975 network included only a handful of notables who were black or female, and these were confined within a very limited region of the network, indicating the salience of those characteristics. In the 1995 data, many more notables were minorities and women, and both were more widely distributed in the space, though still largely concentrated in the top half (not in the corporate sector). Idiosyncratic characteristics of individual notables—such as their personalities—appear to play less part in placing them within the network than do their organizational affiliations, the nature of their clients, or the identity of the politicians with whom they cast their lot in state and local government. The location of particular notables can be accounted for, quite persuasively, in general structural terms.

The network structure may have broader significance for politics within the bar. The fact that there are three distinct sectors, rather than more or fewer, has implications for the extent of the coherence of the bar—that is, for the degree of consensus within it and for the likelihood of accommodation and bargaining among the sectors. If there were a considerably greater number of well-defined clusters, concerted action would probably be even more difficult, and if the network were more unified, then consensus or common action might be more likely. Moreover, the arrangement of the three sectors is also significant. This structure was not inevitable. We might, for example, have found the three sectors lined up in a row, which would then suggest that the constituencies on the respective ends of the row were less likely to interact. Perhaps the liberal sector and the corporate sector might have been antagonists, with liberals at one end and the corporate sector at the opposite end, and the leaders of the organized bar in the middle, where they would be in a position to mediate. Instead, we found the CBA and ISBA presidents firmly embedded in the constituencies of the personal injury and criminal defense lawyers, suggesting that they were aligned with those interest groups. Thus, the network structure indicates that liberals within the bar can (and perhaps do) reach their own accommodations and understandings with the corporate sector, without seeking the intervention of bar leaders. Similarly, the corporate sector may independently strike bargains with the trial lawyers, or the trial lawyers may reach out to either of the other two sectors, in a fluid situation with shifting alliances. Or, as is perhaps the case most often, each of the three sectors might simply choose to go its own way, pursuing its own agenda and remaining largely indifferent to the activities of the other sectors. The network structure, therefore, has implications for the integration of the bar—or, more likely, for the lack of it.

Appendix: Notables' Biographies (as of 1994–95)

Bar Presidents (CBA and ISBA)

Bard. A solo practitioner specializing in the representation of plaintiffs in personal injury cases, especially medical malpractice and products liability. He was president of the Illinois State Bar Association in 1991–92 and a member of the board of managers of the Illinois Trial Lawyers Association (an organization that speaks for plaintiffs' lawyers). He is forty-seven; law school: Indiana University.

Behan. The most prominent plaintiffs personal injury lawyer in Chicago, he is the senior partner of a small firm. He was president of the Chicago Bar Association more than twenty years ago and was a member of the House of Delegates of the ABA and chairman of its litigation section. He is general counsel of the Illinois Democratic Party. Age seventy; Irish Catholic; law school: Loyola University (Chicago).

Benvenuti. Partner in a large Chicago firm. His specialty is consumer finance law, and he represents banks and other financial services firms. He was a justice of the Illinois Appellate Court in the 1970s and a representative in the Illinois legislature in the 1960s. Just before going on the bench, he served as president of the Illinois State Bar Association (1975–76). He is executive vice president and general counsel of the Illinois Financial Services Association. Age sixty-three; Republican; Catholic; law school: De Paul University.

Braddock. A sole practitioner specializing in the representation of plaintiffs in class actions and in mass tort product liability cases. He was president of the Chicago Bar Association in 1981–82, and he shares a suite of offices with two other former CBA presidents. He chairs the Illinois Compensation Review Board, which recommends to the legislature salary increases for judges and other state employees. Age thirty-six; Regular Democrat; law school: Loyola (Chicago).

Braff. A senior partner in a small general-practice firm. She does primarily real estate work, probate, and some litigation. She was the first woman to become president of the Chicago Bar Association (1977–78), and she has also served as president of the Women's Bar Association of Illinois. She is a member of the board of trustees of the Illinois Institute of Technology and was the first woman on the board of Illinois Bell Telephone. Age seventy; law school: Chicago-Kent College of Law.

Brown. Partner in a small firm with a business litigation practice. She specializes in securities broker fraud cases and commodity futures trading regulation. The second woman to serve as president of the Chicago Bar Association (1991–92), she has also held leadership positions in several commissions and committees dealing with law reform, especially in juvenile justice, and now chairs the American Bar Association's Commission on Women. She is in her midforties, earned her JD from Loyola (Chicago), and has ties to the Democratic Party.

Corporate Lawyers

Calderon. Managing partner of a large corporate firm. (She is the only woman who is managing partner of a major Chicago law firm.) She specializes in banking law, particularly in international transactions. She is a member of the boards of the Evanston Hospital, the YMCA of Metropolitan Chicago, and the Chicagoland Chamber of Commerce, and is assistant Chancellor of the Episcopal Diocese of Chicago. Age forty-one; Episcopalian; Wellesley undergraduate; law school: Harvard University.

Callender. A long-time member of the faculty of Northwestern Law School and its former dean, he has just returned to full-time teaching after retiring as a partner of a large multinational law firm headquartered in Chicago. His specialty is securities law. In the late 1980s, he chaired the federal Securities and Exchange Commission. Age sixty-five; Republican; law school: University of Wisconsin.

Cerdan. Vice president of Motorola, in charge of cellular overseas investments. She found fame early in her career as an assistant special prosecutor in the Watergate investigation. During the Carter administration, she served as general counsel of the Department of the Army, and in the mid-1980s she was deputy attorney general of Illinois. From 1987 to 1990 she was executive director of the American Bar Association. Age fifty-one; law school: Columbia University.

Chaloff. Executive vice president and general counsel of the First National Bank of Chicago (First Chicago Corporation). He oversees a staff of seventy-six lawyers. Age fifty-three; law school: University of Cincinnati.

Cherry. The senior partner of a major, new Chicago-based law firm that has grown quickly to include offices in Washington, New York, and Los Angeles. His specialty is corporate tax law. He is a member of the boards of Amalgamated Bank, Roosevelt University, and IIT Chicago-Kent College of Law. Age fifty-eight; law school: John Marshall (Chicago).

Christian. A senior partner of a major corporate law firm headquartered in Chicago. Although he has been at the firm since 1956, in the 1980s he served as vice president and general counsel of International Harvester, then (briefly) as special counsel to Ameritech and then as general counsel and executive vice president of General Motors, all while remaining a partner in the law firm. He is chairman of the board of the Chicago Lighthouse for the Blind and a trustee of the University of Chicago and the Aspen Institute. Age sixty-two; Republican; Presbyterian; law school: University of Chicago.

Cless. Chairman of the executive committee at a major Chicago law firm. He is principal outside counsel for McDonald's Corporation and is a member of the McDonald's board. He is also a director of several other corporations and of civic and cultural organizations, including the Art Institute and the Orchestral Association. Age sixty; law school: Harvard University.

Cohn. A senior partner of a ninety-five-lawyer firm. He specializes in corporate tax and in merger and acquisition work. This is the kind of work that lawyers call "doing deals." He regularly represents, among others, the Pritzker family, owners of the Hyatt Hotel chain and of numerous other properties. Age fifty; University of Illinois, both undergraduate and law school.

Cole. President and director of the Metropolitan Planning Council, a nonprofit organization that advocates policies on health care, housing, transportation, and other civic issues. Before taking this position, she was a partner in a major corporate law firm in Chicago. Before that, she was vice president for business and finance at the University of Chicago, and in the 1960s was general counsel (inside counsel) for the Maremont Corporation. She is on the boards of Commonwealth Edison, LaSalle National Bank, and other companies, and was a founder and first chair of the Chicago Network, a group of highly placed women executives and lawyers. Age seventy; law school: University of Chicago.

Coleman. Chairman of a firm that has four hundred lawyers in its Chicago office and about three hundred in other cities. He does corporate securities and public utilities work, and has chaired the ABA's section on public utilities law. He is a director of the Chicago Stock Exchange, the Northern Trust Company, and several other corporations. He was president of the Legal Assistance Foundation of Chicago 1973–75, has chaired the lawyers' division of the Jewish United Fund in Chicago, and is a trustee of the Chicago Council on Foreign Relations and the Aspen Institute. Age sixty; Jewish; law school: Northwestern University.

Condon. Senior partner in a seven-hundred-lawyer firm. Until September 1993, when he reached age seventy, Condon was chairman of the firm's executive committee, a post that he had held for eighteen years. He is the chairman of the board of Northwestern University. He has represented the Chicago Tribune Company, among many other corporations. From 1980 to 1986, he was vice president and general counsel of AT&T while retaining his position in the law firm. Age seventy-one; law school: Northwestern University.

Conn. Vice president and general counsel of FMC Corporation (a Chicago-based chemicals and defense conglomerate) and, formerly, of Montgomery Ward. Chairman of the board of Northwestern University's corporate counsel center and a member of the board of regents of Georgetown University. Age sixty-two; Democrat; Catholic; law school: Georgetown University.

Cox. A senior partner of one of Chicago's leading firms, he is a tax specialist. He is chairman of the board of trustees of the University of Chicago and a director of *Encyclopaedia Britannica*. Age sixty; law school: University of Chicago.

Deans of Law Schools

Davern. Dean of the University of Chicago Law School 1987–94. (He became provost of the university just before the survey.) His specialty is constitutional law, especially civil liberties issues. He has been a member of the board of the Illinois division of the ACLU, and he strongly criticized the ideological judicial appointments of the Reagan and Bush (George H. W.) administrations. He was one of Justice Brennan's clerks at the U.S. Supreme Court in 1972–73. Age forty-eight; law school: University of Chicago.

Desmond. The dean of the Loyola (Chicago) University Law School and former chair of the ABA's Section on Legal Education and Admissions to the Bar. She teaches in the area of torts and products liability. Before joining the

Loyola faculty twenty-one years ago, she was an administrator at Stanford. Age late fifties; Jewish; law school: Columbia University.

Dickenson. Dean of the De Paul University Law School. His principal field is administrative law. Before becoming dean at De Paul in 1986, he was dean of Wayne State's law school and before that, he was associate dean at Yale. From 1977 to 1980, he was general counsel of the Armed Services committee of the U.S. Senate. He is a member of the advisory committee of the Illinois ACLU. Age fifty-four; law school: Yale University.

Lawrence (see below).

Liberals

Presidents of the Chicago Council of Lawyers (La)

Lang. A senior partner in a small firm specializing in representing plaintiffs in employment discrimination cases. He also represented a group of minority and independent aldermen in an effort to overturn a redrawing of ward boundaries that was supported by the second Mayor Daley. During a portion of Harold Washington's tenure as mayor, he was head of the city's legal department. He was a founder and first president of the Chicago Council of Lawyers. Age fifty-three; Jewish; law school: University of Chicago.

Langford. A partner in the Chicago office of a large firm that started in Cleveland and now has offices in several cities. He does securities and corporate work. He is president of the Legal Assistance Foundation of Chicago and was president of the Chicago Council of Lawyers in 1981–83. He has been a member of several law reform commissions and of the boards of the Lawyers' Committee for Civil Rights Under Law and the American Judicature Society. Age forty-four; Democrat; Presbyterian; Rhodes scholar; law school: Harvard University.

Larkins. A partner in a thirty-lawyer Chicago firm. He started his career in the civil rights division of the U.S. Justice Department. His specialty is litigation, and the firm has a general civil litigation practice. From 1991 to 1993, he was president of the Chicago Council of Lawyers. Age forty; Yale undergraduate; law school: Harvard University.

Lawrence. Dean of the Northwestern University Law School. He teaches contracts and constitutional law and formerly worked both in broadcast regulation and in poverty law. He was the second president of the Chicago Council of Lawyers (in the early 1970s) and has been a member of the Northwestern faculty for twenty-five years. Age fifty-four; Jewish; liberal Democrat; law school: Harvard University.

Other Liberals (L)

Lee. General counsel of the American Bar Association. Before going to the ABA in 1988, he was a litigation partner at a major Chicago firm. He is president of Leadership Greater Chicago and a member of the board of the Migrant Legal Action Program. Age thirty-nine; African American; Harvard University, both undergraduate and law school.

Levinsky. Legal director of the ACLU of Illinois. A recent political cartoon showed him walking over dead bodies as he tried to protect the rights of public housing residents who objected to warrantless searches of their apartments. Age forty-seven; law school: Northwestern University.

Liebling. For the past twenty-four years, he has been executive director of Business and Professional People for the Public Interest, a "public interest law firm" that pursues reform on a number of fronts—public housing and environmental pollution being most prominent among them. Before moving to this organization in 1970 (the year after its founding), he was a highly successful partner in a major Chicago law firm, where he had been for seventeen years. Age sixty-seven; Jewish; law school: University of Chicago.

Long. Director of the legal clinic at Chicago-Kent College of Law. He formerly directed the legal clinics at Northwestern and at Boston College, and he has long been prominent in issues concerning the delivery of legal services to persons of limited means. Age fifty-seven; law school: University of Miami.

Lopez. The current president of the Mexican-American Lawyers Association. He is an associate at a very large firm that specializes in international business transactions. He has been an outspoken supporter of the appointment of Latino judges and strongly advocated the elevation of a Latino appellate judge to a seat on the U.S. Supreme Court. He is a member of the board of the Legal Assistance Foundation of Chicago. A 1988 University of Michigan Law School graduate, at age thirty-one he is the youngest person on the notables list.

Lord. Executive director of the Legal Assistance Foundation of Chicago, an agency providing legal services to indigent clients. The agency is supported by private charity and by grants from the federal Legal Services Corporation. Age fifty-three; law school: Washington University.

Loughran. The director of the Reproductive Rights Project of the Illinois chapter of the ACLU. She has been the lead counsel in several high-profile abortion cases. Age thirty-nine; law school: University of Iowa.

Louis. Director of the legal clinic at the University of Chicago. He was formerly the chief public defender for Cook County, after having served as deputy director of the public defender service in Washington, D.C. He recently chaired the Criminal Justice section of the ABA, and he is a member of the advisory board of the Neighborhood Defender Service of Harlem. Age forty-eight; African American; law school: University of Wisconsin.

Lowe. Director of the Environmental Law and Policy Center of the Midwest, a new public-interest group. Until recently, he was general counsel of Business and Professional People for the Public Interest. An environmental law specialist, he is the son of an executive in a local steel company. The Chicago newspapers called him "a consumer hero" because of his leading role in negotiating $1.34 billion in rebates by Commonwealth Edison, the largest utility rate refund in history. He is a director of the Jewish Council on Urban Affairs. Age thirty-nine; Michigan undergraduate; law school: Harvard.

Lunceford. President of the Cook County Bar Association (the African American lawyers' association) and a partner in a major Chicago law firm. She does corporate and insurance work, and in 1987 she cofounded the Chicago Committee on Minorities in Large Law Firms. Age thirty-eight; African American; University of California (Berkeley) Law School.

Lukas. He was executive director of the Illinois Supreme Court's Special Commission on the Administration of Justice, which recently completed its work. (The commission was appointed in the wake of judicial corruption scandals and was chaired by Trillin; see below.) Lukas now holds a research position at the De Paul Law School, and he formerly held a similar post at Northwestern's Institute for Policy Research. During the 1980s, he served as staff director of another law reform commission chaired by Trillin, and he then became director of administrative operations for the Cook County Public Defender's office. He is a former vice president of the Chicago Council of Lawyers. Age forty-eight; law school: De Paul University.

Lynch. Partner in charge of the Chicago office of a large law firm headquartered in New York. He was a delegate to the Illinois Constitutional Convention in 1970 and chaired its drafting committee. His wife was director of programs and policy on the staff of a Republican governor, but he has given money and advice to Democratic candidates. He specializes in corporate financial transactions, including mergers and acquisitions. Age fifty-five; law school: Northwestern University.

Republicans and Regular Democrats

Rainey. Chairman of the executive committee at a major Chicago law firm. He was governor of Illinois 1977–91 and now specializes in government regulatory work. Earlier in his career, he was a criminal lawyer—he started his career as an assistant state's attorney, and he taught criminal law at Northwestern. In the early 1970s, he was the U.S. Attorney for the Chicago region. He is a director of the Board of Trade, FMC Corporation, the Sun-Times Company, other corporations and several arts organizations including the Lyric Opera and the Museum of Contemporary Art. Age fifty-eight; Republican; law school: Northwestern University.

Rich. Probably the most prominent zoning lawyer in Chicago. He was a partner in a major Chicago law firm 1970–94. He has just moved to a smaller firm. *Chicago* magazine called him "a fixture in the intersecting worlds of Chicago building construction and politics" and noted that he has been a friend and campaign worker for both Mayor Daleys. From 1975 until 1987, he chaired the city's zoning appeals board. Age fifty-six; Democrat; law school: Yale University.

Rinkus. Partner in a major Chicago firm. He specializes in litigation, both criminal and civil. In the early 1970s, when Rainey was the U.S. Attorney, Rinkus was an assistant in that office. In 1985, he became the U.S. Attorney, succeeding Ross in the post. In the early 1990s, he chaired a state commission on crime and corrections, which recommended the construction of a new, supermaximum security prison. Age fifty-two; law school: Northwestern University.

Robinson. The senior partner of a small firm, he is a trial lawyer. In recent years, his firm has done bond issue work for both the City of Chicago and the State of Illinois. He has also handled zoning cases for local real estate developers. He was president of the board of trustees of the University of Illinois (a statewide elective office), commissioner of the Chicago Housing Authority, and president of the Chicago Metropolitan Housing Development Authority. Age sixty-six; African American; Democrat; law school: University of Michigan.

Rollins. Partner in a major corporate law firm. He was Attorney General of Illinois from 1980 to 1983 and chairman of the state's Judicial Inquiry Board (the body that investigates misconduct by judges) 1988–92. A litigator, he has represented the Illinois Republican congressional delegation in a redistricting case and the Chicago Board of Trade. Age fifty-two; Republican; Lutheran; law school: JD from Wayne State University, LLM from Northwestern University.

Ross. Partner in a major Chicago firm. During Reagan's first presidential term, he served as the U.S. Attorney for the Chicago district, but in 1990 he was a special counsel in the Iran-Contra investigation and prosecuted Admiral Poindexter, Reagan's national security advisor. In recent years, he has represented several politicians accused of crimes, including former U.S. Representative Dan Rostenkowski (D-Ill.), and has handled civil litigation as well. Like Rollins and Rinkus, he served in the U.S. Attorney's office in the early 1970s when Rainey headed the office. Age forty-nine; Republican; law school: Loyola (Chicago).

Specialists

Salzman. A senior partner at a small firm specializing in the representation of plaintiffs in antitrust cases. He and his partners also have an "of counsel" relationship with a general practice corporate law firm. He was one of the lawyers for plaintiffs in an antitrust class action against the manufacturers of folding cartons, which resulted in a $200 million settlement in 1979. Age fifty-seven; University of Chicago, both undergraduate and law school.

Serra. Senior partner in a twenty-five-lawyer firm representing defendants (primarily insurance companies) in personal injury cases. The firm also does some health care and municipal bond work. He is a member of the boards of Wheelabrator Technologies, Metropolitan Bank and Trust, Holy Trinity High School, Holy Cross High School, Illinois Benedictine College, and several civic organizations. He was a founder of the Mexican-American Lawyers Association and of the Latin-American Bar Association. He served as president of the Trial Lawyers Club of Chicago and as secretary of the Hispanic National Bar Association. Age forty-seven; law school: University of Pennsylvania.

Shavers. Partner in a large Chicago firm. His specialty is municipal bond work. He was acting head of Chicago's legal department in 1986 and chair of its Planning Commission from 1986 to 1990. He is a trustee of the Goodman Theatre and of Columbia College of Chicago and a member of the National Forum for Black Public Administrators. Age forty-two; African American; law school: Harvard University.

Silver. Professor at the University of Chicago Law School. His fields are constitutional law and administrative law. After clerking for Justice Thurgood Marshall at the U.S. Supreme Court, he worked briefly for the Justice Department before joining the University of Chicago faculty in 1981. Age forty; law school: Harvard University.

Sims. A labor law specialist representing unions and employees, he is the senior partner of a fifteen-lawyer firm. Author of several scholarly articles on labor law. Age sixty-two; University of Chicago, both undergraduate and law school.

Spector. A senior partner in the same firm where Cless is chairman of the executive committee and where Cole was long a partner. He is a labor law specialist, representing the management side in employment and labor relations cases. Among his clients is the Yellow Cab Company. Age fifty-six; law school: University of Chicago.

Stitt. The senior partner of a seventeen-lawyer firm with a varied commercial practice. He specializes in real estate and commercial lending work. His firm, founded in 1981, is one of a small handful of prominent minority-owned law firms in Chicago and has represented Montgomery Ward, Amoco, General Motors, Ford, and Allstate Insurance, especially in real estate and breach of warranty cases. Age late forties; African American; law school: De Paul University.

Trial Lawyers

Tanaka. An associate in a thirty-five-lawyer firm. She specializes in litigation. She was a founder of Chicago's Asian American Bar Association and was its president 1992–94. In 1989–90, she was the central region governor of the National Asian Pacific American Bar Association. Age thirty-five; law school: Harvard University.

Tate. Partner in a major Chicago law firm. She is a corporate litigator and served as chair of the ABA's litigation section. She has also been a member of the ABA's House of Delegates (the governing body) and chaired the committee on "character and fitness" that reviews applicants for admission to the Illinois bar. Age fifty-five; law school: Yale University.

Tatum. A senior partner of a divorce specialty firm. His partners have been quoted as saying that the firm "rarely" takes a case where the assets at stake are less than $1 million—ordinarily, the assets are much greater. He was elected to the state legislature at the age of thirty-one and at thirty-eight became presiding judge of the domestic relations (divorce) division of the Circuit Court of Cook County. Age fifty-five; law school: Valparaiso University.

Teagarden. Senior partner in a five-lawyer Chicago firm. In recent years, he has represented plaintiffs in class action litigation. In the 1960s, during the administration of the first Mayor Daley, he was head of Chicago's legal department, and he later served as president of the Chicago Park District. He is president of the Helen Brach Foundation (the Brach candy company family), a $70 million foundation that primarily supports Roman Catholic educational institutions. Age sixty-two; Democrat; law school: Loyola (Chicago).

Terrell. One of the most prominent criminal defense lawyers in Chicago. He recently joined a seventy-lawyer firm, after having practiced in his own small firm for twenty-five years. He specializes in white-collar crime and has represented accused lawyers, judges, and organized crime figures. Age fifty-seven; law school: University of Illinois.

Terry. The senior partner of a small firm specializing in the representation of plaintiffs in personal injury cases, especially medical malpractice. She began her career as a prosecutor in the state's attorney's office, and she has been an officer of the Chicago and Illinois bar associations, the Illinois Trial Lawyers Association, and the Association of Trial Lawyers of America. She chaired the judicial evaluation committee of the Chicago Bar Association, a politically sensitive post. Age late forties; JD from Notre Dame University.

Teschmacher. Partner in the Chicago office of a large New York–based firm specializing in corporate takeovers, real estate syndications, and other major financial transactions. She is a litigator and a former federal district judge who resigned from the bench in 1987, saying "it's not where the action is." She represented the president of the Cook County Board of Commissioners when his authority to order the resumption of abortions at the county's public hospital was challenged. Age fifty-five; law school: Loyola (Chicago).

Timmons. A trial lawyer who is best known for his criminal defense work and for his prominent role in local politics. He is a former justice of the Illinois Appellate Court, and he made an unsuccessful run for the mayor's office. Age sixty-nine; African American; Democrat; law school: Northwestern University.

Tough. A founding partner of a small personal injury firm, he represents plaintiffs in medical malpractice, product liability, and other personal injury cases. He has been president of the Illinois Trial Lawyers Association, a member of the board of directors of Trial Lawyers for Public Justice, and chairman of the Insurance Practices Committee of the Association of Trial Lawyers of America. In 1989, when he was the youngest person on *Forbes* magazine's list of the nation's highest paid lawyers, Tough claimed to have never lost a case. Age midforties; University of Notre Dame undergraduate; law school: Loyola (Chicago).

Trillin. Chairman of a major Chicago law firm. He specializes in complex corporate litigation, including merger and acquisition work. He chaired two blue-ribbon commissions created by the Illinois courts to recommend reforms (and to assuage public opinion) in the wake of judicial corruption scandals. He has also chaired the Cook County Judicial Advisory Council. Age sixty-four; Jewish; law school: Harvard University.

Tucker. The senior partner of a small firm specializing in personal injury work for plaintiffs. She formerly worked in the office of Behan (see above). She has a radio call-in talk show where she answers questions concerning medical malpractice, product liability, and general negligence law. She has been a member of the governing boards of the Illinois Trial Lawyers Association and of the Illinois State Bar Association and has chaired the tort law section of the Association of Trial Lawyers of America. Age forty-five; law school: De Paul University.

Tunney. Senior partner of a sixty-lawyer litigation specialty firm. He represents defendants in personal injury cases—thus, most of his clients are insurance companies and corporations. He served as president of the American Board of Professional Liability Attorneys in 1985–87 and of the International Association of Defense Counsel in 1993–94. Age fifty; law school: Northwestern University.

Turner. A partner in a medium-sized litigation firm, he specializes in criminal law. Now doing high-profile criminal defense work, he began his career as an assistant public defender and then worked as a prosecutor for thirteen years, ending as First Assistant State's Attorney of Cook County 1983–85. In 1990, he was appointed chairman of the Illinois Gaming Board. He is probably best known for his work as chief prosecutor of mass murderer John Wayne Gacy. A strong advocate for the death penalty, in 1983–84 he was president of the Association of Government Attorneys in Capital Litigation. Age fifty-three; Republican; law school: Northwestern University.

Turpin. A solo practitioner specializing in criminal defense work. More than twenty years ago, he was president of the Cook County Bar Association (the African American lawyers association). When Harold Washington first became mayor, he headed the city's legal department. (Lang was his successor in that position.) More recently, he represented Jabir Herbert Muhammad, Muhammad Ali's former manager, in a contract dispute with Ali. Age sixty-two; African American; law school: University of Illinois.

Chapter 11
A Satisfying Profession?
With Kathleen E. Hull and Ava A. Harter

There is a widespread perception that a crisis of morale afflicts the legal profession. The dean of the Yale Law School defined the crisis: "It is the product of growing doubts about the capacity of a lawyer's life to offer fulfillment to the person who takes it up. Disguised by the material well-being of lawyers, it is a spiritual crisis that strikes at the heart of their professional pride" (Kronman 1993, 2). The complaint, then, is not merely that there has been a decline in lawyers' ethics, altruism, and professionalism, but that this degeneration has made lawyers unhappy in their work.

For at least the past century, critics within the profession have decried the deterioration of the bar (Gordon 1988). Every generation of lawyers appears to think that the golden era of the bar occurred just before they entered it (understandably, however, they never make the cause-and-effect inference). In 1907, John Dos Passos the elder (a lawyer, the father of the more famous writer) observed: "The lawyer stands before the community shorn of his prestige, clothed in the unattractive garb of a mere commercial agent—a flexible and convenient go-between, often cultivating every kind of equivocal quality as the means of success" (1907, 33). Dos Passos said that the "Augustan age" of professionalism was before the war—the Civil War, that is (1907, 31). Going to hell in a handbasket is, apparently, a long, slow journey.

Both the popular and the professional press have featured stories about burnout, career abandonment, and general despair in the bar. A headline in the *Los Angeles Times* read, MISERABLE WITH THE LEGAL LIFE; MORE AND MORE

LAWYERS HATE THEIR JOBS, SURVEYS FIND (Dolan 1995, A1). The story noted that: "A RAND Corp. study last year concluded that California attorneys were 'profoundly pessimistic' about the law, with only half indicating that they would choose again to be a lawyer. Seven in 10 lawyers responding to a 1992 California Lawyer magazine poll said they would change careers if the opportunity arose." A law professor published a provocative article in the *Vanderbilt Law Review* characterizing the American legal profession as "one of the most unhappy and unhealthy on the face of the earth" and observing that "lawyers seem to be among the most depressed people in America" (Schiltz 1999, 872–74). Consider this: "Almost a third of lawyers in a Florida survey reported feeling depressed once a week, and a university study in North Carolina revealed that 11 percent of attorneys in the state considered taking their own lives at least once a month" (Muir 1995, 16).

Maybe Chicago lawyers are special. In the 1995 survey, 84 percent of the respondents reported that they were either satisfied or very satisfied with their jobs—about 10 percent were neutral, 5 percent were dissatisfied, and only 1.6 percent were very dissatisfied. We analyze those findings below, with particular attention to differences among the lawyers by gender, race, and practice setting, but, because our findings are at variance with the popular view and with some research based on samples with relatively low response rates, we think it important to note first that the Chicago findings are, in fact, consistent with most of the scholarly literature.

Research on Job Satisfaction

Previous research on occupational satisfaction indicates that most employed persons, in all professions and in all types of positions, are satisfied with their careers. Glenn Firebaugh and Brian Harley, using the General Social Survey data for 1972 through 1991, found that six out of seven American workers reported being "moderately" or "very" satisfied with their jobs, and that this remained steady over the twenty-year period (1995, 87). Given competing family and career demands on women and their generally lower salaries and occupational rank, one might expect more women to be dissatisfied with their jobs, but several studies have found that women's attitudes toward their jobs are at least as favorable as, and in some cases more favorable than, those of men (Hodson 1989).[1] Racial differences in job satisfaction, however, have been found in several studies. In Firebaugh and Harley's analysis, the lower job satisfaction reported by blacks[2] was largely attributable to the lower satisfaction of black women, who reported significantly higher discontent than white women (see also Austin and Dodge 1992, 579).[3]

Older workers consistently report greater job satisfaction than younger workers. This is the case for men, women, blacks, and whites (Alwin and Krosnick 1991; Felton 1987; Firebaugh and Harley 1995, 45). Since Firebaugh and Harley found that average satisfaction remained steady (102), the higher job satisfaction of older workers appears to be an age effect and not a cohort effect.[4] Lower satisfaction in more recent cohorts would result in a decrease in average satisfaction over time.

Although there are differences between types of work settings, previous research suggests that to a large extent each occupation faces similar problems and derives similar satisfaction, and lawyers are no exception. A study of job satisfaction among lawyers, doctors, engineers, and teachers in Australia found that the four professions exhibited similar satisfaction/dissatisfaction tendencies (Malinowska-Tabaka 1987).[5]

In sharp contrast to most of the occupational satisfaction literature, some studies of women lawyers argue that gender is significantly associated with contentment within the bar. A study of the 1983 graduates of twenty law schools found that 26 percent of women, but only 15 percent of men, expressed general career dissatisfaction (Tucker, Albright, and Busk 1990). A survey of 892 Stanford law school graduates found that both female and male graduates were very satisfied with their jobs, and that their scores on an overall satisfaction measure were not significantly different, but that women were more likely to report symptoms such as overeating, nightmares, crying, loneliness, and depression (Taber et al. 1988).[6] A number of studies suggest that women experience greater conflict between work and family roles than do their male counterparts, largely because women assume a heavier burden of family responsibilities (Epstein 1981; Liefland 1986; Taber et al. 1988). Because of actual and anticipated work-family conflicts, women are said to adopt various coping strategies only rarely employed by men, including delayed marriage and childbearing, lengthy leaves of absence from paid employment, and part-time work arrangements. Employers' assumptions about women's future behavior and work commitment may further exacerbate the situation (W. Bielby and D. Bielby 1989).[7]

In a major study of Toronto lawyers, however, John Hagan and Fiona Kay found no significant difference between male and female lawyers in their levels of overall job satisfaction (1995, 155). Of the 692 lawyers in their 1991 sample, 78.3 percent of the women and 79.4 percent of the men were found to be satisfied with their jobs.[8] A 1987 survey of 521 Minnesota law graduates from the classes of 1975, 1978, 1982 and 1985 found that only 7 percent of the respondents reported being either "dissatisfied" or "very dissatisfied" with their jobs and that there was no significant difference in this between men and women (Mattessich and Heilman 1990). A large study of graduates of the University of Michigan law school found that more than three-quarters of the alumni were "satisfied overall with their careers" (Lempert, Chambers, and Adams 2000, 445, table 21) and that, again, men and women did not differ on this measure (485–86, table 33). A survey sponsored by the *New York Law Journal* produced similar findings (Adams 1994); the sample included 401 lawyers throughout New York State, and found no significant difference in the job satisfaction of men and women. Women, however, reported working fewer hours than men and were more likely to feel that their jobs interfered with their private lives. Almost three-fourths of female lawyers said that their families had to deal with work-related stress at home, while 55 percent of men said that this was true for their families. A majority of the women reported that, despite the demands of their careers, they spent more time with their children than did their spouses, but only 4 percent of male attorneys made the same claim. Four percent of the men in the sample and 15 percent of the women said that the demands of their careers made them decide not to have children.

An earlier study of graduates of the University of Michigan law school, by David Chambers, also found that women with children continued to bear the principal responsibilities for child care, but these women were more satisfied with their careers and with the balance of their family and professional lives than were other women or men (Chambers 1989). The study included more than a thousand graduates from the 1976–79 law school classes. Chambers speculates that the women's multiple roles "provide satisfaction by offering variety and relief, by allowing a sense of mastery, and by providing a broader perspective on the problems in any one setting" (254). The ABA Commission on Women in the Profession also found that having children added to the career satisfaction of women lawyers (Tucker and Niedzielko 1994, 30–36). Nevertheless, when Chambers asked an open-ended question about balancing work and family, women voiced many complaints about the competing demands (265). In sum, the literature on the relationship between gender and lawyers' job satisfaction is inconclusive. Studies report contradictory findings—that gender is not correlated with satisfaction, and that it is. Moreover, some studies find that balancing family and career has a negative impact on women's happiness, while other studies produce opposite results. In analyzing the Chicago data, we look not only at general correlations between gender and job satisfaction but at the particular factors that contribute to satisfaction and whether those factors differ by gender.

The Chicago Findings

As already noted, most Chicago lawyers reported that they were satisfied with their jobs. Respondents were asked to rate their overall job satisfaction on a five-point scale, ranging from 1 for "very dissatisfied" to 5 for "very satisfied." Among practicing lawyers, the mean response was 4.21. Like most of the previous scholarly research on occupational satisfaction, but unlike some of the prior studies of lawyers, the Chicago survey did not find a statistically significant gender difference in overall satisfaction. Women scored an average of 4.13 on the five-point scale and men an average of 4.24. Forty-two percent of the women and 46 percent of the men reported that they were very satisfied with their jobs, and only 2 percent of the women and 1 percent of the men reported that they were very dissatisfied. But there were some large differences among other categories of lawyers. Not surprisingly, for example, of the 178 lawyers in the sample who earned $125,000 or more in 1994, only two individuals were either dissatisfied or very dissatisfied, but of those who earned less than $60,000 about 13 percent were dissatisfied or very dissatisfied. Age has an even stronger effect on job satisfaction (some of the age effect, of course, may be attributable to the fact that older lawyers tend to have higher incomes). None of the respondents older than 55 reported being dissatisfied. No doubt this is, at least in part, due to self-selection—lawyers who continue to practice to the age of 56 or beyond are likely to have been reasonably happy with their lot. Among the youngest lawyers, those 35 and younger, 6 percent were already dissatisfied. Lawyers in the 36–45 age bracket (the stage at which partnership decisions are made) were the most likely to be dissatisfied, but only 11 percent of them were either dissatisfied or very dissatisfied.[9]

There are also differences among the employment settings. The percentage of "very satisfied" respondents is lower in the two larger firm categories than in any of the other practice settings, but the percentages of dissatisfied lawyers are also notably low in the larger firms (fig. 11.1). Thus, job satisfaction in large firms might be characterized as relatively moderate. Solo practitioners had the highest percentage of "very dissatisfied" values, but that percentage amounts to only three respondents. Government-employed lawyers were the most likely to be unhappy—eleven percent of them were either dissatisfied or very dissatisfied—but salaries are low in government, and the dissatisfaction may reflect the income differential. Because a comparatively high percentage of women lawyers work in government (18 percent of female respondents were employed by government, but only 6 percent of males), the finding that overall satisfaction among women was not sig-

Figure 11.1. Overall Satisfaction by Practice Setting, 1995 (percentages)

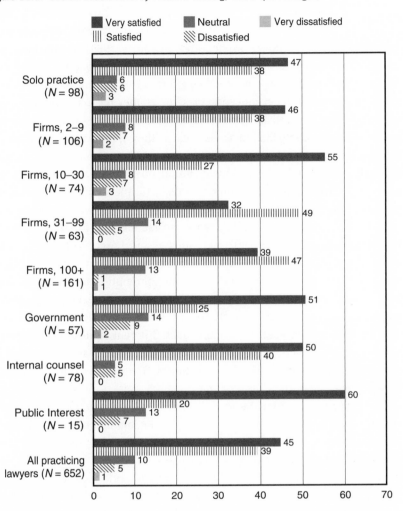

Note: Only 1.4 percent of practicing lawyers but 3 percent of those not practicing were "very dissatisfied" with their jobs.

nificantly lower than that of men is all the more remarkable. Nonetheless, note that the great majority of government-employed lawyers were satisfied in their jobs. Thus, even practice settings where scores are relatively low appear to provide satisfying jobs for most.

At least four broad explanations have been advanced in the literature to account for the general finding that women's job satisfaction is equivalent to or greater than that of men: reference group differences, relative deprivation (emphasizing expectations), role spillover (as hypothesized by Chambers, noted above), and a thesis that men and women value different aspects of their work. The first suggests that, in assessing their circumstances, women usually compare themselves to other women (Crosby 1982; Hodson 1989; Loscocco 1990; and Varca, Shaffer, and McCauley 1983). Karlyn Loscocco and Glenna Spitze, however, noted the importance of organizational context in determining choice of reference groups (1991). As blue-collar women move into more gender-balanced work settings, they begin to compare themselves to male as well as female coworkers, Faye Crosby suggested that women have high satisfaction levels because they approach work with lower expectations or with feelings of deserving certain outcomes or conditions of work (1982), but Randy Hodson found no support for the thesis that lower expectations underlie women's satisfaction levels (1989). Chambers' research provides support for the idea that satisfaction with domestic roles "spills over" to increase women's work satisfaction, and Crosby also credits this explanation (1987, 39–40), but Hodson and Loscocco found little evidence for it. Carrie Menkel-Meadow, citing work in psychology, suggests that "men are 'vertically' ambitious, seeking promotion up the hierarchical ladder, whereas women are 'horizontally' ambitious, seeking to explore a variety of interests simultaneously—work, family, and friends" (1989, 227). Several scholars suggest that women attach different values than do men to various characteristics of work (Bigoness 1988; Martin and Hanson 1985; Murray and Atkinson 1981; Neil and Snizek 1988). This last thesis is addressed by some of the Chicago data.

After inquiring about the overall level of job satisfaction, the Chicago survey asked a series of questions concerning more specific attributes of the respondents' job situations. Respondents were asked to rate their level of satisfaction (on the same five-point scale, from "very satisfied" to "very dissatisfied") with each of twelve aspects of their work: their level of responsibility, recognition for work, content of work, chances for advancement, salary, relations with supervisors, control over the amount of work, control over the manner in which work is performed, relationships with colleagues, opportunities to do pro bono work, the prestige of their organization, and the policies and administration of their organization. On eleven of these twelve measures, the satisfaction scores of female respondents are lower than those of males (fig. 11.2). On eight of the twelve, the differences between men and women are large enough to be statistically significant. The only significant variable on which women are more satisfied concerns relationships with colleagues. These findings suggest a variation of the paradox of the contented working woman: despite being less satisfied with most specific aspects of

Figure 11.2. Mean Satisfaction Scores by Gender, 1995

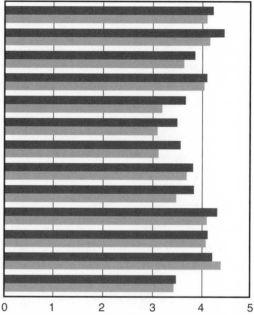

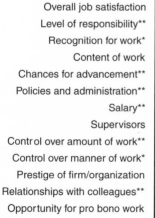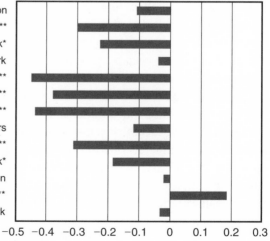

*p < .05 (t-test)   **p < .01 (t-test)

their work, women lawyers report overall job satisfaction that is equivalent to men's satisfaction.

One might ask whether men and women give differing weights to these more specific elements of job satisfaction—so that, when the more detailed variables are used to predict overall satisfaction scores, we would find that the elements that make the most substantial contributions to the prediction differ for men and women. This does not appear to be the case. In multi-variate analyses modeling high satisfaction scores, there was no evidence that women's overall satisfaction ratings were affected more heavily than were men's by particular factors (Hull 1999b).[10] In some related measures, however, we did find significant differences between men and women. Men appear to value professional autonomy more highly than do women; see text at note 24.

As already noted, some studies suggest that women's careers in the law are likely to be affected adversely by child care and other family concerns. It is certainly plausible that lawyers who find it difficult to meet both the demands of their work and the needs of their families would tend to be less satisfied with their choice of career, and that such conflicts might more often be perceived by women. In the 1995 Chicago survey, therefore, respondents were given a series of questions concerning potential conflicts between their personal or family priorities and their jobs. The questions were presented in five sets of opposing statements, and respondents were asked to indicate on a five-point scale whether they more nearly agreed with one statement or the other. Responses to three of the five pairs are significantly correlated with overall satisfaction scores. In one of these, the alternatives were "In planning my career, it has not been necessary for me to base my job choices on personal or family considerations" versus "The career choices or opportunities that were open to me were limited by the need to accommodate personal or family priorities." Respondents who said that their experience was closer to the first alternative, in which career and personal demands did not conflict, were significantly more likely to express high job satisfaction.[11] On a similar question put in terms of "responsibilities to clients," the correlation is less strong, but the same tendency is observed. The alternatives were "My responsibilities to my clients have sometimes made it necessary for me to sacrifice the quality of personal relationships with family or friends" versus "I have found it possible to balance the competing demands of my work and my personal life so that one seldom interferes with the other." As one would expect, the latter alternative is associated with higher satisfaction.[12] The third significant correlation with satisfaction is found on the following pair of statements: "When important deadlines are near, I am willing to work

overtime to meet the needs of my clients or my office" versus "I am not willing to work overtime repeatedly if that means sacrificing my availability to
my spouse, children, or those close to me." Respondents who indicated that
they were more willing to work overtime were more likely to be satisfied.[13]
On all three questions, then, respondents who were less likely to perceive
conflicts between their jobs and their personal circumstances were more
likely to express satisfaction. The remaining two sets of statements, which
dealt with avoidance of overnight travel and with career effects on decisions
about whether to marry or have children, were not significantly correlated
with overall job satisfaction.

There are statistically significant differences between men's and women's answers on two of these five questions and a difference of borderline
significance on a third. Women were more likely than men to report that
their career choices or opportunities had been limited by personal or family
priorities[14] and that their decisions about whether to marry or have children
had been influenced by career considerations.[15] The variable of borderline
significance is the one concerned with willingness to work overtime—men
appeared to be somewhat less likely to find that overtime work conflicted
with family needs.[16]

When we separate respondents with children from those without, however, we see an even more striking pattern. For lawyers with children, the
gender difference is strongly significant on four of the five variables. (The
only one on which it is not is the variable concerning whether "responsibilities to . . . clients have sometimes made it necessary . . . to sacrifice the
quality of personal relationships.") For lawyers without children, however,
there are significant gender differences on *none* of these variables. This suggests an interaction effect between gender and the presence of children.
Among parents, women were much more likely than men to perceive conflicts between their family duties and the demands of their jobs. But among
lawyers without children, the two sexes were equally likely to perceive these
conflicts.

These findings raise yet another version of the persistent question: Since
gender differences, when they appear in these variables, indicate that women are more likely to perceive conflicts between work and family demands
and, presumably, to experience stress in trying to balance those competing demands, why does the overall job satisfaction reported by women not
differ significantly from that of men? Perhaps the overall job satisfaction
question is simply too crude to capture the real differences. When the Chicago survey asked a somewhat different question—whether the respondents
would choose to become lawyers "if they had it all to do over again"—

differences between men's and women's attitudes toward the practice of law emerge.

Although 84 percent of the lawyers reported that they were "satisfied" or "very satisfied" with their jobs, somewhat fewer (77 percent) said they would again choose to become a lawyer. This is similar to the findings in Hagan and Kay's surveys of Toronto lawyers (1995). Their respondents were asked: "Given a choice, would you take the same job again?" In 1985, 78.7 percent of women and 77.7 percent of men said they would; in a 1991 survey, 74.4 percent of women and 75.8 percent of men gave this response (169, table 7.1). We found a more substantial gender difference than did Hagan and Kay, however: 79 percent of the male lawyers but only 71 percent of the women in the 1995 Chicago survey said they would again choose to become a lawyer.[17] We also found some ethnoreligious differences on this question. The percentage of respondents who would choose to become lawyers again was highest among those of northern European descent (85 percent) and lowest among Jews (71 percent). Thus, we might interpret this as evidence that lawyers in categories that are more likely to be privileged—males and northern Europeans—are more likely to be happy within the legal profession, while those in categories more likely to experience discrimination—females and Jews—are more likely to have second thoughts about their choice of career. We should not exaggerate the extent of this unhappiness, however. Even in the less privileged groups, 71 percent of the lawyers would choose the same career again.

It is entirely possible, of course, for one to be "satisfied" or mostly happy in one's job and yet feel that another career might have been even more rewarding. This sort of question is an invitation to dream—one might choose instead to become a philosopher, or a cabinetmaker, or a rock star.[18]

It is also possible, however, that answers to both the satisfaction and the career choice questions are biased toward the positive side of the scale by the respondents' desire to present themselves as successful persons. They may be reluctant to admit, to others or to themselves, that they made poor choices. But our research, like the newspaper stories quoted at the beginning of this chapter, deals only with expressions of satisfaction or dissatisfaction.

The 1995 Chicago survey collected data on relationships between these expressed feelings and the lawyers' practice contexts. Respondents were given nine sets of opposing statements regarding characteristics of their work and were again asked to place themselves on a five-point scale. Some analyses of responses to these questions were presented in chapter 5 (discussion of fig. 5.5). As noted there, one of the items read, "The nature of my practice is such that it is often necessary to accept clients whom I would prefer not to have." The opposite was, "In the course of my practice I have rather wide latitude in selecting which clients I will represent." On this question, not surprisingly, lawyers who indicated greater latitude in selecting clients were significantly more likely to express high job satisfaction.[19] Five of the nine variables are correlated with overall satisfaction. Of those five, three (including the client choice variable) deal with some aspect of autonomy, i.e., personal control over the circumstances of their work. Another autonomy question asked respondents to choose between "Strategies that I pursue are largely of my own design and execution" and "I work closely with others to design and execute strategies in my work." Respondents who placed themselves closer to the first alternative were significantly more likely to be satisfied with their jobs.[20] The third autonomy variable read, "One of the things I like about my area of practice is that I can do largely whatever I like without having someone looking over my shoulder and directing my work," versus "In my practice of law I work closely with more senior lawyers who provide relatively close guidance in the nature of my work." Respondents with higher satisfaction scores were, again, likely to indicate greater autonomy.[21] Thus, autonomy appears to be associated with expressed satisfaction.

The other two variables that are correlated with job satisfaction dealt with the rapidity of change in the law involved in the respondents' areas of practice and with the extent to which their tasks were the exclusive province of lawyers. The former read, "My area requires a great deal of reading of legal material to keep abreast of new developments" versus "Things don't change too rapidly in my area of the law, so there is little need for constant revision of my knowledge and activities." On this variable, lawyers who indicated that they needed to read to keep abreast were more likely to express high satisfaction.[22] Perhaps the lawyers who said that "things don't change too rapidly in my area" felt that their work was boring or repetitive. The remaining significant variable read, "The type and content of my practice is such that even an educated layman couldn't really understand or prepare the documents" versus "A para-professional could be trained to handle many of the procedures and documents in my area of law." Respondents closer to the first alternative were likely to have higher satisfaction scores.[23] Thus, lawyers may find their work more satisfying if they believe that it is more purely professional—that is, that it requires special expertise and arcane knowledge (see the discussion of Abbott's "professional purity" thesis in chap. 4).

When we examine gender differences in these variables, we find that the responses of men and women differ significantly on all three of the autonomy measures, and on those only.[24] On all three, women report less autonomy in their work than do men. Since these variables are correlated with overall satisfaction, and since women report less autonomy, the question once again arises as to why women report job satisfaction equivalent to that of males. The answer could be that women place a lower value on autonomy. By computing the correlations of these nine variables with satisfaction for men and women separately, we find that the correlations do differ by gender. For men, the significant variables are autonomy measures; for women, they are not.[25] Thus, it appears that autonomy plays a stronger part in males' than in females' assessments of their degree of overall job satisfaction.

The lower degree of autonomy reported by women—and, perhaps, the lower value placed on it by women—is consistent with the finding that women are more likely to work as employees of government, corporations, or other large organizations, rather than in law firms or as independent practitioners (see chaps. 3 and 5). While 27 percent of the practicing lawyers overall are women, 53 percent of the government lawyers and 47 percent of those employed as house counsel are women. Women may also have a lower expectation of autonomy than do men because the women are younger, on average, and thus are at earlier stages of their careers. But women appear to be at least as likely as men to wish that they had greater autonomy (see fig. 11.2; "control over amount of work" and "control over manner of work"). Perhaps the lack of autonomy has less impact on the overall job satisfaction of younger lawyers because they believe (or hope) that more autonomy will be acquired as they become more senior.

Differences in satisfaction scores among racial categories are more pronounced than the gender differences. Even though few of the practicing lawyers in the Chicago random sample are African American, the differences between blacks and whites are large enough to be statistically significant. Of the white practicing lawyers, 6 percent were either dissatisfied or very dissatisfied. Of the blacks, 18 percent were. Among the whites, 84 percent were satisfied or very satisfied; among the blacks, 71 percent were.[26] Asian and Latino lawyers are more similar to whites in their satisfaction scores than are African Americans. When lawyers of Asian and Latino descent are added to the blacks to create a broader "minority" category (N = 48 among practicing lawyers), and this category is then compared to whites, the difference in job satisfaction is not statistically significant.

Some of the difference between African Americans and whites may be explained by their work settings and earnings. Recall that lawyers employed by government had the lowest satisfaction scores, on average. Of the white practicing lawyers, only 7 percent were employed by government agencies; by contrast, of the black lawyers, nearly a third (32 percent) were. The negative satisfaction scores of some blacks may be attributable, therefore, to characteristics of government employment that produce dissatisfaction. One of those characteristics may well be that government work is relatively poorly paid. Even among lawyers employed by government, however, there appears to be a racial difference in satisfaction. Of the forty-three white government lawyers in the sample, only two (5 percent) were dissatisfied or very dissatisfied. Of the nine black government lawyers, four (44 percent) were dissatisfied.[27]

Income inequality was analyzed in greater detail in chapter 7, but let us note the disparities that are most relevant to the differences in satisfaction. If we compare the reported income of white and black Chicago lawyers during the year preceding the survey (1993–94), we find that 36 percent of the whites reported incomes of less than $70,000. For the "minority" category (including Asian, Latino, and African Americans), this percentage doubles (to 72 percent). For blacks alone, 85 percent reported annual incomes below $70,000.[28] When we examine the scores of white and minority lawyers on the variables assessing satisfaction with specific aspects of lawyers' jobs, we find that the biggest difference, by far, occurs on the salary question (fig. 11.3). For black respondents, the difference is even more pronounced than it is for the more inclusive "minority" category. Black lawyers have an average salary satisfaction score of 2.61, nearly a full point lower than that of whites.[29] As indicated in figure 11.3, there are also significant differences between whites and minorities on four more of these variables,[30] and the satisfaction of whites is consistently higher than that of the minorities, regardless of the issue.

The income difference between male and female lawyers is also striking (see chap. 7)—the percentage of men who earned $100,000 or more in the year preceding the survey was 48 percent; the comparable percentage of women was 16 percent.[31] Because some of this income difference might be explained by the relative youth or inexperience of the women in the sample, we did a regression analysis predicting income with both gender and years of practice as independent variables.[32] The relationship between gender and income remained significant.[33] Figure 11.2 indicated that women were significantly more likely than men to express dissatisfaction with their salaries. On the five-point scale, the average salary satisfaction score of females was 3.14, compared to 3.58 for males and 2.74 for minorities of both sexes.

To sort out the relationships among job satisfaction and several of these other variables, including gender, age, race, income, and practice setting, we did additional multivariate analyses. Because the distribution of the satisfaction scores was so highly skewed (i.e., the respondents' scores are

Figure 11.3. Mean Satisfaction Scores by Race, 1995

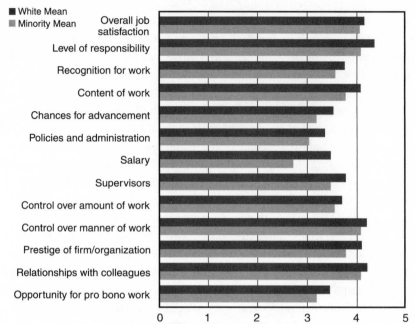

Mean Scores

■ White Mean
■ Minority Mean

| Overall job satisfaction |
| Level of responsibility |
| Recognition for work |
| Content of work |
| Chances for advancement |
| Policies and administration |
| Salary |
| Supervisors |
| Control over amount of work |
| Control over manner of work |
| Prestige of firm/organization |
| Relationships with colleagues |
| Opportunity for pro bono work |

0 1 2 3 4 5

Difference (Minority minus White)

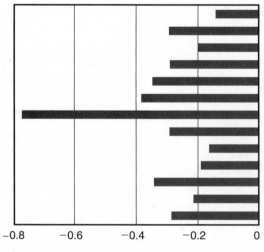

Overall job satisfaction
Level of responsibility*
Recognition for work
Content of work*
Chances for advancement
Policies and administration*
Salary***
Supervisors
Control over amount of work
Control over manner of work
Prestige of firm/organization*
Relationships with colleagues
Opportunity for pro bono work

−0.8   −0.6   −0.4   −0.2   0

*p < .05 (t-test)   ***p < .001 (t-test)

concentrated at the high end of the scale), ordinary linear regression models will not produce valid estimates of the magnitude of the effects. In one analysis, therefore, we split the satisfaction scale into two categories—very satisfied versus anything less. Since 45 percent of all respondents reported that they were very satisfied, this divided the sample into two groups of roughly equal magnitude. We then used logistic regression, an analytic technique that is appropriate for dichotomous dependent variables. In the resulting multivariate model, neither race nor gender nor age was a significant predictor of being very satisfied.[34] Income and practice setting, however, were significantly associated with high satisfaction. Lawyers practicing in large law firms were less likely to be highly satisfied than lawyers practicing anywhere else. This is what one might expect given the data reported in figure 11.1. But recall that, as figure 11.1 shows, the dissatisfied percentage is also small among lawyers in large firms—the greatest number of large-firm lawyers report that they are merely satisfied. When we did another logistic regression analysis, this time predicting scores at the lower end of the satisfaction scale (the lower category included "neutral" "dissatisfied," and "very dissatisfied,"), practice setting was not a significant predictor. The only significant variable in that analysis was income. Thus, when we control for the effects of several variables, considered simultaneously, race and gender do not appear to be significantly associated with the degree of job satisfaction among lawyers, but income is consistently found to be a significant factor.

Happy Hour at the Bar?

Our findings regarding the high degree of job satisfaction within the Chicago bar essentially match those in careful studies of lawyers in Toronto (Hagan and Kay 1995), Minnesota (Mattessich and Heilman 1990), and New York State (Adams 1994), and of graduates of the University of Michigan Law School (Lempert, Chambers, and Adams 2000). The truly cynical will say that all lawyers dissemble, wherever situated. But the level of job satisfaction reported by lawyers is not higher than that in other occupations. Lawyers, on average, claim about the same degree of satisfaction as people in other lines of work (Firebaugh and Harley 1995). It is not immediately apparent why one should expect lawyers to be more disgruntled than people who sell cars or fix teeth.

As we have seen in our analyses of the Chicago findings, one of the persistent puzzles is why the overall job satisfaction of female lawyers, in spite of their unfavorable circumstances (work setting, income, work/family conflicts), is equivalent to that of males. When we examined their evaluations of more specific aspects of their employment, such as their chances for advancement, salary, and level of responsibility, we found that women were consistently less satisfied with those job characteristics than were men. Moreover, women were significantly (though not hugely) more likely than men to say that they would not again choose to become a lawyer. So we should be careful not to overstate the equivalence of men's and women's job satisfaction. Here again, however, the findings regarding lawyers mirror more general findings. Women's job satisfaction, regardless of occupational setting, has usually been found to be equal to—sometimes, greater than—that of men.

A possible contributing factor is self-selection: Unhappy lawyers may have left the field. Lawyers who were not licensed at the time of the survey were not observed. If women leave the bar at a greater rate than do men, this might result in an unrepresentative selection from among the lawyers who had entered. Of dissatisfied men and women, a higher proportion of the women would leave, while more of the men would remain.[35]

It is plausible that women find it easier to leave the legal profession. Society probably still exerts greater pressure on males than on females to maximize earnings. Therefore, a mother who is a lawyer may more often find it acceptable to take a job with shorter hours, or perhaps find part-time work, while a father in similar circumstances would feel compelled to continue to practice law. Many women lawyers are married to professionals, and some may be willing to let their husbands make the more substantial contribution to the family income. The evidence concerning whether women are, in fact, more likely to leave the practice of law is meager and mixed, however. Hagan and Kay's Toronto study concluded that "women are more likely to leave than men" (1995, 166), but Mattessich and Heilman's survey of Minnesota law graduates found that women were retained in the profession at the same rate as men (1990, 87–88). The percentage of female lawyers who can choose not to practice their profession is probably much larger than the percentage of women who feel they can choose not to work at all; so the similar job satisfaction of employed men and women outside the legal profession, in the total labor market, probably cannot be explained by the exit of women from the world of work. This should make us wary about attributing a large effect to self-selection among lawyers.[36]

As we have observed, there is a greater difference in overall job satisfaction between blacks and whites than between men and women. Again, we should consider the possible effect of self-selection (or lack of it). Many of the factors that might lead us to expect selection effects among women lawyers do not apply to racial and ethnic minorities. Women lawyers may have several possible options—to pursue other enterprises, to work part-time, to rely upon their husbands for support—but these options are less likely to be available to members of minority groups. An African American who becomes a lawyer has often achieved a substantial advance in his or her social status and economic circumstances. To then abandon the legal profession and choose other work would often mean surrendering much of the benefit of that achievement. The other work available will probably be a step down in status and economic rewards. If this is so, then black lawyers who are unhappy in the profession may feel compelled, as a practical matter, to remain there. The result would be retention within the bar of a larger share of unhappy black lawyers. Both low income and weaker self-selection effects, then, may contribute to the greater dissatisfaction.

The strongest and most consistent effect on lawyers' overall job satisfaction is produced by neither gender nor race, however. It is produced by the lawyers' income levels. But to say that race and gender do not have significant effects independent of income is not to say that women and minorities bear only their proportionate share of the misery produced by low income. They clearly bear a disproportionate burden. Women and minority lawyers (blacks, especially) make significantly less money than do white males. To the extent that low income is associated with dissatisfaction, therefore, women and minorities will be most likely to feel that effect. On average, women and blacks are also younger than white males and are employed in less prestigious practice settings. The regression analysis tells us that the job satisfaction levels of women, minorities, and white males are not inconsistent with the extent to which they are relatively advantaged or disadvantaged with respect to income, age, and practice setting.

The most striking finding, however, is the generally high level of satisfaction reported by all categories of lawyers. Even among African Americans, 71 percent were satisfied or very satisfied. This is at variance with the common wisdom. The popular belief that lawyers are unhappy may reflect notions of desert: if we regard lawyers as rats (Galanter 1994), then the story that the rats are suffering fits the pervasive hypothesis that this is a just world (Lerner 1980).

The Chicago findings suggest that the attitudes of lawyers toward their work are not greatly different from those of most people in the labor force. We have good days and bad days. Some tasks are more desirable than others.

But, for the most part, we gravitate toward work that we can handle, work where the nasty bits can be limited, and work that may, all in all, give us some sense of satisfaction. People who become lawyers usually have other career options. Those who consider the options and then choose to practice law appear, in most cases, to find the work rewarding.

PART IV
Transformation

Chapter 12
The Processes of Change

What are the processes—in the bar, in the market for lawyers' services, or in the broader society—that contributed to the changes we have observed in the Chicago bar? Do lawyers and the organizations in which they work simply accommodate demand and restructure their practices accordingly, or do professional norms or organizational politics influence the ways in which the varying segments of the bar practice law? Was law firm growth inevitable? Is there any limit on the eventual size of the firms, or will they just continue to burgeon? How does the size of the organizations that deliver legal services affect their management? Are the power relationships among lawyers altered? Do law firms behave like businesses, or do professional service organizations manifest a distinct style or culture? Are lawyers of differing race, gender, or ethnoreligious background differentially affected by these changes? All of these questions are addressed in this chapter, but some of the answers are, of course, more complete or more satisfactory than others.

The preceding chapters analyzed data from the 1975 and 1995 Chicago surveys in some detail in an effort to assess patterns of change and stability. This chapter seeks to put those findings in a larger context by drawing upon the work of other scholars, census data, newspapers that serve the legal profession, and the advertising or promotional materials through which law firms present themselves to potential clients. It also speculates about the directions in which the profession might move in the future. The chapter concludes with a review of some of the principal findings of the Chicago surveys, placed in the context of three recurring themes: autonomy, integration, and stratification.

Those three characteristics interact, in some tension. Both stratification and autonomy are inconsistent with integration. If lawyers are divided into systematic strata, they are unlikely to perceive themselves to be, or to act as, a community of common fate and common purpose, and lawyers who are entirely free to pursue their own interests and inclinations may just choose to do so. Moreover, autonomy is limited if lawyers are divided into strata—the stratification system constrains individual choice and opportunity. But the manner in which and the extent to which each of the phenomena is manifested depends upon the contexts in which lawyers work.

The great majority of urban lawyers work in organizations, are subject to constraints that the organizations impose, and benefit from advantages that they confer. Even lawyers who practice alone, however, are not the masters of their own fate. Indeed, their professional opportunities are usually more narrowly circumscribed than those of lawyers employed by large enterprises. Regardless of their credentials, solo practitioners and lawyers in small firms are seldom able to secure major corporate clients or to work in the fields of law serving those clients (e.g., securities work, corporate tax, complex civil litigation). Big law firms and corporate legal departments dominate the markets for such work.

Autonomy and Influence

Lawyers are often said to be especially powerful, but where does their power reside? Although they hold a disproportionate share of public offices, most lawyers are neither public officials nor lobbyists, and the bar surely possesses even greater potential for influence in its private work. As counselors to clients, lawyers commonly give advice that changes the distribution of things that people value highly. A lawyer may persuade a client with marital problems to pursue a divorce or to make do with the status quo (to "lump it," as Felstiner has put it; Felstiner 1974, 81), or perhaps advise a real estate developer that there will be tax advantages if a shopping mall is built in location B rather than location A.

The way in which lawyers (and other consultants) most commonly affect outcomes, however, is by refusing to take the client's case. Large numbers of potential plaintiffs in personal injury cases are told, in effect, that their cases are not worth the lawyers' time. The plaintiffs' lawyers interviewed by Sara Parikh reported that, of all the potential cases brought to them, they accepted less than half—"low-end" practitioners accepted 49 percent, on average, and the elite of the personal injury bar accepted only 24 percent (Parikh 2001, 75–78, table 5). The chairman of a major law firm told us that, because of potential conflicts of interest, his firm declines more than a third of all the business it is offered.[1] The rejection of clients and cases is, of course, more likely to occur when they will be unprofitable—for example, when the amount at stake is small or the lawyer cannot be certain the fee will be paid. In practice, this means that the frustration that occurs when a potential client has been deprived of counsel is less likely to affect major corporations than abused spouses, petty criminals, defrauded homeowners, or injured drivers. Large, powerful clients usually know what their options are, they are sophisticated consumers of legal services, and they know how to choose lawyers so as to achieve their goals. Weak clients have fewer options; they are therefore likely to be more malleable, more subject to persuasion. Lawyers can push them around. But much the same is true of the relationships between clients and their bankers, accountants, consultants, and contractors.

There is a tendency to think that big cases must be consequential, and thus that the lawyers who handle such matters must also be consequential. If enough money is involved, the deal is assumed to be one that will change the world, and the lawyers are therefore people of consequence because they make it happen. But many people make it happen—the investment bankers, the venture capitalists, the insurers, the boards of directors, the executives, the engineers, and the construction companies, shipping companies, manufacturers, and/or scientists on whom the deal depends. Lawyers are less likely to have discrete roles in corporate transactions than in child custody, or criminal, or political asylum cases. In the latter contexts, lawyers' roles probably also have greater impact on the eventual outcomes.

In charting their courses, some lawyers have more autonomy than others. As we have seen, solo practitioners and those in the largest firms report the greatest latitude in client choice, and solos, lawyers in the smallest firms, and inside counsel are most likely to report a high degree of control over the nature of their work (chap. 5, fig. 5.5). Some scholars have been eager to emphasize the power of lawyers, especially in business contexts, in order to make it clear that lawyers are morally responsible for the consequences of their actions (Gordon and Simon 1992; Kagan and Rosen 1985; R. Rosen 1984; Simon 1998). Exceptional powers are not a precondition to these moral judgments, however. Even if the ability of lawyers to influence clients and potential clients is not essentially different from that of other occupations, lawyers nonetheless have important roles in the allocation of scarce resources (including authority and deference, as well as wealth). But the extent of lawyers' powers is enhanced or limited by their particular social and organizational contexts.

The Decline of Professional Dominance

In 1970, in *Professional Dominance*, Eliot Freidson asserted that the medical profession possessed a "special position of dominance" in the health care system and that "structural characteristics of the profession have far more influence on the nature of medical care in the United States than either the good intentions and skills of individual members of the profession or the economic and administrative arrangements that are usually the focus of attempts at reform" (77).[2] In the legal profession, we argue, the "economic and administrative arrangements" have a very important role.

The bar of the early 1970s and before might be characterized as a system of professional dominance. Lawyers practicing in the personal client sector were then protected from the rigors of competition by a ban on professional advertising, minimum fee schedules promulgated by local bar associations, and limits on the entry of new lawyers into the profession (imposed through the bar admission process [Abel 1989, 269, table 17] and through restriction of law school enrollments). In the corporate sector of practice, because the markets for legal services were local and the options available to clients were few, competition was limited de facto. Lawyers could not practice corporate law successfully without obtaining employment in one of the relatively small number of firms doing such work in any given locality. Relationships between law firms and their corporate clients tended to be long-term, in large part because both the firms and the clients wanted to avoid duplication of the costs of acquisition of knowledge specific to the relationships.

But the power of the bar associations declined. The percentage of Chicago lawyers who belonged to no bar association nearly doubled from 1975 to 1995, and only a third of the respondents to the 1995 Chicago survey reported that they regularly attended any bar association meetings.[3] As noted in chapter 3, specialty bar associations grew at the expense of the general membership associations, which also weakened the solidarity of the bar and its ability to take concerted action. By 1995, the regulation of practice had changed substantially. Minimum fee schedules were struck down by the U.S. Supreme Court in 1975,[4] and in 1977 the Court relaxed the restrictions on advertising.[5] Limits on entry into the profession, never entirely effective (Abel 1989, chap. 3, passim), loosened, the floodgates opened, and the bar grew rapidly. As a result, competitive pressure on lawyers in personal client practice increased markedly and their incomes suffered (see chap. 7; see also Sander and Williams 1989). Competition also increased in the corporate sector of practice as the markets for such services broadened, eventually becoming national and international. To compete effectively in these new markets, law firms expanded the range of their services, added personnel, opened new offices, merged, and adopted new, aggressive marketing strategies.

The "large" New York law firms of the late 1950s that were examined in Erwin Smigel's classic study, *The Wall Street Lawyer* (1969), had an average of 22 partners each. In 1969, however, Smigel observed that "[l]aw firms have, in fact, grown to such proportions that when reference is made in Wall Street to 'large firms' it is beginning to mean offices of 100 or more attorneys" (359). By 1995, there were 124 law firms in New York State with more than 100 lawyers.[6] The largest firms now have 1000 or more lawyers. In both Chicago surveys, respondents were asked the number of lawyers in their firms—in 1975, the average was 27; in 1995, it was 141.[7] The largest firm represented in the 1995 sample then employed 1,800 partners and associates.

Until the last decades of the twentieth century, almost all law firms were locally based. In the late 1950s, there was considerable controversy within the bar over the prospect that Adlai Stevenson's newly merged firm would have offices in three cities—Chicago, Washington, and New York. Referring to that firm, a 1961 book noted that "[t]he bar was startled recently by the announcement of the formation of a nation-wide firm. . . . The setup was so unusual that it had to be approved in advance by the Bar Association; and it occasioned considerable comment among local lawyers" (Galanter and Palay 1991, 23; B. Levy 1961, 20). By the 1980s and 1990s, however, it had become commonplace for firms to have offices in several major cities in the United States and abroad (Silver 2000). Lincoln Caplan quotes a senior partner of the Skadden Arps firm, summarizing the firm's reasons for opening offices in other countries: "that corporations are multinational, that our U.S. corporate clients have significant opportunities overseas, that our competition has set up offices there, and that we have to do the same thing to meet the competition . . . that there is going to be an increasing amount of cross-border work, in M&A [mergers and acquisitions] and related areas, and that we ought to be in position to get our fair share of it" (Caplan 1993, 295).

Before 1970, only two U.S. law firms had offices in London; during the 1970s, fifteen New York firms and eight other U.S. firms opened offices there. By the end of 1999, fifty-seven of the seventy-two U.S. firms studied by Silver had London branches, including firms headquartered in Chicago, Los Angeles, Boston, Houston, Dallas, Philadelphia, Washington, Minneapolis,

St. Louis, Cleveland, San Francisco, Seattle, and Richmond (Silver 2000, 1111–13).

The increase in the scale of law practice organizations was not confined to private firms. Between 1975 and 1995, the size of corporate inside-counsel offices represented in the Chicago samples increased from an average of 17 lawyers to 55 lawyers, and government law offices (national, state, and local) grew from 64 lawyers each to 399. The office of the Cook County State's Attorney (called "district attorney" in many places) employed 850 lawyers in 1995.

The growth in the size and scope of law firms and the other organizations that deliver legal services, the consequent concentration of control of lawyers' work in those organizations, the increasing specialization in legal work, and the decreasing relevance of general bar associations suggest that the coherence of the bar as an entity has waned and that the collective voice of the bar is less likely to be heard—or heeded. Professional dominance has been replaced, at least in considerable measure, by organizational dominance.

Demand

When there are increases of this order of magnitude in organizational scale, significant consequences are likely to follow—and they did. But we should attend not only to the consequences but to what drove the increases and to whether the growth was uniform across the full range of the profession. In chapter 2, we estimated that the percentage of lawyers' effort devoted to the corporate sector increased from 53 percent in 1975 to 64 percent in 1995, while effort devoted to individual clients and small businesses declined from 40 percent to 29 percent (see table 2.1). But both sectors of the market for legal services grew in absolute terms as the total number of lawyers in Chicago roughly doubled (see chap. 1). Therefore, our estimate is that the amount of lawyers' time devoted to individuals and small businesses increased, but not nearly as substantially as the time devoted to corporations and government. These findings are generally consistent with data for many (but not all) major U.S. cities, as reported by the Census of Service Industries (see chap. 2).

The relatively modest increase in demand for legal services to individuals and small businesses is largely a function of simple growth in the size of the population. In spite of public discussion of a "litigation explosion" and the correlative demand for "tort reform"—some of it stimulated by an advertising and public relations campaign by the insurance companies (Daniels and

Martin 1995; Glaberson 1999)—there is little evidence of a major change in community norms concerning disputing behavior or resort to litigation (Galanter 1993). With the exception of mass tort suits (such as the asbestos cases), often brought as class actions on behalf of large categories of individuals, much of the increase in litigation is attributable to suits brought by businesses against other businesses (Dunworth and Rogers 1996). The Chicago surveys found that the percentage of effort devoted to personal injury work for plaintiffs, 6 percent, was unchanged from 1975 to 1995 (see table 2.1). Changes in law that affect individuals (e.g., increasing use of the condominium form of ownership) have not generally increased the rate at which people use lawyers. Indeed, lawyers now appear to be involved in sales of residences less often. In the two Chicago surveys, the estimated percentage of effort devoted to personal real estate transactions declined from 6 percent in 1975 to 3 percent in 1995 (table 2.1). Some new laws have created novel rights and remedies (regarding employment discrimination, for example), but most of the regulatory legislation of recent decades (e.g., regarding occupational safety and health) has primarily given rise to government enforcement proceedings rather than private law suits.

The relative stability in the nature of the legal work done on behalf of individuals and in the rate at which claims are brought on their behalf meant that there was less impetus to alter the form and character of the organizations providing such services. Legal work for individuals and small businesses is still ordinarily done by small firms and solo practitioners (see table 3.2). Carroll Seron (1996, 87, 168) found evidence that some small firms have adopted an entrepreneurial approach to this market segment, but that traditionalists still far outnumber innovators. Although a few firms operating nationally or regionally attempted to use advertising to acquire a brand-name identity in the market for routine wills, divorces, and residential real estate sales, and then to exploit that asset by selling rights to use the name or by contracting with lawyers to provide services in the name of the firm (Van Hoy 1997), these firms did not succeed in capturing a large share of the market. Some "group legal service plans" provide services to members of unions or other organizations, often using lawyers employed on a contractual basis, but again these plans have not acquired much of the market for personal legal services.

A part of the increase in law firm size in the corporate sector is the result of mergers of existing firms, but most is accounted for by overall growth in the number of lawyers doing corporate legal work, in response to a great increase in demand for such services. Some of this demand is cyclical. When the economy slowed in the early 1990s, after the rapid growth of the 1980s, corporate law firms reduced their hiring of new lawyers and many of them discharged excess lawyers, both associates and partners. Kirkland and Ellis, a Chicago-based firm, reportedly dismissed fifty-five associates and nonequity partners (K. Hall 2000). When the economy accelerated again in the mid- and late 1990s, those firms resumed their expansion. Thus, much of the demand for corporate legal services is attributable simply to the rate of business activity: if more business transactions take place, more legal services will be needed. But changes in law or in government enforcement strategy may also affect demand. In the 1980s, the Reagan administration took a newly permissive view of the antitrust laws. As a result, corporations had greater freedom to pursue mergers and the acquisition of other companies, and large law firms then created M&A departments. New employment discrimination laws, occupational safety regulations, and tax reporting requirements also created new legal problems for corporations, much more than they did for individuals.

Changes in the character of American business enterprise, however, had even more impact on the demand for corporate legal services. When the largest sectors of the U.S. economy were agriculture and heavy industry, those enterprises probably generated fewer demands for legal services, per dollar of product, than does the present economy (Nelson 1994). In a survey of companies headquartered in the Chicago area, Robert Bell (1999, 22–24) found that "companies dealing with financial services and insurance and those in the transportation industry are the most intensive consumers of legal services" and that "manufacturers in heavily science-dependent fields are considerably more likely than others to make extensive use of lawyers."

Service businesses typically create a larger number of transactions, with personal contact among a larger number of players, than do manufacturing or agribusiness. Businesses that create a relatively small number of transactions, and where there is greater concentration in a smaller number of companies, generate fewer points of contact that may give rise to disputes. Moreover, where the number of suppliers of a product is small, the consumers of that product will be more highly dependent upon continuing relations with their suppliers and therefore less disposed to initiate legal action against them than will purchasers who may choose from many potential suppliers. Thus, where ease of entry into a business is greater, litigation will be more likely—purchasers of computer services may be more willing than automobile dealers to sue their suppliers (Macaulay 1963). Changes in the mix of types of businesses represented in the economy, then, may alter the volume of transactions, the likelihood that those transactions will be conducted with the participation of lawyers, and the likelihood that the transactions will result in formal disputes.

Reasons for Growth

But why does the larger demand for corporate legal services result in larger law firms? The work groups within the firms, handling each of the particular cases or issues, may be no larger than they were when demand was lower and law firms were smaller. Where are the economies of scale? Although access to electronic communication technology is now essential to an efficient and effective law practice, that technology is not so expensive that large numbers of lawyers must share it in order to make it a sensible investment. Computers, fax machines, and copying machines, once costly items, are now in the offices of even the smallest law firms. The 1995 Chicago survey found that 89 percent of solo practitioners and 98 percent of respondents in firms with two to four lawyers had access to computers, while 97 percent of the solos and 100 percent of the lawyers in very small firms had access to fax machines. But computerized legal research tools such as Lexis and Westlaw were available to only about half of those lawyers; 52 percent of the solos and 48 percent of those in small firms lacked these tools. A firm will not need to be very large, however, before it will be able to afford to purchase Lexis or Westlaw and thus eliminate that competitive disadvantage. But personnel costs for receptionists, secretaries, paralegals, messengers, and an around-the-clock word-processing staff (not to mention accounting, information technology, and marketing departments) are substantial, and such staff costs are probably more efficiently borne by larger operations. As we noted in chapter 5, big law firms employ an average of about 1.5 support staff persons per lawyer (*Illinois Legal Times* 1997, 20). Smaller firms may need greater staff-to-lawyer ratios in order to provide comparable levels of service. Similar economies of scale in personnel costs occur in government law offices and in the internal legal departments of corporations.

One explanation for the growth of private law firms is provided by "portfolio theory" (Gilson and Mnookin 1985). That is, a larger number of clients, bringing work in a larger number of fields of law, helps to spread economic risk. It makes the firm less dependent upon any one client or any one area of practice. If a big client goes out of business or takes its legal work elsewhere, the larger, diversified firm will have work from other clients to fill the void. If there is a downturn in the economy, so that the amount of corporate transaction work declines, it will be advantageous for the firm to have a bankruptcy department to handle work arising from business failures. Thus, firms add clients and specialty areas in order to diversify.

Another reason for law firm growth is that the firms perceive client demand for "one-stop shopping." Many firms believe that corporate clients find it advantageous to have one law firm deal with all their legal problems—taxes, securities issues, labor and employment matters, or litigation. This spares the client the expense of educating additional lawyers about the nature of its business and the trouble of shopping around to find several firms to handle the various types of work, and it permits the client and the firm to develop a continuing relationship of trust and confidence. It also, not incidentally, maximizes the amount of the client's business that the firm is able to obtain and retain. If a firm sends a client to other lawyers—for litigation services, for example—the client will be thrust into the arms of the firm's competitors and may decide to stay there. The client may find the lawyers in the second firm preferable, perhaps not only for litigation but for transactional work as well. When a law firm finds it necessary to refer a matter that it lacks the expertise to handle—a patent law issue, for example—the firm will often seek to send it to a "boutique" specialty firm that will not be a competitor for other work. Thus, a firm may well prefer to create a broad range of competencies under its own roof, having its own lawyers do as much of the client's work as possible.

Marc Galanter and Thomas Palay (1991) argue that law firms must grow in order to satisfy the imperatives of their own internal labor markets. They suggest that, whenever a new partner is admitted to the firm, associates will be hired to support and feed the work of the partner (in order to exploit the assets or "human capital" of the partner fully), and eventually some of these associates must be made partners so that the firm will be able to recruit and motivate new associates. This process creates a growth pyramid—indeed, Galanter and Palay argue that it typically results in a geometric rate of growth in the number of lawyers per firm (1991, 87–91). But we are skeptical about this thesis. Large law firms appear to grow at widely varying rates—some grow rapidly, some slowly, and some persist while growing not at all (Nelson 1988, 49). Galanter and Palay hypothesize that, because it is difficult or costly for firms to monitor the work of their associates and then adjust salaries to reflect individual productivity, firms offer the prospect of a future prize in order to motivate associates to use their best efforts: at the end of a period of years (now, usually, seven to ten years), a percentage of the associates (the percentage being within an understood, relatively stable range) will be rewarded with partnership in the firm. Galanter and Palay refer to this as the "promotion-to-partner tournament." But Kevin Kordana argues that associates are not, in fact, difficult to monitor, and that the firms do so routinely (1995, 1914–17). He observes that promotion-to-partner rates at large law firms vary widely from year to year, which is inconsistent with the existence of an implicit contract to promote a stable percentage of each cohort of associates (1995, 1921–22). There appears to have been an abrupt increase in the growth rate of the firms in 1970 (Galanter and Palay 1991, 78), which is not explained by the tournament theory. The rate change is not fatal to the theory, but it is not accounted for by the logic of the tournament.[8] This is important because about half of all the growth after 1970 is attributable not to the hypothesized geometric rate of increase but to the sudden change in that rate (Galanter and Palay 1991, 88; Heinz 1992, 9). Indeed, the amount of growth attributable to the unexplained 1970 change is so great that the fit to the observed data of a geometric growth rate (growth by x percent per year) is not significantly better than the fit of a simple linear rate (growth by x lawyers per year) if each takes into account the 1970 increase (Nelson 1992, 742). Since geometric growth is a necessary consequence of the hypothesized tournament, this is of considerable importance.

If there was a sudden change in the trend of the growth rates in 1970, there must have been either a change in the level of demand for corporate legal services, or mimetic tendencies in the management of large law firms, causing several firms to follow the growth strategy of some industry leader (DiMaggio and Powell 1983). For the latter to persist, the increase in firm size would at least need to be supported by a sufficient augmentation of demand (and, thus, of firm revenues) to permit the firms to cover the costs of the additional lawyers and support staff. We believe that the primary explanation for the increasing size of law firms is that the volume of corporate financial transactions, and of the litigation that sometimes is occasioned by those transactions, increased substantially[9] and that firms already present in the market for corporate legal services had a substantial competitive advantage in capturing the resulting demand. Existing firms possessed established relationships with corporate clients (a considerable marketing advantage) and, perhaps more important, the clients had already invested in the firms' acquisition of detailed knowledge about their business. Unless a new firm included lawyers who had previously done work for the client, either the client would need to pay start-up costs once again or the law firm would have to absorb those costs. This creates a disincentive to switching. Nonetheless, corporations do seek new suppliers of legal services, not infrequently, in order to stimulate competition for their work.

Changes in Firm Structure and Management

When the demand for corporate legal services was growing most rapidly, some law firms found it difficult to recruit enough lawyers to supply the demand. Large firms were then hiring seventy or more new lawyers per year (Stracher 1998, 29),[10] and the need for bodies led the firms to hire from a broader range of law schools than they had previously. As reported in chapter 3, the 1975 Chicago survey found that although 45 percent of all respondents had attended one of four "local" law schools (DePaul, Kent, Loyola, and Marshall), only 15 percent of the respondents in firms with 31 to 99 lawyers and only 7 percent of those in firms of 100 or more came from the four schools (see table 3.1). In the 1995 survey, about the same percentage of the Chicago bar had been produced by those schools (44 percent), but their share of the lawyers in large firms had increased substantially—26 percent of respondents in firms with 100 to 299 lawyers and 17 percent of those in firms with 300 or more had attended the local schools. So, although graduates of local schools were still underrepresented in the largest firms in 1995, their presence in such firms had increased substantially.

One of the consequences of this broader recruitment was that the firms opened their doors to categories of lawyers not previously represented in large numbers, notably women. Abel (1989, 91) observed that "because the absolute number of male law students had not increased since 1973, *all* subsequent growth of law school enrollments is attributable to the entry of women" (emphasis in original). Although women are overrepresented in the legal departments of corporations and government agencies (see chap. 6; see also Hagan and Kay 1995), a considerable number of the new women lawyers were hired by law firms. Another area of change was the ethnic composition of the large firms. The 1975 Chicago survey found evidence of pronounced ethnoreligious stratification within the bar. Protestants were more likely to be found in the large firms and Catholics and Jews were more likely to be in solo practice and local government (see chap. 3), as had been found in previous studies (Carlin 1962; Ladinsky 1963a, 1963b; *Yale Law Journal* 1964), but there were also large differences among particular fields of practice. Catholic respondents were three times more likely to be prosecutors than were Protestants or Jews. Catholics were also overrepresented in personal injury work, on both the plaintiff and defense sides, and were underrepresented in banking, securities, and labor union work. Jews were significantly overrepresented in divorce and commercial law, and underrepresented in antitrust defense, patents, probate, and business litigation. Lawyers in type I Protestant denominations, (Episcopalians, Presbyterians, Congregationalists; see chap. 3), which traditionally are more socially elite, were heavily overrepresented in securities work, substantially overrepresented in patents, banking, and tax work, and underrepresented in divorce and personal injury work (Heinz and Laumann 1982, 446–49, table B.5). Earlier in the twentieth century, leaders of the organized bar had strongly opposed the entry into the bar of immigrants from southern and eastern Europe, or their children (Abel 1989, 85; Auerbach 1976), and, in the mid-1970s, the social structure of the profession still displayed the effects of these exclusionary attitudes and practices.

But the great demand for corporate lawyers in the 1980s did much to break down the barriers. In addition to hiring women and recruiting the high-ranking graduates of less prestigious law schools, large law firms began to hire substantial numbers of Catholics and Jews. In the 1995 Chicago findings, ethnoreligious differentiation across fields and practice settings is greatly diminished. The overrepresentation of high-status Protestant denominations among securities lawyers, for example, had disappeared by 1995—in 1975 36 percent of the securities lawyers were high-status Protestants (compared with only 13 percent of the bar overall), but by 1995 only 11 percent of securities practitioners were from those type I Protestant denominations (as compared to 12 percent of the full random sample of Chicago lawyers) (see fig. 3.1). Multivariate analyses presented in chapter 3, however, indicate that in 1995 Jewish respondents were still significantly less likely to have become partners in large law firms, and women, African Americans, and Hispanics were underrepresented among partners in law firms of any size and among respondents with an income in the top quartile.

When outside lawyers were in direct and frequent contact with the top levels of corporate management, law firms often asserted that corporate officers preferred to deal with lawyers who resembled themselves—that is, white males, usually Anglo-Saxon Protestants (Baltzell 1964, 1966, 1976). This was alleged to make the clients feel more comfortable and thus facilitate a close relationship. Whether these assertions ever had a sound empirical foundation, or were merely a convenient excuse, is beside the point. In either case, when inside counsel began to select the outside firms, move business from one firm to another, and mediate the relationships between outside lawyers and corporate executives, and when corporate legal departments themselves became more diverse, the argument for social homogeneity lost much of its force. Besides, the law firms needed bodies: there were not enough WASPs to go around.

Law firms, of course, seek to employ lawyers who are especially widely acquainted or notably influential in the hope that they may be useful in recruiting and retaining clients. (These lawyers are called *rainmakers*.) For this reason and others, there is now more movement of senior lawyers among the firms than there was a few decades ago (see chap. 6). Until the 1970s, a partnership in a major law firm was generally assumed to be a lifetime job: once one became a partner, the lawyer had secure employment. It was difficult for lawyers to get reliable information about the earnings of partners in other firms (and, generally, whether the grass was greener). Firms did not discuss such matters with outsiders, and even within the firms compensation information was closely held. This changed. The senior partner of one of the major Chicago law firms told us that, in his firm, each partner gets a written report of exactly how much every other partner will be paid that year. With the advent of newspapers specializing in coverage of the legal profession, information about salaries has also become more generally available. The *National Law Journal* now publishes an annual survey of lawyers' compensation (*National Law Journal* 1999). Some income data are also available on the internet at a Web site maintained by the Altman and Weil consulting firm (www.altmanweil.com). Lawyers who want to maximize their earnings will have information about the possibilities. Law firms actively recruit both partners and associates from other firms, especially if they are likely to bring along with them the business of a client or group of clients (referred to in the trade as "a book of business"). If enough business is to be gained, firms will even recruit whole "practice groups"—a group of lawyers serving a particular client, or a group with special expertise in an area of law in which the acquiring firm perceives an opportunity for new business. For example, the Greenberg Traurig firm, based in Florida, grew from 120 lawyers in 1990 to 401 in 1998 by acquiring practice groups in New York, Washington, and other major cities (Goldhaber 1999). The *National Law Journal* reports the following:

> In Washington, DC, the firm started with international partner Howard Vine and one associate. Soon, the firm started an info-tech cluster in Tysons Corner, Va. In recent weeks, it has added a telecom team from Fleischman and Walsh and the big-league litigation group of Joe Reeder, from Patton Boggs L.L.P. Its presence in greater Washington has grown from the two attorneys in 1993 to 46 lawyers and consultants today. The hallmarks of Greenberg's expansions are patience and opportunism. It looked on and off in Atlanta, Tampa, Fla., and London for years but refused to overpay or settle for a bad fit. Ultimately, it acquired an entertainment boutique in Atlanta; in Tampa and London, it's still looking. Philadelphia is an unpopular place for branches, but when Michael Lehr came along, Greenberg snapped him

up along with his eight-lawyer group at Ballard, Spahr, Andrews & Ingersoll
L.L.P. (1999, A8)

In his study of Wall Street lawyers, based on research done in the late
1950s, Erwin Smigel (1969, 57–58) observed that "Competition for lawyers
among the large firms in New York City is limited in two major ways: the
firms will not pirate an employee from another law office, and they maintain
a gentleman's agreement to pay the same beginning salary, commonly called
the going rate." No longer.

As the demand for corporate legal services grew and law firms perceived
the opportunity for rapid growth, competition among the firms both for new
clients and for new lawyers became intense. "Grow or die" and "bigger is
better" were articles of faith. Although some firms managed to survive while
growing slowly or very little and others failed because they had expanded
too rapidly (Nelson 1988, 49), these facts appeared to give most law firms
only a little pause. Clients had legal problems to be solved, and the firms
feared, perhaps quite reasonably, that if they did not provide the solutions
the clients would take their business elsewhere. Many clients were, at the
same time, spreading their legal work around among several firms. This
might well have led firms (and did lead some) to attempt to retain only
a portion of the business—the firms with slow rates of growth were often
highly prestigious ones that were especially concerned to maintain the quality of their personnel and especially confident of their ability to retain clients;
Nelson (1988, 49) cites Sullivan and Cromwell, Dewey Ballantine, White
and Case, Covington and Burling, and Hogan and Hartson as examples.
But most law firms perceived these prominent examples to be exceptional
cases.

The competition for personnel drove the firms to pay higher salaries,
and the higher compensation then created a need for ever greater levels of
earnings. In the Chicago surveys, the median income of associates in large
firms, in constant (1995) dollars, increased from $70,828 in 1975 to $85,000
in 1995 (see chap. 7). The median real income of partners in such firms
increased from $198,318 to $225,000 over the same interval. In the largest
firms, those with 300 or more lawyers, the median partner income in 1995
was $350,000. In small firms and solo practice, however, the pattern was
quite different. For partners in small firms, median income decreased from
$127,490 in 1975 to $112,500 in 1995, and for solo practitioners it decreased
from $99,159 to $55,000, in constant dollars. Thus, the income gap between
lawyers in large firms and those in small firms and solo practice widened
considerably (chap. 7).

At the end of the 1990s, the salaries of lawyers in the largest firms increased even more dramatically. The stock market was booming, and U.S. companies—especially, Internet-based businesses (the dot-com companies)—were expanding rapidly and needed skilled personnel. Earnings in such companies, with opportunities to acquire stock options, became more attractive than law firm salaries, and law firms came to be regarded as talent depositories that could be raided (Skertic 2000, 1). The *New York Times* reported that at a San Francisco–based firm "turnover among associates rose to 25 percent last year [1999], from 12 percent in 1998, as lawyers jumped ship for both legal and executive jobs at eBay, E*trade and an array of Web start-ups" (Leonhardt 2000b, C14). Law firms in Silicon Valley and the San Francisco Bay area responded to these pressures first, but firms in New York and other major cities quickly followed. At the most prestigious firms, salaries of first-year associates jumped from the $95,000–$105,000 range to the $125,000–$140,000 range, plus bonuses (Leonhardt 2000a and 2000b; Skertic 2000). Fourth-year associates at these firms were given a raise to $200,000 or more (Leonhardt 2000b, C14). Some of the firms also began to take a portion of their fees in stock or stock options in client companies, and the firms then created "equity pools" in which associates were permitted to invest, in order to provide their lawyers with opportunities for capital appreciation. The value of the shares held in 1999 by the largest Silicon Valley firm, Wilson Sonsini, "on a per-partner basis was more than the average profits per partner, which reached about $700,000" (Orenstein 2000, 154). The founder of a firm called the Venture Law Group described his organization as "a hybrid of a startup law firm, a venture capital firm, a consulting firm and an investment bank" (Orenstein 2000, 154).

The increasingly vigorous competition among large law firms, as clients became more likely to move from firm to firm, pushed the firms to cut costs so they could price their services attractively and maintain or increase market share. To recruit and retain the lawyers they needed to handle the work, however, they could not reduce costs by reducing compensation. The firms, therefore, sought to achieve economies through "rationalization" of their production systems. The goal, of course, was to achieve greater output per employee or other unit of cost. One way to do this is to devote fewer resources to training new personnel. In an earlier day, firms had rotated associates among the various departments or practice groups so that the newly recruited lawyers could try various kinds of work and decide what they liked best, and so that the firm could evaluate the associates' particular abilities. But most lawyers become more productive when they specialize, and pressure for productivity thus became pressure for the associate to specialize early. In most large law firms today, therefore, lawyers are hired for a specific department or area of practice within the firm. When Smigel did his research on Wall Street lawyers, firms were committed to training their recruits—the firm's role in socializing and "molding" their lawyers was an accepted part of the professional ideology (Smigel 1960, 63). Now firms demand that law schools produce graduates who are able to "hit the ground running"[11] (this is a popular phrase used by the firms).

At the same time, management changes were implemented to promote efficiency. In the older, smaller firm model, a relatively small set of powerful senior partners presided over separate hierarchies within the firm (Nelson 1988). These work groups, consisting of associates and junior partners working under the supervision of one or more seniors, typically served the needs of a particular, limited group of clients. The law firm's relationships with these clients were tended and nurtured by the seniors, and the work group often dealt with the full range of the clients' problems. In the newer, larger firm model, specialized departments replace these personal hierarchies (see chap. 5). Instead of being built around dominant seniors, the departments are defined by substantive expertise or skill types—for example, tax, litigation, real estate, and mergers and acquisitions. Typically, the allocation of work within each department is managed by a chairman, assisted by a second level of supervisors.

When most law firms were simple partnerships of ten or twenty lawyers, they were governed informally. The partners saw each other often or daily, and important decisions could be made over lunch or in the hallways. But now that many lawyers practice in complex organizations with hundreds of lawyers and even larger numbers of support staff, management of the firms has become a major concern. As the size of the organization increases, formal votes tend to replace informal consensus as the typical governing mode, and the freedom of action of individual lawyers becomes limited by rules and procedures. Many of the firms employ professional managers,[12] and most are governed by a committee of partners operating within detailed rules set forth in the partnership agreement (see chap. 5). In the 1950s, many of the most prestigious firms did not even have written partnership agreements. Smigel (1969, 199) quotes a New York lawyer: "We do not have a partnership agreement. Mr. De Gersdorff of Cravath used to say, 'We don't want people for partners with whom we need written agreements.' "

Traditional hierarchies tend to be relatively inefficient because the importance of personal relationships in the maintenance of such hierarchies makes the decision makers more tolerant of waste. Thus, a partner in a major Chicago law firm observed that firms were formerly willing to accommodate lawyers who had "retired in place." Now, even if they are partners, such lawyers will be sent away.

The increase in scale of law firms and other law practice organizations also led to other changes in personnel management practices. In the older model, lawyers in private firms were divided simply into partners and associates. Although, in rare cases, lawyers were employed as "permanent associates," for longer terms, associates were almost always junior lawyers who hoped to become partners in due course. To be a "partner" in this older model meant that the lawyer was one of the owners of the firm— a partner shared in the profits. Now, however, many large law firms have two classes of partners. Some lawyers called *partners* are not owners of the firm. Thus, although they enjoy the title, they are not really partners in the traditional sense. Those who do have an ownership interest are referred to as equity partners. The 1995 Chicago survey found that 68 percent of the respondents in firms of 30 or more lawyers reported that their firms had adopted this three-tiered system—associates, nominal or income partners, and equity partners.

A variety of other terms, such as *of counsel* and *senior attorney*, are sometimes used to refer to lawyers who have nonstandard roles in the firm. These terms can mean whatever the firms and the lawyers choose to have them mean. In 1975, the largest Chicago firms typically had three to five lawyers with the title "of counsel." These lawyers were often retired or semiretired partners or prominent political figures, often former officeholders, and these categories are still found among the counsel, but many more lawyers now occupy this ambiguous status. In 2001, the largest Chicago firms reported from thirty to forty lawyers listed as "of counsel" (*Chicago Lawyer*). The category includes a variety of types—lawyers (especially women) who prefer to work part-time, former partners who were pushed out at a relatively early age, law professors, specialist experts who serve as consultants, and so on. Much of the growth in the number of lawyers with this status is attributable to the firms' encouragement of (or insistence upon) early retirement. Some law firms now also use the services of temporary or "contract" lawyers, permitting the firm to add or subtract personnel as demand may dictate (Cherovsky 1991; Frederick 1995; Hackney 1996; Scheffey 1995). If the firm gets a big case, it buys the services of additional lawyers for the duration of that case, with no obligation to retain them longer. We were told that, in some firms, these independent contractors amount to as much as 10 or 15 percent of the total number of lawyers at times of peak workload. Some firms now also contract out particular pieces of work, especially legal research; a few send work to India.[13] Thus, law firms are behaving more like corporations and less like traditional, collegial partnerships.

In recent years, many large firms have adopted an organizational form known as limited liability partnership (LLP; Romley and Talley 2004). In a traditional, old-style (general) partnership, all of the partners are personally liable for the debts of the firm. If a large malpractice suit were to bankrupt the firm, therefore, the assets of the individual partners would be at risk and would be available to satisfy the debt. In an LLP, however, each partner is responsible only for his or her own misdeeds. The general partnership provides a form of assurance to clients: every partner stands behind the work of every other, and this helps to assure quality. Given the growth in the size of these firms, however, many of the partners now have very little contact with colleagues in other departments or work groups, especially those in other cities and countries, and thus they may be increasingly uncomfortable about guaranteeing the competence (or even character) of these unknown quantities. The type of partnership adopted by the firm, then, both reflects and shapes relationships among the lawyers. In an LLP, partners may be less willing to assist in the work of another lawyer—if they do so, they may then become personally responsible for that work—and for any bad outcome. Cooperation and consultation within the firm, then, come only at a potential price. Instead of being responsible for one another, the partners have incentives to mind their own business, exclusively (Glater 2003a). Perhaps surprisingly, corporate clients are reported to be insensitive to these changes (ibid.).

Lawyer-Client Relationships

As the demand for corporate legal services increased and law firms grew in response to that demand, the nature of the relationships between corporate clients and the leading partners of the firms began to change. Three factors contributed to a weakening of the ties. First, long-term personal relationships became less common as players on both sides became mobile; turnover of personnel, both in the law firms and in corporate management, made it more difficult for the officers of the corporations to maintain close personal relationships with their lawyers. Second, the growth stimulated a further division of labor: as the volume of legal work grew, law firms found it efficient to disaggregate the client's business and to assign particular pieces of the work to specialized groups within the firms. Third, the sheer number of lawyers and the resulting complexity of firm management made it more difficult for clients to penetrate the layers. When a law firm expands from thirty lawyers to fifty, to one hundred, and then to three hundred or eight hundred, the corporation executive can no longer count on access to the personal advice of the firm's senior partner on all legal issues. Tax matters go to the tax department and litigation to the litigation department, while the senior partner may be tied up with staffing decisions for the firm's new office in Prague. The firm will continue to cultivate personal relationships with corporate officers who are in a position to bring substantial business, but as the law firm grows and the number of clients increases, it becomes more and more difficult for the firm's leaders to give personal attention to every CEO or general counsel. Some will get their telephone calls answered much more quickly than others.

The great increases in firm size and volume of business led to increasing rationalization of the organization of work within firms, especially through specialization of function. The particular form of departmentalization of the law firm often reflects the character and organization of its dominant clients: if the firm represents a large bank, it may well have a banking law department. But corporations realize that, if law firms are able to divide the tasks, clients can do it as well. This means that large businesses can parcel their tasks out to separate law firms if they think that doing so will be more effective, efficient, or inexpensive than bundling all those tasks at one firm. Thus, although big law firms try to encourage one-stop shopping, corporate clients may have incentives to shop around. Long-term personal relationships with particular lawyers once helped to tie the clients to particular firms, but when such relationships dwindled, the ties were loosened.

We should note, however, that durable relations between law firms and corporate clients remain important. In the 1975 Chicago survey, there was no clear relationship between size of firm and the percentage of stable clients—that is, larger firms did not consistently have a greater or lesser percentage of clients represented for three years or more. Lawyers in firms with 30 or more lawyers then reported that 56 percent of their clients had been with them at least three years. In 1995, however, the percentage of stable clients (as defined) increased steadily from 41 percent for solo practitioners to a high of 60 percent in firms of 100–299 lawyers, but then dropped to 45 percent in firms with 300 or more lawyers. This may indicate that firms in the 100–299 category were still relatively likely to represent companies headquartered in Chicago. Client mobility appears to be greater in the largest law firms, which operate in several cities and which represent national or multinational corporations. But, because an individual case, government investigation, or legal transaction may take three or more years to come to fruition (especially in major corporate matters), these statistics do not provide an ideal measure of the stability of client relationships. Nonetheless, the available data are consistent with the proposition that many large corporations follow a hybrid strategy in retaining firms: they maintain long-term relationships for some of their work and distribute another portion adventitiously. W. E. Baker (1990) found that corporations followed a similar strategy with investment banks—they maintained a relationship with a lead bank to conserve on information costs and gain volume discounts, while they placed some business at many other banks to gain additional information on innovations in the field and to keep the lead bank competitive.

A key factor in weakening the ties between law firms and their clients was the changing role of corporate inside counsel. To manage their growing inventory of legal issues, corporations hired more lawyers for their internal legal staffs (although those staffs did not grow as rapidly as did large law firms) and they also sought to enhance the level of sophistication and experience of those lawyers—some top partners in prominent law firms agreed to take leaves of absence from their firms, or to spend part of their time working within corporations, in order to reorganize and strengthen the corporations' legal departments.[14] From the point of view of the law firms, of course, these arrangements might also serve to solidify their relationships with their corporate clients. Inside counsel make decisions about how to divide and allocate the corporation's legal work: about which work should be done inside and which should be sent to outside law firms, and then about which outside firms to use. If the inside lawyers (the chief one is often called the *vice president for law*) know, respect, and like the lawyers in an outside firm, that firm will clearly have an advantage in securing some of the corporation's legal work. If those conditions are not present, the firm will have a difficult time in making its attributes known to corporate management. The networks of relationships among inside and outside counsel are thus a principal determinant of the distribution of legal work (Nelson 1988, 68).

Inside counsel now mediate the relationships between outside lawyers and corporate management, monitor and evaluate the performance of outside lawyers, review billings from law firms, and exercise judgment about whether the charges are excessive (Ruder 1986). They establish rules or standards for outside counsel concerning the number and kinds of personnel used by the firms for certain purposes, such as discovery or depositions (Nelson 1998, 782). In many cases, inside counsel also consult with the outside lawyers about strategies to be used in handling cases. In the 1970s and earlier, corporate house counsel were regarded as second-class citizens of the legal profession—they were sometimes lawyers who had failed to make partner in a major law firm, and were then sent by the firm to the corporation in order to cement the ties between the two (Slovak 1980; Ruder 1986). (But see the discussion in chap. 6 regarding the frequency of Golden Age careers.) As the power of inside counsel increased, their status within the profession increased as well.

To assess the changing status of inside counsel, we can compare their income and law school credentials to those of other lawyers in both 1975 and 1995. Focusing on inside counsel who worked for businesses[15] (that is, excluding those at unions and not-for-profit organizations), we find that in 1975 their median income was only $25,000, versus $35,000 for the full random sample. In 1995, however, this reverses—the median for the full sample was $75,000, while business inside counsel had a median of $112,500.[16] This improvement in the relative income of inside counsel occurred despite an increase in the percentage of women (who tend to receive lower pay; see chaps. 3 and 7) among inside counsel.[17] The difference in law school credentials is consistent with the income difference. In 1975, the percentage of graduates of elite and prestige schools among business inside counsel was slightly lower than that of other lawyers (36 percent versus 38 percent), but in 1995 their elite and prestige school percentage was slightly higher than that of others (31 percent versus 27 percent). Thus, the representation of high-status graduates among inside counsel improved by 6 percentage points relative to other members of the bar. This improvement also occurred despite the increased percentage of female inside counsel—in 1995, only 9 percent of women had attended elite schools (versus 15 percent of men) and women were somewhat overrepresented in both the regional and local school categories.

In selecting outside lawyers, clients seek competition on both price and quality of service. In a marked departure from the earlier model of firm-client relations, many corporations now require law firms to bid on their work. Previously, firms usually devoted as many hours to the work as they thought it required, and they billed for those hours at more-or-less standard rates. Discounts were possible but relatively uncommon. In the 1995 Chicago survey, however, 61 percent of the respondents in firms with one hundred or more lawyers reported that their firms bid for work.[18] (In 1975, this was so infrequent that the survey did not inquire about it.) Some potential clients invite competing firms to make presentations, sometimes referred to as dog and pony shows or beauty contests. For most types of work, corporate clients do not confine this competition to firms in one locale, and large firm practice has thus become more national in character. In the Chicago surveys, we found that in firms of thirty or more lawyers the percentage of clients located outside the Chicago metropolitan area doubled from 1975 to 1995—from 20 percent to 40 percent.

The growth of the power of corporate inside counsel is related to the emergence of the trend toward multicity law firms. Until about the 1970s, if a Wall Street firm decided that it would be helpful to have a Chicago firm handle a problem involving a Midwest transaction, the New York lawyers would send the matter to Chicago counsel in whom they had confidence (and with whom, quite probably, they had a personal relationship). When that was the practice, the Chicago firm had reason to stay out of New York: if it had opened a New York office, it would have become a direct competitor of the New York firm and thus a less likely referral partner. Once control of the allocation of legal work shifts from the outside firm to corporate inside counsel, however, the client makes its own decision about the choice of Chicago lawyers. Since Chicago firms are then no longer dependent upon the goodwill of New York firms for referral (and vice versa), there is less reason to refrain from direct competition.

Organizational Boundaries

The outcome of the processes of change in the bar is not yet clear. Will the organizations that deliver legal services to large businesses continue to be devoted exclusively to the practice of law, as traditionally conceived, or will they encompass a broader range of expert services? Will law firms simply continue to grow—from three hundred lawyers to five hundred to a thousand or two thousand (as some already have), and then to five thousand? If so, will this growth occur primarily through mergers or through continuing expansion in the size of the overall market? In 1992, the eight largest accounting firms earned 28 percent of the total national receipts for accounting services, but the eight largest law firms received only 2.4 percent of the spending for legal services; the 50 largest law firms had only a 9 percent market share (U.S. Bureau of the Census 1996a). Concentration in the markets for architecture and advertising services has also been much greater than that in law (ibid.).

There is probably nothing inherent in the nature of legal work that would prevent a substantially greater concentration of it in larger organizations. At present, however, rules concerning conflicts of interest are a significant impediment to the acquisition of new clients by major firms. A firm may not take on a client if it represents another whose interests are or may be materially adverse to those of the potential client (Hazard and Schneyer 2002, 602–6). This is based in the lawyer's ethical obligation of loyalty to the client and the duty of confidentiality in communication with the client. There is a difference between law firms and accounting firms in this respect—the rules of the accounting profession permit the firms to erect screens or walls within the firm, separating the knowledge, roles, and decisions of accountants working for one client from those working for others, while the ethical rules of the legal profession impute the knowledge and loyalties of each lawyer to every other lawyer in the firm, even in its offices in other cities. A law firm with several hundred lawyers, much less thousands, therefore has great difficulty managing and avoiding conflicts (Shapiro 2001). But the legal profession's ethical rules are subject to change, and they probably respond to market forces to some degree.

Perhaps some clients flex their muscles when dealing with law firms on conflicts issues because they know they can get away with it. The big corporate clients are many times larger and more powerful than their law firms, and those clients know that their lawyers will be attentive to their wishes. In dealing with accounting firms, however, corporations have less room for choice—the degree of concentration in that market means fewer options. In the early 1990s, the Big Six accounting firms (now further consolidated as the Big Four) audited 98 percent of the Fortune 500 industrial corporations (Cook et al. 1992).

In the 1990s, accounting firms increasingly competed with law firms—for tax work, the structuring of financial transactions, and even the preparation of business litigation.[19] What would happen if consulting firms or financial services companies moved into the market for legal services to an extent that threatened the livelihood of law firms? The judges who ultimately set the ethical rules for the legal profession are, of course, lawyers—they came from the practicing bar, and some will return to it. If the survival of law firms were seriously threatened, would judges then modify the rules to permit law firms to compete more effectively?

Law firms are vulnerable to better financed competitors. Major financial services firms, for example, are more wealthy than any law firm. Law firms are undercapitalized, live on annual earnings, and cannot sustain many years with net losses. Before the Enron-Andersen scandal damaged the accounting firms, they made substantial inroads into the practice of corporate law (Van Duch 1997). Some commentators believe that the complicity of the Arthur Andersen accounting firm in the Enron fraud and the firm's consequent dismantling extinguished the competitive threat to the law firms (Schauerte and Hernandez 2002). The subsequent Sarbanes-Oxley Act and new SEC regulations effectively put auditing firms out of the legal services business except with respect to tax matters (but see Garth 2004). The year before its collapse, however, Andersen employed 2,734 lawyers in thirty-five countries (Campo-Flores 2000). In 1997, Deloitte and Touche reported that it employed 1,104 tax lawyers and another 384 nontax lawyers worldwide (Van Duch 1997). In the late 1990s, Phillip L. Mann, former chair of the ABA's tax section, said: "[It] isn't so much the issue of who has the smarter or the harder-working lawyers on their staffs. . . . The real footsteps we're hearing is the scale of competition . . . the vast amount of money and capital that the Big Six [accounting firms] can spend on marketing. . . . They apparently have become convinced that the existing parochial jurisdiction-by-jurisdiction approach to the licensing of the legal profession will be considered just another barrier to international trade and, like tariffs, will one day come down" (Van Duch 1997, A13). As Mann's comment indicates, the globalization of law practice[20] is one of the factors making it more difficult to maintain traditional lines of distinction among the professions. Although ethical rules in all U.S. jurisdictions except the District of Columbia prohibit nonlawyers from having an ownership interest in law firms, the rules in many other nations do not. Consulting and financial services firms are affiliated with law firms abroad. Most American lawyers would prefer to retain their separate professional identity and to work within contexts that are controlled by their own profession (New York State Bar Association 2000). But some are quite ready to defect: one, commenting on his decision to leave his law firm and join an accounting firm, was quoted as saying " I didn't want to be the last one off the boat" (Van Duch 1997, A13).

The most sophisticated work done in the top Wall Street firms and in their counterparts in other major cities requires a level of experience and expertise that is difficult to duplicate, and it therefore seems unlikely that consulting firms or financial services firms will threaten the livelihood of the elite of the bar in the foreseeable future. Corporations are likely to continue to take their most complex and consequential work to such law firms. But this is a relatively small part of the legal profession, important though it may be. The corporate work done by midrange and lesser law firms—and, perhaps, the more routine work done by large firms—is likely to be squeezed by competition from consulting firms, banks, and other financial-services firms (*The Economist* 2000, 81; Gibeaut 2000, 18) . Clients will make choices. The market is more likely to determine the outcome than are the regulators of the bar.

As law firms become international, American firms will find that their options are limited if they are prohibited from sharing fees with entities in which management consultants, investment bankers, or other nonlawyers have an ownership interest. Mergers of law firms with such entities (creating so-called multidisciplinary practices or MDPs) have taken place abroad for several years (Dezalay 1992). If lawyers practice across national boundaries (as is increasingly the case), then it will be difficult for local licensing authorities to enforce restrictions on multinational firms (Garth and Silver 2002).

Large law firms now devote great care and substantial resources to the effort to avoid conflicts of interest. They do so not only because of ethical rules but because of the expressed preferences of some clients (Shapiro 2001). The firms are understandably wary of giving offense to important clients by taking on the representation of the clients' adversaries (Heinz and Laumann 1982, 371–73). But it is not at all clear that corporations value exclusivity of representation as much or as often as the official ideology of the legal profession may suggest—clients, in fact, commonly waive their right to object to conflicts of interest, and the alternative approach to conflicts that is used in accounting firms does not appear to have stemmed the flow of legal work to multidisciplinary practices in Europe (Campo-Flores 2000). The *Wall Street Journal* reported that "European corporate clients who have used the Big Five's [referring to accounting firms] legal services praise the efficiency and cost savings" (M. Jacobs 2000). It is not apparent why the preferences of American businesses should be markedly different. Indeed, some of the work sent to MDPs in Europe came from U.S.-based companies.

It is possible, however, that some substantial segment of the market for legal services deals with matters in which the client has a preference for stringent conflict-of-interest rules. Some work may be of especially great sensitivity, so that a stronger assurance of confidentiality is desired, or may be especially vulnerable to adversarial interests, as in the planned acquisition of a real estate tract or the assemblage of a block of stock. In such matters, the client might prefer to consult an American law firm rather than an MDP that could also advise an adversary. Indeed, a rational choice model might suggest that the greater attention given by law firms in recent years to the monitoring and avoidance of conflicts helped the law firms differentiate their services from those offered by accounting firms. Thus, by adopting rules and practices that distinguish them from consultants in situations where conflicts of interest may be especially worrisome, law firms have created a market niche that is relatively secure from incursion. But the question is, how large is that niche? Is it big enough to employ most of the corporate bar?

Some lawyers doubt that the present conflicts rules of their profession truly serve the interests of clients (Fischel 2000). The system designed to prevent conflicts is expensive, it causes delay, and it may sharpen conflict by requiring lawyers to serve as champions rather than as mediators (Shapiro 2001). Sophisticated clients, therefore, might choose to place their work within that system only when they believe the work to be sensitive or when the necessary skills are not available elsewhere. The examples abroad are available for all to see—lawyers and clients alike. As the globalization of business transactions and corporate law practice proceeds, it is unlikely that multidisciplinary practice could be a success in Europe, South America, and Asia, and a failure in the United States. The large American law firm has been a distinctive form, which has had considerable success and has been copied abroad, notably by the British solicitors firms. It remains to be seen whether the form will endure.

Business Methods

The expansion of corporate law firms and the lengthening of their client lists changed not only the relationships between lawyers and clients but those among the lawyers themselves. Although lawyers had long worked on complex matters in teams that combined specialties, the nature of those teams changed (R. Rosen 2002, 641–47). In 1970, a big firm might have had forty or so lawyers and perhaps three or four dominant partners, and each of those senior partners would have headed a "practice group." Mr. Cabot's group would serve the clients for whom Cabot was the principal outside counsel. The group therefore included lawyers with sufficient expertise in various specialties to meet the regular needs of its particular clientele. If that clientele was narrowly defined, the lawyers dealt with a relatively limited set of problems and they probably acquired a large amount of expertise or "capital" that was specific to the clients. Because the group was relatively small, some degree of movement across specialties was highly desirable— the lawyers needed to learn enough about each others' fields to be able to step in if necessary. In the larger firms of the 1990s, by contrast, dominant partners were more numerous, less clearly defined, and more transitory, and the departments within the firms were more likely to be defined by function or expertise than by client group. Thus, a partner in the tax department would be asked to consult on a Walmart real estate deal one week and on the United Airlines bankruptcy two weeks later, and she and her associates in the tax department might work with different teams from other departments on each of these matters. There was therefore less continuity in the sets of lawyers working with one another, and the tasks addressed by each lawyer were increasingly restricted to his or her specialty (see chap. 2). In such a system, the organization controls the work: it assembles the teams, and it determines how much support (from associates, paralegals, and other staff) the senior lawyers receive.

When work groups are relatively stable, they may become "communities": they tend to develop their own ways of working, distinct sets of interpersonal relationships, and norms that are specific to the group (Regan 2004). But if the lawyers are assembled into teams that differ from transaction to transaction, then distinct procedures, relationships, and norms are much less likely to form. A continuing team has at least the potential to become an independent power base. On particular issues, such as a decision on which of two candidates to hire for a position within its area of concern, the group may be able to overcome the preferences of the firm leadership. When the membership of work groups is transitory, however, the central management of the organization is strengthened.

Lawyers could, of course, choose to serve their own interests at the expense of the firm—for example, by leaving the firm and taking clients, or by failing to use their best efforts on the firm's work (Galanter and Palay 1991, 94; Gilson and Mnookin 1985, 330–39)—and firms therefore try to prevent such opportunistic behavior. If the firm or work group is small, informal norms may inhibit conduct that would harm the collectivity. Norms are more likely to develop and to be communicated in contexts where there is close and continuing interaction among the parties, and the parties will be less likely to transgress the norms if they know they will be working with the same colleagues in the future. Informal sanctions are most effective when reputation, affect, and civility matter. If the work groups do not provide effective informal sanctions, however, the management of the organization will need to create mechanisms of control—such as, perhaps, the "promotion-to-partner tournament" hypothesized by Galanter and Palay (1991). Controls generated centrally are likely to be more formal and to rely on administrative enforcement. They are often codified in a manual of guidelines and procedures. Informal norms, by contrast, are more variable, and the loci of both the norms and the sanctions are more likely to be dispersed. The change from informal norms to formal rules, then, implies a transfer of power from particular constituencies to the organizational management.

During the 1980s and 1990s, when law firms were growing rapidly, the firms had to assimilate large numbers of new lawyers who differed in significant respects from those who worked there previously. Many of these new lawyers were women, an increasing (but still small) percentage were minorities, a large share had been trained at law schools from which the large firms had not recruited in the past, and a substantial number were drawn from ethnoreligious groups that had been markedly underrepresented in such firms. These new lawyers had reason to feel that they were different from the seniors, and their differences bred anxiety about their status and their future. Could they expect to become partners in due course? If not, then they owed no great duty of loyalty to the firm.

The socialization of new recruits was, indeed, a more general problem for the organizations in which lawyers worked. Marc Galanter has analyzed changes in the age distribution of the profession during the latter part of the twentieth century (Galanter 1999). As he points out, the rapid increase in the number of lawyers in the 1970s and 1980s meant that the distribution changed from one in which senior lawyers were only modestly outnumbered by juniors to one in which the great majority of lawyers were relatively young. A preponderance of younger lawyers, with less experience, less thorough assimilation, and narrower networks of relationships, meant that a smaller percentage of the bar was committed to the established ways of recruiting clients, hiring lawyers, making partners, dividing profits, and (generally) managing their firms. The change in the age distribution was, in itself, an additional source of instability in the profession.

In the late 1990s, a firm of perhaps four hundred lawyers, which probably had only half that number a decade before, would find itself trying to instruct scores of new recruits each year in the ways of the firm. Very soon, the recruits outnumbered the veterans, and the organizational culture changed. Old, informal norms were no longer understood and accepted by all. Mobility across firms increased. Turnover among associates became so great in the 1990s that firms sponsored symposia and "studies" addressed to the problem of retention. One product was a volume called *Keeping the Keepers*, published by the National Association for Law Placement, an organization funded by large law firms (NALP Foundation for Research and Education 1998). As the old norms broke down and bureaucratic structures replaced collegiality, partners as well as associates became less secure. Large law firms continued to have higher retention rates than any other practice setting (see chap. 6), but partnership no longer guaranteed permanence. Partners moved. Partners were terminated. Firms that had once refrained from courting talent at other firms now did so freely. The new legal press, especially Steven Brill's *American Lawyer*, celebrated the "modernization" of law firms, the adoption of aggressive business methods, and the explicit disparagement of "gentlemanly" management, which was seen as stolid and inefficient (Powell 1985). In the 1980s, several consulting firms began to specialize in advising law firms about how to conduct their business.[21] The consultants sped the transformation of the firms from traditional partnerships into small bureaucracies operated on the corporate model (see chap. 5). A common theme was the rationalization of the ways in which work was distributed and controlled. As we noted above, the old hierarchies, each headed by a prominent senior partner ("Mr. Cabot's group"), were replaced by departments organized around particular specialties. In the older model, each of the hierarchies was a power center within the firm, and they often competed for control. In the newer model, power was centralized in a chairman of the firm, a managing committee, department chairs, and a professional administrator, with a formal chain of command. An organization supplanted the competing hierarchies.

In the old model, leadership came with seniority. Both control of the firm and income share were usually determined by the percentage of the partnership owned by each partner, often expressed as the number of "points" that each held. The partners would vote their shares (or points) in firm decisions, and income was distributed according to the same hierarchy. Share ordinarily increased with age.[22] At many firms, as younger lawyers increasingly outnumbered older ones, the age cohorts began to struggle for control. Younger lawyers felt that the elders were taking a bigger piece of the pie than they deserved. Senior lawyers were characterized as unproductive and/or dictatorial. Each cohort portrayed the other as greedy.

The change in the age distribution altered the balance of power in law firms, and may in the future change it once again. According to Galanter, in 1970 there were 127 lawyers in their thirties for every 100 in their fifties (Galanter 1999, 1085). The seniors were not then so outnumbered as to overcome the substantial advantages of seniority, and older lawyers could, therefore, set the rules of the game. But by 1985 there were 284 in their thirties for every 100 in their fifties (ibid.). As the lawyers in the younger cohort became partners, seniors began to lose the struggles for power—for example, in selecting members of the managing committee and then in votes within the managing committee. Ambitious new partners in their late thirties and early forties began to push the senior partners out of the way (Ripley 2000; Schmeltzer 1999). Before the age distribution had shifted, the juniors would not have dared to attempt this.

In some firms, juniors succeeded in deposing seniors. In others, seniors managed to suppress dissent and maintain control, and in still others one group bought off the other (Rovella 1997). Some firms lowered the mandatory retirement age—typically, from sixty-eight or seventy to sixty-five or sixty-three (Singer 2000).[23] A consequence of this was that the firms paid pensions for a greater number of years per retiree (e.g., from age sixty-three until death instead of from age sixty-eight until death). Often, the pension plans were unfunded (pensions were paid by the firm out of current income) and, when they were funded, they had been premised on shorter periods of retirement. If the firm was obligated to pay a fixed pension rate, therefore, earlier retirement imposed a heavy financial burden upon the remaining lawyers, which created yet another point of contention between juniors and seniors (Singer 2000). In some cases, retirement benefits were reduced (McDonald 2000).

One of the oldest and most prestigious Chicago law firms, the Sidley firm, demoted thirty-two partners to "senior counsel" or "counsel" status in 1999. The chairman of its management committee said that the demotions of lawyers "mostly in their mid-50s and early 60s . . . will expand opportunities for younger partners and associates" (Taylor 2002). *The American Lawyer* quoted the chairman of the firm's executive committee as saying: "When we laid this out to associates, they understood that the overall plan would create significant opportunities for them" (Ripley 2000). The U.S. Equal Employment Opportunity Commission pursued an investigation of the firm, seeking to determine whether the former partners were "employees" within the meaning of federal law and whether the demotions amounted to age discrimination.[24] At Cadwalader, Wickersham, and Taft, an old-line firm based in New York, a 1994 plan known as Project Rightsize sought to eliminate seventeen partners from the firm. This was referred to in *Crain's New York Business* as a "dramatic power struggle between old and young partners" (McDonald 2000). It also resulted in litigation (Rovella 1997). In a less confrontational style, another prominent Chicago firm initiated what it calls the "senior tour," in which each lawyer who has reached age fifty-eight is interviewed by the firm management and is asked to reflect upon his or her future plans, to consider whether the time has come to slow down a bit, to work part-time, or to indulge a taste for travel. It is presented not as a request to leave but as an invitation to consider the possibilities.

The age distribution of the profession is changing once again. The very large numbers of lawyers who entered the bar in the late 1970s and the 1980s are reaching middle age. Galanter projected that by 2005 there will be only 126 lawyers in their thirties for each 100 in their fifties, and by 2020 there will be 104 per 100. When that happens, will the assets of seniority begin to be reasserted? Senior lawyers do have advantages. Over the course of their careers, they acquire ties to important clients and important politicians. Seniority will also, ordinarily, enhance firm-specific knowledge and, unless the senior is incompetent, his or her due bills for favors done will outweigh debits for enemies made. If the law firms of the future face increasing competition from MDPs and other sorts of consulting firms, the business-getting connections of senior lawyers may, in that environment, become even more highly valued. And if the seniors exploit their capital, corporate law firms might then be governed by smaller hierarchies once again, or perhaps split apart. Or some of these firms may be absorbed by MDPs and thus become even more bureaucratic.

We do not suggest that changes in the market for legal services will, through some automatic or impersonal process, inevitably result in change in the structure or governance of the firms. Rather, the effects of market factors are mediated by the perceptions, interpretations, norms, and biases of the various actors. No doubt the firms seek to make rational choices, but what is rational may be contested. Interest groups within the firms compete for power, as illustrated by the struggles between age cohorts, and observations about the market are mobilized by the groups to support arguments in favor of one or another position. The players will seek to interpret market facts to their own advantage. Thus, Neil Fligstein has demonstrated that control of top management positions in large U.S. corporations shifted among varying constituencies within the companies during the twentieth century (1987, 1990). During 1919–39, a time when "the dominant strategies of [business] firms were oriented toward the manufacture of a single product group," the businesses tended to be controlled by "entrepreneurs, lawyers, and manu-facturing personnel" (Fligstein 1987, 48). After 1939, executives in sales and marketing gained power at the expense of manufacturing personnel because the latter "were not able to deliver on increases in sales or profitability" (1987, 57) and because the firms were then diversifying and entering new markets (1987, 49). After 1959, finance personnel became dominant as the success of the firms was increasingly determined by decisions regarding the allocation of capital among multiple product lines and as corporate mergers became more common (1987, 49, 55–56). Although the changes in leader-ship reflected changes in the companies' business strategies, the strategies were themselves outcomes of political processes within the firms. Fligstein concluded: "All large organizations contain an internal power struggle over claims from various actors over the goals and resources of the organization" (1987, 45).

The signals sent by the market are not unambiguous. It is entirely pos-sible to misread the portents. In the late 1990s, when new technology com-panies were flying high and their lawyers were busy with the financing of the emerging companies, some law firms notified long-term clients that they would no longer represent them—the firms could make more money rep-resenting start-up companies and taking all or part of their fees in stock, which was seen as having great growth potential. The steady fees paid by established companies were unspectacular by comparison. Partners who had been responsible for the old, terminated clients were often injured and an-gered by the decrease in their billings. When the stock market fell a few years later, the old clients were not there to cushion the blow. Several large law firms had invested heavily in increasing their capacity to do intellectual property work, with a particular focus on clients engaged in developing and marketing computer technology. When the dot-com bubble burst in 2001, most of those law firms found that they then employed many more intellectual property lawyers than they had any use for. Some of the firms incurred substantial losses. Because law firms do not accumulate capital, they lack the resources necessary to carry them through lean times of long duration. They must adjust to changed circumstances quickly.

One of the more conspicuous casualties was Brobeck, Phleger, and Harrison, a large, prestigious firm headquartered in San Francisco. It dissolved in 2003 after having prospered for seventy-seven years (Glater 2003c). The Brobeck example is instructive. Its failure was precipitated by the sudden economic downturn, but was exacerbated by a power struggle within the firm. In 1998, the partners elected a new chairman, Tower Snow, who had come to Brobeck only three years before (Beck 2002). Snow, a securities litigator who has been described as "charismatic, handsome, articulate, and visionary," was highly ambitious and presided over major growth at the firm (ibid.). According to the *San Francisco Chronicle*: "Snow craved prominence among the nation's elite firms, and he sought it through breakneck expansion into high-tech, intellectual property and securities litigation. . . . He launched a national advertising campaign that included $3 million-per-year television ads on CNN [and] ads in the *Wall Street Journal*" (Holding, Chiang, and Berthelsen 2003). In three years, the firm more than doubled in size—from 400 lawyers (1998) to more than 900 (2001); at its peak, its annual profits per partner were $1.17 million (ibid.). But the firm went down even faster than it went up. By the end of 2002, profits per partner dropped to $550,000 and the number of lawyers fell to 493 (ibid.). When the bubble burst, Snow's enemies and rivals in the firm, including the former chairman, John Larson, sought to displace him (Beck 2002). In consequence, Snow resigned as chairman before the end of his term (Holding, Chiang, and Berthelsen 2003). A few months later, as Snow arrived at the San Francisco airport after a flight from London, he was handed a letter written by the new chairman of the firm, a litigator from the Los Angeles office. According to the *American Lawyer*, it read:

> Dear Tower: You have been expelled as a partner in Brobeck, Phleger and Harrison LLP pursuant to [Brobeck's] partnership agreement. You are not to go to the offices of Brobeck, Phleger and Harrison LLP unless accompanied by a person designated by me. Your access to the firm computer network

has been shut off and your building and office access cards have been deactivated. (Beck 2002).

A law firm consultant concluded: "Ultimately, it came down to a battle between two big egos. One was Tower's, and the other was (former chairman) John Larson's" (Holding, Chiang, and Berthelsen 2003). But Tower Snow landed on his feet: ten days after he was expelled from Brobeck, he was named head of the new West Coast office of Clifford Chance, a London-based solicitors firm (Beck 2002). Brobeck fared less well. Having borrowed $90 million in an attempt to stay afloat, it sank, less than a year after Snow's departure and only two years after the decline began.

The leadership role played by litigators in the Brobeck battle and the personal styles of the major players exemplify broader changes in law firm leadership. In 1975 and earlier, litigators were seldom found in top leadership positions. In traditional, old-style firms, trial lawyers were often regarded as flamboyant, and too idiosyncratic to guide and represent the firm. Firms cultivated an image of gravitas, sagacity, and quiet dignity. Even if the lawyers were not all descended from old money, they could at least emulate the style. At a time when corporate management was dominated by families that controlled the companies, this matched the lawyers to the clients. But, as marketers and MBAs came to prominence in the corporations, a new-style lawyer was called for. Like Tower Snow, leaders of large law firms are now more likely to be openly ambitious and aggressive. Many of them are litigators, and they are prepared to play hardball. At both times, then, lawyers have tended to emulate their clients. Snow reportedly "believed that a law firm could be run like a successful company" (Beck 2002). His firm's fate demonstrates, of course, that it is also possible for it to be run like a failing company.

In 1933, Karl Llewellyn said "the practice of corporation law not only works for business men toward business ends, but develops within itself a business point of view . . . toward the way in which to do the work" (Llewellyn 1933). When he wrote that, it was not quite true. Not yet. The mid-twentieth-century histories of law firms (Dean 1957; Swaine 1948) describe enterprises that do not much resemble General Motors, even a primitive form of General Motors (Chandler 1962). In 1933, when Llewellyn's article was published, White and Case, Shearman and Sterling, and the Cravath firm,[25] all major New York law firms, had fourteen, fifteen, and sixteen lawyers, respectively (Martindale-Hubbell 1933). That same year, the Sidley, Winston, and Kirkland firms, all big Chicago players, had eleven, twelve, and nineteen (ibid.). Of the private practitioners enumerated in the 1952 *Lawyer*

Statistical Report, 68 percent were still working alone (Martindale-Hubbell 1952). Even in 1975, there were only three law firms in the United States that had as many as two hundred lawyers (Abel 1989, 312, table 46). Smigel described the culture of the Wall Street firm in the late 1950s:

> A number of lawyers who were born in the Midwest but trained at eastern law schools found they still had something to learn about eastern, upper-class, social mores, and remarked that they quickly learned by imitation. One reported, for example: "When I first came into the firm, I noticed what older associates wore, one in particular. I thought he was typical of the successful Wall Street lawyer. I found out where he bought his clothing . . ."
>
> A senior associate recalled, "There was a partner who was involved in a difficult, unpleasant divorce case. He left. I think he was requested to do so. In the law you have to become circumspect." (Smigel 1969, 318–19)

C. Wright Mills' use of the term *law factories* was fanciful, at the time that he used it (Mills 1956). In the last quarter of the twentieth century, however, American law firms did, indeed, develop "a business point of view toward the way in which to do the work."

Bingham and Dana, founded in Boston in 1891, thrived for a hundred years as a conservative corporate firm that specialized in representing banks (Carter 2002). In the 1990s, however, as more and more banks merged into large holding companies, it became clear that there would be fewer such clients. Accordingly, the firm perceived a need to diversify (ibid.). To do so, Bingham established three "ancillary businesses"—that is, businesses that provide services other than legal advice or representation (Zimmerman and Kelly 2004).[26] One is a consulting firm that advises companies dealing with state regulatory agencies, another advises small to medium-sized companies on mergers and access to venture capital, and the third is a joint venture with Legg Mason, a Baltimore financial services company, creating a money management firm (Hines 2001). The managing partner of Bingham said that they sought to emulate the strategy of the major accounting firms, which had taken advantage of "their two main assets—reputation and client base—and leveraged them by looking at the needs and effectively cross-selling, creating a whole line of businesses which became very lucrative" (ibid.).

The Holland and Knight law firm, based in Florida, owned nine subsidiaries as of 2001, including a detective agency, a firm that provided environmental consulting, a money management firm, and a real estate firm (ibid.). In Chicago, the Seyfarth Shaw firm, which specialized in the employer side of labor and employment law, owned Seyfarth Shaw At Work, a company that offered training classes for corporate managers, and Lucid Consulting, a personnel management consulting firm; in 2001, these two businesses had 125 employees (Palmer 2001). Other Chicago law firms also owned ancillary businesses—Mayer Brown had an international trade consulting firm, Baker and McKenzie had a finance and trade company, Hinshaw and Culbertson (a PI defense firm) had a company offering technology risk analysis, and Katten Muchin owned a concern doing customs and international trade work. The vice chairman of McDermott Will, another Chicago law firm that planned business ventures, said: "The line between traditional legal services and general business advisory services is getting blurrier by the minute" (ibid.).

In 2002, Bingham and Dana merged with the McCutchen law firm of San Francisco, resulting in a firm known as Bingham McCutchen. In one of its first advertising pieces (printed in four colors on heavy stock and mailed widely), it characterized itself this way:

> *Dedicated to achieving your business objectives*—Building on a proven track record in hundreds of high-stakes, precedent-setting cases, we focus on what makes sense for your business and develop our strategy accordingly. . . .
>
> For issues that can't be predicted, we can help you quickly devise an effective and cost-efficient strategy, driven by your objectives and the realities of your business.

Note the emphasis on the lawyers' understanding of the client's business. The message is: these lawyers speak your language; they aren't theoreticians; they get the job done, efficiently. To deliver on this promise, of course, the lawyers will have to know how the business works (R. Rosen 2002, 657–58, 672).

Because of the increasing value to lawyers of prior work experience in the business world, some law schools, including Northwestern in Chicago, made it clear that they now preferred applicants for admission who had worked for a year or two after college. Northwestern's dean said that his goal was to admit only students with work experience (Strahler 2001). This emulated graduate schools of business, which had for some time required students to have prior experience in business or management. Law schools also changed their curricula, adding courses in business planning and corporate finance. Their students and prospective students, presumably reflecting perceptions of the job market, generated demand for these offerings (Gest 2001). The number of students applying to Northwestern's graduate business and law program—which offers degrees in both fields, pursued simultaneously—increased from

44 in 1995 to 182 in 2002 and 209 in 2003. As we saw in chapter 8, the views of the youngest lawyers were more sympathetic to business, more opposed to government regulation, than were the views of those who entered practice twenty and thirty years earlier.

Shearman and Sterling, based in New York and one of the largest law firms in the world, distributes compilations of "league tables," which are listings of law firms ranked by some criterion, usually by the number or value of a particular type of transaction handled by the firms. These are called league tables because they resemble the obsessive statistics tabulating the performance of baseball teams. The cover of Shearman and Sterling's brochure for 2000 read: "Shearman & Sterling is ranked among the top five law firms in more than 200 league tables published in 2000, more than any other law firm in the world." The booklet compiled tables originally published in a variety of trade journals, for example: "Leading IPO Counsel to First-Time Issuers" (from the *Daily Deal*, May 9, 2000); "Telecom Project Finance Deals by Deal Value" (from *Privatisation International*, September 1999); "Top Middle Market M&A Legal Advisors in 1999: Drugs, Medical Supplies and Equipment," (from *Mergerstat*, January 2000); "Hostile Acquisitions of Foreign Targets, Representing Target Side," ranked by value (from *Thomson Financial Securities Data*, February 2000). League tables have been used by investment banks for many years as a way of demonstrating their prominence and competence. Law firms adopted the practice more recently, as only one of several new advertising techniques. The Legal Marketing Association was formed in 1985; by 2002, it had 1,250 members (Carter 2002). In 2001, Piper Rudnick, a merger of a Baltimore and a Chicago firm, hired the top administrative officer of the Leo Burnett Company, a major advertising agency, and the Holland and Knight law firm had thirty-eight employees in its marketing department (ibid.). Corporate firms no longer rely solely on word-of-mouth or on contacts made on the golf course or at the University Club. The methods they use to sell their wares increasingly resemble those of their clients.

The growth of corporate law firms reflected the evolution of their clientele. Businesses now operate in many locales, from multiple offices, and seek markets abroad; companies consolidate through acquisition and merger, often creating conglomerates engaged in disparate enterprises—for example, broadcasting and the manufacture of electrical equipment (NBC and General Electric). Although the start-up costs incurred when a client engages a new law firm remain substantial and still inhibit firm switching, such costs loom less large as clients diversify. Prior relationships among lawyers and corporate executives are of little value when the corporation acquires a new business, with new management. Different lawyers may handle those separate lines of work in any event—expertise in the law of broadcasting does not have much utility in the electrical equipment business. If the corporation has offices in twenty major cities around the world, it may want to have convenient, regular access to local counsel in each of those cities. From the client's point of view, the duplication of cost attributable to using several suppliers of legal services may be more than offset by the advantage of competition among law firms for its business. The development of broader (national and international) markets for legal services meant that corporations could choose from many more firms.

When businesses increasingly divided their legal work by subject, locale, or transaction and spread that work among multiple law firms, this decreased the dependence of the client upon a single law firm, but it also decreased the dependence of the firm upon the client. Thus, as law firms opened branches and began to deliver services in broader markets, the pressure to indulge every client preference was alleviated. Moreover, when the firm's clients became more varied, it became more probable that the particular social background characteristics preferred by one client would not suit another. In relationships that are ad hoc, social homogeneity is less likely (Laumann 1973). If a lawyer-client relationship is long-term and one set of lawyers deals with the full range of the business, the preference for lawyers who share the clients' social characteristics has greater force—regardless of whether those preferences come from the client or from the law firm. As we have noted, ethnoreligious exclusivity was once a part of the system of the profession. The social organization of the bar was built upon it. By 1995, however, although some of the effects of that system remained (see chap. 3), ethnoreligious distinctions had in large measure been replaced by stratification based upon gender and race. The demand for corporate legal services peaked in the 1980s and again in the latter 1990s, and the need for lawyers was then so strong that ethnicity was seldom seen as a relevant consideration. In seeking lawyers to process the transactions, businesses became more businesslike.

Individual fate is shaped by organizational constraints. Individual lawyers, or even small groups of them, cannot easily reach clients when markets are national or international. The lawyers need a brand name (a reputation for quality) that is widely recognized, an extensive staff to support the work of senior lawyers, and capital sufficient to fund multiple offices and to underwrite the risk of opening a new office or undertaking a new venture. Lawyers can and do draw upon established relationships with clients to strengthen their own positions within their organizations or, occasionally, to move to a new organization, taking clients with them. For the latter to occur, however, the client must be persuaded that the lawyer's new venue will provide support services of sufficient range and quality to permit the lawyer to deliver good work. Thus, when law firms became larger and more capital intensive, and the mobility of clients increased (and relationships between lawyers and clients therefore became less stable), lawyers became ever more dependent upon the organizations in which they worked.

Conclusion

As the individual organizations that deliver legal services changed and the constraints that they impose on lawyers' work and careers intensified, the broader social structure of the urban bar was transformed. In Chicago, between 1975 and 1995, the bar doubled in size, the percentage of women increased from 4 percent to 29 percent, and the share of the profession practicing in firms with one hundred or more lawyers tripled (from 8 percent to 25 percent).[27] At the same time, solo practitioners and firms with fewer than ten lawyers continued their long-term attrition, and the percentage of lawyers employed in government or as house counsel remained relatively constant. The women who entered the bar came to occupy subordinate positions, for the most part, and most minorities held jobs that were even less prestigious. In the two decades between the Chicago surveys, social stratification within the bar increased while professional autonomy and the integration or coherence of the bar decreased.

The autonomy of lawyers is limited, in the first instance, by constraints imposed by the job market. As we saw in chapter 3, a hierarchy of law schools channels graduates to a hierarchy of practice settings. Lawyers who attend prestigious schools are much more likely to secure prestigious employment—the four "local" law schools train about 45 percent of all Chicago lawyers, but only 17 percent of the 1995 respondents working in firms with three hundred or more lawyers had been educated at those schools, while two-thirds of those in government jobs and in firms of two to nine lawyers were their graduates (see table 3.1). Exceptional lawyers can beat the odds, but only by being exceptional. The autonomy of Chicago lawyers further diminished from 1975 to 1995 as their careers became less stable and they became more dependent upon the employing organizations. In 1995, lawyers in private practice had changed jobs more often than those in 1975 (figs. 6.1 and 6.2), but they usually moved among employers within the same sector of practice—indeed, there was a considerable increase in the tendency of private practitioners to move from a partnership in one law firm to partnership in another (fig. 6.5). Their range of options became even more restricted.

The lawyers who were most likely to report autonomy in their work were those in the practice settings that were declining; only in solo practice and in the smallest firms did more than a fifth of the lawyers report that they had ever refused to accept a client or a work assignment, and lawyers who represented corporate clients were significantly less likely to design their own work strategies (see fig. 5.5). Thus, the types of practice that were growing most rapidly were those where lawyers enjoyed the least autonomy. By 1995, the corporate sector of practice was more than twice as large as the personal client sector—from 1975 to 1995, while the estimated percentage of all lawyers' time devoted to corporate client fields increased from 53 percent to 64 percent, the percentage devoted to fields serving individuals and small businesses decreased from 40 percent to 29 percent (fig. 2.1).[28] Moreover, as law firms grew, they became more bureaucratic and participation in policy decisions concerning the management of the firms narrowed. In firms with a "corporate" style of management, lawyers reported less participation in firm governance than did those in "traditional" or "hybrid" firms (fig. 5.4). Because these types of autonomy are less often manifested in the context of corporate practice, it is perhaps not surprising that expert ratings of the degree of autonomy of the various fields of practice were negatively associated with practitioners' ratings of the prestige of the fields within the profession (table 4.3). Lawyers were faced, significantly, with a choice between autonomy and professional prestige.

Even the personal interaction and the political views of lawyers appear to be importantly influenced by their work context. Lawyers' views on economic issues corresponded to the nature of their clientele (fig. 8.4). For example, when asked whether consumers were more effectively protected by competition or by federal regulation, the lawyers were strongly split (fig. 8.2) and the division reflected the interests of their clients. When asked to identify persons with whom they "most enjoy discussing law related matters," 78 percent of the 1975 respondents named colleagues who worked in the same type of practice setting; in 1995, this grew to 88 percent (chap. 5). Thus, organizational context had a large and increasing effect on these collegial relationships. Ties to a selected set of notable Chicago lawyers were also found to be organized by field of practice, as well as by party politics. One segment of the network of relationships was largely restricted to corporate practitioners, another was dominated by trial lawyers (including many leaders of the local bar associations), and the third included lawyers engaged in legal services work and liberal reformers (see fig. 10.3).

The decreasing autonomy of Chicago lawyers was associated with increasing differentiation of lawyers' roles—boundaries within the profession became more well-defined and difficult to cross. The separate sectors of the bar were even more separate. In 1975, when firms with one hundred or more lawyers employed 8 percent of the practicing bar, those lawyers earned 9 percent of the bar's total income, but in 1995, when the percentage of lawyers working in firms of that size had increased to 25 percent, their income share reached 37 percent (see fig. 5.1). Government lawyers constituted 11 percent of the practicing bar in 1975 and earned 6 percent of the total income; in 1995, they were still 11 percent of the bar but received only 4 percent of the income. Solo practitioners declined from 21 percent to 15 percent of practicing lawyers, but from 19 percent to 10 percent in income share. The gulf between the wealthiest lawyers and the less fortunate widened considerably. In 1975, lawyers in the bottom quartile of the income distribution earned an average of $43,231 (in 1995 dollars). That had dropped by almost $10,000 in 1995 (to $33,816). In the top quartile, however, average income (again, in constant dollars) increased from $266,733 to $325,030. In 1995, the 25 percent of lawyers with the highest incomes received 61 percent of total practice income, while the bottom 25 percent received only 6 percent (fig. 7.1).

As the income hierarchy grew steeper, the effects of demographic characteristics on lawyers' places in the profession, always strong, were reinforced by the entry into the bar of substantial numbers of women and minorities. Ethnoreligious stratification, seen clearly in the 1975 data, was greatly diminished in 1995 (see fig. 3.1), but women, African Americans, and Hispanics replaced the disadvantaged ethnoreligious groups on the lower rungs of the professional ladder. Analyses of the probability of achieving partnership in a large law firm (controlling for age) or an income in the top quartile (again controlling for age) found that these newer entrants to the bar were much less likely to experience these types of success (chap. 3). In 1995, white males from high-status Protestant denominations had a 26 percent probability of being a partner in a firm of one hundred or more lawyers by the time they reached the mean age (forty-three), but for white females the probability was only 6 percent and for African Americans only 3 percent. Gender and race are more obvious markers than ethnoreligious background, more easily observed, and therefore make the social boundaries within the profession clearer, more distinct.

The stratification of the bar extends beyond the profession to the lawyers' roles in civic, business, religious, and political organizations (chap. 9). Lawyers who had high incomes, were Protestants, and were older (but not elderly) were the most likely to be active in such organizations, and those who had ties to the elites of the bar were significantly more likely to have leadership positions (see fig. 9.2). Thus, although membership in the bar may have been an asset in securing invitations to participate and in the competition for leadership roles, it did not serve to equalize social advantage. Rather, attributes that determine social standing in the broader society operated to enhance or diminish the lawyers' potential for influence in their communities.

Social stratification divides the bar and weakens its coherence—lawyers with differing personal characteristics live in different social worlds and play different roles both in the bar and outside it. Moreover, the growing specialization of lawyers' work is increasing the separation among those roles. Our analysis of the degree to which lawyers practiced in more than one field found that connections among the fields were less strong in 1995 than they had been in 1975 (see figs. 2.1–2.3). Specialization of lawyers' practice increased in twenty-three of the twenty-seven fields in which we have comparable data for the two years (fig. 2.4). The hemispheres of the bar, identified in the 1975 study, became further subdivided into smaller, more discrete clusters of fields, and the separation between the sectors was greater than ever. This differentiation of labor lessens solidarity within the profession: as more lawyers work within functionally based departments in large firms or in specialized firms, lawyers' contacts within the bar narrow. Lawyers' colleagues are now, more than ever, likely to do the same kind of work they do, and the cohesion within the bar that is produced when lawyers address the same sorts of problems has diminished. The income inequality previously noted will also, of course, tend to create (or to reinforce) social separation. Lawyers earning $35,000 per year are unlikely to mix with those making $350,000 and up.

The extent of the difference in the lawyers' incomes is itself a measure of the extent to which they are in different markets. Income inequality reflects client differences. Increasing specialization and increasing income inequality indicate that the markets for lawyers' work have become more separate, that the distance between them has grown. And, as the fields differentiate, the social meaning of lawyers' presence in them becomes more distinct. We saw in chapter 4 that the prestige ratings of the fields became more extreme. In 1975, 75 percent of the respondents rated securities law above average in prestige; in 1995, that increased to 85 percent. By contrast, only 9 percent of the 1975 respondents thought that divorce work had above-average prestige, but this decreased even further to only 4 percent of the 1995 respondents (see table 4.2). Of the fields where prestige ratings changed significantly from 1975 to 1995, most of those in the top half of the 1975 prestige order enjoyed an increase in prestige, while the prestige of most of those in the lower half declined. Thus, the disparity between the fields widened. Furthermore, there was a relationship between the prestige of a field and the characteristics of its practitioners. Graduates of elite law schools were significantly more likely to work in fields with high prestige scores, and the fields in which African Americans and women practiced tended to have lower prestige (fig. 4.1). It is probably the case that the latter finding reflects the opportunities open to women and blacks within the profession rather than that their presence in a field adversely affected its prestige, but the latter hypothesis cannot be totally discounted.

The differing views of lawyers on social and political issues, often corresponding to differences in their clientele, further divide the bar. For example, in 1995 Chicago lawyers were evenly split on affirmative action, with 40 percent supportive of it, 39 percent expressing a negative view, and 22 percent neutral or undecided (see fig. 8.3). This dissensus makes it difficult to mobilize lawyers for collective action and has probably contributed to the declining influence of the organized bar (chap. 8). The inability of bar associations to speak effectively for the full range of the profession is, itself, a consequence of the variety of lawyers and their lack of cohesion (chap. 3).

In the last quarter of the twentieth century, practice organizations became a primary engine of change in the social structure of the bar. The autonomy of lawyers, including the extent of their freedom to refuse work or reject clients, varies by organization type (see fig. 5.5). Lawyers' satisfaction with the conditions of practice and their plans to move or to stay in the same job are also associated with organizational context (fig. 11.1). The income of lawyers correlates strongly with the types of organizations in which they work (figs. 7.2 and 7.3). And women and lawyers of color are disproportionately allocated to less prestigious practice settings (fig. 6.6). Management, governance, and work group arrangements vary by organization—thus, whether lawyers have an opportunity to participate in management decisions depends upon organizational structure and policies (fig. 5.4). The nature of lawyers' work (the presence or absence of a hierarchical division of labor, the degree of specialization, the number of hours worked) is shaped by the organizations (chap. 5). The needs and norms of the organizations that deliver legal services have profoundly altered the work and careers of lawyers.

Organizations hire. Organizations assign work. Organizations form, regulate, and terminate relationships between lawyers and clients. Organizations decide which lawyers will become supervisors or partners and how much they will be paid. The preferences of the organizations, therefore, determine whether the bar will be stratified and, if so, the character of that stratification. Organizations decide whether legal work will be done by teams, who the members of the teams will be, who will lead them, and the degree to which particular wishes of the clients will be accommodated. Organizations set the relative value of several types of lawyers' work that are only loosely governed by markets, including pro bono work, organizational management, and the task of serving as a mentor for younger lawyers. But the organizations are not free to do whatever they may wish. They are, themselves, constrained by the market, by local politics, and by powerful social norms. Organizations that survive adjust their strategies accordingly.

Increase in scale has been the most popular strategy by far. In private practice, large firms have succeeded in commanding an ever greater share of lawyers' revenues, redefining the division of labor in legal work, and inculcating a new professional ideology. The needs of the organizations, as perceived and defined by the organizations, shape lawyers' careers, direct their work, and influence their prospects for success—financially, professionally, and perhaps even in their personal lives. The priorities that determine the future of the legal profession are likely to be organizational priorities.

Notes

1. The population of the county decreased from 5,369,000 in 1975 to 5,137,000 in 1995 (U.S. Bureau of the Census 1977, 927; 1996b, 940–41).

2. In constant (1992) dollars, Census data indicate that U.S. expenditures on legal services increased from $32 billion in 1972 to $101 billion in 1993 (U.S. Bureau of the Census 1976, table 4–36; 1996a, 4–443, 4–446, table 49).

3. For the 1975 survey, names were drawn from *Sullivan's Law Directory for the State of Illinois, 1974–75* and the *Martindale-Hubbell Law Directory, 1974* (see Heinz and Laumann 1982, 9). In 1995, the names were drawn from the state's official list of licensed lawyers. All lawyers admitted to practice in Illinois must register with and pay an annual fee to the Attorney Registration and Disciplinary Commission, an agency under the supervision of the Illinois Supreme Court. A lawyer who is not registered with the ARDC is not in good standing. The agency agreed to draw a random sample of names and addresses from the list, following our procedures and specifications. We are grateful to the Illinois ARDC and its staff for their cooperation in this project.

4. In the 1994–95 survey, 8 percent of the original target sample had died, were over age eighty (the eligibility limit), had moved out of the Chicago area, or could not be located after an exhaustive search of directories (and thus were assumed to have moved to another region). These persons were therefore excluded from the target sample. In 1975, 8.4 percent of the lawyers in the sample explicitly refused to grant an interview; the remaining 9.5 percent nonrespondents could not be scheduled because of time constraints, the subject's illness, and the like.

5. Note that the percentage of lawyers employed in "nonlegal" practice settings, as shown in figure 1.1, is smaller than the percentage of "nonpracticing" lawyers because the latter category includes retired and unemployed lawyers. There were twenty-one judges and judicial clerks in the 1975 sample and twenty-two in the 1995 sample.

6. In the 1995 sample, 58 percent of the respondents were natives of the Chicago metropolitan area, and a total of two-thirds were from Illinois.

7. The rankings of law schools change over time, and the two samples include graduates from about a seventy-year period (from the early 1920s to the early 1990s). It is therefore difficult (probably impossible) to arrive at categories that are perfectly comparable over the full span of time. For the most part, we have kept the categories constant. Comparison would be difficult if we used different categories for each date or decade. The 1995 sample, of course, includes many lawyers who graduated before 1975. The only school that appears in a different category in 1995 than in 1975 is the University of Wisconsin. It is in the prestige category in the 1975 data and in the regional category in the 1995 data.

8. A small part of this change is attributable to the fact that the University of Wisconsin was moved from the prestige category in 1975 to the regional category in 1995. If Wisconsin remained in the prestige category, the 1995 percentages would then be: prestige = 16 percent, regional = 26 percent.

9. Graduates of the University of Chicago and Harvard are the most numerous in the elite category in both the 1975 and 1995 samples, but the numbers of both decrease, from 67 to 45 for Chicago graduates and from 49 to 21 for Harvard graduates. Graduates of the University of Michigan increase modestly, from 21 to 26. In the prestige category, there are 108 Northwestern graduates in the 1975 sample, but only 61 in 1995. The decrease in the numbers of Chicago, Harvard, and Northwestern alumni probably reflect the fact that the enrollments of those schools grew very little while the size of the bar was doubling in that period. The prestige category includes 12 Georgetown graduates in 1975 and 20 in 1995. In the regional category, there are 48 University of Illinois graduates in 1975 and 52 in 1995, while the number of Indiana University graduates increases from 5 in 1975 to 16 in 1995 and Notre Dame declines from 12 to 6. It also includes 20 University of Wisconsin graduates in the 1995 data. DePaul graduates are the most numerous in the local category in both 1975 and 1995, but decline in number from 155 to 103. The numbers from the other three local schools all increase—Kent, from 68 to 83; Loyola, from 54 to 80; and Marshall, from 76 to 87. Thus, in the 1995 sample, graduates of each of these four schools substantially outnumber those from Chicago or Northwestern.

10. While 30 may appear to some to be a modest size for the largest category, only 7 percent of the respondents in the 1975 sample worked in firms with 100 or more lawyers. In later chapters we analyze firms of 100 or more and 300 or more.

11. In both 1975 and 1995, this category includes 10 respondents who were law teachers of various kinds. We have excluded 18 lawyers who were retired or unemployed in 1995. Thus, the category means "employed but not practicing law." Judges and judicial clerks (see text) are not included here.

Chapter Two

1. Respondents were asked to indicate whether they devoted 100 percent, 50–99 percent, 25–49 percent, 5–24 percent, 1–4 percent, or none of their time to each field.

2. Since landlord/tenant was defined as one field, it is not possible to separate the work done for landlords from that done for tenants. Because landlords typically have deeper pockets than tenants, however, the work that comes to lawyers more often comes from landlords. In our 1995 data, of respondents who report that they devote 25

percent or more of their time to landlord/tenant work, the median percentage of work time devoted to businesses is 87 percent.

3. These probably cluster because natural gas and electrical lines sometimes cause injuries and because lawyers who do personal injury defense work are sometimes involved in workers' compensation cases in administrative tribunals. Civil rights matters are also often handled by administrative hearing officers.

4. The proximity measure used was an accumulating cross-product matrix.

5. In 1975, a few respondents employed by government agencies regulating labor relations indicated that they worked on both sides (i.e., they were in the middle), which accounts for the overlap of the two fields in that survey. The 1975 interview used the labels "labor law (unions)" and "labor law (management)," while the 1995 interview used "employment law (representing unions and employees)" and "employment law (representing management)." That difference may also play a part in the difference in findings.

6. When we took time in field into account in our analyses of the 1975 data (see text at note 4), we found that the concentration of time in cognate fields resulted in a clustering together of the main litigation fields. But recall that in the original 1975 data (used in those analyses), "civil litigation" was not differentiated by client type—the civil litigation category that clustered with divorce, criminal defense, and personal injury plaintiffs work combined personal and business litigation. Thus, although the 1975 categories were ill designed for the evaluation of the two-hemispheres thesis, the differentiated measure used in 1995 discloses the separation between the business and personal sides of litigation if time is taken into account.

7. The 1995 data concerning organization of work appear to be somewhat less orderly than was the case in 1975. This might be attributable to a higher degree of specialization in 1995. Since there is less overlap among the fields, the clustering analyses are working with less variance, and this may create instability—essentially random events have greater impact on the results.

8. The specialization index was calculated using a procedure developed by Cappell (1979). First, an entropy measure is calculated:

$$\hat{H}_j = \sum_{i=1} P_i \log 1/P_i$$

where P_i is estimated by the proportion of time allocated to practice category C_i by respondent j. It is a measure of "uncertainty" of observing a respondent practicing in legal field C_i. It can also be thought of as a measure of "diversity" of effort across fields. This measure depends on the total number of fields. Therefore, in order to compare two populations (or samples) with unequal numbers of categories, we standardize with an index of specialization (SI) as follows:

$$SI_j = 1 - \hat{H}_j/H_{max}$$

This specialization index ranges from 0 to 1, where 1 is perfect specialization (all time in one field) and 0 is no specialization (time uniformly distributed across fields).

9. In fact, however, even though the respondents were given more field choices in 1995, they chose fewer. After categories chosen by very few respondents were combined with others (e.g., business bankruptcy was combined with commercial law), there were twenty-two field categories in the 1975 data (with tax, litigation, and real estate in their original, undifferentiated form), and thirty-four in 1995. The

mean number of these fields to which respondents devoted 5 percent or more of their time was 2.84 in 1975 and 2.62 in 1995. The medians are 3 and 2, respectively. The difference of means is significant at $p < .02$.

10. Businesses are, of course, defendants in some criminal cases. Although criminal prosecution is supposed to be a full-time job (i.e., prosecutors are not permitted to "moonlight"), our question asked respondents what percentage of their time was spent working for businesses "within the past 12 months." Thus, if the respondent had changed jobs within the past year—moving from the prosecutor's office to private practice or (less commonly) in the other direction—it is possible for a lawyer who had done criminal prosecution work to have had business clients. In the 1995 data, two of the prosecutors had in fact held other jobs during part of the year. This movement among the fields will, then, be a source of underestimation, in a sense, of the degree of differentiation among the fields.

11. But recall that, as reported above, only 22 percent of tax practitioners do both corporate and personal tax work at even the 5 percent level of time commitment.

12. The measure used in 1975, however, was not exactly the same as that used in 1995. The 1975 question inquired about percentages of income rather than time: "During the last 12 months, what proportion of your income was derived from work on personal matters (such as divorce, wills, residential real estate), and what proportion was derived from representing business clients?" In 1995 the respondents were asked, "During the past 12 months, what percentage of your time was spent working for businesses, other kinds of organizations, and on personal matters such as divorce, wills, or residential real estate?"

It is possible, of course, that these two measures could produce systematically different findings. If work for businesses is generally more remunerative than work for individuals, for example, then the 1975 question would produce a higher percentage of business-source income than the 1995 percentage of business-consumed time, even if the division of labor remained the same. Using the 1975 measure, we find that the distribution of fields by percentage of business income does in fact display a grouping of fields at the high end of the scale—seven of the twenty-six fields have percentages of business income in the range from 93 percent to 97 percent.

The 1975 data show a somewhat more distinct division of fields by client type than appears in figure 2.5. In the 1975 distribution of fields, only three of the twenty-six fall into the 22-point interval between 49 percent and 71 percent. Those three fields are public utilities/administrative law, labor union work, and municipal law. Much of the work in those three fields represents clients that are neither fish nor fowl—that is, neither individuals nor businesses. The 1975 data thus do not show a group of fields with a balanced mixture of individual and business clients.

13. In table 2.1, the tax, litigation, and real estate fields in 1975 have again been divided into "corporate/business" and "personal/general" sides, as was done in *Chicago Lawyers*. When client type is not the dependent variable—that is, when we are not trying to determine whether the structure is divided along client lines—then there is little objection to using the differentiated categories. What we want to know here is how lawyers allocate their time, and the distinction between business litigation and personal client litigation, for example, may well be of interest.

14. We have recomputed the estimates for the 1975 data. In most fields, our results correspond exactly to those presented in table 2.1 of *Chicago Lawyers* (Heinz and Laumann 1982, 40). In a few fields, however, there are small differences. We have also

added the two sides of environmental law, which were not included in the earlier table because of the small amounts of time devoted to those fields in 1975.

15. Cook County includes some suburbs as well as the city of Chicago. Unfortunately, the ARDC data are not disaggregated below the county level, so they do not give a separate count for the city. To examine the division between Chicago and suburban Cook County, therefore, we used the *Martindale-Hubbell Lawyers Directory*, which is less inclusive than the ARDC register. According to Martindale-Hubbell, the 1995 breakdown was 24,021 lawyers in the city and 5,065 lawyers in the Cook suburbs (Martindale-Hubbell 1995–96). Since earlier Martindale-Hubbell compilations are not available in a form that permits sorting by computer, we turned to yet another source. *The Lawyer Statistical Report* estimated that there were 19,476 lawyers in Chicago in 1980 (Curran et al. 1985, 320). Comparing that figure to 22,310 lawyers in Cook County registered with the ARDC in 1980, we arrive at an estimate of 2,834 lawyers in the Cook County suburbs in 1980. It is perilous to combine the estimates from the three sources, but it appears to be clear that, although the suburbs show a larger percentage increase (on a relatively small base), the city had a far greater increase in the absolute number of lawyers.

16. Note that "work groups" may be an appropriate term in corporate practice, where teams of lawyers work on the same case or transaction, while "colleague networks" may more accurately describe the relationships in divorce or personal injury practice.

Chapter Three

1. It was founded by General William "Wild Bill" Donovan, a World War I hero and the director during World War II of the Office of Strategic Services, the predecessor of the CIA.

2. Throughout, we have used *Catholic* to refer to Roman Catholics.

3. This difference is not explained by other characteristics of the respondents. In logistic regression analyses controlling for race, gender, age, income, practice setting, law school category, law school class rank, and father's occupation, the religion variables remain significant (Catholic, Beta = $-.599$, $p < .03$; Jewish, Beta = $-.883$, $p < .01$).

4. $\chi^2 = 7.06$, $p < .01$.

5. Of those in firms with thirty one to ninety-nine lawyers, 42 percent regularly attended bar meetings; of those in firms of one hundred or more, 27 percent did ($\chi^2 = 4.51$, $p < .05$).

6. The study counted and classified course offerings listed in the schools' publications. It did not take into account course enrollments, nor whether the course was offered in a particular year (White 2002).

7. These analyses used logistic regression equations. Additional analyses of income, controlling for a larger number of variables, are presented in chapter 7.

8. The difference was significant at the .001 level in both years.

9. Note that the large-firm criterion was inflated from thirty in 1975 to one hundred in 1995.

10. The difference between the dichotomized law school categories was significant at .01 in 1975 and at .001 in 1995.

11. Irish respondents were not underrepresented among Northwestern law school alumni in 1975, however. At John Marshall, the Irish were strongly underrepresented in 1975 but overrepresented in 1995, while Jewish respondents went from a percentage that was nearly the same as that in the overall bar to substantial underrepresentation in the later sample.

12. Note, however, that the percentage of lawyers of Irish descent in the Chicago bar increased somewhat, while the Jewish percentage declined (see totals in fig. 3.2). As noted in chapter 1, however, because of the growth in the overall size of the bar the absolute number of Jewish lawyers did not decline.

13. The list of Spanish surnames was obtained from the U.S. Census. The 1995–96 *Martindale-Hubbell Law Directory*, on CD-ROM, was then searched for those names. A sample was drawn randomly from the resulting list, and letters were sent to eighty-five lawyers. Of those, twenty responded that they were not Hispanic (some other nationalities have the same family names) and two had left Chicago, leaving a total of sixty-three eligible for the Hispanic oversample. Thirty-eight of the sixty-three were interviewed, yielding a response rate of 60.3 percent for the oversample.

14. African American respondents interviewed in the random sample were asked to nominate other African American lawyers in large firms, small firms or solo practice, inside-counsel offices, and government. This produced a list of 220 lawyers in the four categories. Of these, 57 were ineligible because they had already been interviewed, were located outside Chicago, or could not be found in either *Martindale-Hubbell* or *Sullivan's Law Directory*. From the remaining 163 names, random samples were drawn in each of the four practice setting categories in proportion to the percentage of African American lawyers in those contexts in the random sample—21 percent in large firms, 23 percent in small firms or solo practice, 14 percent in inside counsel-offices, and 41 percent in government. Letters requesting interviews were sent to 56 lawyers. One had died, leaving 55 eligible. Thirty-six interviews were completed, yielding a response rate for this oversample of 65.5 percent.

15. The "white" categories here mean "white, non-Hispanic." All respondents included in the male and female Jewish categories here are white. Two Hispanic Jews are included in the Hispanic category.

16. We should note that the sample consists of lawyers located in Chicago in 1995—that is, it does not include those who had departed after attending law school in Chicago or after having practiced there at some point. Because graduates of more prestigious schools have greater opportunities to go elsewhere than do those from less highly regarded schools, elite school alumni might have been drawn to New York, Washington, or Los Angeles in disproportionate numbers, while local and regional school graduates were left behind. This may be true regardless of the race of the lawyers. But we know that some graduates of prestigious schools are drawn to Chicago from other localities, and it is not clear whether minority graduates of prestigious schools were more or less likely to leave the city than were the white graduates of those schools. In response to a question concerning their place of residence during their high school years, 64 percent of African American respondents said that they had lived in the Chicago metropolitan area. The comparable percentages were 59 percent of white males, 51 percent of white females, and 73 percent of Hispanics.

17. Again, these analyses used logistic regression equations. Respondents for whom necessary information (race, religion, gender, or age) was missing were removed from the analysis, unless the missing information was not needed to group them (e.g.,

a white female did not need to specify a religion). In the 1975 sample, 15 individuals were removed, and in the 1995 random sample 5 were. This left a total of 759 cases in 1975 and 778 cases in 1995.

18. The latter was the reference category.

19. The white female difference is significant at $p < .001$. The differences for "other Christian males" and for Jewish males are significant at $p < .01$, and the difference for African Americans is significant at $p < .05$.

20. That is, the .05 level.

21. All of these probabilities were very similar to those in models that included the minority oversamples, except that the probability for African Americans rose from 5 percent to 8 percent, probably because the oversample tended to include lawyers of greater visibility or prominence.

22. Among the practicing lawyers in the 1995 sample, 40 percent of the graduates of elite law schools were equity-holding partners in law firms (see chap. 7) and 38 percent of the graduates of schools in the prestige category were, but only 28 percent of the graduates of "high regional" schools, 14 percent of those from "low regional" schools, and 23 percent of those from "local" schools held equity in their firms ($p < .001$).

23. Prosecution, as a field of practice, has low prestige within the legal profession (see chap. 4) and receives relatively low pay (see chap. 7).

Chapter Four

1. Or, in these days of easier access to all kinds of information, the patient can research the possible treatment, perhaps on the internet. In any event, patients must rely largely on the medical profession to produce, evaluate and interpret medical information.

2. The discussion that follows draws heavily on Sandefur 2001.

3. Additional factors contribute to the esteem enjoyed by an individual. Competence, charm, intelligence, beauty, and noble birth are among the many qualities that may make one esteemed. Here, however, we are concerned with prestige that accrues to roles, positions, and tasks, not with that of individuals.

4. In the 1995 survey, all respondents were given the prestige rating items. In 1975, a randomly selected subset of the respondents ($n = 224$) were asked.

5. In 1975, the fields were civil rights/civil liberties, criminal prosecution, environmental plaintiffs work, personal injury defense, and criminal defense. In 1995, they were civil litigation for individual clients, criminal prosecution and business bankruptcy.

6. The significance test is based on the logit of the prestige increment score, which is $\ln(p / 1 - p)$, where p is the proportion of respondents indicating that the field enjoys "outstanding" or "above average" prestige in the bar (see Hauser and Warren 1997).

7. Differences in the logit of the prestige increment score are noted as significant if $p < .05$, in a two-tailed test.

8. The authors were not among the group of raters in either survey.

9. The specific questions were as follows. *Intellectual Challenge:* "The legal doctrines, cases, statutes, and regulations involved in some types of practice are characteristically more difficult, complex, and intellectually challenging than are those

in others. Would you say that the degree of intellectual challenge presented by the *substance* (as opposed to the strategic considerations) of this type of work is very great, higher than average, average, lower than average, or very little?" *Rapidity of Change:* "The substantive law involved in some areas of practice changes more rapidly than it does in others. The practitioner, thus, may find it more difficult to keep up with developments in the former specialties than in the latter. Would you say that the law involved in this type of work: changes very rapidly, changes relatively quickly, changes at a moderate or average pace, changes relatively slowly, or changes very little or seldom?" *Public Service:* "Some types of legal work are more often done *pro bono publico,* or for altruistic or reformist motives, while other sorts of legal work much more clearly involve a profit motive. Would you say of this type of work that it is: highly money- or profit-oriented, substantially profit-oriented, neither or average, substantially *pro bono,* or mostly *pro bono?" Ethical Practice:* "Some types of legal work have a reputation for 'sharp practice' or for a higher incidence of unethical conduct than is common in some other types of work. Would you say of this type of work that its reputation for ethical conduct is: very good, above average, average, below average, or poor?" *Freedom of Action:* "In the practice of some types of law, the practitioner is, to a considerable degree, a 'free agent,' free to pursue whatever strategic course of action his own professional judgment may suggest. By contrast, the freedom of action of a practitioner of some other types of law is more highly constrained by knowledgeable clients or by organizational superiors who supervise and guide his decisions. Would you say that the practice of this type of law is characterized by: a high degree of freedom of action, above average freedom of action, average, below average freedom of action, or little freedom of action?"

10. The Pearson correlations of the 1975 ratings with the 1995 ratings computed over the twenty-seven fields of law included in both surveys are: .86 for intellectual challenge; .78 for rapidity of change; .86 for public service; .90 for ethical conduct, and .84 for freedom of action.

11. This is an ordinary least squares (OLS) analysis. The measure of prestige employed is the logit of the prestige increment score (see note 6).

12. Because of the way the 1975 data were archived, it is not possible to estimate models that control for lawyers' pay for the 1975 survey. In the 1995 survey, the relationships between the five rated characteristics and prestige remain substantively the same as those presented in table 4.4 when practitioner income is a control variable, whether in the form of the average income for the field, the percentage of effort contributed to the field by lawyers whose incomes are above the mean for the practicing bar, or the percentage of effort contributed to the field by lawyers whose incomes are above the median for the practicing bar. See note 14 for a description of how field-level characteristics were calculated.

13. Public international law and admiralty law, each with only two practitioners, are excluded from these regression analyses.

14. For the measurement of time in field, see chapter 2. Here, in analyzing of the relationship between the prestige of a field and its characteristics, we constructed measures of the characteristics by aggregating the responses of lawyers who worked in that field. To weight each lawyer's contribution to the field, we assigned the lawyer's proportionate time allocation a numerical value equal to the midpoint of the interval indicated. All of the lawyer's time allocations were then normed to sum to 100 percent. For example, a lawyer might report that she typically divided her time across three

fields of law: general corporate law, to which she devoted 50 to 99 percent of her time, and patents and trademark and copyright law, to each of which she devoted 5 to 24 percent of her time. For this lawyer, assigning the percentage intervals their midpoints results in a total time allocation of 103.5 percent = (74.5 percent + 14.5 percent + 14.5 percent). The inverse of the summed time allocations was used as a scaling factor. The sum of the products of the scaling factor and each time allocation is 100 percent by construction (e.g., $(74.5)(.9659) + (14.5)(.9659) + (14.5)(.9659) = 100$). Work effort is thus allocated across fields under the assumption that all lawyers work equally hard. This measure of effort, then, is constructed in a manner similar to the time-token analysis of chapter 2.

15. The measures also contain a degree of error that arises from their construction. For example, we do not have measures of the types of clients who go to lawyers for securities work. Instead, we have measures of the types of clients served by lawyers who do securities work. We also do not have measures of the frequency with which lawyers go to appellate courts for securities cases; we have measures of the frequency with which lawyers who do securities work appear in appellate courts. All fields are subject to this kind of measurement error to some degree, although fields where there is a high degree of crossover or co-practice are more strongly contaminated than fields that require a greater share of a lawyer's time. Exploratory analyses found no relationship between prestige and a measure of dilettantism. To the extent that measurement error is random with respect to the variables of theoretical interest, it will tend to weaken all of their effects on prestige.

16. For a discussion of this measure, see chapter 5 at figure 5.8.

17. We also computed models that controlled for the effects of lawyers' seniority and managerial authority by including the age distribution of the fields and measures of lawyers' participation in management decisions in their organizations. These analyses revealed that seniority and managerial authority have no net relationship to the prestige of fields. Their inclusion in the professional purity model does not affect the estimates for the other coefficients (Sandefur 2001).

18. The frequency of appellate work by the lawyers in a field of practice may also reflect the amounts at issue in their cases; cases in which the stakes are high are more likely to be pursued to the point of appeal.

19. As before, the dependent variable is the logit of the prestige increment score. These are ordinary least squares (OLS) regressions.

20. The Pearson correlations between practitioner age and prestige of practice are .00 for 1975 and .05 for 1995.

21. A third possible explanation for the decline in prestige of these lawyers' portfolios is that the lawyers working in small firms in 1995 were not of the same caliber as their counterparts twenty years earlier, and so attracted less prestigious—and, by extrapolation, less intellectually challenging—work. Such a change is difficult to assess, but lawyers with prestigious educational credentials were significantly less likely to work in firms of two to forty lawyers in 1995. If, therefore, law school reputation is indicative of the quality of legal training, we do find that small-firm practice was less attractive to the best-trained lawyers than it was in 1975. As larger firms began to hire more of the graduates of less highly ranked law schools (see table 3.1), they recruited a disproportionate share of the top graduates of those schools, thus depriving smaller firms of those stars.

Chapter Five

1. In 1975, these were defined as "*e.g.*, Standard Oil, American National Bank, Abbott Laboratories, Playboy Enterprises, Pepper Construction—*i.e.*, over $10 million sales per year."

2. In 1975, these were defined as "*e.g.*, neighborhood stores, local restaurants, local real estate brokers, etc.—less than $250,000 sales per year."

3. In 1995, the categories were defined as follows: *Major Corporations* (e.g., Amoco, American National Bank, Abbott Laboratories, Playboy Enterprises, Pepper Construction—i.e., over $30 million sales per year). *Medium-sized firms* (between $1 million and $30 million sales per year). *Small Business* (e.g., neighborhood stores, local restaurants, local real estate brokers, etc.—less than $1 million sales per year).

4. In 1975, only 8 percent of the top earners came from firms with one hundred or more lawyers.

5. The formula is: $n\,(n - 1)/2$, where n = the number of lawyers.

6. The responses of lawyers from the same firm were compared. In general, there was a high degree of convergence. Discrepancies were resolved by considering the seniority of the respondents and consulting external data. For all cases, on crucial variables we were able to resolve ambiguities in the data.

7. We are indebted to Harris Kim for his expert assistance in these analyses.

8. The difference is significant at $p < .001$.

9. The difference is significant at $p < .001$.

10. The question read: "Is there some issue that is a matter of considerable concern to you, but you feel that the management of this organization would not entertain serious discussion of the issue? [If so] What is it?"

11. In solo practice, the average number of clients per year was 82; in firms of two to nine lawyers, 101; in firms of ten to thirty, 78. In larger firms, however, the number of clients drops. In firms of thirty-one to ninety-nine lawyers, it was 48; and in firms of one hundred or more, 36. This is a measure of the number of clients per respondent, not per firm.

12. Solo practitioners had represented 42 percent of their clients for at least three years, the percentage for those in firms of two to nine was 48 percent, and in the largest firms it was 52 percent.

13. Government lawyers devoted an average of 36 percent of their time to their most time-consuming client, and inside counsel reported 43 percent. (Lawyers in government and in inside-counsel offices commonly refer to the people within their organizations for whom they do legal work as "clients.")

14. The first item read, "In the course of my practice I have rather wide latitude in selecting which clients I will represent," versus "The nature of my practice is such that it is often necessary to accept clients whom I would prefer not to have." The second read, "One of the things that I like about my area of practice is that I can do largely whatever I like without having someone looking over my shoulder and directing my work," versus "In my practice of law I work closely with more senior lawyers who provide relatively close guidance in the nature of my work."

15. The item read, "Strategies that I pursue are largely of my own design and execution." versus "I work closely with others to design and execute strategies in my work."

16. The significance of the Catholic variable was borderline, $p < .06$. The other three variables were all significant at .03 or less.

17. Differences in wording were used to adapt some of the items to the context. Thus, private practitioners were asked about "the division of the profits of the firm," and employed lawyers were asked about "compensation in this office." Similarly, lawyers in firms were asked about "hours billed" and "the decision of a senior partner," and employed lawyers were asked about "hours worked" and "the decision of a single supervisor."

18. The scale achieved an alpha of .62, which indicates only marginal scalability. We used the scale scores nonetheless because they had a track record of effective measurement in Nelson's earlier study and because they appear to differentiate organization types and ranks within organizations.

19. The differences are significant at $p < .001$.

20. These differences were significant in an analysis of variance at .001.

21. The items read as follows: "The office should seek to increase the productivity of lawyers by encouraging specialization." "Lawyers should be directed to choose a specialty soon after joining the office." "The office should be formally organized on a departmental basis, so that work assignments, quality control, and client relationships are the administrative responsibility of the departmental units."

22. These differences, also, are statistically significant at the .001 level.

23. The differences are statistically significant at the .001 level.

24. The median number of hours of legal work is forty-seven for government lawyers (two hours less than total hours), forty-five hours for inside counsel (1.5 less), and also forty-five for public defenders and legal services lawyers (unchanged). The differences in hours across categories are large enough to be significant in an analysis of variance, but are nonetheless smaller than might have been expected.

25. See chapter 6. Table 6.2 indicates that, in both the 1975 and 1995 surveys, lawyers who had started their careers in smaller firms had both more subsequent jobs and more moves per year in the profession, on average.

26. We also asked the respondents about time devoted to managing their personal investments. The medians were one hour per week in all practice settings except state and local government and public defender/legal services. In those categories, it was zero.

27. In this discussion, "frequently" includes both the "frequently" and "very frequently" responses.

28. No respondent had been able to avoid routine paperwork completely, only 7 percent said they seldom did it, and 63 percent said they did it frequently. Perhaps because two of the examples of "routine paper work" used in the question were billing and client intake, lawyers in internal counsel and government offices, especially those in staff positions in such offices, were relatively unlikely to report such work. Half of the lawyers in government staff jobs and 43 percent of inside counsel staff said that they seldom or never did such routine tasks.

29. Seventy-three percent of associates in hybrid firms, 59 percent of those in corporate firms, and 52 percent of those in traditional firms reported doing research frequently. Only 20 percent of internal counsel staff and 29 percent of their superiors did much research, but 54 percent of government staff and 47 percent of the supervisors

in those offices said that they did. Of solo practitioners, 45 percent reported doing legal research frequently.

30. Only 38 percent of staff and 47 percent of supervisors drafted documents frequently.

31. The differences in task dissonance across the full set of organizational position categories are significant at the .01 level.

32. $p < .05$.

33. Of partners, 84 percent of those in traditional firms, 81 percent of those in hybrid firms, and 86 percent of those in corporate firms hoped to remain in their positions; for associates, 39 percent in traditional firms, 48 percent in hybrid firms, and 55 percent in corporate firms. Note that, by this measure, corporate firms had the highest level of satisfaction, among both partners and associates.

Chapter Six

1. The data do include lawyers eligible to practice but working in other jobs or not at all.

2. A striking change, however, is the smaller share of the profession with thirty or more years of experience in the 1995 survey. In the 1975 survey, 19 percent of lawyers had thirty or more years of experience, but only 11 percent did in 1995. In part, this reflects the rapid growth of the profession in the 1970s and 1980s, which swelled its younger ranks. The changing age structure may also reflect higher rates of attrition from the profession among older lawyers as their senior positions became less secure or less desirable (Galanter 1999).

3. In both surveys, respondents reported the number of lawyers in each organization in which they had worked since starting their careers as lawyers. In the 1975 survey, their responses were recorded verbatim. In the 1995 survey, responses for jobs prior to the current job were recorded in the following categories: fewer than ten lawyers, ten to forty lawyers, 40 to 100 lawyers, and more than one hundred lawyers. Thus, in the 1995 survey, respondents could have placed a firm of forty lawyers in either of the two middle categories. For the 1975 survey, we placed firms of forty lawyers in the 11–40 lawyers category.

4. In the 1975 survey, public defenders are not distinguishable from government lawyers and no legal aid lawyers appeared in the sample.

5. The table includes only those lawyers whose first job after completing law school was in the civilian labor force. Lawyers who entered the military directly after law school ($n = 38$) and lawyers who had never held jobs ($n = 2$) are excluded from the table.

6. A three-dimensional log linear model reveals no significant difference between the two surveys in the likelihood that a lawyer who began in private practice would have left private practice by the time of survey ($L^2 = 0.19$, df $= 1$, $p = .66$).

7. A three-dimensional log linear model reveals no significant difference between surveys in the probability that a lawyer who started work in solo practice or a small law firm would be working in a law firm of forty or more lawyers at the time of survey ($L^2 = .96$, df $= 1$, $p = .33$).

8. A three-dimensional log-linear model reveals no significant difference between surveys in the association between starting in a government position and working in a large firm at the time of survey ($L^2 = 2.44$, df $= 1$, $p = .12$).

9. All lawyers (n = 9) who made the move in the 1975 survey started with agencies of the federal government; 58 percent (7 of 12) of those who made the move in the 1995 survey did so.

10. A three-dimensional log-linear model reveals no significant difference between surveys in the association between starting in large firm practice and working in government at the time of survey (L^2 = .03, df = 1, p = .85).

11. A three-dimensional log-linear model reveals a significant difference between surveys in the association between starting in large firm practice and working in a small-firm or solo practice at the time of survey (L^2 = 4.28, df = 1, p = .04).

12. A three-dimensional log-linear model reveals no significant difference between surveys in the association between starting as internal counsel and working in large firm practice at the time of survey (L^2 = .02, df = 1, p = .88).

13. A three-dimensional log-linear model reveals no significant difference between surveys in the association between starting in large firm practice and working in house counsel at the time of survey (L^2 = .01, df = 1, p = .93).

14. Given a five-dimensional log linear model with all two-way interactions and three-way interactions for current and starting position and age, and current and starting position and gender, the addition of a term permitting an interaction between current position, starting position, and survey year yields the test statistic: L^2 = 12.6, df = 1, p = .0003, suggesting the relationship between starting and current position is different in the two surveys, net of changes in age and gender composition.

15. That is, the elite and prestige categories; see chapter 1.

16. In the Golden Age, the vast majority of lawyers were men. During the 1950s, women averaged 3.6 percent of the enrollment of American Bar Association–approved law schools. In the 1960s, women's contribution to the student bodies of these schools averaged 4.5 percent (Abel 1989, table 27).

17. *Regular practice* is defined as civilian work as a practicing lawyer in a law firm or solo practice, for agencies of government, as internal counsel of a private for-profit or not-for-profit organization, or as a public defender or legal aid lawyer. Some lawyers occupied positions after law school but prior to their first jobs in regular practice, including judicial clerkships, military service, and civilian nonlegal positions.

18. This is an overly inclusive identification of Golden Age failure, which involved law firms sponsoring outgoing associates' placement in the internal counsel offices of their clients (Smigel 1964). The Chicago data do not indicate whether the offices of internal counsel these lawyers entered were in clients of their former law firms.

19. p < .05 for chi-square test of difference between periods.

20. p < .01 for chi-square test of difference between periods.

21. In 1975, 25 percent, and 21 percent in 1995; differences between periods are not statistically significant.

22. p < .001 for chi-square test of difference between periods.

23. p = .10. This estimate comes from a logistic regression model of whether a lawyer remained in the large firm setting, as predicted by years since entry into the profession, that quantity squared, gender, whether or not the respondent graduated from an elite or prestige law school, and whether or not the lawyer was in the top 10 percent of his or her graduating class or on the law review at his or her law school (Pseudo-R^2 = .06, n = 209).

24. Logistic regression takes as its dependent variable a natural log transformation of the odds of some event: ln $[p / (1 - p)]$, where p is the share of cases in which the specified event occurs. In most studies of individual-level predictors of job mobility, it has become conventional to use event history analysis, which, rather than modeling only the probability of an event, includes information about the waiting time to that event (Tuma and Hannan 1984; Yamaguchi 1991). We cannot use this technique here because the 1975 survey does not provide the necessary data. Event history analysis requires knowledge of the timing of the job change of interest, such as promotion. The 1975 survey collected information about the dates of moves between organizations or stints of solo practice, but not the dates of title changes within an organization.

25. It would have been desirable to investigate house counsel and government separately, but only 9 of the 55 senior positions held by employed lawyers in the 1995 survey were in government.

26. $\beta = 0.56$, $e^\beta = 1.76$, $p > .10$.

27. 1975: $\beta = -.89$, $e^\beta = 0.41$, $p > .10$; 1995: $\beta = -1.69$, $e^\beta = 0.18$, $p > .10$.

28. $\beta = -0.96$, $e^\beta = 0.38$, $p < .05$.

29. $\beta = -0.58$, $e^\beta = 0.56$, $p > .10$.

30. $\beta = -1.26$, $e^\beta = 0.28$, $p < 10$.

31. 1975: $\beta = 1.11$, $e^\beta = 3.03$, $p < .01$; 1995: $\beta = 1.01$, $e^\beta = 2.76$, $p < .01$.

32. $\beta = -1.32$, $e^\beta = 0.27$, $p < .001$.

33. None of the small number of women ($n = 30$) or blacks ($n = 21$) in the 1975 survey reported careers with no legal jobs. However, the sample sizes are so small that, in comparison with men and nonblacks, the differences do not differ significantly from what one would expect by chance.

34. The single, modest exception is that, in 1995, graduates of local law schools are roughly twice as likely as graduates of more esteemed schools to have spent their careers working outside law (4 percent of local law school graduates had done so versus 2 percent of everyone else, $p = .08$).

35. $\beta = .57$, $e^\beta = 1.77$, $p = .10$.

Chapter Seven

1. According to the most recent U.S. Census data that is available, lawyers' median earnings were $78,000 in 1999 (Sandefur 2004). This was 2.01 times the median income of an American male, full-time, year-round worker and 2.68 times the median income of an American female, full-time, year-round worker (U.S. Bureau of the Census 2002).

2. In the 1975 survey, lawyers were asked to report the share of their income they received from different types of clients. In the 1995 survey, lawyers were asked to report on the proportion of their clients who were of each type. Because work for personal clients is less lucrative than work for business clients, the decline in the number of lawyers serving primarily personal clients is probably understated in these calculations. See chapter 2 for a detailed investigation of shifts over time in lawyers' areas of practice.

3. In the 1975 survey, the only lawyers devoting at least 75 percent of their time to the service of not-for-profit organizations were employed by government. In the 1995 survey, 16 of the 81 lawyers concentrating in service to nonprofit organizations were working outside government agencies.

4. Among lawyers in firms of 2 to 5 lawyers, the ratio of the mean to the median rose from 1.44 ($143,313/$99,159) to 2.01 ($150,434/$75,000), and in firms of 6 to 25 lawyers from 1.41 ($140,258/$99,159) to 1.73 ($155,312/$90,000). Among lawyers in firms of 26 to 100 lawyers, inequality fell from 1.68 ($166,216/$99,159) to 1.34 ($126,884/$95,000), in firms of 101 to 299 lawyers, from 1.46 ($144,985/$99,159) to 1.3 ($156,178/$112,500). Among lawyers in firms of 300 or more lawyers in 1995, the ratio of the mean to the median was 2.42 ($271,706/$112,500).

5. In 1995, there were about 303 persons per lawyer (Carson 1999, table 1).

6. This reduction in the personal client base of solo practice is consistent with, but smaller than, changes in the sizes of the personal and corporate "hemispheres" remarked in chapter 2: as a share of all legal work, work in the personal and small business client sector decreased by 28 percent between 1975 and 1995 (see table 2.3). The decline in service to individuals is likely understated by this comparison, for the reasons noted above (note 2).

7. A second factor affecting the incomes of these lawyers may be the entry of greater numbers of women. Women sometimes choose solo practice because it permits them to control their workload and its scheduling (Seron 1996), thus helping them to balance family responsibilities and paid work. In 1975, women's presence in solo practice was at parity with their presence in the practicing bar, 3 percent. In 1995, women were underrepresented in solo practice relative to their presence in the bar as a whole, but they were a substantially larger proportion than twenty years before, making up 19 percent of lawyers practicing alone. Among solo practitioners in 1995, 45 percent of women and 28 percent of men reported working fewer than 35 hours per week in their job as a lawyer. (The 1975 survey did not collect information about lawyers' work hours.) Child-rearing responsibilities do not appear to be the only reason why female solo practitioners worked fewer hours, however. Women practicing on their own were actually *less likely* than women working in law firms or in offices of house counsel to have children living at home with them. In 1995, 20 percent of female solo practitioners had children living at home, versus 32 percent of the women in the practicing bar overall.

8. The omitted category is firms with 2 to 5 lawyers.

9. The omitted category includes staff attorneys in government and internal counsel offices, law firm associates, and non-owning partners (e.g., "salaried" and "income" partners).

10. The omitted category is lawyers who graduated from regional law schools.

11. The omitted category is white, non-Jewish lawyers. Hispanics were absent from the 1975 sample.

12. The dependent variable in these models is income received from the practice of law in the year prior to the survey, converted to 1995 dollars and then transformed by taking the natural logarithm. When the dependent variable is transformed in this way and the independent variables are left in their natural metrics, coefficients may be interpreted in terms of the proportionate change in income given a one-unit change in an independent variable (Stolzenberg 1980). These are ordinary least squares regressions.

13. Racial and ethnic group membership is indicated by whether the lawyer is African American, Asian, or Hispanic, Jewish, or other white. Hispanics were absent from the sample in 1975.

14. Because of the very small numbers of African Americans and Hispanics in the sample, the coefficients for those variables in the regression models become statistically insignificant once the other variables are controlled.

15. This is the first of the "core values" set forth in the 2001–2006 Strategic Plan of the U.S. Department of Justice: *Equal Justice Under the Law.* "Upholding the laws of the United States is the solemn responsibility entrusted to us by the American people. We enforce these laws fairly and uniformly to ensure that all Americans receive equal protection and justice under the law" (U.S. Dept of Justice 2003, p. ii).

Chapter Eight

1. Perhaps in an effort to demonstrate its lack of bias, however, the ABA judicial evaluation committee, in 2002, unanimously found a conservative, controversial nominee for the federal Court of Appeals to be "highly qualified" (Lewis 2002; Dewar 2002).

2. It would have been interesting to have responses to this question in 2002, following the Enron/Tyco/Arthur Andersen scandals and the decline of the stock market.

3. Tests for reliability indicate that the resulting scale, combining the seven items, satisfies the criterion in both 1975 and 1995 (alpha = 0.70 in 1975; alpha = 0.77 in 1995).

4. The mean scores were 25 to 29 = 2.89, 55 to 64 = 2.92, and 45 to 49 = 3.33.

5. In this measure, a respondent can be included in as many as four field categories. This double counting of respondents thus reduces the variance among the categories.

6. The most liberal average score is that of lawyers in "other" fields in the 40–52 age group. Those lawyers came of age during the Vietnam War and the political ferment of the 1960s and early 1970s. An analysis of data from the 1975 survey, reported in *Chicago Lawyers* (1982, 162, table 5.4), indicated that the economic values of the youngest lawyers then practicing in a set of "conservative" fields were very similar to those of young lawyers in other fields. Since lawyers who were 30 in 1975 were 50 in 1995, that cohort is included in the 40–52 age group in figure 8.4. Unlike the 1975 finding, the difference between the sets of fields for that group is large in 1995. The field categories used in the two analyses are not directly comparable, and this is certainly not a true cohort analysis, but this finding may suggest that lawyers who entered practice in the early 1970s adapted to the values of their clients over time. It is also possible that there was selective attrition from the fields. Thus, lawyers practicing in conservative fields in 1975 may have changed specialties, or even have left the profession.

7. The reference (omitted) categories are male, white, lawyer father, type I Protestant, elite school, solo practice, associates and nonsupervisory positions, other ("non-wealth") field.

8. This category includes the following fields: In 1975, antitrust defense, banking, business litigation, commercial law, employment law (management), general corporate, patents, personal injury defense, probate, public utilities, real estate (business), securities, and tax (business). In 1995, it includes these same fields plus environmental (defense), insurance, and private international law.

9. We used the same procedure to analyze responses to the abortion question, with similar results, except that the amount of variance explained was greater. The model

including only personal background variables accounted for 19 percent of the total variance, and the addition of the profession variables contributed merely an additional 1 percent. Gender was highly significant, as was Catholic (in the opposite direction). Having a father who was employed in an occupation of lower socioeconomic status was also significant (in the antiabortion direction). None of the legal profession variables was significant at $p < .05$.

10. Unfortunately, on many of the items used in the Chicago surveys, directly comparable data drawn from other populations do not exist, so far as we could determine. We offer here the limited comparisons revealed in our electronic search.

11. This differs from our question only in the final word, *nation* as opposed to *country*.

12. It would be highly desirable to have direct comparisons with other professionals.

Chapter Nine

1. The first three of these motivations correspond to Clark and Wilson's typology of reasons for participation in organizations (Clark and Wilson 1961; see also Salisbury 1969, 15).

2. Putnam's thesis derives from and is more fully developed in his influential book, *Making Democracy Work* (1993), which is based on historical analysis of northern Italy.

3. Paxton argues that: "the overall connectedness of a population increases information flows. Increased information flows aid in the maintenance of democracy by ensuring that political participation is tolerant, moderate, and publicly oriented. Tocqueville argued that as individuals participate in associations, they see others who are participating in associations and notice that their interests coincide at a greater level. . . . [W]ith more aggregate-level association memberships, new ideas and opinions are more quickly disseminated throughout the population, yet extremist ideas are more easily challenged , as they have less chance of remaining isolated" (1999, 102–3). But see J. Cohen, 1999, 263.

4. The question asked the respondents to list "business or professional organizations, or trade associations (not including businesses themselves, or bar associations)."

5. These are generally less exclusive in membership than the country clubs and dining clubs. It has been suggested that the real difference between these two categories lies in the degree to which Spandex is visible on the premises. But it is also the case that some of the "fitness clubs" are profit-making businesses rather than not-for-profit associations.

6. Separate questions were asked in both 1975 and 1995 concerning participation in bar associations and other professional legal organizations (see chap. 3). Our present concern is the extraprofessional or "community" roles of lawyers.

7. If educational organizations are included, the overall activity rate in 1995 is 73 percent.

8. If educational organizations are included, the percentage of "leaders" in 1995 is 21 percent.

9. If educational organizations are included, the mean number of leadership positions per lawyer in 1995 is .31.

10. Associations with Illinois addresses increased from 1,102 to 1,512, while the Chicago listings declined from 722 to 672 (*Encyclopedia of Associations* 1975, 94–123; *Encyclopedia of Associations* 1995, 164–201).

11. Among respondents to the 1975 survey, the mean age was 44.5; in 1995, it was 41.9, a significant difference. T-test for equality of means = 4.13, $p < .001$ with a two-tailed test.

12. Chi-square for the cross-tabulation of the age categories and the number of respondents holding at least one leadership position is 27.0 in 1975 and 25.9 in 1995, both significant at .001. Similarly, analysis of variance in the total number of leadership positions held across the age categories produces F statistics of 8.2 in 1975 and 11.1 in 1995, both significant at .001. The age groups used were under 35, 35–45, 46–65, and over 65.

In the oldest age category, the percentage of respondents holding at least one leadership position was the same in 1995 and 1975 (36 percent). In all of the other age categories, however, it was lower in 1995 than in 1975.

13. Across six income categories, $\chi^2 = 9.9$, $p < .05$ one-tailed. The income categories are less than \$20,000 ($N = 54$), \$20,000–\$49,999 ($N = 131$), \$50,000–\$79,999 ($N = 185$), \$80,000–\$99,999 ($N = 96$), \$100,000–\$174,999 ($N = 144$), and \$175,000 or more ($N = 115$).

14. Across four age categories, $\chi^2 = 20.9$, $p < .001$.

15. Across five religion categories, $\chi^2 = 24.1$, $p < .001$. The numbers of respondents in the religion categories are: Catholic, 255; Jewish 195; Nonreligious, 128; Protestant type I, 92; Protestant type II, 109.

16. $\chi^2 = 7.9$, $p < .005$.

17. Across seven categories, $\chi^2 = 8.0$, $p > .05$.

18. Under \$15,000 ($N = 61$), activity rate = 46 percent; \$15,000–\$19,999 ($N = 120$), rate = 40 percent.

19. \$40,000 to \$59,999 ($N = 130$), rate = 69 percent; \$60,000 and over ($N = 122$), rate = 71 percent. Across six income categories, $\chi^2 = 38.2$, $p < .001$.

20. Under 35, rate = 46 percent; 35 to 45 = 67 percent; 46–65 = 65 percent; over 65 = 64 percent. Across four age categories, $\chi^2 = 25.5$, $p < .001$.

21. $\chi^2 = 27.2$, $p < .001$.

22. Across four law school categories, $\chi^2 = 6.4$, $p < .10$.

23. $\chi^2 = 1.9$. Recall that there were only 30 women among the 777 respondents to the 1975 survey.

24. These were OLS regressions.

25. $p < .01$.

26. $p < .01$.

27. $p < .10$.

28. Smith notes that "some researchers have found that length of residence in the community is associated with more volunteer participation" (1994, 250).

29. "Local" law school was the reference category.

30. $p < .01$.

31. In 1975, for Catholic $p < .05$; type I Protestant, $p < .05$; type II Protestant, $p < .001$. In 1995, for Catholic, $p < .10$; type I Protestant, $p < .01$; type II Protestant, $p < .05$.

32. It is plausible, however, that there might have been an increase in educational activity because of the movement for "school reform" in Chicago, which spawned many boards and committees.

33. The large number of World War II veterans was largely depleted by age and mortality by 1995.

34. Note that some of the traditional men's clubs do engage in public service or civic reform activities. The Union League Club of Chicago, for example, was active in the movement to replace elected with appointed judges and it lobbied (successfully) for the construction of a new Chicago public library building. It was also engaged in school reform and a number of other civic and legislative issues; see Union League Club of Chicago 1998, 27–28, and 1999, 27–28.

35. In contrast, religious organizations burgeoned. Most religious organizations do not appear among the most popular choices, however, because any individual congregation or affiliated organization is not large enough to involve a substantial percentage of the overall bar. Some respondents reported "Catholic Church" as an organization, but most reported individual parishes.

36. Males had a higher rate of activity in dining and athletic clubs (30 percent) than females (18 percent) in 1995, whereas the opposite was true of social clubs (females = 11 percent; males = 6 percent). In each of the six categories in which age was significantly associated with activity rates in 1995—dining clubs and business, political, educational, civic, and fraternal organizations—there was a steady increase in the rate across the four age categories.

Activity also increased generally with the income level of the respondents. (There is, of course, a significant correlation between income and age. The bivariate Pearson correlation between income and age in 1995 is 0.298, $p < .001$. In the 1975 data, it is 0.271, $p < .001$). The religious affiliations of the respondents were associated with significant differences in four categories of organizations—dining and athletic clubs, and religious, educational, and ethnic organizations. In dining clubs and religious and educational organizations, Protestants had high rates of activity. For organizations of persons of a particular ethnicity, however, the pattern was quite different—type I Protestants had the lowest activity rate (2 percent), while Jews and Catholics had the highest rates (14 percent and 9 percent, respectively). Graduates of elite law schools were more likely than those from other schools to be active in dining clubs and in civic and educational organizations. In fitness clubs, the pattern was the opposite—graduates of elite schools had the lowest participation rate (3 percent), while regional school graduates had the highest (14 percent) and local school graduates had the next highest (11 percent). Lawyers in large law firms had the highest activity rates in dining clubs (36 percent), while government lawyers had the lowest (7 percent). In business organizations, lawyers in government again were the least likely to be active (9 percent), while house counsel had the highest rate (32 percent) and respondents who were in nonlegal jobs had the next highest (28 percent).

37. We exclude educational organizations because of the difference in the prompts used in the 1975 and 1995 interviews.

38. In 1975, all three of the lower income categories are underrepresented in the top fifth, while all three of the higher income categories are overrepresented (χ^2 = 18.1, $p < .003$). In both 1975 and 1995, the Protestant categories are overrepresented in the top fifth, and all other religion categories are underrepresented (in 1975, χ^2 = 11.1, $p < .05$; in 1995, χ^2 = 24.6, $p < .001$). In both years we find that lawyers who were under 35 years old had the lowest percentage ranking in the top fifth (11 percent in each year), and that the percentages then increase in an orderly fashion through the 46–65 age bracket (25 percent in 1975; 29 percent in 1995). In 1975 (but not in 1995),

the percentage declines in the oldest category. (chi-square is significant at .001 in both years.)

39. The larger number of respondents with scores of zero in the earlier survey may be attributable to the fact that "inactive member" was a possible response in 1975 but not in 1995.

40. In a multiple regression predicting the number of leadership positions held by respondents, acquaintance with notables was highly significant.

41. This was done by dividing the denominator of the 1995 ratio by 2. Thus, in the example given in text, the ratio becomes 3/336 instead of 3/672.

42. Rodney Stark, using data from several sources, estimated that the church membership rate was about 62 percent (1987).

43. Given that Chicago lawyers are urban, predominately male, and predominately white (all of which reduce the rate of adherence), the similarity is even greater (Gallup 1996, 41).

Chapter Ten

1. As noted in chapter 1, the number of lawyers with offices in the city increased from approximately fifteen thousand in 1975 to thirty thousand in 1995.

2. Of the sixty-eight notables on the list, 11 received their law degrees from Harvard, 10 from Northwestern, 9 from the University of Chicago, 7 from Loyola, 5 from De Paul, 4 from the University of Illinois, 3 from Yale, 2 each from Michigan, Columbia, and Wisconsin, and 1 each from the University of California–Berkeley, Chicago-Kent, Cincinnati, Georgetown, Indiana, Iowa, John Marshall, Miami, Notre Dame, Pennsylvania, Valparaiso, Washington (St. Louis), and Wayne State.

3. The interview items were as follows: "So that we can analyze communication among various sectors or segments of the Chicago bar, we would like to have you go through this list of Chicago lawyers and indicate which ones you know. Please place a check in column A by the names of persons you know well enough to call by their first name when you see them."

And, after completion of that task: "Now, please place a second check in column B by the names of lawyers with whom you are more closely acquainted—those you know well enough to be sure that they would take the time to assist you briefly without charging you a fee, if you had a question or minor problem."

4. In the 1975 data, although the list of notables was shorter (forty-three notables) and somewhat less diverse, the likelihood of knowing notables was greater. At the stronger level of connection, only 38 percent of the respondents reported knowing none of the notables in 1975; 37 percent knew one to three, and 25 percent knew four or more. Ten respondents claimed to know half or more of the notables. Thus, in 1995 Chicago lawyers had become less likely to be personally acquainted with the elites of the bar.

5. The correlation between respondents' incomes and the number of notables known is .52 at the weaker level of ties and .53 at the stronger level, both significant at .001.

6. The correlation between age and the number of notables known is .44 in the measure of acquaintance and .37 in the measure of stronger ties, both significant at .001.

7. The analysis uses the data on connections to notables at the weaker, "acquain-

tance" level (i.e., the first question). The principal reason for this choice is that the number of ties falls off considerably at the stronger level of connection, which would require us either to drop several of the notables or run the risk of instability.

The proximity estimator used here is the Jaccard similarity measure, also known as the similarity ratio:

Jaccard $(x, y) = a / (a + b + c)$

where in the contingency table for cases x and y, a is the value for joint presence, and b and c are the values for nonmatches. Note that joint absences (the d cell) are not used in the Jaccard measure.

In two dimensions, the degree of fit (or its opposite, the amount of stress) is unsatisfactory—Kruskal's stress is .27 and the R^2 is .67. In the three-dimensional solution presented here, stress decreases to .20 and the R^2 improved to .76. In solutions with a greater number of dimensions, fit continues to improve—in four dimensions, stress = .16, R^2 = .81; in five dimensions, stress = .14, R^2 = .84.

8. The six outlying cases indicated by arrows account for 33 percent of the total range on the third dimension. The other fifty-nine cases occupy only two-thirds of the range on that dimension.

9. But most of these notables are not famous. Even knowledgeable Chicago lawyers would surely be unfamiliar with many of the names.

10. Calderon has a Spanish name but is not of Latin American ancestry. She is a Harvard Law School and Wellesley alumna who is active in the Episcopal church. See chapter appendix.

11. Compare, for example, Robinson and Turpin with Stitt, Shavers, Lunceford, or Lee; see chapter appendix.

Chapter Eleven

1. For similar findings, see Campbell, Converse, and Rogers 1976; Austin and Dodge 1992; Bokemeier and Lacy 1992; and Mottaz 1986.

2. The difference between blacks and whites was about one-fourth of a standard deviation; Firebaugh and Harley 1995, 99.

3. Steven Tuch and Jack Martin, however, using data from the 1985 and 1987–89 General Social Surveys, found that the lower job satisfaction of blacks was mostly the result of structural factors rather than of differences in the work values of black and white workers (1991, 111–13).

4. Four possible reasons have been suggested for the positive association between age and job satisfaction (Firebaugh and Harley 1995, 89). First, older workers may actually have better jobs because they are more advanced in their careers. Second, self-selection may have occurred, in which older workers, over time, sorted themselves into comfortable positions. Third, expectations may decline with age—this suggests that workers' expectations adjust to conform to their experience, so that older worker's expectations have been "ground down" (Hamilton and Wright 1986, 209–14). Fourth, younger workers and older workers are in different generations, and these cohort or history effects may influence expectations and levels of satisfaction. The last of these propositions, however, is inconsistent with Firebaugh and Harley's findings.

5. The variables analyzed included income, intrinsic rewards, time measures, service to community, prestige, career, and public image of the profession. The study also found that women lawyers were not as much concerned with "intrinsic rewards,"

"career advancement" or the "public image of the profession" as were their male counterparts; at 464. See also Menkel-Meadow 1989.

6. Surveys sponsored by the Young Lawyers Division of the American Bar Association found that, in 1984, 29 percent of female lawyers reported general career dissatisfaction, versus 14 percent of male lawyers. In their 1990 data, dissatisfaction increased for both women and men, to 41 percent and 28 percent, respectively (American Bar Association 1991, 53–54; Lentz and Laband 1995; Tucker and Niedzielko 1994).

7. The prototypical legal career, commentators suggest, continues to be based on a male career model in which total commitment to work is both possible and desirable (Barnett 1990).

Sex discrimination and sexual harassment within the legal profession might also lead to greater dissatisfaction among women (MacCorquodale and Jensen 1993). A survey of 220 women lawyers in a Midwestern state capital also collected information on their experience of discrimination, gender disparagement, and sexual harassment in their work (Rosenberg, Perlstadt, and Phillips 1993). Research on the status of women in the English legal profession was consistent with some of these findings (Spencer and Podmore 1982, 1987).

8. The very small difference between men and women was consistent across practice settings. In a 1985 sample, there was no distinct pattern of difference by gender. The Toronto study also suggested, however, that women tended to express more dissatisfaction than men in group, open-ended discussion settings.

9. The bivariate correlation between age and satisfaction is .147 ($p < .001$).

10. Because the overall satisfaction measure is highly skewed, with most respondents reporting being "satisfied" or "very satisfied," linear regression is an inappropriate method for analysis of these data. This problem was resolved by using logistic regression and treating the overall satisfaction measure as a dichotomous variable: respondents were categorized as either "very satisfied" or not.

11. Pearson correlation = .13, $p < .001$, two-tailed.

12. $p < .02$.

13. $p < .01$.

14. In a t-test, $p < .03$.

15. In a t-test, $p < .001$.

16. In a t-test, $p < .06$.

17. $\chi^2 = 4.7$, 1 df, $p < .05$.

18. The *New York Times* reported an interview with Chief Justice Rehnquist: "Q. If you hadn't become Chief Justice, what other career would you have liked to have? A. An architect. Symphony conductor" (D. Smith 2004).

19. Pearson correlation = .147; $p < .001$, two-tailed.

20. Pearson correlation = .094; $p < .02$, two-tailed.

21. Pearson correlation = .143, $p < .001$, two-tailed.

22. Pearson correlation = .10, $p = .008$, two-tailed.

23. Pearson correlation = .09, $p = .02$, two-tailed.

24. On the client choice variable, $\chi^2 = 12.2$, 4 df, $p < .05$; on the variable concerned with direction or supervision by seniors, $\chi^2 = 30.2$, 4 df, $p < .001$; and on

the variable concerning independence in designing strategies, $\chi^2 = 21.4$, 4 df, $p < .001$. On another variable, concerning the extent to which the problems addressed by the lawyer "go beyond purely legal issues," the difference between men and women just misses the conventional .05 test of statistical significance, but women appear to be somewhat more likely to report that they deal with extralegal matters.

25. The two variables significantly correlated with satisfaction among male respondents are client choice ($p < .001$) and the variable dealing with direction by seniors ($p < .01$). The two that are significant among women are the variable regarding rapidity of change in their areas of the law ($p < .05$) and the one concerning the degree to which exclusively professional expertise is required in their work ($p < .05$).

26. $\chi^2 = 11.7$, 4 df, $p < .05$.

27. Because of the very small numbers of respondents in these categories, the difference is only marginally significant when the chi-square is computed with the Yates correction; $\chi^2 = 7.96$, 4 df, $p < .10$.

28. $\chi^2 = 27.7$, 5 df, $p < .001$. Some of this income difference is attributable to the fact that the black respondents are, on the average, somewhat younger than the whites. The mean age of whites is 41.3 and that of blacks is 37.9; t-test significant at .02.

29. In a t-test, $p < .001$.

30. The differences between whites and minorities on the final two variables listed in table 11.3—relationships with colleagues and opportunity for pro bono work—also come very close to reaching the .05 level of statistical significance.

31. $\chi^2 = 63.6$, 5 df, $p < .001$.

32. Experience was measured by number of years out of law school. In addition to the simple number of years since graduation, we included a term with the square of that value because income returns to experience are probably curvilinear rather than linear. As expected, the latter term was significantly negative.

33. $p < .01$.

34. In a second version of the model, we included an interaction term for gender and race. It was not significant.

35. As indicated in chapter 1, the population from which the respondents were sampled included all lawyers licensed by the state, even those who were retired, unemployed, or doing other sorts of work. Thus, exit from this population would occur only if the lawyers allowed their licenses to lapse. Most lawyers who do other work probably want to retain their licenses, if only as insurance. The respondents to the 1995 survey did, in fact, include 112 lawyers who were not practicing at the time, but most of the analyses discussed here have dealt with only the 675 practicing lawyers. Since the question in the survey asked about present job satisfaction, analysis of the nonpracticing respondents will not reveal their degree of satisfaction in law practice at an earlier time.

36. If we compare practicing to nonpracticing respondents, we find that 9.9 percent of the males and 12.7 percent of the females were not practicing at the time of the survey. This difference is not statistically significant. (For the purposes of this analysis, we excluded judges, judicial clerks, and law professors from both the practicing and the nonpracticing categories. The percentages of men and women in this disparate residual grouping are exactly equal; sixteen men and sixteen women. Thus, women are substantially overrepresented.)

Chapter Twelve

1. This estimate is very similar to that made by a prominent Washington lawyer, Lloyd Cutler (Cutler 1978, 1549).

2. Two decades later, in *Professionalism Reborn* (1994), Freidson argued that the power of third-party payers, hospital administrators, and managed-care organizations had created a need for a revitalization of professional ideals.

3. Because lawyers who were active in bar associations were more likely to respond to the surveys (see chap. 1), these estimates probably overstate the rate of bar association activity somewhat. The 1975 survey did not ask about attendance at bar association meetings.

4. *Goldfarb v. Virginia State Bar*, 421 U.S. 773 (1975).

5. *Bates and O'Steen v. Arizona*, 433 U.S. 330 (1977).

6. This information was compiled by Clara Carson of the American Bar Foundation, using data from the *Martindale-Hubbell Law Directory*.

7. Note that, because the surveys used random samples of lawyers, not firms, the probability that any given firm would be represented in the samples was directly proportional to the number of lawyers in the firm. Thus, the average number of lawyers per firm in a random sample of *firms* would be smaller than the numbers given here, which are instead a measure of the nature of the contexts in which the lawyers practiced.

8. As Richard Sander and Douglass Williams (1992, 406) point out, however, the growth rates of several of the firms examined by Galanter and Palay did not increase in 1970; in fact, some decreased.

9. The pace of certain types of corporate transactions (notably, mergers, acquisitions, and securities work generally) also increased markedly, thus requiring additional staff to process the matters quickly. One Chicago lawyer told us that "A deal that might have taken a month or two in 1975 may take a week or less today."

10. In 1999, the Skadden Arps firm reportedly hired 143 entering associates (Parsa 1999, 31). This does not take into account growth through mergers with other firms.

11. The 1998 *Strategic Plan for Northwestern University School of Law* notes: "Legal employers demand graduates who are able to enter practice with the judgment and the maturity to assume responsibility quickly. Even in large law firms, a new lawyer has little time to develop these traits on the job."

12. The 1995 Chicago survey found that 65 percent of the respondents in firms with thirty or more lawyers reported that their firms had an executive "responsible primarily for administrative policy, rather than doing legal work" (see chap. 5).

13. According to the *Chicago Tribune*, an agency "farms out legal work to a subsidiary with 15 full-time workers in Mumbai, formerly Bombay. Much of the work the staff handles, such as drafting research memos and surveying the law of various jurisdictions, are duties that younger lawyers or paralegals may otherwise have performed at much higher costs" (Sachdev 2004).

14. Chicago law firm examples include Elmer Johnson from Kirkland and Ellis at General Motors, Howard Trienens from Sidley and Austin at AT&T, and Ted Tetzlaff from Jenner and Block at Tenneco.

15. $N = 94$ in 1975 and 67 in 1995.

16. There was a smaller income range among inside counsel in both years. Thus, they had a lower standard deviation.

17. In 1995, 39 percent of the inside counsel were women, compared to only 26 percent of other practicing lawyers. In 1975 there were only three women among the ninety-four inside counsel (3.2 percent of inside counsel were women versus 4.0 percent of other lawyers). The income difference is also not explained by change in the relative age of inside counsel. In both years, the median age of inside counsel was three years older than other lawyers.

18. There is a clear relationship between size of firm and the likelihood of bidding for work. The percentage of respondents who reported in 1995 that they had *not* obtained clients by competitive bidding within the past three years was: for solo practitioners, 97 percent; in firms with 2–9 lawyers, 74 percent; in firms of 10–30 lawyers, 64 percent; firms of 31–99 lawyers, 53 percent; firms with 100–299, 48 percent; and in firms with 300 or more lawyers, only 31 percent ($\chi^2 = 106.7$; $p < .001$).

19. As they entered the market for legal services, the accounting firms encountered conflicts. Auditors of public companies have a duty to disclose problems so investors and potential investors can assess the risks, but clients who go to expert consultants for business, tax, and financial advice have an expectation of confidentiality. The Securities and Exchange Commission (SEC) criticized the accounting firms for compromising the independence of their auditing function through the provision of consulting services to the same clients (Gibeaut 2000). Responding in part to pressure from the SEC, several of the largest accounting firms then separated their auditing divisions from the consulting services. In most cases, the consulting practice became a separate corporation (Michaels and Peel 2000; Tagliabue 2000). In making these moves, the firms were also motivated by the need to raise capital to finance the expansion of the consulting practice (MacDonald 2000; Michaels and Peel 2000, 18). By separating the consulting entity from the auditors, it became possible for the consulting company to raise capital through a public offering or from a private investor. The Sarbanes-Oxley Act later prohibited auditing firms from selling consulting services, including legal services.

20. Carole Silver (2000) analyzes the move of U.S. law firms into foreign markets. She reports that, of the firms on the *American Lawyer* list of the hundred largest U.S. law firms, seventy-one had offices abroad (Silver 2000, 37). See also *The Economist* 2000.

21. Prominent early players in this market were Hildebrandt, Altman Weil, and Price Waterhouse.

22. In some firms, notably in the highly successful Cravath firm in New York and in a few of the other old-line New York firms, income was (and is) distributed solely by seniority—the longer the service, the larger the share (Carter 2002; Elwin 2003).

23. In England, solicitors have recently been pushed into retirement at much earlier ages. According to the *Times* of London: "In most City law firms today, it is unusual to find partners over 55. Few firms admit to a policy of compulsory retirement at 55, but retirement at 55 is seen by most managing partners as a blessing" (Digby-Bell 1999). A law firm consultant was quoted as saying "there has been a shift in the firm's focus, with young partners in their late 30s, early 40s seizing control, either in a velvet revolution or a fairly bloody coup" (Langdon-Down 2001).

24. *Equal Employment Opportunity Commission v. Sidley Austin Brown & Wood,* 315 F.3d 696 (7th Cir. 2002). At the time of the demotions, the firm was known as Sidley and Austin. About a year later, it merged with another firm and became known as Sidley Austin Brown and Wood.

25. The firm, now known as Cravath, Swaine and Moore, was then Cravath, de Gersdorff, Swaine and Wood.

26. The ethical rules of the bar permit this so long as the law firm owns the other business. It is objectionable, however, if nonlawyers own the law firm. The ethics of the legal profession require that lawyers be in control.

27. Since the base on which the percentage is computed was twice as large in 1995 as in 1975, the best estimate is that the number of Chicago lawyers in firms of one hundred or more increased by about sixfold. The percentages given here are for practicing lawyers. The percentage among all licensed lawyers also tripled, from 7 percent to 21 percent.

28. This does not mean that the amount of legal services provided to individuals and small businesses decreased. Because the bar doubled in size, those services grew, but corporate practice grew much more rapidly.

References

Abbott, Andrew. 1981. "Status and Strain in the Professions." *American Journal of Sociology* 86 (4): 819–33.

——. 1988. *The System of Professions: An Essay on the Division of Expert Labor.* Chicago: University of Chicago Press.

ABC News/Washington Post Survey 1989, cited in Galanter 1998, 808.

Abel, Richard L. 1989. *American Lawyers.* New York: Oxford University Press.

——. 1994. "Symposium: The Future of the Legal Profession: Transnational Law Practice." *Case Western Reserve Law Review* 44:737–870.

Abel, Richard L., and Philip S. C. Lewis, eds. 1988–89. *Lawyers in Society.* 3 vols. Berkeley: University of California Press.

Adams, Edward A. 1994. "Legal Career Exacts Steep Personal Price." *New York Law Journal,* February 7, 1.

Allison, Paul D. 1978. "Measures of Inequality." *American Sociological Review* 43:865–80.

Alwin, Duane F., and Jon A. Krosnick. 1991. "Aging Cohorts and the Stability of Sociopolitical Orientations over Life Span." *American Journal of Sociology* 97:169–95.

American Bar Association. 1992. *A Review of Legal Education in the United States, Fall 1991.* Chicago: American Bar Association.

American Bar Association, Young Lawyers Division. 1991. *The State of the Legal Profession 1990,* 53–54. Chicago: American Bar Association.

American Bar Association Commission on Professionalism. 1986. *". . . In the Spirit of Public Service": A Blueprint for the Rekindling of Lawyer Professionalism.* Chicago: American Bar Association.

Attorney Registration and Disciplinary Commission. 1977, 1995, 1996. *Annual Report.* Chicago: Supreme Court of Illinois.

Auerbach, Jerold S. 1976. *Unequal Justice: Lawyers and Social Change in Modern America.* New York: Oxford University Press.

Austin, Roy L., and Hiroko H. Dodge. 1992. "Despair, Distrust, and Dissatisfaction among Blacks and Women." *Sociology Quarterly* 33:579–98.

Baker, W. E. 1990. "Market Networks and Corporate Behavior." *American Journal of Sociology* 96:589–625.

Baltzell, E. Digby 1964. *The Protestant Establishment: Aristocracy and Caste in America.* New York: Random House.

———. 1966. *Philadelphia Gentlemen: The Making of a National Upper Class.* New York: Free Press.

———. 1976. "The Protestant Establishment Revisited." *American Scholar* 45:499–518.

Barnett, Martha W. 1990. "Women Practicing Law: Changes in Attitude, Changes in Platitudes." *Florida Law Review* 42:209–28.

Baron, James N., and William T. Bielby. 1980. "Bringing the Firm Back In: Stratification, Segmentation, and the Organization of Work." *American Sociological Review* 45:737–65.

Beck, Susan. 2002. "The Harder They Fall." *American Lawyer,* August, 64–70, 128–29.

Becker, Gary. 1993. *Human Capital: A Theoretical and Empirical Analysis with Special Reference to Education.* 3rd ed. Chicago: University of Chicago Press.

Bell, Robert. 1999. *Some Determinants of Corporate Use of Attorneys.* ABF Working Paper Series. Chicago: American Bar Foundation.

Ben-David, Joseph. 1963–64. "Professions in the Class System of Present Day Societies: A Trend Report and Bibliography." *Current Sociology* 12:247–42.

Bentley, Arthur F. 1908. *The Process of Government.* Reprint, Evanston, IL: Principia Press, 1949.

Berger, Peter L., Brigitte Berger, and Hansfried Kellner. 1974. "Excursus: On the Obsolescence of the Concept of Honor." In *The Homeless Mind: Modernization and Consciousness,* 83–96. New York: Vintage.

Beverly, Duncan. 1954. "Estimated Jewish Population of Chicago and Selected Characteristics, 1951." *The Chicago Community Inventory.* Chicago: University of Chicago.

Bielby, William T., and Denise D. Bielby. 1989. "Family Ties: Balancing Commitment to Work and Family in Dual Earner Households." *American Sociological Review* 54:776–89.

Bigoness, William J. 1988. "Sex Differences in Job Attribute Preferences." *Journal of Organizational Behavior* 9:139–47.

Blau, Peter M., and Rebecca Z. Margulies. 1974–75. "A Research Replication: The Reputation of American Professional Schools." *Change in Higher Education* 6 (Winter): 44.

Blaustein, Albert P., and Charles O. Porter. 1954. *The American Lawyer: A Summary of the Legal Profession.* Chicago: University of Chicago Press.

Bokemeier, Janet L., and William B. Lacey. 1992. "Job Values, Rewards, and Work Conditions as Factors in Job Satisfaction among Men and Women." *Sociology Quarterly* 28:189–204.

Bourdieu, Pierre. 1984. *Distinction: A Social Critique of the Judgement of Taste.* Cambridge: Harvard University Press.

Bowen, William, and Derek Bok. 1998. *The Shape of the River: Long-Term Consequences of Considering Race in College and University Admissions.* Princeton: Princeton University Press.

Brandeis, Louis D. 1905. "The Opportunity in the Law." *American Law Review* 39 (July–August): 559–61.

Bridges, William P. 1995. "Where Do Markets Go To: An Analysis of Change in Internal and External Mobility Patterns." *Research in Social Stratification and Mobility* 14:71–98.

Burger, Warren E. 1995. "The Decline of Professionalism." *Fordham Law Review* 63:949–58.

Burt, Ronald S. 1992. *Structural Holes: The Social Structure of Competition.* Cambridge: Harvard University Press, 1992.

Cain, Glen G. 1976. "The Challenge of Segmented Labor Market Theories to Orthodox Theory: A Survey." *Journal of Economic Literature* 14 (4): 1215–57.

Campbell, Angus, Phillip E. Converse, and Willard L. Rogers. 1976. *The Quality of American Life: Perception, Evaluations, and Satisfaction.* New York: Russell Sage Foundation.

Campo-Flores Avian. 2000. "Bar Talk: King Arthur." *American Lawyer,* January, 17.

Caplan, Lincoln. 1993. *Skadden: Power, Money, and the Rise of a Legal Empire.* New York: Farrar Straus Giroux.

Cappell, Charles, L. 1979. "Organizations and Specialization of Legal Activity." Memorandum, American Bar Foundation.

Carlin, Jerome E. 1962. *Lawyers on Their Own: A Study of Individual Practitioners in Chicago.* New Brunswick, NJ: Rutgers University Press.

———. 1966. *Lawyers' Ethics: A Survey of the New York City Bar.* New York: Russell Sage Foundation.

Carr-Saunders, A. P., and P. A. Wilson. 1933. *The Professions.* Oxford: Oxford University Press.

Carson, Clara N. 1999. *The Lawyer Statistical Report: The U.S. Legal Profession in 1995.* Chicago: American Bar Foundation.

———. 2004. *The Lawyer Statistical Report: The Legal Profession in 2000.* Chicago: American Bar Foundation.

Carter, Terry. 2002. "Law at the Crossroads." *ABA Journal,* January, 29–34.

Chambers, David L. 1989. "Accommodation and Satisfaction: Women and Men Lawyers and the Balance of Work and Family." *Law and Social Inquiry* 14:251–87.

Chambliss, Elizabeth. 1997. "Organizational Determinants of Law Firm Integration." *American University Law Review* 46:669–744.

Chambliss, Elizabeth, and Christopher Uggen. 2000. "Men and Women of Elite Law Firms: Reevaluating Kanter's Legacy." *Law and Social Inquiry* 25:41–68.

Chandler, Alfred D. 1962. *Strategy and Structure: Chapters in the History of the American Industrial Enterprise.* Cambridge: MIT Press.

Cherovsky, Edwin. 1991. "The Use of Temporary Lawyers Is on the Rise in Many Firms." *New York Law Journal,* March 4, 44.

Chicago Lawyer. 2001. "Chicago Lawyer 2001 Survey: The Largest Law Firms in Illinois." *Chicago Lawyer,* May, 13–33.

Chiu, Charlotte, and Kevin T. Leicht. 1999. "When Does Feminization Increase Equality? The Case of Lawyers." *Law and Society Review* 33 (3): 557–94.

Clark, Peter B., and James Q. Wilson. 1961. "Incentive Systems: A Theory of Organizations." *Administrative Science Quarterly* 6:129–66.

Clogg, C. C. 1995. "Latent Class Models." In *Handbook of Statistical Modeling for the Social and Behavioral Sciences,* edited by G. Arminger, Clifford C. Clogg, and Michael Sobel, 311–59. New York: Plenum Press, 1995.

Cohen, Jean L. 1999. "Does Voluntary Association Make Democracy Work?" In Smelser and Alexander 1999, 263.

Coleman, James. 1998. "Social Capital in the Creation of Human Capital." *American Journal of Sociology* 94 (supp.): S95–S120.

Cook, J. Michael, Eugene M. Freedman, Ray J. Groves, Jon C. Madonna, Shaun F. O'Malley, and Lawrence A. Weinbach. 1992. "The Liability Crisis in the United States: Impact on the Accounting Profession." *Journal of Accountancy* (November): 18–23.

Cornwall, Richard R., and Phanindra V. Wunnava, eds. 1991. *New Approaches to Economic and Social Analyses of Discrimination.* New York: Praeger.

Coulter, Philip, B. 1989. *Measuring Inequality: A Methodological Handbook.* Boulder, CO: Westview Press.

Crosby, Faye J. 1982. *Relative Deprivation and Working Women.* Oxford: Oxford University Press.

———. 1987. "Multiple Regressions and Multiple Roles: A Note for the General Reader." In *Spouse, Parent, Worker: On Gender and Multiple Roles,* edited by Faye Crosby. New Haven: Yale University Press.

Curran, Barbara A. 1986. *Supplement to the Lawyer Statistical Report.* Chicago: American Bar Foundation.

Curran, Barbara A., and Clara N. Carson. 1994. *The Lawyer Statistical Report: The U.S. Legal Profession in the 1990s.* Chicago: American Bar Foundation.

Curran, Barbara A., with Katherine J. Rosich, Clara N. Carson, and Mark C. Puccetti. 1985. *The Lawyer Statistical Report: A Statistical Profile of the U.S. Legal Profession in the 1980s.* Chicago: American Bar Foundation.

Curran, Barbara A., and Francis Spalding. 1974. *The Legal Needs of the Public.* Chicago: American Bar Association and American Bar Foundation.

Cutler, Lloyd N. 1978. "The Role of the Private Law Firm." *Business Law* 33:1549.

Daniels, Stephen, and Joanne Martin. 1995. *Civil Juries and the Politics of Reform.* Evanston, IL: Northwestern University Press.

Dau-Schmidt, Kenneth G., and Kaushik Mukhopadhaya. 1999. "The Fruits of Our Labors: An Empirical Study of the Distribution of Income and Job Satisfaction across the Legal Profession." *Journal of Legal Education* 49 (3): 342–66.

Davis, Kingsley, and Wilbert E. Moore. 1945. "Some Principles of Stratification." *American Sociological Review* 10:242–49.

Dean, Arthur H. 1957. *William Nelson Cromwell, 1854–1948: An American Pioneer in Corporation, Comparative and International Law.* New York: Ad Press.

Demerath, Nicholas J. 1965. *Social Class in American Protestantism.* Chicago: Rand McNally.

Derber, Charles. 1982. "The Proletarianization of the Professional: A Review Essay." In *Professionals as Workers: Mental Labor in Advanced Capitalism,* edited by Charles Derber, 13–34. Boston: G. K. Hall.

Derber, Charles, William A. Schwartz, and Yale Magrass. 1990. *Power in the Highest Degree: Professionals and the Rise of a New Mandarin Order.* New York: Oxford University Press.

Dewar, Helen. 2002. "Senate Panel Rejects Bush Court Nominee." *Washington Post,* September 6, A1.

Dezalay, Yves. 1992. *Marchands de droit: La restructuration de l'ordre juridique international par les multinationales du droit.* Paris: Librairie Arthème Fayard.

Dezalay, Yves, and Bryant G. Garth. 1996. *Dealing in Virtue: International Commercial Arbitration and the Construction of a Transnational Legal Order.* Chicago: University of Chicago Press.

Dieter, Richard C. 1995. *With Justice for Few: The Growing Crises in Death Penalty Representation.* Washington, DC: Death Penalty Information Center.

Digby-Bell, Christopher. 1999. "Plan to Go Out Gracefully and Usefully." *Times* (London), September 21, features sec.

DiMaggio, Paul, and Walter Powell. 1983. "The Iron Cage Revisited: Institutional Isomorphism and Collective Rationality in Organizational Fields." *American Sociological Review* 48:147–60.

Dixon, Jo, and Carroll Seron. 1995. "Stratification in the Legal Profession: Sex, Sector and Salary." *Law and Society Review* 29 (3): 381–412.

Dos Passos, John R. 1907. *The American Lawyer: As He Was, As He Is, As He Can Be.* New York: Banks Law Publishing.

Dolan, Maura. 1995. "Miserable with the Legal Life." *Los Angeles Times,* June 27, A1.

Dunworth, Terence, and Joel Rogers. 1996. "Corporations in Court: Big Business Litigation in U.S. Federal Courts, 1971–1991." *Law and Social Inquiry* 21:497–592.

Economist, The. 2000. "Lawyers Go Global: The Battle of the Atlantic." Feb. 26, 79–81.

Elwin, William. 2003. Telephone interview, April 8.

Encyclopedia of Associations. 1975. 9th ed. Edited by Margaret Fisk. Vol. 2, *Geographic and Executive Index.* Detroit: Gale Research.

———. 1995. 29th ed. Vol. 2, *Geographic and Executive Indexes,* edited by Rebecca L. Turner and Carol A. Schwartz. Detroit: Gale Research.

Epstein, Cynthia Fuchs. 1981. *Women in Law.* New York: Basic Books.

———. 1993. *Women in Law.* 2nd ed. Urbana: University of Illinois Press.

Eulau, Heinz, and John Sprague. 1964. *Lawyers in Politics: A Study in Professional Convergence.* Indianapolis: Bobbs-Merrill.

Evans, Mariah D., and Edward O. Laumann. 1983. "Professional Commitment: Myth or Reality?" *Research in Social Stratification and Mobility* 2:3–40.

Felstiner, William. 1974. Influences of Social Organization on Dispute Processing. *Law and Society Review* 9 (1): 63–94. University of California, Los Angeles.

Felton, Barbara J. 1987. "Cohort Variation in Happiness: Some Hypotheses and Exploratory Analyses." *International Journal of Ageing and Human Development* 25:27–42.

Finke, Roger, and Rodney Stark. 1992. *The Churching of America, 1776–1990: Winners and Losers in Our Religious Economy.* New Brunswick, NJ: Rutgers University Press.

Firebaugh, Glenn, and Brian Harley. 1995. "Trends in Job Satisfaction in the United States by Race, Gender, and Type of Occupation." *Research in the Sociology of Work* 5:87–104.

Fischel, Daniel R. 2000. "Multidisciplinary Practice." *Business Lawyer* 55:951–74.

Fligstein, Neil. 1987. "The Intraorganizational Power Struggle: Rise of Finance Personnel to Top Leadership in Large Corporations, 1919–1979." *American Sociological Review* 52:44–58.

———. 1990. *The Transformation of Corporate Control.* Cambridge: Harvard University Press.

Frank, John P. 1965. "The Legal Ethics of Louis D. Brandeis." *Stanford Law Review* 17:683–98.

Frank, Robert H., and Philip J. Cook. 1995. *The Winner Take All Society: Why the Few at the Top Get So Much More Than the Rest of Us.* New York: Penguin.

Frederick, Samuel A. 1995. "Teaming Up with Temporary Lawyers." *American Lawyer,* May, S58.

Freidson, Eliot F. 1970. *Professional Dominance: The Social Structure of Medical Care.* New York: Atherton Press.

———. 1984. "Are Professions Necessary?" In *The Authority of Experts: Studies in History and Theory,* 3–27, edited by Thomas L. Haskell. Bloomington: Indiana University Press.

———. 1986. *Professional Powers: A Study in the Institutionalization of Formal Knowledge.* Chicago: University of Chicago Press.

———. 1992. "Professionalism as Model and Ideology." In Nelson, Trubek, and Solomon 1992, 215–29.

———. 1994. *Professionalism Reborn: Theory, Prophesy, and Policy.* Chicago: University of Chicago Press.

Friedkin, Noah E. 1999. "Choice Shift and Group Polarization." *American Sociological Review* 64:856–60.

Fritsch, Jane, and David Rhode. 2001. "Two-Tier Justice: Part 1, Facing Life in Prison. Part 2: High Volume Law. Part 3, The Final Stop." *New York Times,* April 8–10.

Galanter, Marc. 1974. "Why the 'Haves' Come Out Ahead: Speculations on the Limits of Legal Change." *Law and Society Review* 20 (Fall): 95–160.

———. 1993. "News from Nowhere: The Debased Debate on Civil Justice." *Denver University Law Review* 71:77–113.

———. 1994. "Predators and Parasites: Lawyer Bashing and Civil Justice." *Georgia Law Review* 28:662–69.

———. 1996. "Real World Torts: An Antidote to Anecdote." *Maryland Law Review* 55: 1093–60.

———. 1998. "The Faces of Mistrust: The Image of Lawyers in Public Opinion, Jokes and Political Discourse." *University of Cincinnati Law Review* 66:805–45.

———. 1999. " 'Old and in the Way': The Coming Demographic Transformation of the Legal Profession and Its Implications for the Provision of Legal Services." *Wisconsin Law Review* 1081–17.

Galanter, Marc, and Thomas Palay. 1991. *Tournament of Lawyers: The Transformation of the Big Law Firm.* Chicago: University of Chicago Press.

Gallup, George H., Jr. 1996. *Religion in America.* Princeton: Religion Research Center.

Garth, Bryant G. 2004. "Multidisciplinary Practice after Enron: Eliminating a Competitor But Not the Competition." *Law and Social Inquiry* 29:591–95.

Garth, Bryant G., and Carole Silver. 2002. "The MDP Challenge in the Context of Globalization." *Case Western Law Review* 52:903–42.

Gartner, Alan, and Frank Reissman. 1974. *The Service Society and Consumer Vanguard.* New York: Harper and Row.

Gawalt, Gerard W., ed. 1984. *The New High Priests: Lawyers in Post–Civil War America.* Westport, CO: Greenwood Press.

Gest, Ted. 2001. "They'd Rather Be in Business: Law Schools are Prepping Future Attorneys for the Corporate Life." In *U.S. News and World Report: America's Best Graduate Schools.*

Gibb, Frances. 2003. "New Broom Looks at Sweeping Legal Changes." *Times* (London), "Law Report," October 21.

Gibeaut, John. 2000. MDP in SEC Crosshairs. *ABA Journal,* April, 16.

Gilson, Ronald, and Robert H. Mnookin. 1985. "Sharing Among the Human Capitalists: An Economic Inquiry into the Corporate Law Firm and How Partners Split Profits." *Stanford Law Review* 37:313–92.

Glaberson, William. 1999. "When the Verdict is Just a Fantasy." *New York Times*, June 6, sec. A4, 1, cols. 1–3.

Glater, Jonathan D. 2003a. "Fearing Liability, Law Firms Change Partnership Status." *New York Times*, January 10, C2.

———. 2003b. "Pressure Increases for Tighter Limits on Injury Lawsuits." *New York Times*, May 28, A1.

———. 2003c. "West Coast Law Firm Closing After Dot-Com Collapse." *New York Times*, January 31, C1.

Glendon, Mary Ann. 1994. *A Nation Under Lawyers: How the Crisis in the Legal Profession Is Transforming American Society.* New York: Farrar, Straus and Giroux.

Goldstein, Amy. 2001. "Bush Curtails ABA Role in Selecting U.S. Judges." *Washington Post*, March 23, A1.

Goldhaber, Michael D. 1999. "How Greenberg Got So Big." *National Law Journal*, April 26, A1.

Goode, William J. 1957. "Community within a Community: The Professions." *American Sociological Review* 22:194–200.

———. 1978. *The Celebration of Heroes: Prestige as a Control System.* Berkeley: University of California Press.

Gordon, Robert W. 1988. "The Independence of Lawyers." *Boston University Law Review* 68:1–83.

———. 1990. "Corporate Law Practice as a Public Calling." *Maryland Law Review* 49:255.

Gordon, Robert, and William Simon. 1992. "The Redemption of Professionalism?" In Nelson, Trubek, and Solomon 1992, 230–57.

Gorman, Elizabeth H. 1999. "Moving Away from 'Up and Out': Determinants of Permanent Employment in Law Firms." *Law and Society Review* 33 (3): 637–66.

Granfield, Robert. 1992. *Making Elite Lawyers: Visions of Law at Harvard and Beyond.* New York: Routledge.

Granovetter, Mark. 1973. "Strength of Weak Ties." *American Journal of Sociology* 78 (6): 1360–80.

Greeley, Andrew M. 1989. *Religious Change in America.* Cambridge: Harvard University Press.

———. 1997. "The Other Civic America: Religion and Social Capital." *American Prospect*, May–June, 68–73.

Greenwood, Ernest. 1957. "Attributes of a Profession." *Social Work* (July): 45.

Greenwood, Royston, C. R. Hinings, and John Brown. 1990. "P2 Form Strategic Management: Corporate Practices in Professional Services Firms." *Academy of Management Journal* 33: 725–55.

Grusky, David B., ed. 1994. *Social Stratification: Class, Race and Gender in Sociological Perspective.* Boulder, CO: Westview Press.

Guttman, Louis. 1968. "A General Nonmetric Technique for Finding the Smallest Coordinate Space for a Configuration of Points." *Psychometrika* 33:469–506.

Hackney, Melissa M. 1996. "Some Large Philadelphia Firms Embrace Contract Lawyers; Degree of Acceptance Varies from Somewhat Reluctant to Not at All." *Legal Intelligencer*, April 15, 1996, 3.

Hadfield, Gillian K. 2000."The Price of Law: How the Market for Lawyers Distorts the Justice System." *University of Michigan Law Review* 98:953–1006.

Haeckel, Stephan H. 1999. *Adaptive Enterprise: Creating and Leading Sense-and-Respond Organizations.* Cambridge: Harvard Business School Press.

Hagan, John. 1990. "The Gender Stratification of Income Inequality Among Lawyers." *Social Forces* 68 (3): 835–55.

Hagan, John, and Fiona Kay. 1995. *Gender in Practice: A Study of Lawyers' Lives.* Oxford: Oxford University Press.

Hall, Karen. 2000. "That Was Then . . ." *American Lawyer,* March, 24.

Hall, Richard H. 1975 [1969]. *Occupations and the Social Structure.* Englewood Cliffs: Prentice-Hall.

Hall, Richard H., Norman J. Johnson, and J. Eugene Haas. 1967. "Organizational Size, Complexity and Formalization." *American Sociological Review* 32:903–12.

Halliday, Terence C. 1987. *Beyond Monopoly: Lawyers, State Crises, and Professional Empowerment.* Chicago: University of Chicago Press.

Haltom, William, and Michael McCann. 2004. *Distorting the Law: Politics, Media, and the Litigation Crisis.* Chicago: University of Chicago Press.

Hamilton, Richard F., and James D. Wright. 1986. *The State of the Masses.* New York: Aldine.

Handler, Joel F., Ellen Jane Hollingsworth, and Howard S. Erlanger. 1978. *Lawyers and the Pursuit of Legal Rights.* New York: Russell Sage Foundation.

Haslam, S. Alexander. 2001. *Psychology in Organizations: The Social Identity Approach.* Thousand Oaks, CA: Sage Publishers.

Hauser, Robert M., and John Robert Warren. 1997. "Socioeconomic Indexes for Occupations: A Review, Update and Critique." *Sociological Methodology* 27:177–298.

Hazard, Geoffrey C., Jr., and Ted Schneyer. 2002. "Regulatory Controls on Large Law Firms: A Comparative Perspective." *Arizona Law Review* 44:593–608.

Heintz, Bruce, and Nancy Markham-Bugbee. 1986. *Two-Tier Partnerships and Other Approaches: Five Alternatives.* Chicago: American Bar Association.

Heinz, John P. 1992. "Review of Tournament of Lawyers." *Law and Politics Book Review* 2:6–10.

Heinz, John P., and Edward O. Laumann. 1982. *Chicago Lawyers: The Social Structure of the Bar.* New York: Russell Sage Foundation and American Bar Foundation.

Heinz, John P., Edward O. Laumann, Robert L. Nelson, and Robert H. Salisbury. 1993. *The Hollow Core: Private Interests in National Policy Making.* Cambridge: Harvard University Press.

Heinz, John P., and Peter M. Manikas. 1992. "Networks among Elites in a Local Criminal Justice System." *Law and Society Review* 26:831–61.

Heinz, John P., Anthony Paik, and Ann Southworth. 2003. "Lawyers For Conservative Causes : Clients, Ideology, and Social Distance." *Law and Society Review* 37:5–50.

Hengstler, Gary A. 1993. "Vox Populi: The Public Perception of Lawyers: ABA Poll." *ABA Journal,* September, 60. Accessed via ProQuest February 3, 2004.

Hines, Crystal Hix. 2001. "Competition Sprouts One-Stop Law Firms." *New York Times,* May 31.

Hodson, Randy. 1989. "Why Aren't Women More Dissatisfied?" *Sociology Quarterly* 30:385–99.

Hoffman, Paul. 1973. *Lions in the Street: The Inside Story of the Great Wall Street Firms.* New York: Saturday Review Press.

———. 1982. *Lions of the Eighties: The Inside Story of the Powerhouse Law Firms.* Garden City, NY: Doubleday.

Holding, Reynolds, Harriet Chiang, and Christian Berthelsen. 2003. "How High Flying Firm Fell." *San Francisco Chronicle*, February 3, 2003.

Horsky, Charles A. 1952. *The Washington Lawyer: A Series of Lectures.* Delivered under the auspices of the Julius Rosenthal Foundation at Northwestern University School of Law. Boston: Little, Brown.

Hughes, Everett C. 1958. *Men and Their Work.* Glencoe, IL: Free Press.

Hull, Kathleen E. 1999a. "Cross-Examining the Myth of Lawyers' Misery." *Vanderbilt Law Review* 52:971.

———. 1999b. "The Paradox of the Contented Female Lawyer." *Law and Society Review* 33:687–700.

Hull, Kathleen E., and Robert L. Nelson. 2000. "Assimilation, Choice or Constraint? Testing Theories of Gender Differences in the Careers of Lawyers." *Social Forces* 79 (1): 229–64.

Illinois Legal Times. 1997. "100 Largest Law Firms in Illinois." July.

Jacobs, M. A. 2000. "Accounting Firms Covet Forbidden Fruit: Piece of U.S. Legal Market." *Wall Street Journal*, May 31, B1.

Johnston, David Cay. 2003. "Costly Questions Arise on Legal Opinions for Tax Shelters." *New York Times*, February 9, A15.

Kagan, Robert, and Robert Eli Rosen. 1985. "On the Social Significance of Large Firm Practice." *Stanford Law Review* 37:399.

Kahl, Joseph A. 1957. *The American Class Structure.* New York: Rinehart.

Katz, Jack. 1982. *Poor People's Lawyers in Transition.* New Brunswick, NJ: Rutgers University Press.

Kay, Fiona M. 1997. "Flight from Law: A Competing Risks Model of Departures from Law Firms." *Law and Society Review* 31:301–35.

Kay, Fiona M., and John Hagan. 1998. "Raising the Bar: The Gender Stratification of Law Firm Capital." *American Sociological Review* 63:728–43.

———. 1999. "Cultivating Clients in the Competition for Partnership: Gender and the Organizational Restructuring of Law Firms." *Law and Society Review* 33 (3): 517–56.

———. 2003. "Building Trust: Social Capital, Distributive Justice, and Loyalty to the Firm." *Law and Social Inquiry* 28:483–519.

Kordana, Kevin A. 1995. "Law Firms and Associate Careers: Tournament Theory versus the Production-Imperative Model." *Yale Law Journal* 104:1907–34.

Kornhauser, Lewis A., and Richard L. Revesz. 1995. "Legal Education and Entry into the Legal Profession: The Role of Race, Gender, and Educational Debt." *New York University Law Review* 70:829–964.

Kronman, A. T. 1993. *The Lost Lawyer: Failing Ideals of the Legal Profession.* Cambridge: Belknap Press of Harvard University Press.

Ladd, Everett C. 1996. "The Data Just Don't Show Erosion of America's 'Social Capital.' " *Public Perspective,* June/July.

Ladinsky, Jack. 1963a. "Careers of Lawyers, Law Practice and Legal Institutions." *American Sociological Review* 28:47.

———. 1963b. "The Impact of Social Backgrounds of Lawyers on Law Practice and the Law." *Journal of Legal Education* 16:127–44.

———. 1964. "The Social Profile of a Metropolitan Bar: A Statistical Survey in Detroit." *Michigan State Bar Journal* 12 (February).

Landon, Donald D. 1990. *Country Lawyers: The Impact of Context on Professional Practice.* New York: Praeger.

Langdon-Down, Grania. 2001. "One Foot in the Grave?" *Times* (London), September 25, features sec.

Larson, Margali Sarfatti. 1977. *The Rise of Professionalism: A Sociological Analysis.* Berkeley: University of California Press.

Laumann, Edward O. 1973. *Bonds of Pluralism: The Form and Substance of Urban Social Networks.* New York: John Wiley and Sons.

Laumann, Edward O., and John P. Heinz. 1977. "Specialization and Prestige in the Legal Profession." *American Bar Foundation Research Journal* 2 (1): 155–216.

Laumann, Edward O., Peter V. Marsden, and Joseph Galaskiewicz. 1997. "Community-Elite Influence Structures: Extension of a Network Approach." *American Journal of Sociology* 83:598–600.

Lazega, Emmanuel. 2001. *The Collegial Phenomenon: The Social Mechanisms of Cooperation among Peers in a Corporate Law Partnership.* Oxford: Oxford University Press.

Leicht, Kevin T., and Mary L. Fennell. 1997. "The Changing Organizational Context of Professional Work." *Annual Review of Sociology* 23:215–31.

———. 2001. *Professional Work: A Sociological Approach.* Malden, MA: Blackwell Publishers.

Lemann, Nicholas. 1996. "Kicking in Groups." *Atlantic Monthly*, April.

Lempert, Richard O., David L. Chambers, and Terry K. Adams. 2000. "Michigan's Minority Graduates in Practice: The River Runs Through Law School." *Law and Social Inquiry* 25:395–505.

Lenski, Gerhard. 1994. "New Light on Old Issues: The Relevance of 'Really Existing Socialist Societies' for Stratification Theory." In Grusky 1994, 55–61.

Lentz, Bernard F., and David N. Laband. 1995. *Sex Discrimination in the Legal Profession.* Westport, CT: Quorum Books.

Leonhardt, David. 2000a. "And Let the Lawyers Sing: 'Glory to the Salary King.'" *New York Times*, February 4, C8.

———. 2000b. "Law Firms' Pay Soars to Stem Dot-Com Defections." *New York Times*, February 2, 1.

Lerner, Melvin J. 1980. *The Belief in a Just World: A Fundamental Delusion.* New York: Plenum Press.

Levy, Berryl H. 1961. *Corporation Lawyer: Saint or Sinner?* Philadelphia: Chilton.

Lewis, Neil A. 2001. "White House Ends Bar Association's Role in Screening Federal Judges." *New York Times*, March 23, A1, col. 2.

———. 2002. "Democrats Reject Bush Pick in Battle Over Court Balance." *New York Times*, September 6, A1, col. 1.

Liefland, Linda. 1986. "Career Patterns of Male and Female Lawyers." *Buffalo Law Review* 35:601–31.

Litan, R. E., and S. Salop. 1992. "More Value for the Legal Dollar: A New Look at Attorney-Client Fees and Relationships." Unpublished paper presented at American Bar Association annual meeting, San Francisco.

Llewellyn, Karl M. 1933. "The Bar Specializes 'With What Results?'" *The Annals: of the American Academy of Political and Social Sciences* 167:177–92.

Los Angeles Times. 1995. Telephone survey. June.

Loscocco, Karlyn A. 1990. "Reactions to Blue-Collar Work: A Comparison of Women and Men." *Work and Occupations* 17:152–77.

Loscocco, Karlyn A., and Glenna Spitze. 1991. "The Organizational Context of Women's and Men's Pay Satisfaction." *Social Science Quarterly* 72:3–19.

Luban, David J. 1988. *Lawyers and Justice: An Ethical Study.* Princeton: Princeton University Press.

M/A/R/C Research 1999. *Perceptions of the U.S. Justice System.* Chicago: American Bar Association. www.abanet.org/media/perception/perceptions.pdf (accessed February 9, 2004).

Macaulay, Stewart. 1963. "Non-contractual Relations in Business: A Preliminary Study." *American Sociological Review* 28:55–67.

———. 1979. "Lawyers and Consumer Protection Laws." *Law and Society Review* 14:115–71.

MacCorquodale, Patricia, and Gary Jensen. 1993. "Women in the Law: Partners or Tokens?" *Gender and Society* 7:582–93.

MacDonald, E. 2000. "Grant Thornton Set to Restructure Consulting Division." *Wall Street Journal*, February 25, C16, col. 1.

Malinowska-Tabaka, Elzbieta. 1987. "Complex Measures of Job Satisfaction/Dissatisfaction among Professionals." *Social Indicators Research* 19:451–73.

Manza, Jeff, and Clem Brooks. 1999. *Social Cleavages and Political Change: Voter Alignments and U.S. Party Coalitions.* Oxford: Oxford University Press.

March, James G., and Herbert Alexander Simon, with Harold Guetzkow. 1958. *Organizations.* New York: John Wiley & Sons.

Martin, Jack K., and Sandra L. Hanson. 1985. "Sex, Family Wage-Earning Status and Satisfaction with Work." *Work and Occupations* 2:91–103.

Martindale-Hubbell. Various years. *Martindale-Hubbell Law Directory.* New Providence, NJ: Martindale-Hubbell Inc.

———. 1975–76, 1995–96. *Martindale-Hubbell Law Directory.* Winter, CD-ROM edition. Reed Reference Publishing.

Mather, Lynn, Craig A. McEwen, and Richard J. Maiman. 2001. *Divorce Lawyers at Work: Varieties of Professionalism in Practice.* New York: Oxford University Press.

Mattessich, Paul W., and Cheryl W. Heilman. 1990. "The Career Paths of Minnesota Law School Graduates: Does Gender Make a Difference?" *Law and Inequality* 9:59–114.

McBrier, Debra Branch. 2003. "Gender and Career Dynamics within a Segmented Professional Labor Market: The Case of Law Academia." *Social Forces* 81 (4): 1201–66.

McCutcheon, Allan L. 1987. *Latent Class Analysis.* Newbury Park, CA: Sage Publications.

McDonald, Michael. 2000. "Older Lawyers Put Out to Pasture: Firms Pare Costs by Retiring Higher-Paid, Lower-Billing Staff." *Crain's New York Business,* December 4, 28.

Melone, Albert P. 1977. *Lawyers, Public Policy, and Interest Group Politics.* Washington, DC: University Press of America.

Melville, Herman. 1996. *Bartleby, the Scrivener: A Story of Wall Street.* In *The Piazza Tales,* edited by Harrison Hayford, Northwestern Newberry Edition. Evanston, IL: Northwestern University Press.

Menkel-Meadow, Carrie. 1986. "The Comparative Sociology of Women Lawyers: The 'Feminization' of the Legal Profession." *Osgoode Hall Law Journal* 24 (4): 897–918.

———. 1989. "Feminization of the Legal Profession: The Comparative Sociology of Women Lawyers." In Abel and Lewis 1988–89, 3:196–255.

———. 1994. "Culture Clash in the Quality of Life in the Law: Changes in the

Economics, Diversification and Organization of Lawyering." *Case Western Reserve Law Review* 44:621–63.

Menkel-Meadow, Carrie, and Robert Meadow. 1983. "Resource Allocation in Legal Services." *Law and Political Quarterly* 5:237–56.

Merrion, Paul. 2000. "Auditors at Law: Attorneys Fret as CPA's Encroach on Their Turf." *Crain's Chicago Business,* January 17, 15.

Michaels, Adrian, and Michael Peel. 2000. "PwC Plans Ground-Breaking Split." *Financial Times,* February 18, companies and markets sec., 1.

Michelson, Ethan, Edward O. Laumann, and John P. Heinz. 1997. "Chicago Lawyers and their Clients 1975–1995: A Client-Based Approach to the Social Transformation of the Bar." Paper presented at the Management of Durable Relations: Theoretical and Empirical Models for Households and Organizations conference, Zeist, The Netherlands, June 26–28.

Miller, Mark. 1995. *The High Priests of American Politics: The Role of Lawyers in American Political Institutions.* Knoxville: University of Tennessee Press.

Morello, Karen. 1986. *The Invisible Bar: The Woman Lawyer in America: 1938 to the Present.* New York: Random House.

Mortimer, John. 1993. *The Best of Rumpole.* New York: Penguin.

Moscovici, Serge, and Marisa Zavalloni. 1969. "The Group as a Polarizer of Attitudes." *Journal of Personality and Social Psychology* 12:125.

Mottaz, Clifford. 1986. "Gender Differences in Work Satisfaction, Work-Related Rewards and Values, and the Determinants of Work Satisfaction." *Human Relations* 39:359, 360.

Muir, Kate. 1995. "Counsel for the Depressed and the Stressed." *Times* (London), July 13, 16.

Murray, Michael A., and Tom Atkinson. 1981. "Gender Differences in Correlates of Job Satisfaction." *Canadian Journal of Behavioral Sociology* 13:44.

NALP Foundation for Research and Education. 1998. *Keeping the Keepers: Strategies for Associate Retention in Times of Attrition.* Washington, DC: NALP (National Association for Law Placement) Foundation.

National Association for Law Placement. 2002. "Women and Attorneys of Color at Law Firms '2002.' " www.nalp.org/nalpresearch/mw02sum.htm (accessed July 25, 2003).

National Center for Education Statistics. 2000a."Table 274. First-professional degrees conferred by degree-granting institutions, by racial/ethnic group and sex of student: 1976–77 to 1997–98." *Digest of Education Statistics, 2000.* United States Department of Education. http://nces.ed.gov/pubs2001/digest/dt274.asp (accessed July 25, 2003).

———. 2000b. "Table 261. First-professional degrees conferred by degree-granting institutions in dentistry, medicine, and law, by sex, and number of institutions conferring degrees: 1949–50 to 1997–98." *Digest of Education Statistics, 2000.* United States Department of Education. http://nces.ed.gov/pubs2001/digest/dt261.asp (accessed July 25, 2003).

National Law Journal. 1999. "What Lawyers Earn." June 14, B7–B10.

Neil, Cecily C., and William E. Snizek. 1988. "Gender as a Moderator of Job Satisfaction." *Work and Occupation* 15:201, 213–14.

Nelson, Robert L. 1988. *Partners with Power: The Social Transformation of the Large Law Firm.* Berkeley and Los Angeles: University of California Press.

————. 1992. "Of Tournaments and Transformations: Explaining the Growth of Large Law Firms." *Wisconsin Law Review* 733–50.

————. 1994. "The Futures of American Lawyers: A Demographic Profile of a Changing Profession in a Changing Society." *Case Western Reserve Law Review* 44 (2): 345–406.

————. 1998. "The Discovery Process as a Circle of Blame: Institutional, Professional, and Socio-economic Factors That Contribute to Unreasonable, Inefficient, and Amoral Behavior in Corporate Litigation." *Fordham Law Review* 67:773–808.

Nelson, Robert L., and Laura Beth Nielsen. 2000. "Cops, Counsel and Entrepreneurs: Constructing the Role of Inside Counsel in Large Corporations." *Law and Society Review* 34 (2): 457–94.

Nelson, Robert L., and David M. Trubek. 1992. "Arenas of Professionalism: The Professional Ideologies of Lawyers in Context." In Nelson, Trubek, and Solomon 1992, 177–214.

Nelson, Robert L., David M. Trubek, and Rayman L. Solomon, eds. 1992. *Lawyers' Ideals/Lawyers' Practices: Transformations in the American Legal Profession.* Ithaca: Cornell University Press.

New York State Bar Association. 2000. *Preserving the Core Values of the American Legal Profession: The Place of Multidisciplinary Practice in the Law Governing Lawyers.* Report of the NYSBA Special Committee on the Law Governing Firm Structure and Operation. Albany, NY.

Olson, Daniel. 1992. "The Changing Shape of American Religion." Unpublished lecture, Indiana University (South Bend), February 5.

Orenstein, Susan. 2000. "Lawyers Need Equity, Too." *Industry Standard*, April 10, 142.

Palmer, Ann Therese. 2001. "Law Firms Take Steps Out of the Box." *Chicago Tribune*, August 12, sec. 1, 1, cols. 2–5.

Parikh, Sara. 2001. "Professionalism and Its Discontents: A Study of Social Networks in the Plaintiff's Personal Injury Bar." Ph.D. diss., University of Illinois at Chicago.

Parsa, T. Z. 1999. "The Drudge Report." *New York*, June 21, 24–31.

Parsons, Talcott. 1962. "The Law and Social Control." In *Law and Sociology: Exploratory Essays*, edited by William M. Evan, 56–72. Glencoe, IL: Free Press of Glencoe.

————. 1968. "Professions." In *International Encyclopedia of the Social Sciences*, edited by David L. Sills, 12:536–47. New York: Macmillan Company and The Free Press.

————. 1969. *Politics and Social Structure.* New York: The Free Press.

Paxton, Pamela. 1999. "Is Social Capital Declining in the United States? A Multiple Indicator Assessment." *American Journal of Sociology* 105:88–127.

Phillips, Damon Jeremy. 2001. "The Promotion Paradox: Organized Mortality and Employee Promotion Chances in Silicon Valley Law Firms, 1946–1996." *American Journal of Sociology* 98 (4): 829–72.

Pierce, Jennifer L. 1995. *Gender Trials: Emotional Lives in Contemporary Law Firms.* Berkeley and Los Angeles: University of California Press.

Pitkin, Hanna F. 1972. *The Concept of Representation.* Berkeley: University of California Press.

Pope, Liston. 1948. "Religion and the Class Structure." *Annals of the American Academy of Political and Social Sciences* 256:84.

Powell, Michael J. 1979. "Anatomy of a Counter-Bar Association: The Chicago Council of Lawyers." *American Bar Foundation Research Journal* 4 (3): 501–41.

————. 1985. "Developments in the Regulation of Lawyers: Competing Segments and Market, Client, and Government Controls." *Social Forces* 64:281.

————. 1986. "Professional Divestiture: The Cession of Responsibility for Lawyer Discipline." *American Bar Foundation Research Journal* 11 (1): 31–54.

————. 1988. *From Patrician to Professional Elite: The Transformation of the New York City Bar Association.* New York: Russell Sage Foundation.

Putnam, Robert. 1993. *Making Democracy Work: Civic Traditions in Modern Italy.* Princeton: Princeton University Press.

————. 1995. "Bowling Alone: America's Declining Social Capital." *Journal of Democracy* 6:65–78.

————. 2000. *Bowling Alone: The Collapse and Revival of American Community.* New York: Simon and Schuster.

Reed, Alfred Z. 1921. *Training for the Public Profession of the Law.* New York: Carnegie Foundation for the Advancement of Teaching.

Reeves, Arin Nadimpalli. 2001. "Gender Matters, Race Matters: A Qualitative Analysis of Gender and Race Dynamics in Law Firms." Ph.D. diss., Northwestern University.

Regan, Milton C., Jr. 2004. *Eat What You Kill: The Fall of a Wall Street Lawyer.* Ann Arbor: University of Michigan Press.

Rehnquist, William H. 1994. Remarks on the dedication of the North Carolina Bar Association Center, October 21 (unpublished).

————. 1997. Keynote address at the dedication of the David A. Harrison III Law Grounds, University of Virginia, November 8 (unpublished).

Reichman, Nancy J., and Joyce S. Sterling. 2002. "Recasting the Brass Ring: Deconstructing and Reconstructing Workplace Opportunities for Women Lawyers." *Capital University Law Review* 29 (1): 923–77.

Reiman, Jeffrey. 2001. *The Rich Get Richer and the Poor Get Prison.* 6th ed. Needham Heights, MA: Allyn and Bacon.

Reiss, Albert J., Jr., ed. 1961. *Occupations and Social Status.* New York: Free Press of Glencoe.

Reskin, Barbara F., ed. 1984. *Sex Segregation in the Workplace: Trends, Explanations, Remedies.* Washington, DC: National Academy Press.

Ridgeway, Cecilia L. 1997. "Interaction and the Conservation of Gender Inequality: Considering Employment." *American Sociological Review* 62:218–35.

Ripley, Amanda. 2000. "Seniority Complex." *American Lawyer,* June, 83.

Rogers, Jackie Krasas. 2000. *Temps: The Many Faces of the Changing Workplace.* Ithaca, NY: Cornell University Press.

Romley, John, and Eric Talley. 2004. "Uncorporated Professionals." Unpublished paper. RAND Corporation and University of Southern California Law School.

Roper Center. iPOLL (public opinion surveys), www.ropercenter.uconn.edu/ipoll.html (accessed October 4, 2004).

Rosen, Robert Eli. 1984. "Lawyers in Corporate Decision-Making." Ph.D. diss., University of California, Berkeley.

————. 1989. "The Inside Counsel Movement, Professional Judgment and Organizational Representation." *Indiana Law Journal* 64:479–553.

————. 1999. "Proletarianizing Lives: Researching Careers." *Law and Society Review* 33 (3): 703–12.

————. 2002. "Educating Law Students to Be Business Leaders." *International Journal of the Legal Profession* 9:27.

————. 2002. " 'We're all Consultants Now': How Change in Client Organizational Strategies Influences Change in the Organization of Corporate Legal Services." *Arizona Law Review* 44 (3–4): 637–83.

Rosen, Sherwin. 1992. "The Market for Lawyers." *Journal of Law and Economics* 35 (October): 215–46.

Rosenberg, Janet, Harry Perlstadt, and William R. F. Phillips. 1993. "Now That We Are Here: Discrimination, Disparagement, and Harassment at Work and the Experience of Women Lawyers." *Gender and Society* 7: 415–33.

Rosenthal, Douglas. 1974. *Lawyer and Client: Who's in Charge.* New York: Russell Sage Foundation.

Rovella, David E. 1997. "Buying into the Buyout." *National Law Journal,* March 24, A1, col. 2.

Ruder, D. S. 1986. *The Evolving Role of Corporate Counsel.* Unpublished paper, Corporate Counsel Institute, Northwestern University School of Law.

Rueschemeyer, Dietrich. 1973. *Lawyers and Their Society: A Comparative Study of the Legal Profession in Germany and in the United States.* Cambridge: Harvard University Press.

Rufford, Nicholas. 1998. "Barristers Lose Court Monopoly in Bid to Cut Legal Costs." *Sunday Times* (London), June 21.

Rutherford, M. Louise. 1937. *The Influence of the American Bar Association on Public Opinion and Legislation.* Philadelphia: Foundation Press.

Sachdev, Ameet. 2004. "Law Firms Slow to Outsource." *Chicago Tribune,* January 19, sec. 4, 1.

Salisbury, Robert H. 1969. "An Exchange Theory of Interest Groups." *Midwest Journal of Political Science* 13 (1): 1–32.

Sandefur, Rebecca L. 2001. "Work and Honor in the Law: Prestige and the Division of Lawyers' Labor." *American Sociological Review* 66:382–403.

————. 2004. "Transformation of an Occupational Internal Labor Market: The Case of American Law." Manuscript in Preparation. Department of Sociology, Stanford University.

Sandefur, Rebecca L., and John P. Heinz. 1999. "Winner-Take-All Markets for Legal Services and Lawyers' Job Satisfaction and Occupational Commitment." ABF Working Paper Series. Chicago: American Bar Foundation.

Sandefur, Rebecca L., Edward O. Laumann, and John P. Heinz. 1999. "The Changing Value of Social Capital in an Expanding Social System: Lawyers in the Chicago Bar, 1975 and 1995." Chap. 12 in *Corporate Social Capital and Liability,* edited by Roger Th.A.J. Leenders and Shaul M. Gabbay. Norwell, MA: Kluwer Academic Publishers.

Sander, Richard H., and E. Douglass Williams. 1989. "Why Are There So Many Lawyers? Perspectives on a Turbulent Market." *Law and Social Inquiry* 14:431–79.

————. 1992. "A Little Theorizing about the Big Law Firm: Galanter, Palay, and the Economics of Growth." *Law and Social Inquiry* 17:391–414.

Sarat, Austin. 1997. "Studying American Legal Culture: An Assessment of Survey Evidence." *Law and Society Review* (Winter): 427–88.

Sarat, Austin, and William L. F. Felstiner. 1995. *Divorce Lawyers and Their Clients: Power and Meaning in the Legal Process.* New York: Oxford University Press.

Sarat, Austin, and Stuart Scheingold. 1998. *Cause Lawyering: Political Commitments and Professional Responsibilities.* New York: Oxford University Press.

————. 2001. *Cause Lawyering and the State in a Global Era.* New York: Oxford University Press.

Schaafsma, Marjorie B. 1998. "Disruptive Ambitions: Women Lawyers in Large Law Firms." Ph.D. diss., Northwestern University.

Schauerte, Mark, and Nathaniel Hernandez. 2002. "Enron Throws Fuel on Hot Debate over Multidisciplinary Practices." *Chicago Lawyer,* April, 8.

Scheffey, Thomas. 1995. "Turning Lawyers' Hourly Services into a Commodity." *Legal Times,* May 22, 529.

Schiltz, Patrick J. 1999. "On Being a Happy, Healthy, and Ethical Member of an Unhappy, Unhealthy and Unethical Profession." *Vanderbilt Review* 52:871–952.

Schleef, Debra. 2000. "That's a Good Question! Exploring Motivations for Law and Business School Choice." *Sociology of Education* 73 (3): 155–74.

Schmeltzer, John. 1999. "Sidley Shuffles Partners' Status: 30 Attorneys Wind Up at Lower Level," *Chicago Tribune,* December 8, 1.

Schneyer, Theodore J. 1983. "The Incoherence of the Unified Bar Concept: Generalizing from the Wisconsin Case." *American Bar Foundation Research Journal* 8 (1): 1–108.

————. 1989. "Professionalism as Bar Politics: The Making of the Model Rules of Professional Conduct." *Law and Social Inquiry* 14:677–737.

Schwartz, Carol A., and Rebecca L. Turner, eds. 1995. *Encyclopedia of Associations.* 29th ed. Detroit: Gale Research Inc.

Seron, Carroll. 1996. *The Business of Practicing Law: The Work Lives of Solo and Small-Firm Attorneys.* Philadelphia: Temple University Press.

Shapiro, Susan. 2001. *Tangled Loyalties.* Ann Arbor: University of Michigan Press.

Shils, Edward. 1994 [1968]. "Deference." In Grusky 1994, 197–203.

Sikes, Bette H., Clara N. Carson, and Patricia Gorai. 1972. *The 1971 Lawyer Statistical Report.* Chicago: American Bar Foundation.

Silver, Carole. 2000. "Globalization and the U.S. Market in Legal Services—Shifting Identities." *Law and Policy in International Business* 31:1093–50.

Simon, William. 1998. *The Practice of Justice: A Theory of Lawyers' Ethics.* Cambridge: Harvard University Press.

Singer, Amy. 2000. "Way Out: Special Report, The Graying of the Bar." *American Lawyer,* June, 73.

Skertic, Mark. 2000. "Dot-Coms Lure Lawyers." *Chicago Sun-Times*, February 14, 1.

Slovak, Jeffrey S. 1979. "Working for Corporate Actors: Social Change and Elite Attorneys in Chicago." *American Bar Foundation Research Journal* 4 (3): 465–500.

————. 1980. "Giving and Getting Respect: Prestige and Stratification in a Legal Elite." *American Bar Foundation Research Journal* 5 (1): 31–68.

Smelser, Neil J., and Jeffrey C. Alexander, eds. 1999. *Diversity and Its Discontents: Cultural Conflict and Common Ground in Contemporary American Society.* Princeton: Princeton University Press.

Smigel, Erwin O. 1960. "The Impact of Recruitment on the Organization of the Large Law Firm." *American Sociological Review* 25:56–66.

————. 1964. *The Wall Street Lawyer: Professional Organization Man.* Glencoe, IL: Free Press of Glencoe.

————. 1969. *The Wall Street Lawyer: Professional Organization Man.* Bloomington: Indiana University Press.

Smith, David H. 1983. "Synanthrometrics: On Progress in the Development of a General Theory of Voluntary Action and Citizen Participation." In *International Perspectives* on *Voluntary Action Research*, edited by David H. Smith et al., 80–94. Washington, DC: University Press of America.

————. 1994. "Determinants of Voluntary Association Participation and Volunteering: A Literature Review." *Nonprofit and Voluntary Sector Quarterly* 23:243–63.

Smith, Dinitia. 2004. "Rehnquist's Book on a Disputed Election (No, Not That One)." *New York Times*, March 6, A17, cols. 1–6.

Smith, Reginald Heber. 1919. *Justice and the Poor.* New York: Carnegie Foundation.

Southworth, Ann. 1993. "Taking the Lawyer Out of Progressive Lawyering." *Stanford Law Review* 46:213.

————. 1996. "Lawyer-Client Decisionmaking in Civil Rights and Poverty Practice: An Empirical Study of Lawyers' Norms." *Georgetown Journal of Legal Ethics* 9:1.

————. 1999. "Collective Representation for the Disadvantaged: Variations in Problems of Accountability." *Fordham Law Review* 67:2449.

Spangler, Eve. 1986. *Lawyers for Hire: Salaried Professionals at Work.* New Haven: Yale University Press.

Spencer, Anne, and David Podmore. 1982. "Women Lawyers in England: The Experience of Inequality." *Work and Occupations* 9:337–61.

————. 1987. "Women Lawyers—Marginal Members of a Male-Dominated Profession." In *In a Man's World: Essays on Women in Male-Dominated Professions*, 113–33, edited by Anne Spencer and David Podmore. New York: Tavistock Publications.

Spilerman, Seymour. 1978. "Careers, Labor Market Structure, and Socioeconomic Achievement." *American Journal of Sociology* 83:551–93.

Spillenger, Clyde. 1996. "Elusive Advocate: Reconsidering Brandeis as People's Lawyer," *Yale Law Journal* 105:1445.

Stark, Rodney. 1987. "Correcting Church Membership Rates: 1971 and 1980." *Review of Religious Research* 29:69–77.

Stolzenberg, Ross M. 1980. "The Measurement and Decomposition of Causal Effects in Nonlinear and Nonadditive Models." *Sociological Methodology* 11:459–88.

Strahler, Steven R. 2001."Rewriting the Rules: Reaching for the Top." *Crain's Chicago Business*, November 26, 13, 15–16.

Stracher, Cameron. 1998. *Double Billing: A Young Lawyer's Tale of Greed, Sex, Lies, and the Pursuit of a Swivel Chair.* New York: William Morrow.

Stouffer, Samuel. 1995. *Communism, Conformity and Civil Liberties.* New York: Doubleday.

Sullivan's Law Directory for the State of Illinois, (1974–75). 1975. 99th ed. Chicago: Sullivan's Law Directory.

Swaine, Robert T. 1946–48. *The Cravath Firm.* 3 vols. New York: privately published.

Szelényi, Ivan, and Bill Martin. 1989. "The Legal Profession and the Rise and Fall of the New Class." In Abel and Lewis 1989, 3:256–88.

Taber, Janet, Marguerite T. Grant, Mary T. Huser, Rise B. Norman, and James R. Sutton. 1988. "Project, Gender, Legal Education, and the Legal Profession: An Empirical Study of Stanford Law Students and Graduates." *Stanford Law Review* 40:1209, 1251–52.

Tagliabue, John. 2000. "Cap Gemini to Acquire Ernst & Young's Consulting Business." *New York Times*, March 1, C1, cols. 3–6.

Taylor, T. Shawn. 2002. " 'Partners' Put Law Firms in Labor Bind: EEOC, Chicago Firm Do Battle," *Chicago Tribune*, April 7, business sec., 1.

Tocqueville, Alexis de. 1945. *Democracy in America.* Translated by Henry Reeve, as revised by Francis Bowen and Phillips Bradley, with a foreword by Harold J. Laski. 2 vols. New York: A. A. Knopf.

Tolbert, Pamela S., and Robert N. Stern. 1991. "Organizations of Professionals: Governance Structures in Large Law Firms." *Research in the Sociology of Organizations* 8:97–117.

Toobin, Jeffrey. 2004. "Annuls of Law: A Bad Thing." *New Yorker*, March 22, 60.

Trillin, Calvin. 1978. *Alice, Let's Eat.* New York: Random House.

Trubek, David, Yves Dezalay, Ruth Buchanan, and John R. Davis. 1994. "Global Restructuring and the Law: Studies of the Internationalization of Legal Fields and the Creation of Transnational Arenas." *Case Western Reserve Law Review* 44:407–98.

Truman, David B. 1951. *The Governmental Process.* New York: Alfred Knopf.

Tuch, Steven A., and Jack K. Martin. 1991. "Race in the Workplace: Black/White Differences in the Sources of Job Satisfaction." *Sociology Quarterly* 32:103.

Tucker, Marilyn, Laurie A. Albright, and Patricia L. Busk. 1990. "Whatever Happened to the Class of 1983?" *Georgetown Law Journal* 78:153–95.

Tucker, Marilyn, and Georgia A. Niedzielko. 1994. *Options and Obstacles: A Survey of the Studies of the Careers of Women Lawyers 32* (citing Commission on the Status of Women in the Legal Profession, North Carolina Bar Association, 52). Chicago: American Bar Association; Commission on Women in the Profession.

Tumin, Melvin. 1953. "Some Principles of Stratification: A Critical Analysis." *American Sociological Review* 18:387–94.

U.S. Bureau of the Census. 1976. *1972 Census of Selected Service Industries.* Vol. 1. Washington, DC: U.S. Department of Commerce.

———. 1977. *Statistical Abstract of the U.S.* 98th ed. Washington, DC: GPO.

———. 1986. *1982 Census of Service Industries.* Washington, DC: U.S. Department of Commerce.

———. 1996a. *1992 Census of Service Industries.* Washington, DC: U.S. Department of Commerce.

———. 1996b. *Statistical Abstract of the U.S.* 116th ed. Washington, DC: GPO.

———. 2002. Table P-45, Occupation of Longest Job—Full-Time, Year-Round Workers (Both Sexes Combined) by Median and Mean Earnings: 1982 to 2001. www.census.gov/hhes/income/histinc/p45.html (accessed June 13, 2003).

U.S. Department of Justice. 2003. "Fiscal Year 2002 Performance Report and Fiscal Year 2003 Revised Final Performance Plan, Fiscal Year 2004 Performance Plan." Washington, DC: Department of Justice. www.usdoj.gov/ag/annualreports/pr2002/TableofContents.htm (accessed June 16, 2003).

Union League Club of Chicago. 1998. "State of the Union," Annual Report.

———. 1999. "State of the Union," Annual Report.

Van Duch, Darryl. 1997. "Big Six in Hot Pursuit of Legal Biz: Major Law Firms Lose Stars, Market Share to Accountants." *National Law Review,* August 18, A1, A13.

Van Hoy, Jerry. 1997. *Franchise Law Firms and the Transformation of Personal Legal Services.* Westport, CT: Quorum Books.

Varca, Phillip E., Garnett S. Shaffer, and Cynthia D. McCauley. 1983. "Sex Differences in Job Satisfaction Revisited." *Academy of Management Journal* 26:348–53.

Veblen, Thorstein. 1994 [1899]. *The Theory of the Leisure Class: An Economic Study of Institutions.* New York: Penguin Books.

Wallace, Jean E. 1995. "Corporatist Control and Organizational Commitment among Professionals: The Case of Lawyers Working in Law Firms." *Social Forces* 73:811–39.

Warner, R. Stephen. 1999. "Changes in the Civic Role of Religion." In Smelser and Alexander 1999, 229.

Waters, Malcolm. 1989. "Collegiality, Bureaucratization, and Professionalization: A Weberian Analysis." *American Journal of Sociology* 94 (5): 945–72.

Weick, Karl E. 1976. "Educational Organization as Loosely Coupled Systems." *Administrative Science Quarterly* 21:1–19.

White, Ryan. 2002. "Legal Education in Chicago: How Differences in Course Curricula Shape Occupational Opportunity in the Bar." Unpublished paper, Northwestern University.

Wilkins, David B., and G. Mitu Gulati. 1996. "Why Are There So Few Black Lawyers in Corporate Law Firms? An Institutional Analysis." *California Law Review* 84:493–625.

———. 1998. "Reconceiving the Tournament of Lawyers: Tracking, Seeding, and Information Control in the Internal Labor Markets of Elite Law Firms." *Virginia Law Review* 84:1581–705.

Wilson, John, and Marc Musick. 1997. "Who Cares? Toward an Integrated Theory of Volunteer Work." *American Sociological Review* 62:694–713.

Yale Law Journal. 1964. "The Jewish Law Student and New York Jobs—Discriminatory Effects in Law Firm Hiring Practice." 73:625–60.

Yamaguchi, Kazuo. 1991. *Event History Analysis.* Newbury Park, CA: Sage Publications.

Yanas, John J. 1990. "President's Message." *New York State Bar Journal,* May.

Zimmerman, Jay S., and Matthew J. Kelly. 2004. "MDPs May be Dead after Enron/Andersen, But Subsidiary Businesses Thrive." *Law and Social Inquiry* 29:639–53.

Index